Mind's Landscape

B

Mind's Landscape

An Introduction to the Philosophy of Mind

Samuel Guttenplan

BLACKWELL
Publishers

Copyright © Samuel Guttenplan 2000

The right of Samuel Guttenplan to be identified as author of this work has been asserted in accordance with the Copyright, Designs and Patents Act 1988.

First published 2000

2 4 6 8 10 9 7 5 3 1

Blackwell Publishers Inc.
350 Main Street
Malden, Massachusetts 02148
USA

Blackwell Publishers Ltd
108 Cowley Road
Oxford OX4 1JF
UK

Library of Congress Cataloging-in-Publication Data

Guttenplan, Samuel D.
  Mind's landscape: an introduction to the philosophy of mind / Samuel Guttenplan.
    p. cm.
  Includes bibliographical references and index.
    ISBN 0-631-20217-X (hardcover: alk. paper)—ISBN 0-631-20218-8 (pbk. : alk. paper)
    1. Philosophy of mind. I. Title.
BD418.3. G88 2000
128'.2—dc21

                                                        00-022955

British Library Cataloguing in Publication Data
A CIP catalogue record for this book is available from the British Library.

Typeset in 10.5 on 12.5pt Bembo
by Best-set Typesetter Ltd., Hong Kong
Printed in Great Britain by TJ International, Padstow, Cornwall

This book is printed on acid-free paper.

Contents

For Jennifer

Preface

It has become commonplace for authors to use introductory books in philosophy to argue for their own most cherished views. There need be no harm in this, and indeed there is much to be said for it. At the very least, being taken through a subject by an author who has some sort of an agenda – perhaps even an axe to grind – might well make the journey more lively. Moreover, in a subject as vast as the philosophy of mind has become, difficult decisions have to be made about what to leave out, so a bias in favour of a certain view might well bring relief from what would otherwise be a surfeit of options.

In a general sense, *Mind's Landscape* is no exception to this trend, but its philosophical biases are different in kind from those that animate other introductory books. Many writers now feel confident enough to plump for one or other detailed account, even if this threatens the loss or distortion of what might be called our everyday conception of the mind. I have no such confidence, finding instead that all accounts have what look like serious weaknesses. But neither do I think that everyday thoughts must be defended at all costs against philosophical theorizing. It seems obviously right that genuine philosophical problems must *begin* with – be traceable back to – our most ordinary thoughts, but this does not mean that they end there. And this is especially so given that our ordinary thoughts about the mind can seem to dissolve into incoherence on close examination.

Since my view is that we can neither rest content with our first thoughts about the mind nor leave them behind, I have tried to write a book that keeps both the ordinary and the philosophical in focus. In so far as I have succeeded, the result is more a narrative account of where we have got to in our understanding of the mind than it is a compendious survey of the subject. There are several evident consequences to this. First, the chapters which follow do not bristle with references to the literature, though the further reading lists given at the end of the book should provide all you need to pursue any given topic.

Secondly, some topics that are now hotly debated, and fill up many journal pages, are only lightly sketched, whereas others that might now be regarded as passé take somewhat more of the centre stage. In both cases, the shape of the whole has been driven by my desire to tell as coherent and as plausible a story as I could manage. My hope is that I will in this way encourage independent thought, rather than merely providing summaries of the thoughts of others. But, that said, my narrative does aim to reveal the overall shape of the philosophy of mind, using where appropriate what I hope are memorable pictorial representations of the relevant options.

Writing this book made me realize even more than I had before my debt to Birkbeck students. As the classification has it, they are typically 'mature' students, meaning thereby that they are studying for degrees whilst earning their living during the day. But I have found this classification to be one of merit as well as description. Having to lecture about the philosophy of mind to these motivated and mature students during the past twenty-five years has taught me about what will – and will not – pass as plausible, and for these lessons I am genuinely grateful.

It is also with pleasure as well as gratitude that I dedicate this book to Jennifer. Her contribution as a critic and proofreader was material, and she made a real immaterial difference by lifting my spirits when writing was less than easy.

La Taillède,
March 2000

Introduction

You might have expected that this book would be called 'Mind's Portrait'. After all, portraits typically depict individual human beings and their characteristic psychological features, whereas landscapes depict . . . well, landscapes. When it comes to a philosophical depiction of the mind – something typically, even if not exclusively, human – a portrait would seem just the thing.

Here I disagree. Apart from suggesting a pleasing ambiguity between depiction and depicted – a landscape being both   I think the metaphor I have chosen is better. It might not have the immediate resonance, the directness of 'portrait', but it is ultimately more informative. Indeed, if it is taken wholly seriously, something I strongly recommend, it might even dissuade you from making various erroneous assumptions which have done more damage to the philosophy of mind than is often recognized. Below, I shall say in a little more detail why I think this is so, but these introductory remarks about the title are only intended to suggest a certain line of thought, for this is a case in which the title can only be properly judged by the book.

A landscape – the thing itself, not its depiction – is a stretch of countryside set out before a spectator. Three related but distinguishable features are suggested by this characterization: the first is the idea of being an expanse, of being something spread out; the second is of being something apt for viewing; and the third is the idea of being a surface – something outermost – under which there are other layers. With the license appropriate to metaphor, each of these features can, or should, teach us something about the mind.

Talk of the mind almost inevitably brings with it the idea of an inner reality, of things going on, as it were, inside human, and possibly other, creatures. This idea is natural, and though it is not simply mistaken, it can be thoroughly misleading. It is my hope that speaking about mind's landscape will act as an obstacle, something standing in the way of jumping too quickly to this narrow conclusion. If it does nothing else, the metaphor should encourage us to think of the mind as something whose features are part of a scene extended across space and time, one which is of course different from, but in this respect just like, the rolling hills and picturesque streams of any literal landscape. Books and buildings, the sounds of language, the anger of a crowd, a scientific theory, churches, states, and societies themselves, are some, perhaps not even the best, examples of the extendedness of mind. That it is possible to see these things in other ways – perhaps as mere outer evidence of the inner mind – I do not doubt. But remember that, like all metaphors, talk of mind's landscape is intended to suggest and encourage, not to convince.

No less important than the possibility of conceiving of the mind as in some sense spread out is the idea of its being visible. A landscape is not merely a stretch of countryside, it is a stretch set out before a spectator, and, though we will have to think hard about what is meant by 'spectator', something of this carries over to mind's landscape. In taking seriously the fact that landscapes and points of view are made for each other, we will have to consider the familiar different points of view – that of a subject herself and that of an observer – which figure in our conception of the mind.

Finally, there is the idea of a landscape as a surface, an outermost layer supported and given its character by what lies underneath. This feature of real landscapes reminds us of the methodology we would use in any thorough investigation of a terrain. Such a study would inevitably begin with a sketch or map, some depiction of how the landscape with all its features and landmarks would appear to a spectator. (A landscape in the artistic sense might serve.) This would then set the agenda for the further geological work which follows. The first task here would be exploration (and recording) of what lies most immediately under the surface, and which contributes to its characteristic shape. In this task, the hard work of excavation rather than the application of geological theory is likely to play the bigger part. But in the second task – the provision of an account of how the whole of the landscape is supported on the deepest layers, on the tectonic plates of bedrock – an appeal to theory is inevitable.

With suitable adjustments, I recommend just this methodology in the study of the mind. The sketching or mapping of the mental terrain – part I of the book – comes in chapter 1. Here an attempt is made to describe what would be present to even the most naive of spectators, so the result is bound to seem superficial. But of course, so long as all the major features of the landscape are displayed, superficiality is just what is wanted.

Next, in part II, the aim will be to see what lies underneath. Here digging will be required rather than appeals to anything deserving the title of theory. Using little more than our ordinary intellectual tools, the aim will be to explore what lies under the major landmarks of the mind. The results of this exploration will be reported in chapters 2, 3 and 4, though I should note here that these results are disturbing. Under the mental landscape there are faults and fissures not evident to the naked eye, and it is our struggle to make sense of these that has set the agenda for much of the purely philosophical study of the mind.

Finally, in part III we shall get to what is, in many people's reckoning, the very bottom of things. The mysteries of what lies just under the surface of our initial map might well be thought work enough for philosophers of mind. But sometimes it is necessary to go even deeper in order to understand the contours of the upper layers, and in doing so we usually have need of various theories. In particular, it has seemed to many philosophers that we can never really be certain of what the mind is like without understanding how the whole of the structure sits on the relatively stable bedrock of the physical world. This is the world of material stuff, of atoms and molecules weaving their patterns in accordance with physical laws. We know that at the extreme limit of physical complexity are such things as biological organisms and the physiological structures that make them up. We know also, or at least strongly suspect, that certain of these physiological structures – brains and their attendant neurophysiological mechanisms – are deeply implicated in the very possibility of a mental life. But how? How, if at all, does what was charted in parts I and II fit on to the bedrock of physical reality described by sciences such as physics, chemistry and biology? This will be the third and final stage of our investigation, and it will fill chapters 5 to 9.

Part I

Surveying the Territory

1

The Mental Landscape

The starting-point is description. With the minimum of philosophical sophistication, we need to describe the features that make up the mental landscape. Fortunately, this task will not require field trips. Equipped as we are with minds, each of us is perfectly well-placed to do the job with little more (but no less) than thought. Of course, it may well be that the proximity of mind can, in the end, be a source of error. As you will come to appreciate, there can be two views here: one stresses that the mind is special precisely because it is knowable from the 'inside', whilst the other view, insisting that real knowledge must be observer-independent, demands that we study the mind from somewhere more objectively 'outside'. Exactly what the 'inside/outside' metaphor comes to will be considered in later chapters, but for the present we will proceed without worrying too much about this.

Ideally, I should like to ask you to think about how to answer the following question: what things or phenomena count as mental, as showing the presence of minds? These answers would then serve as the starting-point of our investigation. Though circumstances do not allow me to gather this information directly, I can do the next best thing. Over the years, I have handed out a questionnaire to students before they have done any philosophy of mind, asking them to list the sorts of things that they would count as showing the presence of minds. Below is a lightly edited collation of their answers:

ability to learn	acting intentionally	agency
awareness	believing	building a house
ability to represent	choosing	ability to value
consciousness	deciding	desiring a holiday
dreaming	emotions	experiencing a pain
experiencing happiness	feelings	getting the point of a joke
having a point of view	having free will	hearing a violin
imagining	intending to write an essay	introspecting

loving	melancholy	painting a picture
perceiving	perceiving	pleasure
reasoning	reflecting on a problem	remembering
seeing a tree	self-consciousness	speaking
theorizing	the self	thinking
understanding language	understanding symbols	wanting
will-power	anger	

No doubt one could think of ways in which this list could be altered. First, the list seems to include a lot of unnecessary redundancy. For example, *seeing a tree* seems to be at the same level of generality as *hearing a violin*, and both would count as *perceiving* something. It is thus not clear why we need to have all three in the list.

Secondly, it should be remembered that the list I have given is a collation of the answers given by many different students, and you may not agree with a number of the choices. Most importantly, you might feel that some item does not belong on the list – is not genuinely mental. For example, a number of students argue that actions should be counted as at most the *outcome* of what goes on in minds, and therefore as not deserving the same status as feelings. To this I can only say that further discussion is needed to decide whether this is a reasonable view, for many students are convinced that human action is just as important to the characterization of the mind as other phenomena, and we must not begin our inquiry by closing off the possibility that they are right.

Let us call the subject-matter which is partly defined by the above list the 'mental realm'. This somewhat grand-sounding title has a certain vagueness, but the items on the list are such a heterogeneous bunch that any less vague term would prejudice further discussion.

Order out of Chaos

The first thing to note about the list is that it contains broadly two sorts of item: (i) activities, that is, things which are naturally reported by verbs; and (ii) the products or outcomes of these activities which are reported by nouns. For example, *thinking of a number between 1 and 10* is certainly something done, whilst *the thought of a number between 1 and 10* could be considered the product or upshot of some such activity. We use a verb to describe the former and a noun phrase to describe the latter. (But don't think of 'product' in its most literal sense. Certainly, I do not want to be taken as saying that a thought is *manufactured* by thinking.)

Leaving 'products' on one side for the moment, it seems to me – and to the students with whom this was discussed – that there are three importantly different kinds of mental activity, which are represented in the list with more or less general entries. With several specific examples of each, these main categories of mental activity are as follows:

Experiencing   (having a pain, 'seeing' stars when you bump your head),
Attitudinizing   (wanting chocolate, believing that the Earth is round),
Acting   (signing a cheque, making a chair, reaching for a glass).

Each of these is a recognizable activity of mind, at least in so far as we count verbs as markers of activity. Admittedly, there might be some puzzlement about the second of these items. Experiencing and acting are themselves represented in the original list, and I have simply drafted them in to be the names of general categories. But we do not ordinarily speak about 'attitudinizing' (at least in the way intended) and this term requires, and will be given, further comment. However, everyone has some idea what it is to want or believe something, so I shall let the examples serve for the moment, returning later to the mysterious 'attitudinizing'.

In so far as each of the above is an activity, each of them will have a characteristic or associated 'product'. They are as follows:

Experiencing → **consciousness**,
Attitudinizing → **attitudes**,
Acting → **actions**.

It might be thought odd that I have used the word 'consciousness' as the outcome of experiencing, rather than using the obvious word 'experience'. In fact, nothing much hangs on this, and my reason for having broken the symmetry is simply that 'experience' can be either a noun or a verb, whereas what was wanted was something more clearly a noun. Also, the point of the strange word 'attitudinizing' might now be a little clearer. Speaking of such things as beliefs and wants as attitudes is closer to ordinary usage. None the less, to want something − to *adopt* that attitude − is a kind of doing; it is something we report with a verb. All I did was to use a more general verb.

As you will come to see, these three pairs are particularly important to anyone trying to chart the mind's landscape; like mountains, they constitute fixed landmarks in that landscape. Yet before we allow ourselves to use them in our map-making activities, we need to know in more detail what they are like. Considering that they all figure, at least initially, in most people's list of contents of the mental realm, they are surprisingly different from one another.

Experiencing and Consciousness

> The laughter of the class, graduating from the first shrill bark of surprise into a deliberately aimed hooting, seemed to crowd against him, to crush the privacy that he so much desired, a privacy in which he could be alone with his pain, gauging its strength, estimating its duration, inspecting its anatomy. The pain extended a feeler into his head, and unfolded its wet wings along the walls of his thorax, so that he felt, in his sudden scarlet blindness, to be himself a large bird waking from sleep. The blackboard, milky slate smeared with the traces of last night's washing, clung to his consciousness like a membrane. The pain seemed to be displacing with its own hairy segments, his heart and lungs; as its grip swelled in his throat he felt he was holding his brain like a morsel on a platter high out of hungry reach.[1]

Perhaps the most persistent view that I have come across from students is that our ability to experience, and in so doing to be conscious or aware of something, is a central activity of the mind. Indeed, some consider that consciousness is the very essence of the mind. But what sort of things figure in this awareness? As the above quotation shows – graphically – there seems to be a special kind of awareness of the state of our bodies and an awareness of our perceptual interactions with the world. If you have been injured, as the teacher was in the Updike story, or if certain bodily events are taking place, then this will usually result in consciousness of pain or pleasure, pressure or fatigue, hunger or satiation. Or, if you are seeing something, this perceptual activity is often accompanied by particular conscious activity that determines what it is like to have such a perception. The teacher described in the passage sees the blackboard and, in seeing it, experiences it in a particular way. The phrase 'milky traces smeared with last night's washing' is a description of the blackboard, but it is also a description of the teacher's experience; the blackboard is said to have 'clung to his consciousness like a membrane'.

In addition to bodily and perceptual awareness, there is a kind of experience that seems related to these, but does not seem to depend on there being a specific change to the body, or an object of perception. Think of the moods and feelings that rise in us and accompany our other activities, often for no obvious reason. Among these are, for example, a sense that all is well with the world, or a lurking anxiety that what you are doing is doomed to failure. In being features of our consciousness these are like pains and perceptions, but they do not seem to have the more narrowly oriented roles of bodily awareness or perception. They somehow float free of any particular business in our mental life, whilst colouring it in more shades than we can name.

An important thing to notice about all of the above phenomena is that they count as experience of what goes on 'inside', even when, as in the case of perception, they also embrace something external to our consciousness. Walking down a city street in the cool of March, you feel the wind in your face as it is funnelled through the gaps in the taller buildings, you have the experience of greys and browns of drab buildings and leafless trees, and you hear the hum of the traffic punctuated here and there by louder sounds of impatient drivers using their horns, or trucks accelerating away from traffic lights. The wind, buildings, trees and traffic are 'outside' of us, but we none the less count our experience of them – what goes on when we perceive them – as 'inside'.

This whole show of experience – inside and outside, repeated in thousands of varying ways as we move from place to place – is what counts for many as the core of the mental realm. The view of some of my students tends to be: to have a mind is nothing other than to have what is often described as a 'stream of consciousness' – a kind of show that is going on most of the time when we are awake. And the metaphor of a show is the one that crops up most often when I ask for a description of experience – a description of what it is like to be the possessor of a stream of consciousness. 'It is as if you were in a cinema watching a film from so close and with such involvement that you were only aware of *what* was happening and not *that* it was happening on a film in an auditorium.' Fine, I say to this recurrent sort of answer to my question, but it seems to require us to understand what it is to be *aware* of a film in some particularly close way, so it is not all that much help in telling someone what awareness itself is. Moreover, this account seems to apply exclusively to our perceptual experience, to the awareness – itself inside – of what is happening outside. But what about such things as pains and other wholly inner sensations and moods? The needed revision often runs as follows: 'Well, it's not exactly like the show in a cinema, but it does seem to involve witnessing various things – observing them, paying attention to them – even if from an only metaphorical distance. When I have a pain, I direct my attention to it, just in the way that I direct my attention to my present experience of, say, colours in my visual field. This is sort of like a film or theatrical performance which I can witness, and with respect to which I can differentially direct my attention from one character to another.'

Does this sort of metaphorical description help? Perhaps it points you in the direction of what I mean to speak about under the heading of 'experience', but I doubt it is much more informative than that. Indeed, it raises more questions than it answers: for example, who or what does the directing of attention in this case? 'The self' comes the reply. But this reply also gets us into very deep waters. Is the self separate from experiential activity and its attendant consciousness or are they united rather like the dancer and the dance? Here we are beginning to see some of the problems that lie just beneath the surface of our conception of experience and consciousness, and for the present we shall leave well enough alone. In any case, perhaps there is not much more that one can do in directly characterizing experience than to reach for metaphors like those found in Updike's wonderfully lurid description.

Attitudinizing and Attitudes

All this was lost on Alice, who was still looking intently along the road, shading her eyes with one hand. 'I see somebody now!' she exclaimed at last. 'But he's coming very slowly – and what curious attitudes he goes into!' (For the Messenger kept skipping up and down, and wriggling like an eel, as he came along, with his great hands spread out like fans on each side.)

'Not at all,' said the King. 'He's an Anglo-Saxon Messenger – and those are Anglo-Saxon Attitudes. He only does them when he's happy.[2]

In the subtle shift of perspective in this passage – the shift from attitude as posture to attitude as a feature of a mind – Carroll has given us several important hints about mental attitudes. We are invited to imagine the Anglo-Saxon Messenger as taking up odd postures, setting his limbs in awkward or uncomfortable positions. However, in ways it is perhaps more tactful for me to leave unsaid, the Anglo-Saxons have the reputation of having odd, sometimes downright 'uncomfortable', attitudes – by which is meant beliefs, desires and expectations – in respect of a variety of subjects.

The appeal of this passage is that it effortlessly manages to shift our attention from a set of bizarre postures to a set of perhaps equally bizarre attitudes towards life. In using the two senses of 'attitude' in the same context, Carroll succeeds in getting us to pause over something that we don't usually bother much about – the aptness of the word in its 'posture' sense for characterizing such things as beliefs and desires.

A posture is something we manoeuvre ourselves into, and which is therefore observable in our behaviour. Similarly, we usually tell what someone believes or desires by things done and said – by behaviour; an attitude in this sense is a mental state which we often 'read' off from behaviour. Moreover, it is true of attitudes, even in the posturing sense, that they can be directed to, or indicative of, something. When someone is said to adopt a menacing attitude, what is in question is not merely how a person is standing, though some such bodily position is being described. Rather, what is special about a 'menacing attitude' is that it is a posture directed towards someone or something. And of course, this is precisely what is typical of such things as beliefs and desires. They are not merely states of mind we discern through behaviour, they are states of mind that have a special kind of directedness. I don't just believe or desire, I believe that something is the case, or I desire someone or something.

The two crucial defining features of attitudinizing displays are:

(a) A kind of behaviour which is typically characteristic of the particular atti-tude in question. (Imagine how you could tell the difference between someone who desired something, believed something, intended some-thing, etc.)

(b) A 'something' towards which the attitudinizing is directed, as when we say that:

> Harry believes *the telephone is out of order*,
> Jane desires *a new car*,
> Bill intends *to boil a kettle*.

Note that the items towards which an attitude can be directed are quite various. In the above three examples we have these three items:

> the telephone is out of order,
> a new car,
> to boil a kettle.

Focusing on the sentences we use to report attitudes, and borrowing a term from grammar, we shall call the 'something' towards which attitudes are directed the *complement* of the attitude. That is, in the sentences given in (b) there are complement phrases which report the particular direction of the atti-tude. Note that the first of these has a declarative sentence as a complement. This is important because sentences like this are typically used to say, truly or falsely, how things are; they report what philosophers call 'propositions'. More-over, it seems possible (even if it might sound awkward in given cases) to report virtually all attitudes using declarative sentences as complements. We could have expressed the other examples in (b) as:

> Jane desires that she has a new car.
> Bill intends that he will make the kettle boil.

Because complements of belief reports typically contain a complete declara-tive sentence that expresses a proposition, and because the other attitudes can apparently be twisted into this shape, philosophers have settled on the idea that the products of attitudinizing can all be called *propositional attitudes*. So, what Carroll has shown us is that the Anglo-Saxon messengers strike odd postural as well as propositional attitudes.[3]

We can also call the item to which an attitude is directed its *content*. The notion of a 'complement' seems to many to be too grammatical and too closely tied to the report of an attitude, whereas the word 'content' seems to capture something about the attitude itself. But for the present it won't matter much whether you think of the attitudes as having complements or contents.

The above is little more than a sketch, and much more remains to be said about the role of the attitudes in the mental realm. However, even this sketch is enough to make obvious just how important a part they play in our characterization of that realm. And this comes as a bit of a surprise to those who are convinced that experience is the central feature of the mind. For, whatever else we come to say about them, the propositional attitudes are not obviously items of experience. For example, suppose someone were to ask you, out of the blue, whether the present government will be returned to power at the next election. I have no doubt that your answer would be readily forthcoming and might well begin like this: I believe that . . . But to get to this answer did you have to search the elusive stream of consciousness we just discussed? Does that stream contain a sort of banner on which is written 'the present government will not be returned to power at the next election'? This is highly unlikely. Of course, I don't doubt that images of governments – a sort of collage of images of politicians, government buildings, television coverage of elections and perhaps even images of words – might be prompted by the original question. Yet these do not constitute the belief itself. In fact, those not so wedded to the experiential picture of the mind as to rule out everything else tend to report that consciousness plays very little role in our ability to know and say what attitudes we have. (This is not to deny that we might think consciousness, or the capacity for consciousness, is a prerequisite for a creature who can be said to adopt attitudes.)

These observations point the way down a number of difficult roads. If consciousness figures less (and sometimes not at all) in our apprehension of our beliefs, how do we tell what we believe, want, intend, etc.? We certainly don't do it in the way we tell these things about other people, that is, by looking at what they do and say. Moreover, what relation is there between the 'self' which made its appearance in our discussion of experience and the item which is the subject of attitude reports? In what way is the 'I' of 'I am in pain' related to the 'I' of 'I believe that it will snow'? These sorts of question are typical of the next stage of investigation. But our interest at present has only been in the kind of thing that comes under the headings 'attitudinizing' and 'attitude', and we have completed that task. The activity of attitudinizing results in our having attitudes with contents. Each attitude has typical manifestations in behaviour, and all of them seem suitable for treatment as propositional attitudes, as allowing their contents to be reported by declarative sentences.

Acting and Actions

> The astonishing thing about action is that it is possible at all. For, if a man is making a chair, you will find a physical causal explanation of the movement of each piece of wood from its initial to its final setting; everything that happens is in accordance with law; but you will look throughout this world or universe forever in vain for an analogous physical explanation of their coming together in the form they did, a form that mirrors human need and the human body itself. (Try it.)[4]

As I mentioned earlier, there is a strong tendency to overlook actions when thinking about what to count as items in the mental realm. Those who find themselves only reluctantly admitting attitudes into the fold, dig in their heels at what they regard as too physical a thing to count as anything mental. Such is the pull of the idea that the mental consists in the 'inner' – the show of experience and consciousness – that actions can seem just too far removed from this centre to count as anything more than the mind's wake as it moves through the physical world. But this view is by no means universal, and one would do well to listen to those who oppose it.

The passage above emphasizes the difficulty of fitting actions into the picture of the world encouraged by science. Thus, whilst each movement of the arms and hands, hammer and nails might well be explicable in terms of science, the fact that all these things come together as the making of a chair can seem quite mysterious. Discussion of how the mental realm fits in with the scientific picture of the world will figure later. But the situation described in the passage can be used to illustrate something more pertinent to our present concerns.

Begin by supposing that everything is as described in the passage, except that the agent making the chair is invisible. To an unsuspecting witness, the pieces of wood seem to rise up and be nailed and glued into place; the chair just seems to come unaided into existence. This would of course be astonishing, but we can leave this on one side for the moment. What I want to ask is this: would the witness actually observe the action, the making of the chair? Clearly, by hypothesis, the agent goes unseen, but if you are one of those who think of the action as nothing but some sort of change in the physical world, you should be prepared to say that the action is seen, even if not the actor. Yet surely that is not how we would describe it. Why? Well, the very idea of an action – even of a purely 'physical' action – seems to require us to identify some sort of mental component. As the passage notes, were there not human desires and needs at work, as well as the further beliefs, desires and intentions to fulfil them, then we would not have the faintest idea of what was going on. When we do see the actor, we see some or all of these attitudes *in* the transformation of the materials, and unless we can see the mind in the process unfolding before us, we simply don't count that process as an action; for all we know it might just be the accidental product of some strange cosmic wind.

The idea that an action is in this way at least partly a mental phenomenon is what one of my students had in mind with the astute comment: 'actions are the mind's purposes seen in the movement of matter.' But those who insist that actions are not themselves mental still have something to say. Here is a typical rejoinder:

> What the example shows is that you couldn't imagine the pieces coming together unless there was some mind *orchestrating* the movements. But the action itself – the physical movement of the pieces – is not mental. What happens is that you see these movements – the action – and then *infer* that there are mental states directing them. In seeing the action, you don't literally *see* the mind.

This rejoinder throws up many intricate problems and these must await further discussion. However, whatever we end up saying about an action such as making a chair, it must be pointed out that the class of things called actions is much broader than we have so far allowed.

Making a chair is usually called a 'physical action' – an action in which some change is effected in some physical object or event. Examples of this kind of action are what most people think of when they are asked to imagine an action taking place, and it is this kind of action that leads to the greatest disagreement in measuring the boundaries of the mental realm. However, there is another kind of action that has been staring us in the face, the mental status of which must be beyond doubt. I have in mind here the very activities of experiencing and attitudinizing. Recall that I was careful to insist that the main categories of the mental realm had both an activity and a product sense: *experiencing* and consciousness, *attitudinizing* and attitudes, as well as *acting* and actions. But surely, for example, to direct one's attention to some item in the stream of consciousness – to experience it – is nothing short of an action, and a purely mental one at that. Moreover, once you begin to think about it, there seems to be a whole host of other things that we do which are 'in the mind' in this way. Think of your favourite colour! Work out (but don't say) the sum of 15 and 22! When you accede to these requests, you are certainly doing something – acting – only in neither case is there any ordinary change wrought in your physical environment. These episodes of thought and inference would thus seem to be the tip of a very large iceberg consisting of actions whose claims to belong in the mental realm are unimpeachable.

As with experience and attitudinizing, each case of an action comes with a subject, or, perhaps more appropriately in the case of action, an *agent*. Indeed, just as for particular items of consciousness or attitudes, it is simply impossible to have an action without an agent. The kind of impossibility here seems to be conceptual: we cannot conceive of an unowned pain, a subjectless belief, nor can we conceive of an action that lacks an agent. And now we have another element to add to the problem raised earlier: what relations obtain between the 'I' of 'I am in pain' and 'I believe that my keys are in the cookie jar' and the 'I' of 'I pruned the ceanothus too late in the year'? Clearly, there is an enormous pull in favour of saying that the items picked out by each pronoun are one and the same person or self. Indeed, this tends to be such a universally held view among my students that it takes them some time to see that there might be a problem – that the differences between experiencing, attitudinizing and acting might make it less than obvious why one and the same thing does all three.

Estimating Distances

My thumbnail sketches of consciousness, attitude and action are useful starting-points, but they must be supplemented if we are to have any hope of using them in a realistic ordering of the mental realm. However, even before we do this, it is important to get clear about how the ordering is to be achieved.

One way – perhaps the obvious way – of bringing order to a large list is by putting items in the list under various headings. The game of sorting things into animal, vegetable and mineral is a model here, but this is inappropriate for the mental realm. Take an emotion like anger, which is certainly a mental phenomenon if anything is. If we were to play the sorting game here by trying to decide whether anger was a phenomenon of consciousness, attitude or action, we would not only distort our understanding of the emotion itself, but the headings used. For anger has features of all three; it is, so to speak, in some respects animal, vegetable and mineral.

What this suggests is that we should think of the three categories, not as headings, but as poles towards which the phenomena of mind are more or less attracted. Anger is in some respects a conscious phenomenon, in some an attitude and in still others a pattern of action; it is in these ways pulled toward each of the poles. Order is generated then not by headings under which we sort, but by estimating the distance of each item from the three polar categories.

This sort of ordering depends crucially on our being able to say more about the respects in which something is like experience, attitude or action. But what are these respects and where do they come from? The list is as follows:

> Observability,
> Accessibility,
> Expressibility,
> Directionality,
> Theoreticity.

As with everything at this surface-mapping stage, this list has its basis in the untutored judgements of my students. However, I have had to invent my own names for these respects, and some of the discussion will seem more committed to this or that philosophical view than has heretofore been the case. This is perhaps inevitable, given that I pushed my informants for their views about the underlying nature of various mental phenomena; after all, philosophical theorizing does not necessarily need professional philosophers. Still, even if what follows reveals what might seem only prejudice when exposed to proper philosophical scrutiny, it is fairly widespread prejudice. And that makes it no less part of the mental landscape than our original list. Indeed, after some clarification of the labels, I expect you to recognize, perhaps even agree, with much of what is said. Deeper investigation of the phenomena and the scheme of classification will come in part II of our inquiries.

(i)   Observability

Confronted with a mind (someone else's), how easy is it to tell whether you are in the presence of experiencing, attitudinizing or acting? This is not meant to be a deep question. There is a long tradition in philosophy of considering how, if at all, we can justify our faith in the mindedness of others. This is not what we are up to here. Assume that others do have minds, that the extreme sceptical stance is inappropriate, and ask yourself this: how easy is it to tell just by looking that some mind is experiencing something, maintaining an attitude towards something, or acting? To many, at least part of the answer is straightforward. Philosophical argument might well shake our convictions in respect of all three, but it is certainly easier to wreak sceptical havoc in respect of experiencing than in respect of acting. The usual thought is that we can conceal what we experience, sometimes with no effort at all, but that what we do – our actions – are there for the looking. However, we must be careful not to read too much into this apparently obvious conclusion.

There are experiences which would be regarded as easily observable and actions which are not. It is natural to think that the victim of a serious accident can be seen to experience pain, whereas someone can do something completely away from even the possibility of prying eyes – something like adding up two numbers, as we say, 'in the head'. That is, there would seem to be cases where experiences are out in the open, and also cases of actions that are 'inside'. Moreover, the idea of observation that is in play here cries out for further elucidation. Still, having agreed that the proper place for this elucidation in our part II investigations, let us say for now that 'in general and for the most part' experience comes at the low end of the observability spectrum, while action lies at the other. A typical case of experiencing something – having an ache in a limb – is usually counted as fully discernible only to the subject of the experience, whereas a typical case of acting – signing a will – is rated as something anyone in the right place can witness.

But what about attitudes? How easy is it to see that someone wants an ice-cream or believes that it is about to rain? The temptation is to say: it all depends. If the circumstances are right, for example, if there is enough behaviour to go on, it would seem to be quite easy. The child irritably resisting his parents' best efforts to distract him from the ice-cream vendor can be clearly seen to want an ice-cream, whereas the academic comfortably engaged in reading a book might well believe that it is about to rain without giving our observational abilities any purchase at all. Still, if we abstract away from special cases and, as in respect of experiencing and acting, think only in general and for the most part, the attitudes seem to be somewhere in between the two extremes in respect of observability. It is easier to see what people do than what they believe, but it is also easier to see what they believe than what they experience.

(ii)   Accessibility

How easy is it for you to tell of *yourself* that you are experiencing, believing or doing something? That is, how accessible is your own portion of the mental realm? Do we always know what we are doing, or what we believe and want? No, but perhaps this is because we don't always attend to these things; the idea would be that if we did attend, we would know. Yet couldn't there be cases in which no amount of thinking about it would lead us to acknowledge particular actions or beliefs and wants as our own? Indeed, aren't such cases perfectly familiar? Smith sets out to help Jones dig the garden; he believes that he is doing this from the goodness of his heart, and that is what he would avow after reflection. But, to those who know him, what he is doing seems more appropriately described as competitively displaying his horticultural superiority over Jones; the way in which he goes about 'helping' seems to give him away. Ask Smith what he is doing, believing and wanting and you get one answer. Ask his friends and you get another. Perhaps Smith could be brought to see himself in the way others do, but that is not really relevant. All that I want this example to remind us of is the perfectly ordinary fact that we don't always have instant accessibility to what we believe, want or are engaged in.

Experiencing, however, seems to be in stark contrast to these. Not only do we think that such things as pains and itches are highly accessible, we would find it difficult to imagine cases in which there was any attenuation of accessibility. Could you be in pain, for example, and not notice that you were? And here, by pain, I mean some fairly robust example of the kind, not a barely perceptible sensation which comes and goes too fleetingly to count as one thing or another. You could of course be stoical about it, not show others that you were in pain; you could even push it into the background so that it didn't interfere with your present activities. But could you have a pain and not notice it at all? This is a difficult question, a question whose very status has been debated. In particular, is it a question about how things are as a matter of fact in respect of pains, or is it somehow a more conceptual question: is the very concept of pain such that it is logically impossible to have an exemplar of it without noticing?

As in the case of observability, nothing we are engaged in just now requires us to deal with these worries. Whatever is to be said in the long run when we start to dig deeper, here it is enough to note what seems the unvarnished truth to most people (and, in particular, to the students who so forcefully expressed this view): we have a much greater degree of access to items of experience than we do to attitudes and actions.

How do attitudes and actions compare in respect of accessibility? There is a tendency to think that we know more about what we believe and want than about what we do. The reason most often given for this is that acting requires some co-operation on the part of the world: we have greater accessibility to what we intend to do (an attitude) than what we are actually doing or achieving, because we are only doing or achieving something if certain worldly events are actually taking place, and we may be in error about whether they are. Dreams illustrate the point nicely.

If, in a dream, you are about to sign a cheque then you seem to have the intentions, desires and beliefs appropriate to that commonplace action. But if you were actually signing a cheque, not only would there have to be this attitudinal background, your hand would have to hold the pen and move in some appropriate way. And it is precisely the latter that is missing in a dream. When you dream that yet another bill is overdue and, in a state of generalized anxiety, reach for your cheque-book and write out a cheque, hastily and without due care and attention to the balance remaining in your fragile account, you have a keen awareness of the attitudinal background – it seems wholly accessible to you. But, as you often come to realize on waking, one thing that didn't happen was that you signed a cheque.

Dreams are the extreme case here, but there are less dramatic cases of actions being inaccessible in ways that the attitudes are not. So, summing up: we usually rank experiences at one extreme – immediate and pretty full accessibility – whereas attitudes come somewhat further down the line with actions bringing up the rear.

(iii) Expressibility

It would seem equally easy to tell someone that you have a pain in your arm, that you believe right will triumph over wrong, and that you are cooking your dinner. But many feel that this way of putting things misses an important feature of these categories. In particular, there is a prevalent idea that, though we can tell someone *that* we have a pain in the arm, we cannot express or communicate the experience itself. Put colloquially, 'what it is like' to have a particular pain seems something that escapes even the most imaginative use of language. As we have found with other respects, intuitions like this one raise more questions than they answer. For example, what exactly would it be like to express an experience if we could? What would constitute success in this apparently difficult task? If we don't know even that much, then perhaps our conviction that experiences cannot be expressed is less interesting than it seems. Still, we must not stop just yet at such deeper questions; there is a consensus that experiences are very low on the expressibility scale, and that is good enough for the present.

But what about attitudes and actions? Actions seem to be straightforwardly expressible: in so far as you know what you are doing, you just put it into words – you describe your action in some appropriate way, chosen from amongst all the ones available to you. In appropriate circumstances, you just say: 'I'm signing a cheque,' 'paying the gas bill' or 'practising my signature on this already ruined cheque'. To be sure, there are cases where it is not quite that easy. I can imagine myself engaged in some intricate physical manoeuvre which is necessary to the well-being of my bicycle, but which I cannot properly describe – it is just too complex, even though the aim of the action itself is simple. Of course, I could always just say: 'I am adjusting the brakes' or 'fixing my bicycle' and this might do. Telling someone what I am doing does not always require detailed description. In the end, then, there doesn't seem to be much of a problem about expression here.

With belief, want, and other attitudes, the problem comes down to getting hold of some appropriate sentence to use in the complement place in the attitude report. In most cases, this is straightforward. To be sure, there are times when you are not quite sure whether you believe something to be the case, or merely hope that it is. And there are also bound to be times when, for example, you expect something to happen, but would be hard put to find the exact sentence which captures the content of your expectation. (I am assuming here that expectation is a specialized form of belief – belief about some future course of events.)

In sum, there are problems for both actions and attitudes in respect of expressiblity – problems which make them about equal in this dimension. But they are nowhere near as severe as the problems encountered in respect of one's experiences.

(iv)   Directionality

An attitude is a mental item which can show itself in activities and behaviour. Of course, this is not invariably so; one can easily conceive of beliefs, desires and the like which happen never to leak out into the realm of action. Still, it is not unreasonable to think of the attitudes as having particular and typical kinds of manifestation in activity. A desire to buy a new coat, for example, will 'look' very different to observers from a belief that coats keep you warm in winter.

However, what is particularly characteristic of the attitudes is that they are attitudes *about* something – they are reported in sentences which contain complement clauses, or, using the other idiom, they have *contents*. Yet another way of putting this is to say that attitudes are never merely expressed in behaviour, they are also, and essentially, *directed* to, or at, something. For example, compare desire with, say, vanity. Both have a claim to be the kind of thing appropriate to the mind, but there is an important difference between them. A vain person, like a desirous one, is disposed to act in various ways, but to understand the desire fully, we must know what it is a desire *for*. There is no counterpart to this directedness in the case of vanity.

On the face of it, directionality is virtually absent in those items that most naturally group themselves around the category of experience. Taking pain as the first example, imagine that you have overdone some exercise and that you are now suffering for it. You have various aches and pains and these seem to be located in various parts of your body. They are located – and they have specific characteristics, each different from one another – but they don't seem to be *about* anything; they lack directionality. Your aching thigh is not an ache *for* anything – it is not reported in a sentence containing a complement clause, and thus it does not have a content.

One must be careful here. The notion of content as just used is somewhat specialized. It is that item to which an attitude is directed. The content of the desire that you have a new coat is, roughly, the state of affairs of your having a new coat. If you had it badly enough, one could describe your state – somewhat fancifully – as an ache for a new coat. In a more general sense of the word 'content', of course it is true that a pain has a content. But this is not the sense of the word in question.

I said that directionality is virtually absent in typical cases of experiencing such as the pain case. Certainly, there is nothing that corresponds to the robust use of complement clauses with which we report beliefs. But why only 'virtually'? Well, it seems to many as if there is a kind of directionality in the pain case which it is easy to overlook. It is a lower grade of directionality than we have in connection with the attitudes, and it may in the end be nothing more than the result of an attitude being linked to an experience, but it is worth remarking on. Certainly, pain is not usually a neutral item of experience: it is something unpleasant and which we seek to avoid. The directionality of an experience of pain may be no more than 'would that it would go,' but it is at least possible to see this as a primitive version of the kind of directionality we have in full-fledged attitudes. Of course, one might take the view that pains just happen to have (in us, and for the most part) a kind of *connection* to the attitudes. On this view, it is not the pain that has any kind of directionality, it is just that pains bring with them desires to get rid of the pain. The idea is that the desire, not the pain, is directed.

Somewhat different from the pain case is this: think of what it would be like to be standing just in front of a blue wall, looking squarely at it. Your perception would be directed: it would be described as a perception of a blue wall. But that is not quite what is at issue. Try to forget about the fact that you perceive a blue wall (which is surely directional, like an attitude), and think instead of the conscious experience occasioned by the expanse of blue. Clearly, this is something that you are aware of when you perceive the blue wall, but it is distinct from the latter. It is the experience found, as is said, by introspection in the stream of consciousness, and it can be separated from what causes it (the wall), or what it is about (the blueness of the wall). As the struggles of the last few sentences show, it is not an easy matter to use words to point to the phenomenon in question. But most people are, on reflection, only too eager to admit that there is such a thing as the what–it–is–like–to–see–blue sensation in their stream of consciousness when they direct their attention to a blue object.

Does the qualitative experience you have when you are perceiving a blue wall constitute a case of pure, non-directed experiencing? It certainly doesn't seem to have even the most primitive form of directionality. Unless the colour is particularly shocking, your experience of blueness does not come with the feeling: 'would that it would go away.' So perhaps the colour perception case is a better example than pain of non-directedness. Or perhaps the pain case really constitutes just as good an example, which only seems different because pain is hooked up *in us* to genuine attitudes such as the desire to get rid of the pain? Well, whether pain has a kind of primitive directionality is not something we need to settle here. For whatever we end up saying, it seems that directionality is typical of, and central to, attitudinizing, and is only of marginal importance to experience.

What of the third category – acting? We have briefly discussed the question of the degree to which actions are mental items. Our discussion was admittedly inconclusive, but it was suggested that even a physical action could not be thought of simply as a sequence of physical movements: the mind is either actually present in the action or is intimately involved in it in some way. Thus, signing a cheque certainly involves various hand movements, but these are (at least) mind-directed. The movements have as their aim, for example, the payment of the electricity bill.

As always, there is much more to be said here. But for now it is enough to note that, with respect to directionality, attitudes have it as a central feature, actions include elements which are directional, and items of consciousness have at most a minimal kind of directionality.

(v)   Theoreticity

Is it possible to see electrons? Not an easy question, nor one we have to settle definitely here. But this much seems true: whether or not one can stretch the notion of 'seeing' sufficiently to allow it to be said that we see electrons, any seeing of them would be a wholly different kind of thing from our seeing of tables and chairs. Though not a precise business, it does seem that some items count as immediately or directly observable, whereas others are less directly observable (if observable at all). What have been called 'middle-sized dry goods' – taking tables and chairs to be representative – falls under the first heading, whereas electrons fall firmly under the second.

Recognizing that electrons are at best indirectly observable, the next question to ask is: do they really exist? Here again, brushing aside the deeper ruminations of certain philosophers, the answer is surely 'yes, there really are electrons.' But having admitted that electrons are only indirectly observable, what grounds do we have for saying that they exist? Undoubtedly, many people regard the best grounds for something's existence to be its direct observability, but there are other grounds. For instance, one could say this: the notion of an electron forms an essential part of a theory we have about the nature of matter – a theory which is by now established in the scientific community. Even though we may never be able (even in principle) to observe electrons directly, we are generally happy (give or take a few philosophical qualms) to say that they exist. They exist because they are integral to our well-established *theoretical* understanding of the universe.

Against this background, here are some things we can say about the feature of theoreticity: chairs and tables – things we regard as directly observable – have a *low* degree of theoreticity. We don't believe in the existence of these things on the basis of our theory of the universe – we just see them. On the other hand, electrons have a *high* degree of theoreticity: their very existence is bound up with our theoretical understanding of nature.

What about the items in the mental realm? There is generally a consensus (one that some philosophers have challenged) for the view that, whatever else we say about other items, experiences have a very low degree of theoreticity. We do not regard a pain, a visual appearance, an experience of a sound, the changing coloured image which comes before our closed eyes just after we have seen a bright light, as things whose existence depends in any way on a theory we may have about how things work. Items of experience seem to be immediately apprehended. Indeed, there is a tendency, which has been encouraged, though not invented, by some philosophers, to consider items of experience as *more* directly observable than the middle-sized dry goods which surround us. Introspection can seem a more direct and reliable guide to what exists than modes of 'extrospection' such as seeing, touching and hearing.

Allowing strength of opinion on this to be our guide, and leaving on one side any investigation of the basis of that opinion, we shall count experiencing as at the lowest end of the scale of theoreticity. But what about the other two categories: attitudes and acting? Here matters get more complicated. In discussing the accessibility of the attitudes, it was noted that, whilst we *sometimes* either make mistakes as to the direction of our attitudes, or, on occasion, just fail to register attitudes that others can more accurately gauge from our behaviour, we *often* have fairly immediate access to what we desire, intend, believe, etc. But one thing we also noticed was that, even when the access we have is fairly immediate, it doesn't appear to be like the access we have to such things as pain. For example, if asked whether next Sunday was the 15th, you would surely do some kind of ruminating before answering. However, compare this rumination with what you would go in for if I asked whether you could feel the pressure exerted by the chair you are now sitting on. Your answer in the second case seems something like a case of looking and discovering; that is why the expression 'intro*spection*' seems so apt. But this kind of introspection seems the wrong sort of method for discovering whether you believe next Sunday to be the 15th.

In cases of the attitudes and experiences of others, the contrast seems even more pronounced. You find out what someone's attitudes are by being sensitive to behaviour. Of course, you may be told point-blank what someone believes, but even this may not settle the issue. Perhaps they are not facing up to things, or are trying to see things in a better light. In cases more complicated than the one about Sunday the 15th, perhaps they are mistaken about what they believe. However, in the case of experience, it would seem that the verdict of the subject is both necessary to an accurate judgement and final.

How can one explain this difference? One way is this: an experience is something that is directly observable – though only by the person whose experience it is – whilst an attitude is something not directly observable by either the subject or his friends. On this view, attitudes are items we attribute to ourselves and each other as part of trying to make sense of – to explain – behaviour. One way of putting this would be to say that attitudes are part of our *theory* of human nature. (There will be more about this later in this chapter and in subsequent ones.) Clearly, a consequence of this view would be that attitudes are more theoretical than experiences. Of course, this is not to say that they are just like electrons. After all, the explanatory theories of physics do seem different from the 'theories' with which we explain human activities. But the discussion of electrons was only meant to illustrate the notion of theoreticity.

Accepting then that attitudes come out as more theoretical than conscious experiences, what about actions? Do we directly observe actions, or do they have a somewhat more theoretical and less directly observable nature? Here the old wounds open up again. Those students who regarded actions as not much more than physical movements would see them as directly observable. Those who considered them to be 'purposes embodied in movement' would demur, since a purpose is an attitude. And, of course, one must not forget actions which are generally classified as mental – actions such as thinking of a number between 1 and 10. Without even trying to sort all this out here, I shall take the easy way out by placing actions somewhere in between attitudes and experiences on the theoreticity scale.

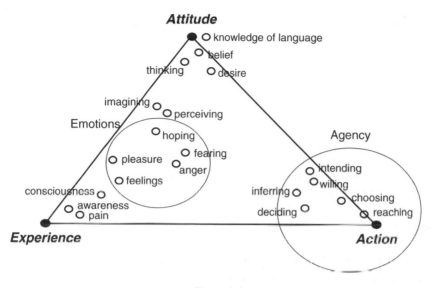

Figure 1.1

The Inventory of the Mind

Without suggesting that it is either complete or uncontroversial, figure 1.1 illustrates how the five features just discussed can be used to order the original list. It displays what we can call a proper *inventory* of the mind.

The main categories are represented as three poles equidistant from one another. Perhaps more in keeping with the landscape metaphor, we should think of them as mountains (seen from above) whose summits mark extreme points; the location of any given mental item is fixed by the degree to which it approaches these summits in one or other of the five respects. For example, experience is a peak where one would put any feature of the mind that was wholly accessible, not observable, not expressible, not directional and not theoretical. Of course, no actual feature of the mind has this stark profile. Pain tends to be cited as the paradigm case of an experience, but there are ways in which even it falls short of being what might be called a 'pure' experience. First, whilst pain is thought of as highly accessible to its sufferer, there is arguably room in our idea of the mind for pain that is not noticed at a given time. Secondly, we do think of pain as sometimes observable − think of the accident victim − even if in many other cases it is difficult for an observer to discern. Thirdly, it is not easy to express (describe) pain, but it is not impossible to go some way towards it; one need only return to Updike's description of the teacher in pain to appreciate this. Fourthly, as was noted, there is a kind of directionality that seems to accompany a painful experience – a sort of 'would that it would go away' content. Finally, it is possible to imagine cases in which pain was appealed to more on theoretical than observational grounds. Thus, a doctor might explain why you seem always to be tired by citing the fact that you have had a pain in your leg which causes you to walk and sit awkwardly. When you protest that you felt no such pain, the doctor might well say that the pain never expressed itself – that it remained, as is often said in medical circumstances, 'sub-clinical'. Given these considerations, pain must be placed short of the summit of Experience; its dimensional profile shows it to be some little way towards both Attitude and Action.

Other features of the mental realm are assigned places on this same basis, though I don't want to insist that I have got these locations precisely right. More than a little of the philosophical literature is taken up with what are represented here as orientational questions. Once known as 'philosophical psychology', this branch of philosophy is responsible for many acute observations about the rich and subtle connections that exist among the phenomena in the mental realm. Against this background, you should see figure 1.1 as providing no more than an idea of how to order the mental realm, not as a definitive statement of that ordering. Nevertheless, before we move on, here are a few notes explaining some of the reasons for various placements.

(a)   To keep the inventory uncluttered, I have left out some of the items which figured in the original list, but it should be obvious where they would go. Thus hope, fear, anger are placed more or less centrally and they mark out a region within which one would put other emotions. This central location seems right because emotions look towards each of the peaks without being markedly closer to any one of them. Certainly, one can be, for example, angry *that such-and-such is the case* – anger is certainly something like an attitude with a content. Yet anger is often spoken of as a feeling, as something accessible in the stream of consciousness. And finally anger not only causes us to do various things, it is itself said to be *expressed* in action.

Of course, differences will emerge as soon as one moves from anger to one or other of the emotions, so you should think of the central location labelled 'emotions' as a region within which more accurate placements can be made. Perhaps a 'calmer' emotion like regret will be closer to the attitudes than anger, and further away from the other two fixed points, whilst love might be closer to experience and further away from attitude.

Note also that feelings are placed slightly closer to experience and further away from action than emotions. In some contexts, 'emotion' and 'feeling' are used interchangeably, but in others, feeling hints more at experience. Its location near the edge of the region is meant to cater for both of these possibilities.

(b) It may not be obvious why pleasure comes just within the emotion region, whilst pain is firmly outside, closer to experience. After all, don't we speak of 'pleasure and pain' as a contrasting *pair*? Yes, there is this cliché, but there are also certain more pressing considerations which favour the placements in figure 1.1. In particular, we often speak of pleasure without suggesting anything about what is happening to our bodies. Thus, when we use 'being pleased that' or 'taking pleasure in', pleasure here comes closer to an emotion than to any sort of bodily sensation. When, for example, you find yourself saying that you are pleased to have gone to the dentist, it is unlikely that you are suggesting that such pleasure is felt in any particular part of your body, though of course any pain that the dentist caused certainly does show up in this way. This is not to deny that 'pleasure' can describe bodily sensations, nor that 'pain' can be used to describe a specially intense kind of sorrowful emotion. But the more typical use of both justifies my having placed them as in figure 1.1.

(c) Why is consciousness not shown in exactly the same place as awareness? Admittedly, I have at times used the two expressions interchangeably, but there is a reason — so far unremarked — that is responsible for this placement. One can use the word 'conscious' and its related forms of speech in two ways: either as a synonym for 'awareness' or 'experience', or as adverb qualifying the verbs of attitude and action. In this second sense, one says such things as: 'he consciously decided to . . .' or 'she consciously believed that . . .' or 'he consciously inferred that . . .' Here the contrast is with cases in which decisions, beliefs and actions are somehow not directly available to the subject. Thus, a conscious decision is one that has been reflected upon, taken after due deliberation, and is one to which the subject has the kind of access required for reporting the decision to others. However, it is not necessary for a belief or decision to be conscious for it to be experienced in the way that a pain is. (In any case, it is difficult to imagine what such an experiencing would be like.)

Some writers think that this distinction in the use of the word 'consciousness' points to the conclusion that there are really two kinds of consciousness. The one associated with pains and bodily sensations is called 'phenomenal' consciousness, and the other, the one that goes with the adverbial uses, is called 'access' consciousness. Not intending to take sides here, I still wanted figure 1.1 to reflect something of the dual nature of our appeals to the notion of consciousness. This was done by placing consciousness just that little bit closer to attitude and action than awareness. (The point can be put linguistically: 'aware' does not lend itself to adverbial use in the way that 'conscious' does.)

(d)   Reaching – stretching out one's hand and arm – is about as central a case of bodily action as one could have, and its location in the inventory reflects this. On the other hand, inferring – as in 'noticing that the shutters were closed, he inferred that they were not home' – is a clear example of an act that does not involve the body. For this reason it is placed further from action and closer to experience.

Intending, willing, choosing and deciding are intimately connected with actions of all sorts, and, according to some accounts, they are themselves forms of mental act. I have included these, and the more typical cases of action, within a region labelled 'agency' because, though I haven't discussed it at any length yet, these are the notions which together give us our idea of an agent – the person or self who initiates actions.

(e)   Finally, as has been noted, we are not always the best judge of our attitudes, nor of our actions and decisions; sometimes our states of mind are hidden from us. Sometimes this happens because the states of mind in question are as a matter of fact inaccessible to us, and sometimes because we have in some sense made them so. Examples of the first sort usually involve a sort of knowledge that we have and use, but do not, and largely cannot, remark upon. For example, when we hear the sounds of our language, we are able to interpret them – indeed it is impossible not to – because of, it has been claimed, the vast number of things we know about the sounds, grammar and meanings of that language. Yet many skilled listeners (most of us in fact) are unable to describe these crucial bits of knowledge. They guide us though they remain in some way tacit. To mark this kind of circumstance, I put knowledge of language near the attitudes but on the other side from experience. (The whole idea of tacit knowledge, especially in connection with language, has been heatedly discussed by linguists and philosophers, and we will have occasion to return to it in later chapters.)

The second way we can lose track of our own states of mind revolves around the notion of the *unconscious*, as this notion is used in psychoanalytic theory. The idea here is that some of our attitudes, decisions and actions are undertaken for reasons which we somehow manage to conceal from ourselves. Why we do this — and how — are questions that form the subject-matter of psychoanalytic theory. Unconsciousness is a bit difficult to draw on the map — and I have therefore not tried to do so — because it could pop up pretty much anywhere; one hears talk of unconscious beliefs, desires and intentions, anger, grief, etc. Looked at in this way, there is a kind of complementarity between so-called access consciousness and the unconscious: both are adverbial, though in the one case access is granted, whereas in the other it is denied. (Note the difference between things we might know tacitly and the unconscious. Tacit knowledge is simply not accessible, whereas, on one view, the unconscious involves some kind of deliberate denial of access.)

Putting it Together

The inventory of the mind in figure 1.1 was framed in quite deliberately superficial terms: care was taken to avoid philosophical doctrine, though some has no doubt crept in, no deep commitment to doctrine is necessary to comprehend it. However, an inventory falls far short of the proper guide to the mental landscape promised at the beginning of this chapter. Imagine your disappointment if someone, having promised you a guide to the countryside, produced instead a mere list of the main hills and mountains. Even if this list included descriptions of each feature, you would have been sold short.

Turning the inventory of the mental realm into something more useful requires an understanding of how experiences, attitudes and actions fit together; some idea of what they do, or, rather, what we do with them. As before, the aim is to come to this understanding with minimum philosophical preconception. So, let us work up to it slowly by considering a series of different ways in which we might describe some quite specific situation in which human beings play a central role.

Description I
There are four human beings in a room. A female is seated with a male child on her knee. A second female is seated in front of a three-legged wooden stand, and is facing the first female and male. Another adult male is standing off to one side of the two females. He moves towards the female seated at the wooden stand, and she contracts her facial muscles.

What is going on here? I don't expect it to be easy for you to answer this question, nor is the situation easy to visualize. (I base these judgments on the kind of informal experimentation with students that has already been used as the source of the inventory of the mental realm.) What we have here is an unvarnished account of the situation of four human beings and some events that they participate in. Yet there is a tendency to be confused by it, to find it opaque even though it purports to contain 'nothing but the facts'. Why is this? Well, part of the reason is that what has been described involves inter-action between human beings, and we expect description of such interaction to be framed in terms that have been at least lightly 'varnished' by the mental realm. Description I is difficult to construe precisely because it confounds this expectation. Such confounding of expectations can occur even when human activity is not directly involved. Imagine someone describing a scene in these ways:

> As you look straight ahead, you see a structure made of cellulose, copper–zinc and silicon dioxide. This structure is resting on flat square-cut sheets of complex naturally occurring minerals.

> As you look straight ahead you see a bright light blue in the middle of your visual field, with some dull yellow lower down, shading into orange, and then disappearing into a brown-black.

We expect a scene to be described, not by talk of chemical composition or colour patches, but by an account of the *objects* (a wooden, bronze and glass table) and *relations* (the table is sitting on a stone patio) that figure in it. So, except for very special purposes, both of the examples are confusing, even if in some sense highly accurate. (Special purposes might include: a book on the chemistry of everyday objects or a description suited to a painter, in which the flow of colours is more important than what is depicted.)

But mere confounding of expectations is not the whole story of what is wrong with Description I, for, in this latter kind of case, it is not merely that we are surprised that certain descriptive vocabulary has been left out. Rather, we think that any description of human activity given solely in 'object and relation' terms is bound to be distorting and downright inaccurate. Compare Description I with this one:

Description II
Lily Briscoe is an artist, seated in front of her easel, painting a picture of her friend Mrs Ramsay who is herself holding her child on her knee. Mr Bankes is near Mrs Ramsay, looking on at the proceedings. He then moves across the room, taking up a position behind Lily Briscoe, so that he can have a look at her painting. As he does this, Lily Briscoe winces.

Here we feel more at home with the vocabulary, and feel also that previously suppressed facts have been revealed. In contrast to Description I, even a casual reading of this description makes it easier to visualize the situation. This is because it gives us information about the characters described and their actions. Artists in the midst of painting tend to look at their subject; the subjects posing for a picture tend to have a slightly self-conscious air, though perhaps this is not so of a child; an onlooker needs to move behind an artist in order to see what is being painted; wincing, as opposed to mere contraction of facial muscles, might well be something done rather than a mere tic.

All of these things are so natural and obvious that we tend to overlook them. Moreover, the improvement effected by Description II is not simply the result of its providing detail left out by Description I. What we are given is not simply some further factual information so much as a new way of understanding the same facts. This point could be put in terms of descriptive frameworks within which the situation is embedded: Description I uses a framework of objects and events – it tells us what things there are, and how they move – whereas Description II embeds that same situation in the frame-work of persons and actions. And with this second sort of embedding comes a kind of insight. Though the explicit language of explanation – the use of words like 'because' and 'therefore' – does not figure in Description II, we none the less come away with more of an understanding of what is going on.

Description II provides more of an understanding, but still leaves much unclear. The framework of persons and actions is rooted in our inventory of the mind; actions are after all one of the major categories of the mental realm. However, Description II doesn't, as we might put it, *really* tell us what is going on in the situation described. Against this background of puzzlement, consider this further account:

Description III
This ray passed level with Mr Bankes's ray straight to Mrs Ramsay sitting reading there with James at her knee. But now while she still looked, Mr Bankes had done. He had put on his spectacles. He had stepped back. He had raised his hand. He had slightly narrowed his clear blue eyes, when Lily, rousing herself, saw what he was at, and winced like a dog who sees a hand raised to strike it. She would have snatched her picture off the easel, but she said to herself, One must. She braced herself to stand the awful trial of someone looking at her picture. And if it must be seen, Mr Bankes was less alarming than another. But that any other eye should see the residue of her thirty-three years, the deposit of each day's living mixed with something more secret than

she had ever spoken or shown in the course of all those days was an agony. At the same time it was immensely exciting.

The language of this description is not easy, but certainly better than anything I could have produced. It is a passage from Virginia Woolf's *To the Lighthouse*.[5] Like the transition from the first to the second description, the move to this one makes what is essentially the same situation more intelligible, but it does so in a somewhat different way. We now know not only who did what, we have some clearer idea of *why* at least the central incident in the story took place. At the risk of labouring the obvious, we know now that Lily winced because the thought of someone looking at her work – work that up until then she had kept from others – frightened her. But we also know that she did no more than wince, she did not try to stop what was happening, because she believed that there was some importance, even value, in the judgemental gaze of someone else. And more than this, we know too of the complex attitudes that she had to her painting, described as it was as the deposit of each day's living over thirty-three years.

Notice that the passage, like Description II, does not contain any explicit explanatory claims. We are told various truths about the situation, rather as we were in the other descriptions, but the inclusion of Lily Briscoe's attitudes and feelings allows us to get, as it were, inside the head of the main protagonist; knowing these attitudes and feelings from the inside, from her point of view, makes it easy for us to elaborate on Description III in an explanatory way. We can say such things as:

> She winced *because* she believed that Bankes' gestures meant that he was about to look at her painting, and having her paintings looked at frightened her.

> Her not removing her painting, or covering it up, is *explained* by her belief that a real artist ought to expose her work to the judgement of others, together with the belief that Bankes was likely to be a gentle, or perhaps a not threateningly knowledgeable judge of such work.

> Whether or not she was conscious of it before, she discovered a frisson of excitement in knowing that Bankes was about to look at her work, and this together with her other attitudes towards him and her work was *her reason* for allowing the incident to develop in the way it did.

The italicized words in the first two of the above suggest that the explanations given are of the same form as explanations not directly concerned with the understanding of human action. We say that a dish cracked *because* it was moved too quickly from the freezer to the oven; that the higher incidence of leukaemia in young children is *explained* by the radiation from the nuclear reprocessing plant located nearby. But the words of the third – the idea of someone's having a reason for doing something – does differ markedly: it simply makes no sense to say that the quick move from freezer to oven gave the dish a reason to break.

Clarifying the notion of explanation as it applies to everyday objects and events, to human actions, and as it is used in more systematic scientific contexts, will be business for later chapters. Moreover, even as this brief discussion suggests, it is important business. Efforts to integrate the mental into the realm of science depend for cogency, or lack of it, on this issue. (For this reason, it is an issue that we will return to more than once.) Here my ambitions have been much more circumscribed: the aim has been simply that of displaying certain further facts about the mental realm. The move from Description I to II, and then to III, shows us what is done with the items in the inventory in figure 1.1. What we see is that the vocabulary of the mental realm enables us to reconceive certain situations. At a basic level this vocabulary makes it possible for us to see certain movements and events as human actions. But, when fully deployed, it lends itself to more than mere redescription. When, as in the passage from *To the Lighthouse*, all the elements of the mind are knitted together, they enlighten, explain, make intelligible the action previously described.

Noting the way in which the elements of mind are used in the description and explanation of human behaviour finally allows us to progress beyond the inventory stage. We must no longer view the mental realm as captured by a list of different, though related, phenomena, since we have seen how these phenomena can be descriptively combined to give a special sort of insight into events that feature human beings. That I have introduced this idea using a literary example should not be surprising since literature depends almost wholly on this activity. Novels contain stories about things that people (or similar characters) do, and for the most part they contain descriptions of these doings which allow the reader to understand at least some of them. (This is not to say that the ultimate purpose of novels is to tell an explanatory story about some bits of human behaviour; novels can have as many different purposes as conversations.) Moreover, literary examples are often richly realistic, and this is in contrast to the rather shallow sort of case that one comes across in philosophical discussions.

The explanatory interanimation of items in the mental realm has been called many different things in the philosophical literature, but perhaps 'belief–desire psychology', 'common-sense psychology' and 'folk psychology' are the three most common labels. However, none of them is particularly apt.

The use of the term 'psychology' is intended to point towards the explanatory role of descriptions like the one taken from *To the Lighthouse*, and there
is no doubt that we use the term in something like this way. None the less,
contemporary psychology aims to be a more or less scientific discipline, and
thus might well have explanatory aspirations that do not overlap with those
evident in the Woolf passage. Until we have got clear about the notion of
explanation, we must therefore be careful; we must not let the use of the word
'psychology' foist on us an unrealistic picture of what is going on when we
write and talk about ourselves.

The name 'belief-desire psychology' has its origin in the fact that, though
virtually all our explanatory narratives at some point make essential use of the
attitudes in general, belief and desire play a central role. To see some event as
a human action seems to require us to see it as *intended* in some way, and intentions are generally intelligible only against a background of *beliefs* and *desires*.
Lily Briscoe could have prevented Bankes from seeing her painting, but she
quite intentionally stopped herself from doing this because she believed that
artists should be exposed to criticism and, in spite of some misgivings, desired
Bankes to be that critic. All this is true and important, but nevertheless it can
be distorting. The idea of 'belief-desire psychology' as working in this way suggests a picture of the attitudes as levers, the pulling and pushing on which
somehow causes actions to pop into existence.

As we saw, there is no doubt that we can distil explanations from descriptive narratives: the passage from *To the Lighthouse* encourages, even if it doesn't
employ, the use of words like 'because' and 'explains'. However, as we also saw,
it is by no means clear what is involved in this distillation. In particular, we
have yet to say anything about the explanatory value of the notion of a reason.
Looked at carefully, the passage does not say that a belief and desire caused
Lily to sit tight. Rather, it suggests that things she knew, believed, saw and felt
came together to be her reason for acting in the way she did. Until we know
more about how all the items in the mental realm can come together in this
way, we must be careful about attributing causal powers to this or that specific item. Unfortunately, the label 'belief-desire psychology' can encourage us
to throw such caution to the wind.

Talk of 'common-sense psychology' suggests that the kind of descriptive-
explanatory narrative we have been discussing is pretty much common property, that more or less anyone can both provide and understand it. Up to a
point, of course, this is true. A creature who lacked the ability to see actions
in events, and who failed to understand why actions take place, is simply not
human, or at least not completely human. However, the fact that our human-

ity consists partly in this ability shouldn't lead us to think that it is shared equally, or that there could be no innovative development. To the extent that these expectations are implied by the label 'common-sense', that label is misleading.

To see just how off-beam the label is – but not just for this purpose – consider the following story (which is in all essentials absolutely true). Some thirty years ago, a marriage took place between two people who had known each other since early childhood (and who were known to me through a mutual friend). Their two families lived near one another, took holidays together, and both families were pleased when, in their early twenties, the couple announced their engagement. There was no familial pressure for this to happen, though there was little surprise. After all, the two had been inseparable during their teens, and had travelled together during university vacations. What did surprise both families and friends was what happened next: the marriage lasted a single day.

As far as anyone could tell – though no one felt able to ask them directly – the separation was completely without rancour, though it was certainly final; no attempt to patch things up took place, the house they bought together, and all of their shared possessions, were divided without lawyers, and the couple are now married to others, living in the same city, but seeing nothing of one another.

Everyone who knew them, and even those who only heard about what had happened, had a 'theory'. That is, everyone suggested a narrative which might make this strange event intelligible. A first thought, one that occurred to almost everyone, was that sex was the key. However, a moment's thought showed this to be implausible. The shared holidays almost certainly included sexual relations, and, even if not, what could have happened to rule out the possibility of staying together – even for a matter of a few months or weeks – whilst trying to deal with any sexual problems? A second line of thought could be summed up this way: they came to realize all of sudden that they should never have got married in the first place; that being childhood sweethearts had swept them along a path they should never have taken. Whilst there is something to be said for this view, it too does not stand up to close scrutiny. The first day and night of a marriage is bound to seem strange, is bound to provoke fears and questions. But why would otherwise sensible people let these fears lead immediately to separation? A third theory centred on the likelihood that one or both had met someone else, and had gone through with the marriage out of some misguided sense of loyalty. (It was even imagined that the wedding night might have been taken up with a tentative and painful mutual confession of infidelity.) Yet subsequent events did not really confirm this view: each married someone else, but only much later, and in each case it was someone met for the first time after the disastrous wedding ceremony.

None of the theories seemed quite right (and the matter remains a mystery). Yet a great deal of creative effort went into formulating them, and some people were clearly better at it than others. Also, some were better than others when it came to judging whether a given theory was plausible. As the word is normally taken, it would therefore have been simply wrong to characterize what went on in these discussions as 'commonsensical', if this implies that more or less anyone is as good as anyone else at contributing.

Of course, someone might defend the label 'common-sense psychology' by pointing out that the words and concepts used in formulating theories about the failed marriage were not technical: after all, these discussions were not like those in particle physics. In appealing to notions that we share, it might be said that there is a *common framework* to these theories, even though it would have been wrong to describe the particular theories as themselves commonsensical.

There is certainly something right about this move, but it makes an important concession – one which we must not forget when we return to this topic later – and even with this concession, there is still a deep problem with the label. A common framework for theorizing about human behaviour is not by itself a psychology of any sort. (Imagine someone thinking that the common framework of botany – an accepted classification of plants and their parts – was itself an explanatory theory of plant life.) But even aside from this, something important is overlooked.

The explanations offered for the failure of the marriage were never of the sort involved in the physical sciences, and many of them – as in the examples above – were set in something like the common framework of attitude and experience. But there were some explanations that made use of notions whose relation to that framework is both controversial and very far from being common property. I have in mind here explanations relying on a whole range of concepts drawn from the psychoanalytic tradition. Those who knew the couple better than I did, and who accepted some strands of that tradition, were inclined to pepper their explanations with talk of, amongst others, unconscious desires, repression and projection. I shall not pause here to give specific examples of these explanations; nor to offer a view on their adequacy, but their very possibility shows the hopelessness of the label 'common-sense psychology'. The framework within which we offer explanations of various human actions may be set by the basic inventory of the mental realm pictured in figure 1.1, but this framework can be, and has been, extended in all sorts of ways, amongst which the broadly psychoanalytic approach is perhaps the best known.

(Note: as with everything to do with psychoanalysis, it is controversial whether we should see it as an extension of the 'common framework' or as a completely independent explanatory framework. My hope here was simply to suggest that the extension view is not implausible – after all, one does speak of unconscious desires, beliefs and intentions – and that if we accept it, we have even less reason to take seriously talk of common-sense psychology.)

The space devoted to fretting about the right name for our explanatory/narrative practices might seem excessive. However, inaccurate names can send us off in wrong directions – something particularly true in the philosophy of mind – so we must be careful. Besides, my discussion of names has been in part an excuse for clarifying the nature of the thing we have yet to baptize. The third candidate name happens to be the one most frequently used, and this is ironic, since it was coined to express a critical, even negative, view of the enterprise.[6] 'Folk medicine', 'folk physics', 'folk chemistry' all suggest the primitiveness of views ripe for replacement by proper explanatory schemes, and it is in this spirit that many writers use the label 'folk psychology'. In so far as the 'psychology of the folk' implies both scientific pretensions and unskilled deployment, this label suffers from the same defects as those of 'common-sense psychology'. But it is the suggestion of primitiveness that requires a brief comment.

Given how little we once knew, folk medicine was the best we could manage, but the advance of modern medicine has both supplanted its primitive forebear and, in some cases, revealed why this or that piece of folk medicinal practice has some efficacy. (This is of course the official story; though many do, there is no need to question it here.) The suggestion in the label 'folk psychology' is that the same thing could happen to our narrative/explanatory practices. Put most starkly, the label implies that one day we might well come to hold that human beings do not have beliefs, desires, intentions, nor feel pains, have visual experiences or moods. Beliefs and these other things will turn out to have been merely part of an intelligible, though mistaken, first attempt to understand human beings.

It might surprise you to find that this possibility is taken seriously; that there are some working in philosophy and psychology who accept it, and see no genuine paradox in the claim that they *believe* there are no beliefs. In due course, we will come to consider the background to this sort of 'eliminativist' view, but here the point is simple: we should be very suspicious of any argument for eliminativism which takes off from the label 'folk psychology'. Our current narrative/explanatory practices – the stories we tell as part of making intelligible what people do – are creative, revisable in the light of evidence, and are by no means accessible to everyone. They do not differ in these respects from the explanatory efforts of modern medicine. True enough, the background framework within which these theories fall is in a broad sense available to the folk. But this is no less true of medicine. Modern medicine and folk medicine differ considerably, but both share a framework determined by notions of, among others, disease, cure and health.

None of the labels currently used is without drawbacks, but I do not want to spend the whole of this book speaking of 'our 'narrative/explanatory/intelligibility conferring practices'. In any case, the caveats so far registered give us a certain freedom in the choice of name. So, perhaps perversely, I shall mostly use 'folk psychology', whilst thinking of what it names as not necessarily theoretical in the manner of the science of psychology, nor as something simply given to the folk.

Persons

Narratives that knit together experiences, attitudes and actions confer a special kind of intelligibility on the world. And the key to the unity of these narratives is the notion of a person or self. As has already been noted several times, every item in the mental realm belongs to, or is owned by, some person. Pains have sufferers, beliefs have subjects and actions have agents. Nor is this simply a matter of fact: pains, beliefs and actions do not just happen to belong to persons; it simply makes no sense to think of these mental phenomena without thinking of them as someone's.

Of course, it does not follow from the constitutive nature of the relationship between persons and mental phenomena that the person who experiences, who adopts attitudes and who acts is one and the same kind of thing. Not yet having considered what a person is, it could be that sufferers of experiences differ systematically from subjects who adopt attitudes, whilst both differ from agents of actions. Yet this bare possibility is never one that we take seriously.

The idea that there is one kind of thing which has experiences, attitudinizes and acts is a constitutive presupposition of the coherence of our folk psychological narratives. Just as an exercise, imagine trying to make sense of a narrative in which sufferer, subject and agent are given different names. Told that A did what he did because of what B felt and C believed and desired, we are likely to react in one of two ways. Either we think we are being told that A's own feelings, beliefs and desires happen to have been moulded by the feelings of B and the beliefs and desires of C; or we think that, for some unmentioned reason the story includes three different names of the same person. Only in one of these ways could we make head or tail of the use of 'because' in the original claim.

(Note: there are two questions which could be put to this claim and which might suggest that it is overstated. They are:

(a)   What about the notorious cases of multiple personalities?
(b)   What about the idea that, e.g. perceptual beliefs, do not strictly belong to a person, but belong instead to some subsystem (a visual system) within a person?

A quick answer to these questions is that they both still seem to presuppose – though in a more complicated way – the very claim they are meant to challenge. Thus, when we read about some case of multiple personality, it seems always to be a single person whose misfortune it is to have a special kind of multiplicity. And similarly, talk of beliefs being those of some subsystem seems no less strongly to imply a single owner of this, and other, such systems. However, having so far said nothing substantial about the notion of a person, these answers are too quick to settle matters.)

What has been said so far might make it seem as if the unity of personhood in the context of folk psychological narratives is merely a 'formal' unity. By this I mean a unity that simply requires the narrator to make clear, in order to shed light on an action, that the actor, experiencer and believer are one and the same person. However, this kind of unity is no different from that required in the explanation of events that do not involve persons. If I set out to explain why a billiard ball moved in the way it did, I had better make sure that this same ball is the subject of the causal factors responsible for the final motion.

What has been left out is the important presumption of folk psychological narrative that the required unity of persons can be appreciated from the 'inside' as well as from the 'outside'. Not only can we view Lily Briscoe as at the same time the person who resisted removing her painting, who believed her art should be open to the gaze of others and who felt frightened at the approach of Bankes, we can view Lily Briscoe as somehow taking herself – a single self – to have these feelings and beliefs, and as acting on them. The narrator's and audience's point of view – what is called the third-person perspective – is what I labelled the 'outside'. Lily Briscoe's own point of view – the first-person perspective – is the 'inside'. What distinguishes folk psychological explanation from the explanation of such things as the motion of billiard balls is not merely the fact that the former deals with mental phenomena, nor the fact that a unity of personhood is required. The crucial extra element is that of the first-person perspective.

Woolf's narrative conjured up this perspective: we were made to imagine what Lily Briscoe felt and thought from her own point of view. Of course, it need not have been done this way; we could have been told, as it were from Woolf's point of view, what Lily Briscoe felt and thought. (Many novels adopt this perspective: almost miraculously, the author is able to tell you what a protagonist feels or believes, even though the author is not actually involved in the action.) But even in this case, the third-person narrative would only work – it would only make what Lily Briscoe did intelligible – if we also regarded her as at least capable of adopting a first-person perspective on her actions.

You can get some idea of what is meant here by thinking about the notion of 'having a reason for' that plays such an important part in our narratives. Even when seen from the outside, feelings and thoughts only come together to give reasons for action when we see them as belonging to a single person. This is the unity thesis. But they couldn't be that person's reason for action unless the unity of personhood – something we might recognize from the outside – is somehow available to the agent herself.

Think again about attempts to explain the failed marriage. I have suggested that the couple's being married for a single day, given the background circumstances, is deeply puzzling. But you may feel – as many friends of the couple did – that the mystery only exists because of our reticence. If we could have just asked the bride or bridegroom why they broke up, there would no longer be a puzzle. Now, this might not be true: even a frank discussion with the couple might still leave the event unexplained. However, independently of whether, in this case, it is true, the fact that we tend to think it illustrates in a concrete way the importance of the first-person point of view. Our attempt to explain what happened seems to presuppose that there are first-personal points of view; we seem to count things done as done for reasons only in so far as there are agents who see themselves as having those reasons.

This idea might be called the 'self-consciousness' thesis, and as I have described it, it is *additional* to the idea of a 'formal' unity of personhood in our narratives. But it is by no means obvious that the unity and the self-consciousness theses are quite so separable. In a very often cited passage, John Locke (1632–1704) wrote:

> [a person] is a thinking intelligent being that has reason and reflection and can consider itself as itself, the same thinking thing in different times and places.[7]

And the suggestion seems clear here that some kind of self-consciousness ('can consider itself as itself') is inextricably connected with what I have called narrative unity ('the same thinking thing in different times and places'). However, any further discussion of the issues this passage raises, would exceed my brief.

My aim in this chapter was to describe the role of persons in our folk psychological practices, not to set to work on the project of coming up with a substantive account of personhood.

(Note: throughout this chapter I have insisted that all three of the main categories of the mental realm can be seen as things we *do*. This is of course obvious in the case of acting, but remember that we don't merely have pain, and the belief that right will triumph, we *experience* pain and *believe* right will triumph. There is thus a sense in which our idea of the self or the person is essentially a notion of an agent, and this is reflected nicely in Locke's claim, in which a person is said to be something with a capacity for a certain kind of activity.)

Notes and References

1   From *The Centaur*, by John Updike (London: André Deutsch, 1962), pp. 3–4.
2   From *Through the Looking-Glass*, by Lewis Carroll (London: Macmillan, 1874), p. 140.
3   I have a lot of sympathy for the view that the substitution of whole sentence complements is more than merely awkward, it is downright distorting. But I won't pause here to engage in an extended argument about this.
4   From 'Observation and the Will' (*Journal of Philosophy*, 60, 1963, pp. 367–92) by Brian O'Shaughnessy.
5   New York: Harcourt, Brace and World, 1955, pp. 80–1. First published in 1927.
6   Its earliest use is lost in the mists of time, but Dan Dennett once told me that he *believes* his use was the first, and that he certainly meant it to convey a kind of disdain for the explanatory adequacy of the practice.
7   *An Essay Concerning Human Understanding* (1690). Everyman edn. (London: Dent, 1951), p. 280.

Part II

Digging Deeper

2

Attitude, Experience and Action

Natural historians of the seventeenth century were dismayed that the Earth has so many mountains and hills. They regarded these features as irregular, and hence as disfigurements, some going so far as to think of mountains as God's particular way of telling us of our sinfulness. The mental landscape so far described is no less lumpy, at least in a metaphorical sense. Experience, Attitude and Action, the categories that together partition the mind, seem just very different from one another. These differences are maintained – even highlighted – by the narratives of folk psychology, and unity of persons is made more, not less, problematic by this diversity.

The lumpy nature of the mental realm would seem to rule out the possibility of finding a single general feature which characterizes the mental. This is bound to be a disappointment to those who may have thought that the mind was a unified realm whose core is constituted by the so-called 'stream of consciousness'. But, whether fortunately or not, this expectation cannot withstand the sheer force of the number, character and interanimation of the features of the mental landscape.

The previous chapter gave us a sketch of how the land lies, but this is only the beginning. Not content to be simply tourists, we philosophers take ourselves to be geologists of the mind: we want to understand what lies beneath the surface. However, such understanding cannot come all at once. Recognizing the diversity of the mental landscape, we must first do some preliminary digging, some subsoil testing. This is the work of this and the next chapter, and only when we have finished it will we be able to speculate about how the mental landscape sits on bedrock.

What I propose is that in this chapter we confine our attention to experience, attitude and action, saving folk psychological narrative and persons for the following. In every case, the procedure will be quite simple: certain questions – which are in no sense technical or specialist – will be asked about each of these features. Since our questions presuppose nothing about science, psychology or any specialist discipline, we must count this stage of our investigation as purely philosophical. That is, we call on certain 'naive' intuitions — intuitions that appear to be inherent in the conceptual framework of common sense — in order to pose questions about a realm which is itself part of that conceptual framework. This sounds easy enough, yet, surprisingly, instead of straightforward answers, we will find puzzles, even paradoxes. What lies immediately beneath the mental landscape turns out to be shot through with faults and fissures. Moreover, as will become obvious, there is a pattern to these faults that we find in the mental subsoil, though exactly what we are to make of this will only emerge later.

One last note before we begin. The explicit aim of the material in this chapter and the next is to uncover certain philosophical difficulties raised by attitudes, experience, action, folk psychology and personhood. And this will require us to pursue lines of argument that are narrowly focused on certain specific issues. But the discussions themselves are also intended as introductions to five main areas of the philosophy of mind, and it is suggested that you can pursue these topics using the reading lists provided at the end of the book. In chapter 4 — before we begin our descent to the bedrock of the mental realm — I shall try to bring these topics together by showing certain themes that are common to them.

2.1   Attitudes and Attitudinizing

Attitude Problems

I begin in the middle with the second of the categories — attitudinizing. This is not merely whimsical. Rather, it is because attitudinizing looks both ways: many think that it has roots in experience — both of the bodily and perceptual variety — and it certainly seems to look towards actions in shaping and anticipating them. Besides, the attitudes have so far raised very few awkward questions, and it is now time to be awkward.

What is most striking about attitudinizing is the feature we have called directionality, and this will be the focus of our discussion. The idea that beliefs are directed, that they are reported by sentences that themselves contain sentence complements, that beliefs therefore have contents, these things are so familiar to us that it is easy to overlook just how special they are. When we say that Anne believes she left her coat in the hallway cupboard, we are, one would suppose, saying something true about Anne. Looked at from this perspective, there is a lot in common between our reporting that Anne has a belief, and our reporting – truly – that she has a cold. In each case, there would seem to be a state that Anne is in, albeit it is a mental state in the case of belief and a physical state in the case of the cold. However, from this perspective, we miss the crucial feature that differentiates the one state from the other.

A physical state of a person can be quite complex – it can take many words to describe it accurately. But no matter how complex it is, it never has the feature of directedness that goes with attitudinizing. Anne has a cold – certain unpleasant biological and chemical things are going on in her – but this state is not directed to anything, it is not about anything. Her physical state is somehow complete in itself and can be described without including reference to any other state of affairs. In contrast, Anne's belief is directed to another state of the world – her coat's being in the hallway cupboard. It is this latter state that forms the *content* of her attitude, and there is just no way of describing Anne's belief without referring to this content.

In the literature, the directedness characteristic of the attitudes, and the sentences we use to report them, is often called 'intentionality'. However, I think that there are good reasons, at least for the present discussion, to stick to 'directionality'. For a start, in some of its forms the word 'intentionality' can be misleading. This is not a big problem, but it sounds odd to speak sometimes of an intentional action, meaning one done with a certain intention or deliberately, and at other times of an intentional mental state, meaning one exhibiting intentionality. It seems better to speak of the latter as involving the directionality of the mental state. (Actually, there is a close connection between the attitude verb 'intend' and the idea of intentionality. But, even so, it can be confusing to speak of some belief being *intentional* when we usually reserve such a description for actions.)

Much more important than this possible verbal confusion is the fact that philosophers sometimes speak of intentionality when what they have in mind is the fact that beliefs, desires and other attitudes are reported with complement clauses, whilst at other times it is used in a less restricted sense. Very roughly, in this second sense, the intentionality of the mental concerns the broader relationship between mind and world – a relationship which could in fact characterize conscious experiences as well as attitudes. Unless we use some such term as 'directionality' to keep the complement-requiring nature of attitude ascriptions separate from intentionality in this broader sense, we are liable to end up saying glibly that only the attitudes exhibit intentionality. Many philosophers do just this, but it is a mistake. (We will return to the notion of intentionality later on.)

Whatever we call it, this remarkable feature of the attitudes is so familiar that it is all too easy to be blasé about it; we tend just to take it for granted when we report someone's attitudes. Anne's coat is there hanging in the hallway cupboard. This is as far from being a mental fact as anything can be; it is merely a state of the world at a given time. But Anne is in, or has, a special mental state – she has a belief – and the very description of this second state requires us to make reference to the first. What allows us to connect up these two claims in this way? Even if we are usually unreflective about it, what guides our ways of reporting beliefs and the other attitudes?

The first thought that someone might have here is tantalizingly simple. There is the coat hanging in the cupboard, and Anne is believingly related to this fact. That is, just as she might be owningly related to the house on 23 Elm Street, so is she believingly related to the coat's being in the cupboard. In the one case, she bears a complex physical, social and legal relation to a house, in the other a perhaps no less complex mental relation to something that is going on in the world.

Unfortunately, this simple account is beset with problems. The most obvious fault is that it signally fails to make room for false belief. Anne may truly *believe* her coat is in the cupboard, but it may well not be – her belief may be false. In this perfectly ordinary case, it cannot be the relation between Anne and the coat's being in the cupboard which grounds our attribution of the belief to Anne, for there is no coat there and hence no such relation.

This is even more obvious in the case of desires. Suppose that you have a long train journey ahead, and you absolutely must have a newspaper to make it pass more quickly. You see a shop and desire very much to acquire from it a copy of your usual daily. In the somewhat awkward idiom discussed earlier, we can say:

> You desire that you come to own one of the copies of the *Guardian* in the shop at the station.

But, sadly, there has been a run on *Guardians*, and there simply aren't any in that shop. So you truly have the desire, but the desire can hardly be a relation between you and a newspaper in the shop which is (as you think) waiting there. There simply isn't any newspaper there answering to your desire.

In the face of these difficulties, it might be tempting to try to keep the spirit of the simple proposal by retreating a little. (Indeed, *retreating* is one of the main strategies for dealing with the problems of directionality.) We are prevented from seeing Anne as believingly related to the coat's being in the cupboard because it just isn't there. But why not still insist that she is believingly related to the coat (wherever it is), the cupboard and the relationship described by the words 'being in'. That is, why not invent a complex entity made up of these three items which certainly exist in the world, even if they do not exist together in the way envisaged by Anne? Thus, we can say what her belief state is directed at, without thereby guaranteeing that it is true. (Rather as we can say what an archer's target is without committing ourselves to whether the arrows hit the mark.)

The entity made up of the coat, the cupboard and the relationship is somewhat odd – it is a sort of abstract thing made up from concrete objects and relations – but that in itself is no special problem.[1] After all, one wouldn't expect mental attitudes to be completely straightforward. But oddness is only the beginning of the difficulties with this proposal. Consider, for example, this belief attribution:

Henrietta believes that Macbeth was not misled by a greedy wife.

Are we saying that Henrietta is believingly related to Macbeth, his wife and an appropriate 'misleadingness' relationship? It certainly has seemed to many people as if one of the fascinating things about attitudes is that we can have them towards fictional characters and other non-existents (remember the desire for the newspaper). But doesn't this put a great deal of strain on the idea that belief consists in a relation to a complex of *existing* items?

Actually, whilst the answer to my last question is clearly 'yes', I don't think that worries about fictional entities constitute the main stumbling block to accepting the idea that attitudes are relations to things. Fiction creates havoc wherever it goes – whether in our accounts of language or in our accounts of attitude ascriptions. And it creates havoc for virtually every account in these areas. So, whilst it is worth mentioning, I shall put it on one side. There is a larger obstacle standing in the way of our present proposal regarding the world-directness of the attitudes, and we must deal with it before we can consider such relatively minor matters as so-called 'fictional' objects.

Deeper into Trouble in London and Paris

So far we have been trying to hang on to the idea that beliefs and other attitudes are directed at the things they most certainly seem to be about – the items referred to in the complement sentences of attitude ascriptions. However, we have seen that Anne cannot simply be related believingly to her coat's being in the cupboard because it might not be there. So we have retreated to the idea that she is believingly related to a made-up, complex entity consisting of the coat, the cupboard and the feature of one thing's being contained in another. This seems to make room for falsity, since these items might not actually be in the relationship to each other that Anne thinks they are. But falsity (and fiction) are not the only problems, for the relation between the believer and the believed is much more elusive than we have so far noticed. There is a kind of slack between believers and what beliefs are about which can make one despair of ever coming to understand the directionality of the attitudes. The following two examples will illustrate what I mean.

(i)   London

Monique, on her first visit to London, takes a lightning tour from the top of a double-decker bus. Among the things pointed out to her is the British Museum. As a result of what she is told, and what she can see for herself, she comes to believe that the British Museum has two lions guarding its entrance.

On a later visit to London – this time in order to attend a literary party in a publishing house in Bloomsbury – she notices, as she arrives, that there is a large, sombre building with imposing columns opposite the offices she is to visit. She wonders whether this could be the British Museum (she knows it is in Bloomsbury), but, looking about in vain for the lions (there are none at the front entrance), she dismisses this possibility. But, of course, what she is looking at is simply the British Museum from its south side.

If we construe the belief formed on the sightseeing bus according to the proposal described earlier, we would say that Monique is believingly related to the 'triplex' entity consisting of:

the British Museum,
the two lions,
the relationship of guarding.

On the second visit, one would seem forced to say that she is believingly related to:

the British Museum (she is looking at it),
the two lions (she clearly remembers these),
the absence of the relationship of guarding (she can see that there are none flanking the entrance).

The first belief was attributed using the form of words:

Monique believes that there are two lions guarding the entrance of the British Museum.

and the second:

> Monique believes that the building over there does not have two lions guarding the entrance.

However, 'the building over there' in the second belief attribution is in fact none other than the British Museum, and this is what leads to trouble. What trouble? After all, the story describes in a coherent way the kind of mistake that we can all make, so it may seem that we have not uncovered any particularly shattering gap in our everyday understanding of the attitudes. But this is to forget how we got to the present position. Our question was: what counts as the content of a belief? The eventual answer was: it consists in an amalgam of those items to which the belief is directed. Just describe that amalgam and you have the content sentence of a belief attribution. What the above example apparently shows is that this cannot be right. In Monique's case, the key items that form the content of her two beliefs are the same – it is the British Museum and the lions that figure in both. There is, as one might say, just 'one reality' toward which Monique's beliefs are directed. But Monique has two beliefs about this reality which are simply not compatible. And it would be unfair to Monique to say that she believed both that the British Museum was guarded by lions and that it wasn't. Monique, we can assume, is much too rational for such an attribution to make any sense. So, does she believe that the British Museum is guarded by lions? And if we say 'yes' (or 'no') to this, where does that leave our account of the directionality of the attitudes?

This first example seems to show that one can adopt two different (even incompatible) attitudes toward one and the same set of things, and this introduces a puzzling element of slack into the relationship between our attitudes and what they are about. It is as if our beliefs can slide about whilst still being apparently directed at the same things. Before trying to alleviate this situation, let us consider the second example.

(ii)   Paris

Richard hasn't been to Paris for years. When he was last there, he stumbled on a small brasserie near his hotel which he used to go to every day. In fact, it was in this brasserie that he first met the woman he would now describe as the love of his life. He was sitting at a table near the window, and all the other tables were fully occupied when she came in . . .

Now, all these years later, Richard is in Paris on business, and he decides to see whether the brasserie is still there. Heading to the *quartier* of his former hotel, he has not reckoned on one thing: the tendency, in our times, for successful businesses to try repeating their success by forming chains of identical establishments. So, when he stumbles onto another of the brasseries, he takes it for the one that was the object of his search. Indeed, so close is the resemblance between the two, and Richard's memory is very precise, that he finds the tables and chairs, the metal-covered *comptoir*, the curtains, the menus – everything seems to be just as it was before, give or take a new coat of paint.

On and before entering the brasserie, Richard had many beliefs and other attitudes which together contributed to what we would describe as his feeling of nostalgia. But for the purposes of the example, let us focus on some specific belief. Richard had believed that the chairs in that local brasserie were very comfortable. This belief has not changed in the intervening years, and, as he enters, one of things he thinks is this: I hope they haven't changed the chairs. He is thus relieved to see the same kind of chairs set neatly around the tables. Now he could correctly be described as believing that the chairs in the brasserie he used to go to every day have not changed, they are still comfortable. In short, he continues to believe what he had believed before.

But is what he believes true? This is not an easy question to answer. For the sake of definiteness, let us suppose that the brasserie he actually used to go to – the one he mistakenly thinks he is now in – has *changed* its chairs, and that they are no longer what Richard would describe as 'comfortable' if he were to come across them. In this case, there is some pressure for thinking that his present belief is false: the chairs in the brasserie *to which he used to go* are not comfortable. After all, Richard would be quite insistent that, whatever else was true, he had not changed his belief about the chairs, and *we* know – what Richard has yet to find out – that the chairs have changed. Yet, sitting there in the *new* brasserie, entertaining the thought that these chairs are comfortable, one may be tempted to think that his belief is true. But it is certainly bizarre to describe one and the same belief as both true and false.

On the account of the directionality of beliefs within which we are working, Richard's long-standing belief about the chairs was directed at an amalgam of these things:

the chairs in the original brasserie,
the property of being comfortable.

On the apparently reasonable assumption that Richard's belief hasn't changed, this belief continues to be directed at these things, only it is now false. However, it is difficult to ignore the fact that he is sitting there in a brasserie looking at some chairs and judging them to be comfortable. In this case, his belief seems to be directed at:

the chairs in the new brasserie,
the property of being comfortable,

and it is thus true. So, either he is thinking the same thing and, hence, thinking something false, or he has changed his mind (without realizing it!) and he is thinking something different and true. Neither seems very palatable, but the second alternative seems particularly bizarre.

(iii)   The Moral

The example involving Monique showed that there is one kind of looseness in the directedness of our beliefs: we seem to be able to have quite different beliefs — even incompatible ones — *about one and the same reality*. The case of Richard shows that this looseness can occur the other way around: we can have one and the same belief *about two different realities*. Put together, these two examples put intolerable pressure on the idea that Monique or Richard can be simply described as being believingly related to features of the world. There are standards which must be met by anything we could regard as a genuine relationship, and these examples apparently show that the attitudes do not come up to scratch.

Consider again the ownership relationship between Anne and her house. As was said, this is a complicated legal and social relationship — there may even be problems in telling whether it holds definitively. But this much is true: if Anne really does own a house, then she bears this relationship to it no matter how that house is described. And she bears this relationship to just that house, and not to others, merely because they resemble it.

Admittedly, the cases of Monique and Richard are those involving confusion and mistake, and you might think that they are therefore of less importance than I have made them out to be. But mistakes and confusion are just the things on which we must focus if we want to understand the attitudes. An attitude is a *state of mind* directed towards something or other, and it is therefore liable to go wrong. Indeed, where but in states of mind would you expect to find confusions and mistakes? But it is precisely the possibility of these confusions and mistakes which seems to undermine an account of the content of the attitudes that makes them relations to extra-mental reality.

At this point there are two ways to jump: either agree with the conclusion of the last paragraph when asked what we should make of the directionality of the attitudes, or look for ways to get around the kinds of examples that created the problem in the first place. As one might guess, the philosophical community has tended to go for the second option.

The Way Forward

Actually, though counting here is not a precise art, one can find at least four ways forward: three of them could be understood as ways to improve on the simple proposal of directionality that has led us into trouble, and the fourth as a rather more thoroughgoing revision of that proposal. But one must be careful. As you will discern for yourself, these ways are not completely independent of one another. Each consists in a suggestion of how we might begin to cope with the puzzles about the directionality of belief described above, but there is nothing to prevent – and everything to encourage – taking to heart more than one suggestion at a time. Obviously, if some combination of these strategies can convincingly describe the directionality of the atittudes and defuse the puzzling cases, then there is good reason to plump for it. I have chosen to describe them seriatim, since I want to highlight the essentials, and not because I think that they are exclusive alternatives.

(a)   Language

Nothing could be more obvious than that attributing attitudes to someone involves careful choosing of one's words. To take an extreme example: a five-year-old looking westwards in the late March afternoon may well believe that the sun is setting. But it would be bizarre to say of him that he believes that the medium-sized, fusion-powered star now visible on the western horizon is passing out of the line of sight of the inhabitants of the British Isles. One feels he just doesn't believe *that*. And the reason? Clearly, it is partly a matter of language. The 'sophisticated' way of describing the setting sun uses words that stand for concepts unavailable to a five-year-old. Had we said simply: 'he believes that the sun is setting,' this would have passed as reasonable.

Intuitions such as this suggest that the choice of words (and/or concepts) plays a large part in attitude attributions, and that some mileage can be got out of this. The hope is that if we can get the role of language right, then we can deal with the problems raised by examples such as those involving Monique and Richard. If there is something about the use of the phrases 'the British Museum' or 'the building over there with columns' that makes them function differently in sentences attributing beliefs, then perhaps we can avoid having to say that Anne is believingly related in different ways to the same reality. Maybe this will allow us to regard the apparent slack between Anne's state of mind and reality as due to the language we use to describe the beliefs, and not to the beliefs themselves.

The details of linguistic attempts to deal with the propositional attitudes are too complex to be described fully in this book. Indeed, there is a sense in which this approach takes the problem of the attitudes outside the scope of the philosophy of mind itself, and not merely beyond the reach of this survey of the subject. For the question of how it is that words connect their users with reality – and within what limits – falls squarely within the philosophy of language. Moreover, even a cursory look at the literature here will show just how complicated the story can get. It is enough to make one wonder how we ever do manage to say what people believe. However, for the sake of definiteness we ought to have at least a rough description of how things might go.

In their ordinary employment, phrases like 'the British Museum' and 'the brasserie I used to visit' refer to items in the world. That is, at least part of their linguistic function is, broadly, to bring reference to such items into our conversational exchanges. Yet, in sentences reporting what people believe, we get into trouble if we take these words simply to have that sort of function. Given this, one way to get out of trouble would be to say that, when these sorts of phrases (and indeed, words generally) occur in the context of propositional attitude reports, they change their function somewhat. Perhaps they cease to refer directly to items in the world and refer instead to how these items are thought of by the believer. Here is the proposal put more concretely.

Monique believes that the British Museum is guarded by lions. Think of the words 'Monique believes that' as having a strange effect on whatever it is that follows them. Thus, the underlined space in 'Monique believes that ____' is a linguistic context in which words do not function as they would outside such a context. To keep matters simple, let us just consider the phrase 'the British Museum'. This is a name of that famous building, but in the above-mentioned context, this name does not simply refer to that building. Instead, it refers to Monique's way of thinking about that building – we could say that it refers to the way in which that building is *presented* to her. Thus, we should not think of the building itself as taking its place in the content of her belief. Instead, it is the 'mode of presentation' which is baked into the propositional confection. Calling it 'the British-Museum mode' (for want of a better way to describe it) here is the content of Monique's belief:

the British-Museum mode of thinking of the British Museum,
the two lions,
the relationship of guarding.

Now this will differ significantly from her second belief – the one which we reported by the sentence, 'Monique believes the building over there is not guarded by lions' because the first element in the confection for this one will be:

the building-over-there mode of thinking of the British Museum.

And we can say all of this even though the building her beliefs are about – the one presented by these two different modes – is one and the same.

Of course there are problems with this account, many of them. Just to mention one troublesome area, there is the obvious difficulty we might have in spelling out what a mode of presentation is, and how it can happen that words sometimes refer to buildings and sometimes to modes of presenting them. Still, it is tempting to think that Monique's belief relationship to something or other is like ownership, that is, it is not the slack kind of relationship that it might appear to be. And it would therefore be nice if we could deal with the appearance of slack by attributing it to some more complicated way in which language functions in propositional attitude reports.

How does this kind of move fare in relation to Richard's encounter with the unsuspected change in brasserie? It must first be admitted that the kind of linguistic move described above was worked out with Monique-type cases in mind. But perhaps it could be adapted. For example, one might say that since his belief involves a relationship to the mode of presentation of the chairs rather than to the chairs themselves, his nostalgic belief is about the former brasserie, even though he is no longer in that brasserie, and whatever truth there was in it stays the same. However, the troubles with this suggestion come thick and fast, and they point to certain deeper problems, even in respect of Monique-type cases. For what they all stem from is this: we want beliefs to be about what is around us, and to be made true or false by that reality. Indeed, this is surely a large part of what belief-talk is for. Yet, if we slip too deeply into the mode of presentation way of describing beliefs, we run the risk of making them completely unresponsive to reality. For example, by allowing Richard's belief to be tied to the original brasserie, and to keep its truth value, we risk cutting him off from his new surroundings. Admittedly, one nice feature about the present proposal is that it can explain why Richard would say such things as, 'Nothing much has changed in the old place.' This is because, so far as the content of his beliefs is concerned, nothing much has changed. And as I have emphasized all along, the attitudes are our main tool for explaining what people do and say. Still, we must be careful to preserve both our intuitions about the attitudes: they explain what we do *and* they do this by showing how the world seems to us to be. In other contexts, losing the world may be a good thing to do, but it makes little sense in the present one.

(b)   Styles of Believing

An obvious thought to have, given the problems there are in coping with the two aspects of belief, is that there may well be *two* kinds of belief (and, as needed, two kinds of the other attitudes as well). One kind has Monique believingly related to the relevant items in the world. With respect to this kind, and appearances notwithstanding, Monique's beliefs just are about the British Museum; she just does believe of that famous landmark that it is both guarded by, and not guarded by, lions. In the trade, this kind of belief is called *de re* thereby indicating the connection between the believer and the relevant 'things' (Latin: *res*) in the world.

The other kind, called *de dicto*, is not only sensitive to the choice of words used in attributions, it goes as far as to have believers related not to the things of the world, but to the linguistic items (Latin: *dicta*) that figure in the attributions. With respect to this style of belief, Monique does believe that the British Museum is guarded by lions, but does not believe that the building over there is guarded by lions, even though the building over there is none other than the British Museum.

It is sometimes difficult to get the hang of this, since it sounds so much like the way of putting matters that got us into trouble in the first place. What one has to do is to recognize that the *de dicto* sytle of belief has Monique believing a linguistic item: *the British Museum is guarded by lions*. And it not implausible to regard this linguistic item as quite different from the following one: *the building over there is not guarded by lions*.

The basic idea behind this strategy (though this is very rarely made explicit) is that by discerning two kinds of belief we can cope with the apparently puzzling cases in a divide-and-conquer way. The *de re* attribution shows Monique to have a problem: she has beliefs that make the British Museum a strange building indeed – one that both has and does not have lions guarding its entrance.

By itself this shouldn't be all that surprising. After all, the story I told is essentially one in which Monique is confused. So why shouldn't her confusion take this form? Still, as noted earlier, if this were *all* we could say about Monique's beliefs, things would not be very satisfactory. She is confused all right, but not as totally mad as this attribution makes her sound. And this is where the availability of the *de dicto* style comes in handy. It gives us the chance to add – almost as a qualification – that Monique is not as crazy as all that, since she *de dicto* believes that the British Museum entrance is guarded by lions and that the building over there is not so guarded.[2] These latter claims might well make us less squeamish about the *de re* attribution because the two styles, taken together, seem to give us a reasonable handle on the nature and source of Monique's confusion.

As will be obvious, the detailed working out of the *de dicto* style overlaps with the linguistic attempt to defuse the puzzles. For merely citing the *de dicto* style is not enough. We need to have an account of the *dicta* – an account which makes it plausible that Monique is related in various ways to the relevant bits of language and the world – and this is central to the linguistic approach.

Leaving aside the Byzantine details that have grown up around attempts to deal with the attitudes using linguistic resources, there are a number of more straightforward problems with this second, divide-and-conquer approach. Most of them begin with the obvious and simple question: what is the relationship between *de re* and *de dicto* belief? Note that this is not just an idle question – one that we would like to have answered but which can wait. Our original intuition about the directionality of the attitudes was that it was some kind of relationship between the attitude taker and items in the world. We have been trying to see (in outline) how to spell this out, whilst remaining faithful to our intuitions about how we actually use attitude-attributing sentences in particular cases. On the present approach, it would seem that all the world-directedness is handled by the *de re* style; the *de dicto* form helps us cope with those things we might say about believers when they are confused or ill-informed, though it does so at the cost of *not* being a relationship between believers and items in the world. But so far from helping, this bifurcation of tasks risks losing everything. For unless there is an intelligible relationship between the *de re* and the *de dicto*, each will end up a failure at giving an account of directionality – one because it ignores the attitude taker and the other because it loses the world. We will have two wrong approaches instead of one.

In addition, there is a real question about whether, on the present proposal, what we have are two different attitudes or merely two styles of attribution. If there is only one kind of belief, but it can be attributed in two different ways, then our interest should be in the nature of this belief and not so much in the styles of attribution. And if the proposal is that there are really two kinds of belief (and two kinds, therefore, of each of the attitudes) where is the evidence for this?

The history of attempts to cope with the *de re/de dicto* distinction would require a book in itself. Indeed, the attempt to relate the two generated a thriving industry in philosophy – an industry whose output overlapped with the linguistic approach to the attitudes. Nor has production completely ceased, even though the main markets have moved elsewhere.

(c) Styles of Content

The de re/de dicto distinction (and the use of philosophy of language to clarify it) was historically connected with Monique's kind of problem. But what about Richard's predicament? Does the de re/de dicto distinction, problematic though it is, give us something to say in that case?

The origin of Richard's kind of trouble is a certain thought experiment suggested originally by Hilary Putnam,[3] though it has gone through many variations since. In that experiment, you are asked to suppose that (a) there is a glass of water in front of you and that (b) you believe there to be a glass of water in front of you. Next you are invited to imagine that there is this other place called 'Twin Earth'. The name is appropriate because everything on Twin Earth is a molecule-by-molecule duplicate of things on our planet. In particular, there is a molecular duplicate of you, that duplicate is sitting in front of a glass and has a belief about its content. Crucially, though, there is this one difference between Earth and Twin Earth: on Twin Earth the stuff in rivers, lakes and in the glass is not H_2O but something chemically called 'XYZ'. For reasons which are not really important to the present debate, we can take it that this means that there is no water on Twin Earth, though there is something very much like it which we could call 'twater' (twin water). Now, suppose that you are thirsty. Since you believe that there is water in the glass in front of you, you would probably reach out for the glass and drink it. Similarly, your Twin-Earth counterpart would do the same. Why? Well, if you and the twin were molecularly identical, one would expect that your brains and nervous systems would support the same beliefs and other psychological states. (The proper discussion of brains and belief comes in part III but, for the sake of the argument here, let us accept this claim about the way belief and brain march in step.) But your twin couldn't be described as having the belief that there is water in the glass in front of him, because, as we have assumed, there is no water on Twin Earth. There is only twater. Moreover, assuming that you don't know how to tell the difference (by looking) between water and twater, what do you suppose you would do if you (and your thirst) were miraculously transported to Twin Earth? You would reach for the glass.

What these things are held to show is that you and your twin's beliefs can be, in some respect, the same, even though the world they seem to be about is different. Or, in the case of transportation, your belief remains the same, but what it is about has changed. (The case of transportation is closest to the case of Richard in Paris.) One consequence which has been drawn from Twin Earth cases, is that there may well be two kinds of content. One kind is that which you and your Twin-Earth counterpart can share, even though there are differences in your respective worlds. This is called 'narrow' content. The other is that kind of content that shows your belief, which is after all about water, to be different from your twin. This content is called 'wide' (sometimes 'broad') content. Applying these two kinds of content to Richard's case, we can say that when he walked into the new brasserie, he had a set of beliefs with narrow contents responsible for the things he did and said. In being narrow, these beliefs were not sensitive to the fact that Richard was not in the original brasserie, However, from another point of view, we could view his beliefs as having wide content – as being directed to real-world items and, hence, as sensitive to any swapping of such items. The narrow content of Richard's beliefs was not falsified by the surprising duplication of brasseries, but the wide content was. In so far as Richard widely thought that the chairs in the old brasserie were still comfortable, his belief was false.

Clearly, this proposal echoes some of those previously considered, especially the de re/de dicto distinction. But one should not assume that, for example, narrow content and de dicto content are the same. The problems each were designed to deal with are quite different: narrow content is intended to help with Twin-Earth kinds of duplication of reality; de dicto content is a way of dealing with the possibility of multiple beliefs about a single reality. One could look at it this way: narrow content comes from a kind of subtraction – take away from belief contents whatever it is that makes us think they connect directly to particular things. In contrast, de dicto content comes from a kind of addition – add to belief contents those elements that make them a way some particular person thinks of things. Of course, this subtracting and adding might get you to the same place – to a content which was expressible by dicta – but there is no guarantee of this.

Aside from the problems of understanding how the narrow/wide content distinction is related to the others, there is the even more vexed question of how these styles of content are related to each other and to our ordinary ways of speaking. For beliefs do seem to be about the world; hanging on to that idea in the face of certain problems is what we have been trying to do. Of course, it would be nice if we could simply say that narrow content, entertained in a particular environment, fixed wide content. That is, that what goes on in the relatively narrow confines of our minds serves to attach us to the wider world. But duplication cases like Richard's show that this just won't work; if it did, Richard wouldn't have been in his predicament in the first place. As with de re/de dicto styles of believing, there seems to be a danger that having two styles of content simply pushes our original problem under another part of the carpet.

(d)   Troilism

The approaches considered so far have closely followed our talk about the attitudes in regarding them as essentially relations between attitude takers and some second item. We say:

Anne believes that her coat is in the hallway cupboard,

and this has set philosophers on the trail of that second item — the thing to which Anne is attitudinally related. Mesmerized by the language of attitude reports, they have assumed that whatever else they are, attitudes show them-selves to be two-place relations. But some things work better in threes. Perhaps we could regard Anne's belief as really a three-place relation: one which holds between Anne, the set of items consisting of the coat, the cupboard and the relationship of being in, and a third element such as a sentence. In the prob-lematic case of Monique in London, the proposal would come out roughly as follows:

Monique is believingly related in the *lions-guard-the-British-Museum* sort of way to the British Museum, the lions and the guarding relation.

But this is a different relationship from:

being believingly related in the *building-over-there-is-not-guarded-by lions* sort of way to the British Museum, the lions and the guarding relation.

This is a difficult proposal to come to grips with on first hearing, but the central idea is simple enough. By adding some third element to the belief relation, we give ourselves extra room to manoeuvre – something we can use, in the appropriate circumstances, to get ourselves out of trouble. For example, we can use the above three-place belief relation to say that Monique's two beliefs really relate her to the same building, lions, etc., but that each of them does this in a slightly different way.

Of course, there is an obvious problem here: where does this third item come from? After all, the surface structure of attitude sentences reveals them to have just one thing in the content place, whereas the present proposal requires two. One serves to describe the reality to which Monique is fixed, and a second specifies the way in which she is fixed to it. To be sure, some-times it may be possible to accomplish both of these jobs with a single sen-tence: just pick a content sentence that both shows what the world must be like for the belief to be true, and displays the way in which the believer actu-ally does her thinking about that world. But there are many times when we attribute beliefs without being all that careful. Indeed, there are times when we haven't a clue what sentence would faithfully reproduce the subject's point of view.

The idea that propositional attitude attributions make subtle use of two dif-ferent content sentences has obvious connections with the proposals discussed earlier. One might even think that it was an amalgam of modes of presenta-tion and styles of believing. Unfortunately, it is not that simple. There are cur-rently a large number of different, incompatible and intricate suggestions for how to engage in this particular *menage à trois*, and any attempt to summarize them briefly would be unfair.

(e)   Stepping Outside

I said earlier that retreat was the strategy most often used in trying to deal with the attitude problem. First, we retreated from regarding belief as a relation between a believer and some actual state of affairs, then we considered retreat-ing from the idea that there was only one kind of belief (or style of belief at-tribution) and, most recently, we have seen that we may even have to retreat from the appearance that belief has of being a two-place relation. But I have saved the most dramatic retreat for last.

In one way or another, all of the proposals so far considered begin with the idea that an attitude is a genuine state of a person, albeit a mental and rela-tional one. There is something about Monique that is her mental state of believing and that state is somehow related to the British Museum, or her representation of it, or a sentence, or . . . whatever. But perhaps this is completely the wrong way to go about it. Maybe we are taking our talk about belief and the other attitudes too literally.

Look at it this way. We began with what is apparently a description of a person:

A believes that p,

(where A is a person and p is some belief complement). Then we searched around for something true of A – some state internal to the workings of A's mind – which made the above attribution correct, did so in a way which met various desiderata thrown up by the problem cases and, most importantly, told us something sensible about the relation between A and the topic of the belief. (One must not forget this last thing since what started the discussion in the first place was the need to understand the directionality of the attitudes.) But perhaps we should be thinking of what goes on in attitude sentences in a completely different way.

Consider this sentence:

Henry weighs 80 kilograms.

In it, one seems to be claiming that there is some kind of relationship between Henry and a number of kilograms. After all, the sentence seems to have the same grammatical form as:

Henry is sitting in the armchair.

Yet there is clearly something misleading about this surface appearance. For you wouldn't expect to find the 80 kilograms that Henry weighs in the way you would expect to be able to find the armchair he is sitting on. The difference in the two cases is easily explained. Henry is a certain size. That is just one of his properties; it is not a relation between him and some other kind of object. But when we come to describe that property, we have a special way of doing it: we use a verb ('weighs') which relates Henry to a numerical scale, although the scale is used merely as an *index* of Henry's weight, and not as something that can interact with him like an armchair.

The suggestion in the case of the attitudes is patterned on the case of weight: attitudes are seen as non-relational features or properties of individual human minds. However, when we come to describe these attitudes, we have devised a special scale for the job − a special way of indexing them. We use the sentences of our everyday language. Thus, going back to our first example: at a particular time, Anne is in a certain mental state. Call that state S. Now S is going to be very useful for our understanding of what Anne is likely to do and say, so it would be nice to have some revealing way of characterizing it. What we therefore do is to find some sentence ('The coat is in the hallway cupboard') in our language which, for example, is the likely kind of thing we might say if we were in a state like S. This sentence is then used in a verbal construction ('Anne believes that . . .') so as to provide us with the following useful description of S:

Anne believes that the coat is in the hallway cupboard.

Of course the sentence we choose has a meaning – it is about the way things are or might be – and it is because of its meaning that this sentence is a reasonable one to use in 'measuring' Anne's mental state. But in using it for indexing or measuring her state, we are not committed to regarding that state as intrinsically relational. There is no mysterious kind of thing to which Anne is believingly related, just as there is no mysterious kind of thing called '80 kilograms' to which Henry is related merely because he is of a certain bulk.

Exactly how to choose our sentences to measure people's attitudes is something open to lots of different kinds of interpretation. Above, I suggested that we might choose sentences that reflect what we, the attributer, might actually say when in the same kind of mental state as the believer. But there are other possibilities. For example, the best sentence might simply be the one that the believer would assent to, if asked, though this tends to make it difficult for non-users of language to so much as have attitudes.

As with the other proposed 'solutions' to the problem of directionality, this one has its drawbacks. Aside from the difficulty of giving an acceptable account of how to go about measuring attitudes with sentences, one is left with worries about these 'states' of believing (and desiring, hoping, etc.). Are they something over and above the patterns of action they are responsible for? Or do they just come into being when we measure them with sentences? Dealing with these sorts of worries would take us far beyond the task we have set ourselves in part II.

Conclusion

We started with what seemed a straightforward question: how does the directionality of the attitudes work? In considering answers to it we have now gone inconclusively through a number of proposals: attitudes are relations to the world; to propositions; to modes of presentation; to things (*res*) and/or *dicta*; to wholly self-contained (narrow) contents and/or to wide contents; and, finally, we have even speculated that they might not be relations at all. Moreover, inconclusiveness here just reflects the state of play in the philosophical community: there just isn't a best theory of the directionality of the attitudes.

And things get worse. The aim of part II is to probe our conception of the mind – to ask questions about it and to see what assumptions lie below the surface. What we are not doing – yet – is to see how the mind fits into our wider understanding of the world, into the kind of understanding most often identified with scientific inquiry. But when philosophers talk about the 'problems of intentionality', they tend to run together two things: what exactly is the directionality of the attitudes, and how can anything *like that* exist in the world as described by science. Of course, this is not necessarily a bad thing to do. After all, you've got to know what you are talking about before you see how it fits into your picture of the world's workings. Still, the running together of these questions can lead to confusion, and that is why I have chosen to keep them in separate stages. What I have described here is how one of our most prominent ways of speaking about the mind – the attributing of attitudes – has a feature which is downright perplexing. When we dig just beneath beliefs, desires, etc. there is a labyrinth, and I have tried to supply a thread to guide you, though it is not enough of a guide to show you the way out.

2.2 Experiencing and Consciousness

An Experience

Before it was the usual practice to give injections, my childhood dentist had a method intended to help alleviate the suffering. He would arrange that my right arm rested comfortably on the arm of the chair saying: 'If the pain is really bad, raise your arm and I'll stop drilling.' A fine promise. But, on more than one occasion, having suffered, as I thought bravely and for a long time, but needing a rest from the mounting agony, I would raise my arm only to be told: 'What I am doing to you just doesn't hurt. You are not in pain.'

In retrospect, even I can find the dentist's claim amusing because the thought behind it – if there was one – is so much at variance with both our ordinary conception of mental items such as pain and with the dentist's own affirmation of this conception. As noted in chapter 1, bodily sensations are generally regarded both as highly *accessible* and as only poorly *observable*, where these terms are understood in the somewhat special ways outlined there. Thus, the pain I experienced in the dentist's chair was highly accessible (I was thoroughly and intimately aware of it) and only tenuously observable (the dentist, and any other third parties, could not directly tell that I was in pain). In devising a system to signal him, the dentist apparently recognized these features of the situation, yet his later refusal to count my hand movement as a genuine indicator of pain contradicted that recognition. Perhaps because of his then advanced age and long experience with suffering, he was somehow more expert than most at telling whether someone was having pain. But however much of an expert he took himself to be, it does strike us as bizarre to regard his expertise as more reliable than his patient's, because we are so committed to the idea that our bodily sensations are accessible to us, and not directly observable by others.

The above story brings out something else about the nature of experience. The dentist asked me to 'tell' him when I was in too much pain by raising my arm. Clearly, since I was unable to speak in those circumstances, some such relatively crude signalling device was necessary. But suppose that I could have spoken. Would this have allowed me to communicate my pain to him in any more adequate way? I think we would be tempted to answer 'no'. As was noted earlier, experiences such as pain tend to be very low on the expressibility scale: we can say that we have them and we can say a few things about them, but they have features which – as we commonly say – cannot be put into words. In raising my arm, I was using a prearranged, uncomplicated signal to convey the idea *that* I was in pain. But I was not thereby making the pain itself – the content of my experience – available to the dentist. Nor would such conveyance seem easier, or even in principle possible, if I had been able to use the resources afforded me by the public language I shared with the dentist.

Pain is often taken to be a good example of the category of experience. But when one realizes that this category includes the whole gamut of bodily sensations, as well as the kind of thing that takes place when we perceive the outside world, or introspect our current mood or trains of thought, it may be unreasonable to use the example of pain in this way. For certainly there are differences between pain experiences and the others. Yet pain has in common with these other experiences these features: high accessibility (to their subject), poor observability (by others) and poor expressibility (by the subject to others). And, since it is the conjunction of these three general features that makes so much trouble for our understanding of experience, we need not be worried here about specific differences within that category.

Knowledge

There are many different ways in which such trouble can be made to appear, but perhaps the most direct begins by a brief reflection on what it is to know something. Here is a truth – almost a truism – about knowledge:

> When you know something, there is something that you know.

This claim owes its obviousness to our understanding of what makes something a propositional attitude. For, though knowledge may be special in all sorts of ways, it is after all one among the attitudes, and as such it has content. A specification of a knowledge claim has the standard form 'x knows that p' where x is some knower and p is the knowledge content. So, of course, when you know something, there is something – a content – that you know.

A second claim about knowledge would appear to follow directly on from this:

When you know something, you can say what you know.

Calling this the 'expressibility principle', you should be able to see why it might be thought to be a consequence of the claim about content. If the standard form of knowledge attribution is 'x knows that p', then any such truth comes equipped with what is needed for expressing that knowledge. I know that Tower Bridge is in London, so I have available a form of words ('Tower Bridge is in London') with which I can express my knowledge to anyone who cares to listen.

There are many reasons one might have for resisting the idea that knowledge is essentially expressible, and some of them will emerge in the further discussion of experience. But there is one reason that is not particularly relevant to our concerns, and it can be dealt with by a small qualification to the expressibility principle. There can be things that we know, but only in an implicit way. For example, I might be said to know all sorts of things about the grammar of English, though there would be no point in asking me what I know, since I might lack the requisite grammatical concepts to put my knowledge into words. Usefully, such knowledge is called 'tacit' precisely because it is knowledge that we are unable to spell out. However, though it is clear that tacit knowledge, if there is any, makes trouble for the idea that we can always say what we know, this will not be relevant to the present argument. For it certainly seems plausible that when we know something in a completely explicit way – when we are non-tacitly aware of the content of our knowledge – then we ought to be able to say what we know.

The Problem

Against these background claims about knowledge, the path leading to trouble is uncomfortably straight. When someone has a pain, it certainly seems to be something known to the person whose experience it is. Equally, when I look out at an expanse of forest in the summer, the *experienced* quality of the shades of green, as well as that of the shapes of the trees, seems to be something in my consciousness I not only know, but which I know in a way no one else does or can. Yet the contents of my knowledge in these cases is not something that I can convey to someone else. I can of course say that I am in pain or that I am experiencing a complex range of shades of green. But neither of these would manage to convey the content of what I experience to someone else; neither would they make it apparent what it is like to have these experiences. So it seems that I can know all sorts of things in respect of my conscious or experiential states that I cannot properly express. And this undermines the perfectly ordinary idea that if I know something, then I can say what it is that I know.

Initial reactions to this vary. I can even imagine someone thinking that there isn't much of a problem here – just a case of knowing something we are unable to find words to describe. Here we might be encouraged to think of times when something was so surprising, or passed by so quickly, that we struggled to find adequate descriptive language. And basically the thought here is that I was just wrong in suggesting that we can always say what we know. Perhaps, in spite of first impressions, the principle of expressibility is just not true of knowledge. Unfortunately, the tension between the expressibility of knowledge and the ineffability of experience will not go away so easily. Yet, if you are struggling to keep the tension in focus, perhaps the following example will help.

Simone's Story

Simone was born colour-blind. In her case, this meant that she could not distinguish any colour at all: her colour-discriminative abilities were no better than yours would be if you watched a black-and-white film, and had to answer questions about the colours of the actors' clothes. However, Simone did not accept her 'disability'. Instead, she set about trying to cope with the world of colour by other means. By laborious study, she came to understand the physical and psychophysical basis of ordinary colour perception. In time, and using devices to measure the wavelengths of reflected and transmitted light, as well as allowing for the peculiarities of the way the human brain processes such input, she was able accurately to tell the colour – indeed even the shade of colour – of any object. Had you not been aware of the complex measuring devices, not to mention the theoretical reasoning that went into her judgements, you would not even suspect that her colour perception was inferior to yours.

That is the example. But dwell for a minute on the idea that, in spite of all her research and her uncanny accuracy in describing the colours of objects, there is still something *defective* about Simone's colour judgement. What makes it so natural for us to continue to think of Simone as colour-blind? I don't think it is difficult to offer some kind of answer here. She gets the colours of objects right, but she lacks something enjoyed by a non–colour-blind person – her perceptual experience is markedly different. Speculating a bit, we might imagine that her perceptual experience is something like that we would have if we were watching a black-and-white film. But whether or not this is exactly right, it seems clear that her inner world is markedly different from ours. And one way to summarize this difference is to say that we know something about, for example, seeing the cloudless sky, that she doesn't.

Embellishing the story a little can make this point even more sharply. Suppose that Simone undergoes an operation which makes her experience exactly like ours. In this event, it is natural to imagine her saying something like this: 'I always knew that the sky was blue, but I never knew that blue was like *that.*' And this last word – the demonstrative 'that' – points directly at what we are trying to capture. The story of Simone seems to lead us inexorably to the idea of there being something it is like to perceive colours (and to have pains), and to the further idea that we *know* about this inner realm. We are led to these conclusions because – to repeat – it seems natural to think that Simone comes to know something about her experience of seeing *after* her operation that she didn't know *before.* (Remember that what Simone is said to know after her operation is not a fact about the sky, but one about her experience of it.)

The trouble is, though, that whatever it is that she knows remains strangely inexpressible. For, as we noted, there just doesn't seem to be a vocabulary suitable for giving any precise content to this knowledge. The best that I could imagine Simone as saying about her newly acquired knowledge is: 'I now know that blue is like *that.*' But this doesn't really convey the whole of what we usually expect from someone who is said to know something. Thus, consider how we manage with knowledge about our surroundings. Just now I am sitting in in my study, so I certainly know what it is like. And, given this, you would expect me to be able to tell you – to say things like: 'There is a desk in the middle, a pile of books on the floor,' etc. But what would your reaction be if, instead of these things, I said, 'Well, my study is like *that*'? I suppose that you would think that either I didn't know what I was talking about or I was concealing certain things from you.

Introducing 'Qualia'

It should be obvious that the problem we are having with our knowledge of experience is unlike cases in which we witness something so strange, or so terrifying, that we lack words to describe it. For it is possible to keep your attention fixed on what you are experiencing long enough to know (as we say) perfectly well what it is like. The trouble is that we just don't have words to express this knowledge. Of course, we say all sorts of complicated metaphorical things about our states of mind: 'I felt as if I had been run over *slowly* by a 73 bus' (hangover) or 'I feel as if someone has tied a knot in my stomach and is *twisting* it' (anxiety). But our problem is not met by these sorts of description. What we lack are words for the simplest of experiences, such as the way it is with us when we see a perfectly ordinary shade of colour.

At this point you might be tempted by the thought that this lack is really quite superficial. After all, since we are mostly interested in telling each other what is going on in the world, it is perhaps not surprising that our language has developed without the necessary resources to describe our inner life. However, what is to stop us inventing some terms to fill this gap? Nothing – or so say those philosophers who have taken at least the first step in that direction.

Think of how things are when you look up at a cloudless sky. If you are asked, you will say that it is blue. But, of course, the colour word is used here to describe a feature or property *of the sky*, and no one would think otherwise. It is simply bizarre to say that your experience is blue. But then how can you even to begin to describe how it is with you when you are seeing the blue sky? Here's how. Concentrate on the nature of your sky-directed experience, taking special care to keep fixed on what is happening to you, whilst ignoring as best as you can how things are with the sky. There certainly seems to be something going on in your consciousness – something that has various properties. If you doubt this, just imaginatively compare how different these things would be if you were looking at the same sky, but that its colour began to change, having been made to glow red by the setting sun. No one could doubt your ability to distinguish the experiences of the two differently coloured expanses. And what else could explain this except that the experiences have different properties.

Now, of course, we don't have names for these properties – either the specific ones in the blue-sky case, or even their general category. But – at least in respect of the general category – why not just coin some suitable word? Why not follow the lead of some philosophers by calling the properties of experience (in general) 'qualia' (singular: 'quale')? The name seems apt since what we are dealing with are the *qualitative* aspects of experiences – the 'how it is to us' when we have them. Armed with this term, we can say this much about the blue-sky experience: it has qualia which distinguish it from, for example, the red-sky experience. We could also go on to invent terms for each of the specific qualia that mark our experience – we could say that the relevant quale of my experience when I look at the blue sky is 'blue-ish', though this latter term should not be confused with 'blue'. But what matters in making sense of such words as 'blue-ish' is that they pertain to qualia, so all the weight really hinges on the general term. For example, we can now (apparently) say what is defective about Simone's colour judgements before the operation: it is that she makes them without reference to the qualia of her experiences.

Does the coining of the term 'qualia' solve the problem with which we began? That is, can we now reconcile our knowledge of our experience with the demand that knowledge be expressible? This certainly would be a quick fix to the original problem – almost certainly too quick. Any new word counts as a genuine extension to our language only if we are fairly sure that we can understand what it is supposed to signify. And it is not clear that we have said enough to imbue 'qualia' with a meaning suitable to get over the expressibility problem. For the suspicion is that this new word doesn't do any more for us than the demonstrative 'that' as it occurred in Simone's original judgement: 'So *that* is what blue is like.' Indeed, I suspect that many of the proponents of this new word would be perfectly satisfied with this outcome. They never wanted to use the term to give a definitive answer to the expressibility problem. Far from it. What they wanted was some way to talk about that very problem. The word 'qualia' was invented as a way of answering those who take our lack of expressive means as indicating that there may not be anything it is like to have an experience. However, rather than spending any more time on qualia here, we should now review more complete responses to the expressibility problem. Considerations relevant to our understanding (or lack of it) of the word 'qualia' will be more intelligible against this background.

(Those familiar with some philosophical literature may think that 'qualia' is just another name for what used to be called a 'sense datum'. I don't think this would be quite right, but spelling this out is not appropriate here. Suffice it to say that those philosophers who have found it congenial to speak of sense data have used them in projects different from our present descriptive one.)

Grasping the Nettle

I can imagine someone thinking that we have overlooked the best strategy for dealing with our present trouble in respect of knowledge of experience: what we should do is just brazen it out. If the accessibility and inexpressibility of our experiences do not fit with the idea that knowledge ought to be expressible, then why not just say – as far as experience is concerned – that the expressibility principle just doesn't apply? Why not just say that there is for each of us an inner realm to which we have a directness of access that is denied to anyone else and, further, that it is a mistake to regard the knowledge we have of this realm as expressible in the ordinary way? I can tell you that my study has a desk and books, but that is because the study and its contents are publicly observable – they are part of an 'outer' realm. However, when it comes to experience, the best I can do is to make a sort of gesture: I can tell you (as I did the dentist) that I am in pain. I can tell you that my experience is of that special kind that I have when I see the blue sky or green leaves. And I can invent words like 'qualia' to make it seem easier to refer to these special features of my experience. What I cannot do is to be as fully informative about the inner realm as I am about the outer, but that is just how it is.

In essence, this suggested way with our problem comes under the heading 'grasping the nettle'. One admits that there are features of experience and knowledge that are in tension with one another, but then, rather than allowing this to bother us, we simply count the tension as itself a sign of the special nature of experience. The trouble is that, whatever the common wisdom, grasping nettles – even philosophical ones – is scarcely painless. But before we see just how painful it is in the present case, I should like to point out something about the history of the view just canvassed.

As I have presented it, the view is a reaction to the apparent difficulties that we get into when we add our conception of knowledge to our conception of experience. However, the standard view of the history of these matters does not treat it as in any way a *reaction* to problems. Rather, in the works of René Descartes (1596–1650), it is usually seen as the robust and confident statement of a conception of the mind which has been worked on – and over – during the past 400 years. Indeed, it could be argued that Descartes himself only articulated what anyone would say about these matters; many regard the Cartesian view as the common-sense view. Moreover, the underlying tensions to be found in the conception have been the centre of concerted philosophical attention only in the past fifty years or so. Still, having admitted that my presentation is a-historical, I hope you will come to appreciate that it is none the worse for that.

Grasping the nettle in the way described is tantamount to accepting that there is a sharp divide between our knowledge of the world – the external world of tables and chairs – and the inner world of our experiences which is commonly said to be known by introspection. Of course, the spatial metaphor inherent in the words 'inner' and 'outer' is not mandatory. Less metaphorically, we could describe the Cartesian view as requiring us to recognize the divide as between *first-* and *third-person* knowledge – between what I know of myself, and what I can know of someone else. But whatever words we use, there is a high – and many think an unacceptable – price to pay for maintaining this divide.

First of all, the existence of a sharp distinction between first- and third-person knowledge makes it difficult to understand how we can ever know that our friends and neighbours so much as have mental lives. For the Cartesian, each of the surveys of our feelings, perceptions, sensations and moods takes place in the privacy of our own minds and, though the 'qualia' we thereby come across can be as rich as anything, the attempts to convey these things – to make them present in some way from the third-person perspective – never amounts to anything; all that we have as evidence of each other's mental lives are words issuing from our lips and other bits of behaviour. But these words and behavioural manifestations could issue from creatures completely lacking in any inner life, so a complete scepticism about other minds is made possible by the Cartesian picture. And if we think that any view encouraging such scepticism is unacceptable, then this will be reason enough to look elsewhere to deal with the tension between knowledge and experience.

Of course, there are those who will not react to this kind of scepticism with horror: grasping the nettle a little harder (so to speak) they will insist that scepticism about other minds is perfectly reasonable – at least as a possibility. After all, no one has found a completely satisfying way of showing that philosophical scepticism in general is incoherent. The image of philosophers as people struggling to prove the reality of the kitchen table at which they are sitting is an enduring one. And philosophers know that these struggles can be interesting and helpful to our thinking, though they do not for a minute have any serious worries about resting their elbows on the table. So why not admit that we might be unable to prove conclusively that the sceptic about other minds is wrong, whilst unconcernedly living and acting as if we had no doubt at all about the mental lives of other human creatures? What is to stop us saying that we can never *know* that those around us have minds, but that we can be pretty sure that they do – for practical purposes?

Leaving aside the issue of whether it is ultimately satisfying to deal with the sceptic by conceding even that much, there is a deeper problem which is easy to miss if you concentrate too hard on scepticism. In a nutshell, it is a question of the very coherence of the first-/third-person divide, and it is best approached by investigating the words that figure in our speaking about the mind. Take a specific example: Harry has a pain in his elbow, and he tells you this. Given the Cartesian picture, Harry has not thereby managed to convey fully what it is that he knows; full expressibility is denied to this sort of first-person knowledge. Yet Harry does use the word 'pain', so it is perfectly reasonable to ask what this word means both in his mouth and in his audience's ears. Here is one view: Harry uses the word 'pain' as the label of the experience he is undergoing at present. After all, he judges this experience to be sufficiently similar to other experiences he has previously labelled 'pains'. So the word 'pain' has its meaning fixed by the inner landscape which Harry (and no one else) is in a position to survey.

This won't do. For how would we ever be in a position to understand what Harry said? If the meaning of Harry's remark depends on his own conceptualization of a realm completely unobservable by us, then he might as well have said something like this (with apologies to Lewis Carroll): 'My elbow feels uffish.' And actually the situation is even worse, for the conceptual location of pain depends upon the availability of general terms like 'feeling' of which pain is a subspecies. But the word 'feeling' too must get its meaning from Harry's inner survey, and it is thus no more available to third parties than 'pain'. So Harry's remark might have been, 'My elbow whiffles uffish,' and this certainly leaves us in the dark about what is up with him. (Note that this line of reasoning would apply especially forcefully to the word 'qualia'. Indeed, the preceding sort of reasoning is what grounds some people's conviction that coining terms like 'qualia' does nothing to help us with the original problem.)

What can seem the natural move here is to admit that Harry's word 'pain' labels something unavailable to us, but to note that his use of the word goes with behaviour that *is* observable, and is just like the behaviour we go in for when we have such experiences. Included here is behaviour such as uttering the sounds 'My elbow hurts.' Reasoning then by analogy with our own case, we say that Harry's behaviour shows him to mean pain by 'pain', since when we have pain, we behave in roughly the same way. But this won't do either. What we are asked to imagine is that the word 'pain' applies to me because of what I experience, but that it applies to others because they behave in roughly the ways I do when I feel myself to be in pain. Unfortunately, this appeal to analogy does not take seriously enough the confinement to our own case. For, given what has been described, it may be more sensible to say that the word 'pain' is systematically ambiguous than it is to say that it has the same meaning when I apply it to myself and when others apply it to themselves. This is because I never do manage to experience someone else's alleged pain – my analogical reasoning never gets a single confirmation. Even worse, it is not clear that I could now coherently say what constitutes a confirming instance. For, if I say that it is a case of someone else's having *just* what I have when I use the word 'pain', this never happens – one thinks indeed it couldn't happen. Yet, how could I even begin to say how someone's supposed inner life must differ from mine whilst remaining faithful to the idea that the word 'pain' is used in just the way I would use it? Given this problem, wouldn't it just be a lot more plausible to say that 'pain' means one thing for me and something else when used by others? The trouble is, this makes it wholly mysterious how we ever do manage to communicate with one another.

I have put this point in terms of words and communication, and there are those who might feel that such problems with language are relatively superficial. However, whilst the difficulty is easiest to explain as one about the use of words like 'pain', it is far more serious than that. For, given the Cartesian view, we seem unable even to *think* coherently about experience. If the concepts in terms of which we organize our thoughts about ourselves apply to a range of experiences which are only available from a first-person point of view, then there will be an unbridgeable divide between them and those concepts we use to think about others.

The trouble with scepticism seemed to be that it made knowledge of other minds impossible, though we imagined that we could at least formulate the hypothesis that others enjoy experience like ours. Now it should be apparent that there is a problem with the hypothesis even before we get to scepticism. If our conception of the mindedness of other people is determined by their patterns of action and speech, then of course we will often know that they have minds. But the hypothesis that is the subject of the sceptic's interest is not about publicly available behaviour. Yet how can we characterize the appropriate hypothesis? Is it that others can look inside themselves and see that things are like *this* (where we concentrate very hard on our stream of consciousness)? That can't be quite right. How can they find things to be 'like this' when what that is like is forever hidden from them? (Remember that the word 'this' refers to one's own conscious experience, even though the aim is to give content to the thoughts of others about their experience.) How can I set out to imagine someone else enjoying my stream of consciousness?

To this you may be tempted to reply that I have overstated the case for the incoherence of the hypothesis: what is wanted is not that I imagine someone else enjoying *my* stream of consciousness, but just something *like* it. The trouble is, though, that on the Cartesian picture, the only experiences I ever come across are my own, and the concepts I use in framing my thoughts about that experience are forever bound to it. It is not easy to see what content I could give to the idea of someone enjoying what is not my experience but only very much like it, when the only idea of experience in play is my own. It is easy to miss this, since there is a tendency to think of cases where it makes perfect sense to make the first-/third-person shift. For example, though I have a particular kind of watch, there is no problem in imagining someone else having a watch of the same kind. But this is because the watch in question is in the public domain to begin with; anyone with the relevant discriminatory abilities can frame a concept of that object and then use it to think about an object that would be *like* that one except in respect of ownership. But the Cartesian view makes it difficult to see how this sort of move is possible in respect of any given experience, since ownership in this case is simply not detachable.

The No 'Know' View

Our discussion of the Cartesian attempt to grasp the nettle seems to lead to an impasse. But whether or not the case is proven, the time has surely come to see if there are less painful ways out of the original difficulty. Recall that all our trouble came from the fact that knowledge seems to be essentially expressible, whereas experience seems to be both known and inexpressible. I portrayed the Cartesian as someone prepared to say that we just have to live with the fact that knowledge of experience is an exception; someone prepared to say that there can be an inner realm of things which we can survey, and thereby come to know about, though we cannot properly describe what we know. However, since there do seem to be reasons for thinking that we cannot really live with this picture, we ought to find something else to say about experience and knowledge. And a promising thing to do – almost as a reaction against the Cartesian picture – is to question the very idea of an inner realm known in this way.

The simplest expression of this questioning attitude consists in denying that the word 'know' is appropriate in the first-person case. Typically, when we know something, or are said to know it, we have had to do some looking around and checking. For example, I would now claim to know that there is a bird sitting on the branch I can see from my window. Of course, I could be wrong, and, if it was important, there are steps I could take to check this, among other things, by consulting with others. Putative knowledge is essentially fallible, and it is also intersubjectively checkable. That is why the principle of expressibility seems so apt. However, none of these features seems to apply to what we have been calling 'knowledge' of our own experiences: it is not fallible in the way that my perceptually based knowledge is, and it is certainly not intersubjectively checkable. So maybe the way forward is to deny that we have *knowledge* of an inner landscape of the kind suggested by the Cartesian. I shall call this the 'no-knowledge' view.

Here one must be very careful. It is all too easy to think that the suggestion just made is in effect a denial of the very existence of experience. To take our earlier example: when Harry says that his elbow hurts, the no-knowledge view will insist that Harry is not thereby attempting to express something he knows. And one might be tempted to think this was possible only on the assumption that Harry simply had no inner life – that there was nothing there to be the subject-matter of any sort of knowledge. This temptation may even be further reinforced by remarks made by proponents of the view, when they attempt to spell out just what it is that Harry is getting at. In particular, one suggestion has it that we should count Harry's words only as a piece of behaviour to be put alongside other things he might do in respect of his elbow, such as flinching when it is touched. When he says 'my elbow hurts,' he is in effect just saying 'Ouch!', though in a more complicated way. The one thing he is not doing is *describing* how things are with him, and this can lead one to think that the no-knowledge view is actually denying that there is any way things are with him.

A view that insists that mental concepts are in the end concepts that apply only to people's doings and sayings is usually labelled 'behaviourism', and this view is beset with difficulties of its own. (We will consider various versions of behaviourism later on.) However, more important now is the simple fact that behaviourism is not really much of a help with our problem. We want to be able to say something about both experience and knowledge which makes it reasonable to regard experience as highly accessible, without thereby threatening the expressibility of knowledge. A behaviourist interpretation of the no-knowledge view does not do this, since it just denies or ignores the thought that Harry has experiences that are highly accessible only to him. Of course, if the original problem proves completely intractable, someone might urge us to do the radical behaviourist thing, facing whatever further problems this leads to. However, for now it would be better to resist behaviourism, and see if there is a way to understand the no-knowledge view which does help with the original difficulty. The no-knowledge view is after all the no-*knowledge* view, and, however tempting, this should not lead us too quickly to see it as the no-*experience* view.

As several of my earlier examples indicated, knowledge typically involves the application of our concepts to the objects and properties we come across. Thus, any knowledge I have of the bird sitting in the tree consists in my having concepts of such things as birds, trees and sittings, and my putting them together in appropriate ways in my thoughts. Note, by the way, that the objects and properties mentioned here are publicly available – one might say that they belong to no one and yet to everyone. However, on the Cartesian picture, the objects and properties which make up the inner landscape (experiences and their qualia) are quite different; they belong only to the person whose landscape it is. And this is what upsets the no-knowledge theorist. Such a theorist has nothing against experience or against the fact that experience is in some sense private. What he objects to is seeing the realm of experience as just like the realm of objects and properties that make up our public, intersubjectively available world.

Spelled out a bit more, the thought might be expressed this way: of course we all have mental lives and conscious experiences. And, of course, we inhabit a world consisting of objects and properties which we can come to know about and describe. But the conditions for our having concepts of, and describing, the external world are simply not met by experience. The Cartesian mistake consists in thinking that the 'inner world', for the purposes of knowledge and description, is just like the external one. This mistake is signalled by the willingness to use the word 'knowledge' to describe our relationship to our experiences, but the mistake itself is not merely one about when to use this word. It is based on a deep misconception of the nature of experience. It assumes that our experiences are arrayed in something like a landscape, even though none of the features of real landscapes apply.

The no-knowledge view is not an easy one to keep in focus. It has a tendency either to shift before your eyes into a kind of behaviourism or to disappear altogether. Returning to our example of Harry's pain, we certainly have a right to be told a convincing story about what Harry is up to when he says 'My elbow hurts.' As I mentioned, if this is treated as nothing more than a complicated way for Harry to say 'Ouch!', then we are faced with a kind of behaviourism. Surely (many think) these sounds are not characterizable simply as a kind of ornate flinching. They say something about Harry's present experience – a kind of experience that explains why Harry made his remark and that, if Harry did flinch, would explain that as well. The no-knowledge theorist insists that we must not treat the phrase 'say something about Harry's experience' as just a paraphrase of 'tell us what Harry knows about himself.' For it is insisted that to do this invites the profoundly mistaken Cartesian view that Harry is the only possible *witness* to his 'private' pain, when the very idea of a witness only makes proper sense in respect of things that could be witnessed by others. Yet how else can we take Harry's remark? And, considering again the case of Simone after her operation, what could be more natural than to see her as saying: 'Now I know what it is like to see blue'?

Unless the no-knowledge theory can respond to these demands, it seems to be no more than a warning about how to use certain words. And the pressure on the no-knowledge theorist to let us use the word 'know' seems to many overwhelming. Yet there does seem to be something right about resisting the Cartesian picture and all the difficulties into which it tends to lead us. Given all of this, perhaps the way forward is to work out how we can continue to allow that there is a special kind of knowledge which each of us has in relation to our experiences, but which is at the same time a kind of knowledge that steers clear of any commitment to the Cartesian picture. This is where the 'know-how' theory might come to the rescue.

The Know-How View

When we think of knowledge as essentially expressible, we surely have in mind knowledge having propositional content and characterized by the standard form: 'knows that p'. But there are other sorts. Thus, among his other accomplishments, Harry plays the piano rather well, and it is natural to describe his talent by saying: he knows how to play the piano. But this attribution of knowledge does not require anyone (and this includes Harry) to be able to express what is known in some propositional form. The content of Harry's knowledge is not something like a proposition that is even a candidate for truth. Instead, it is an ability or capacity.

Can the distinction between knowing that something is the case, and knowing how to do something help in our present predicament? Here is a suggestion. Suppose we agree that *knowledge that* is essentially expressible, and that Harry (in pain) and Simone have knowledge of their experiences. But we insist that, in the latter cases and appearances aside, there are no propositions that Harry and Simone know. Instead, they each have a special kind of knowledge *how*. Consider Simone: before her operation, we felt that her vision was in some sense defective even though her judgement about the colours of things was unfailingly accurate. After the operation, her judgements were no different, but it is natural to suppose that something had changed – that she had acquired some kind of perceptual knowledge. Well, why not say that what she had acquired was a kind of discriminatory knowledge – a knowledge of how to discriminate colours in a new way? The old way consisted in her appealing to measuring instruments and theories; the new way just involves looking.

Next consider Harry: he says that his elbow hurts, and it is natural to suppose that he is thereby expressing something he knows about himself. However, instead of telling the Cartesian story about Harry's inner landscape, why not just say that Harry's remark shows him to have a kind of discriminatory ability which is lacking in others? He can tell *just by paying attention* that his body is damaged in some way. Harry's specific ability is lacking in us because we have to examine him to see what the damage is – we cannot tell just by paying attention – though, of course, we each have an analogous discriminatory ability in respect of ourselves. And here the appeal to an analogy between Harry and ourselves is less fraught than it was in connection with the inner landscape view. For what is analogous is a perfectly accessible item: an ability to say – without instruments or detailed investigation – that one is damaged in a certain way.

The appeal of this know-how view is considerable. It allows us to say that the difference between the first- and third-person cases is one of knowledge:

for Harry and Simone do know something. Yet we can say this without fear of contradicting the principle of expressibility of knowledge, since that principle applies only to propositional knowledge – knowledge *that*. Neither Harry nor Simone have that kind of knowledge about their states of mind. In addition, this view gives us something to say about the accessibility and observability of our self-knowledge. For Harry and Simone not only know something – they know something we don't. That is, their abilities to tell what colour something is by looking, or to tell that they have suffered some kind of damage just by a sort of paying attention, are abilities special to them. To be sure, we can also tell what colour something is, and whether their bodies are damaged, but not in the way they do. And it is the particular way – the particular ability – that is at issue here. So we can say of this ability that it is highly accessible to those who possess it, but only low on the observability scale. Finally, as far as expressibility is concerned, it should come as no surprise to learn that it is virtually impossible to express what goes on when we exercise this kind of ability. No surprise, that is, in just the way that it is no surprise that Harry cannot describe his knowledge of piano-playing in any terms but these: 'I know how to do it.' Indeed, one could just about consider Simone's excited claim 'I never knew that blue was like that' as more or less equivalent to: 'I never knew how to tell by looking that something was blue. But now I do know how to do it.'

It is easy to get carried away by the know-how view, but all is not plain sailing. The main problem is that our abilities don't stand on their own: it is usual to ask for some kind of explanation of them. Thus, consider two abilities that Harry has: he can play the piano and he can hold forth about the kings and queens of England. The first of these is, of course, very complex and took years to develop, but it isn't unreasonable to say that it is partly a form of what is sometimes called 'hand–eye coordination'. Harry's eyes take in certain notes on the page and his hands, fingers and arms react to them as a result of the training he has received. Of course, if he is any good at the piano, he will also have the more conscious ability to control these reactions in ways that conform to his musical intentions. But for the moment let us think only of the more basic technical ability that consists in getting from the written to the played notes. How would we explain this? Clearly the answer to this would be enormously complicated (and is probably only known in outline), but whatever the details, we can with great plausibility say this much: our explanation will not have to appeal to anything that Harry explicitly knows or believes. And by 'explicit' I mean things to which Harry has conscious access. Thus, Harry doesn't consult some repository of consciously available information such as: if the black note is on the bottom line, then one must use the middle finger of the right hand. He will certainly know this sort of thing, but consciousness of this knowledge is not what guides his hands. If it did, it is unlikely that he would ever manage to move his fingers fast enough. (He might be guided by such things tacitly, but, whatever this means, we can leave it on one side for the moment for reasons which will become clear.)

Contrast piano-playing with Harry's ability to tell you about the kings and queens of England. The obvious way to explain this ability is by appealing to a whole number of things Harry knows or believes, and to which he has conscious access. It is because he knows that Queen Victoria came to the throne in 1837 that he has the ability to say so. In a case like this, speaking about an ability is really only an indirect way of speaking about what someone knows in a fully propositional way. It is the knowledge of what is true that explains someone's ability to come out with it.

Given these two sorts of case, the obvious next question is which of them is the best model for cases of experiential know-how? That is, what explains the abilities Simone has with respect to the experience of seeing blue and Harry has with respect to his pain? Is it like the piano-playing case? Do they just come out with judgements about colours and pains as if they were producing these in unconscious response to something discerned – a sort of 'mind–mouth' coordinative ability? This seems absurd. What one would most naturally claim is that the ability to say how things are (either with colour experiences or with one's body) is based on a prior awareness of the relevant experiences. It is because it is like *that* to see blue – and because Simone came to know this after her operation – that she has the ability to say of an object, without any use of instruments, that it is blue. And it is because Harry has an awareness of the pain that is undoubtedly connected with the damage to his body that he is able to make the discriminative judgements he does. In short, the more plausible model of our know-how in respect of experience is the one based on some kind of prior – and possibly propositional – knowledge. But, if this is the case, then we are back where we started: the know-how interpretation only hid from view the know-that problem.

Here I should insert a final note about the possibility of an explanation based on tacit knowledge, for it might seem as if this would be the best way to deal with our problem. This is because if tacit knowledge lies behind our abilities, then we would have a kind of knowledge that supported the know-how interpretation but avoided the expressibility problem (we already agreed that expressibility didn't apply to tacit knowledge). This move might seem especially appealing in view of the fact that many theorists of language (and piano-playing) appeal to tacit knowledge to explain the relevant abilities. However, though all this is fine, it leaves out something crucial: we do want to preserve the special kind of access that we have to our experiences. But it is difficult to see how this can be preserved if we think that our experience of colour and bodily conditions is nothing other than a discriminative ability grounded in tacit knowledge. Just imagine being asked how it was that you could tell that the sky had changed colour towards sunset. This would be like asking Harry how he knew to begin the second bar with his right thumb. If, as we imagined, this was just a trained reaction on his part, he would simply say: 'don't know – just happened.' Though we could tell a story about his tacitly knowing a rule that connected the note and the hand movement, this would not be knowledge that Harry was aware of, and consulted, whilst he was playing. And could you really be satisfied by saying that you had no idea why you said the two sky scenes differed – it just seemed right to say that they did?

Conclusion

That we know what we feel, that we know this in a way no one else can, and that we cannot fully convey what it is like to have these feelings – these things just seem obvious to many people. Unfortunately, when these are put together with equally obvious-sounding claims about knowledge, the result is less than coherent. Moreover, as I have been labouring to show, it doesn't seem as if tinkering with our conception of knowledge or experience gets us very far in dealing with the threat of incoherence. So something has to give, something we think about the experiential aspects of the mental realm must be wrong. Or, at least, something we think must be reinterpreted in a fairly fundamental way. Radical solutions seem to be called for, and the philosophical community has not been slow in providing them. Here is a sample:

> We don't really have experiences, we only *think* we do.
>
> We don't really have experiences we only *say* we do.
>
> We certainly do have experiences, and these are known only to us, but we don't know anything *else* including among other things about the existence of other people. (This position is best put in the first person: *I* know about *my* experiences and only about them, etc. It is called 'solipsism' and it is certainly a radical solution to the expressibility problem.)
>
> We do have experiences but these are known as well, or better, to others – at least those who take an interest in the dispositions of our bodies. (On this view, maybe the dentist had a point after all.)

Most of these are not really motivated by local conceptual problems about experience that have been the subject-matter of this section of part II. They arise more directly from the attempt to trace the foundations of experience and other mental items to the bedrock of the physical realm. This will be the subject-matter of part III, but first we must consider the third of the categories, that of acting and actions.

2.3   Acting and Actions

As was mentioned earlier, the mental status of actions is controversial: discussion following my informal questionnaires always shows up sharp disagreement about whether to count actions as mental phenomena. There are those who insist that they are no more than end-products of more genuinely mental items, and others who think that the credentials of actions to be included in the mental realm are just as impressive as those of the attitudes. The first group does not deny the important role that the mind plays in acting, but the point tends to be put this way: actions are the *outputs* of minds. As described earlier, they are the wake our minds leave as they travel through life, and for this reason they do not merit *equal* standing with the categories of experience and attitude. The opposing camp denies this second-class status for acting. On this view, when we see someone engaged in acting we are not merely seeing some sort of output, we are seeing the mind itself.

   Disagreement about the status of acting suggests that there may be some fundamental difficulty in our thinking about actions, but it doesn't prove that there is. After all, supporters of one or the other position may just be wrong, and may change their minds when faced with a persuasive reason for doing so. Yet the aim here – as it was in respect of attitudes and experience – is to uncover any real difficulties infecting our understanding of actions. So, for the time being, I shall ignore the disagreement over status, and start from the beginning. What I intend to show is that there are several theses, each of which would be accepted as obviously true of actions, yet that when these are put together they yield unacceptable – even paradoxical – consequences. It will then be easy to see just how far the problem about status is a real reflection of the trouble with acting.

Four Theses about Action

The world contains lots of things – chairs, houses, people and the like. It also contains things that happen. Indeed, it would be impossible explain what our world was like without saying both what things it contains and what happens in it. Can we sharpen or deepen our understanding by getting more specific – by replacing 'happening' with 'what takes place' or with 'event'?

Perhaps, but any such improvements will not be necessary here, for the first thesis about action requires nothing more than the ordinary, if vague, word 'happen':

Thesis (I)   Actions are things which happen.

Of course, there is a use of the word 'happen' that may seem less congenial to this thesis, for sometimes people speak of a happening as almost accidental. It might even be felt that this use *contrasts* with genuine acting, as in someone's saying, 'there was no action, it just happened.' Yet I suggest that this does not undermine thesis (I). For, when it is claimed that there is a contrast between actions and happenings, the contrast is always between things done and things that *merely* (or *just*) happen. In order to make the contrast some such restriction is needed, and the felt need for this qualification actually supports thesis (I). The supposed contrast between actions and happenings is really a way of saying: look, actions are happenings alright, but they are not *just* happenings. And this shows the next thing we must do. We must supplement thesis (I) with some truth about actions which shows how it can be that the class of happenings is so much broader than that of actions – how it can be that there are plenty of happenings that are not actions. This supplement will take the form of a second thesis:

Thesis (II)   Actions are those happenings involving agents: they are happenings that can be described as things done by agents.

This second thesis is a move in the right direction: it shows us how to draw the line between mere happenings and actions in the broadest sense, but it must be treated with caution. Here are two examples of happenings that count as actions in virtue of thesis (II).

(i) The tide scours a riverbed and deposits the silt outside the mouth of the river. In this case we say that the tide creates a harbour bar – this is something it does. We also say that it acts on the riverbed.

(ii) Harry puts on his left shoe. This is something that he did – it was an action on his part.

Now, clearly our interest is in actions of type (ii), but as stated thesis (II) seems promiscuous enough to allow in both of the above types of action. Of course it might be argued that tides only count as doing something – as agents – in a metaphorical sense. There is a sort of harmless, if not poetic, animism in thinking of tides in this way. And if this is right, then perhaps thesis (II) could be regarded after all as capturing just those cases that interest us: all we have to do is to insist that any metaphorical uses of agency don't count. However, whether we take this way out or not, we are going to have to say more about the kind of agency that does interest us, so it is perhaps just as well not to argue too much about thesis (II). If someone insists that type (i) cases are really (literally) cases of action, so be it. But even such a diehard would have to recognize that there is a world of difference between the kind of 'doing' brought about by tides and the kind that involves what we might call 'personal' agents. So, since there is this difference, and since our interest is wholly in personal (mostly human) agents, we might as well come clean and say:

Thesis (III)   Personal actions are things done by agents who possess minds.

In being explicit in this way, we can from now on economize by using the simpler 'action' and 'agent' in place of having always to say 'personal action' and 'personal agent'. But of course there is much more to be said about what is involved in this kind of agency.

Thesis (II) was unspecific about the relationship between agent and action; all it said was that a happening is an action if it 'involves' an agent, or if it is a 'thing done' by an agent. But neither of these will do. The problem is that there are many things that involve agents, or could be said to be done by them, that we would not ordinarily count as actions. One example should make the point clearly enough. Harry had a bad cold which left him with a rasping cough. On any of the occasions when he gives voice to his affliction, it makes perfect sense to ask: what did Harry just do? And for the answer to be: he coughed. Yet, even though coughing is something that involves Harry – is something that the agent Harry did – we would not count this among Harry's actions. To see this, think of a case in which Harry coughs, but this time because he wants to show his disbelief in what someone is saying. Both kinds of coughing are things Harry does, but only the editorial cough seems up to scratch as an action. And the difference between the cases is as plain as can be: some things we do are done deliberately or intentionally, some are not. Hence the next thesis is:

Thesis (IV)   Things agents do count as actions if they are done intentionally.

There are lots of things to say about this thesis. On the one hand, it would be nice if we could spell out somewhat what is required for something to be done intentionally, and to show how the intentional is connected to the 'deliberate' and the 'voluntary'. There will be more on all this shortly. But there is a more pressing need to say something to block what otherwise might be a devastating objection to thesis (IV), namely that it is false.

Consider again hapless Harry. He is being shown his friend's porcelain collection and, when he reaches out in a suitably admiring way to grasp a figurine, he unbalances another (known to its owner as the 'Hunter and Dog') which smashes on the floor. No one thinks that Harry smashed the 'Hunter and Dog' intentionally, not even those who know he has always thought that porcelain figures were not much better than tacky souvenirs. Even so, smashing the porcelain is surely not like his cold-induced cough; unlike the cough, the breaking was surely Harry's action. In sum, we seem to have a case of an action which is unintentional, thus contradicting thesis (IV).

One way to deal with this counter-example is to think about it a little more carefully. Contrast it with a case in which Harry smashes the 'Hunter and Dog', not by reaching for another piece of porcelain, but by a spasm that causes his arm to thrash out in the 'Hunter and Dog' direction. Like Harry's coughing, this kind of smashing is unintentional, but it seems quite different from the reaching case, and the difference is fairly clear. In reaching, Harry didn't smash the 'Hunter and Dog' intentionally, but he did do something intentionally – he reached for the other piece. This was what brought about the destruction. As so often, what we intend and what we end up bringing about as a consequence are two different things. But it is usual to regard something as a proper case of action, so long as it can be described as intentional from some point of view. With this in mind, we might be able to repair the damage to thesis (IV) by changing it slightly:

> Thesis IV (revised)   Things agents do count as actions if they are done intentionally, or if what they bring about results from something done intentionally.

With thesis (IV) revised in this way, we are finally zeroing in on the essential features of those happenings that would be regarded as actions. What would more or less finish the job would be some account of what makes a doing intentional.

Note the heavy irony in this last sentence, for one of the most complicated topics in the philosophical discussion of action consists precisely in saying what makes an act intentional. However, by sticking to the most general considerations, it should be possible to say something uncontroversial about all this. And given my ultimate aim of showing that our ordinary thought about action tends towards certain incoherencies, it is crucial that whatever is said be uncontroversially ordinary.

When Harry broke the 'Hunter and Dog', he reached for the neighbouring figurine intentionally. Another way to say almost the same thing is to say that he was minded to reach for the relevant object, and this quaint way of putting the matter can tell us quite a bit. For in saying this, we are indicating that there were features of Harry's mental condition directly implicated in the reaching – features that made the reaching intentional. Which features? Well, in the broadest sense, one could say that Harry believed certain things:

there was a reachable figurine in front of him,
it belonged to the collection of his friend,
his handling it in a respectful way would be appreciated,
etc.

and that he wanted certain things:

to put his hand on the reachable object,
to show interest in his friend's collection,
etc.

and finally that it was the combination of these beliefs and wants that constituted something we would call Harry's *reason* for reaching in the way he did. Then all we have to add is that having some such reason is what makes it true that Harry was minded to reach, that his reaching was intentional. That much is surely uncontroversial, though things get sticky when we try to be more specific about the connection between having a reason and acting intentionally. Some are tempted to say that the reason brings about a further mental condition – Harry's having an intention – and it is the presence of this that makes the reaching intentional. Others say that there is no such further mental condition, and that having the appropriately active reason is itself what constitutes the intentionalness of the reaching. Moreover, there are long and contested stories told about the way reasons 'bring about' or show themselves to 'be active'. (Some discussion of this will figure in part III.) But since all we care about here is finding those features that determine which kind of happening is an action, it is perhaps forgivable if we pass over these disputes. For everyone accepts that if a happening can be traced back to a reason, and if that reason suffices to make the happening intentional, then we have a case of action.

Just before we move on, I should tie up one loose end. Earlier I said that being minded to do something would probably not be considered equivalent to doing that thing intentionally, and pointing out why this is so will remove a doubt about thesis (IV) that may have occurred to you. It has to do with the question of our awareness of our reasons. There are, of course, times when we ponder our next course of action, when we call to mind the beliefs and wants that finally figure in our reasons for doing this or that. (Think here of deciding whether to make lunch now.) And there are other times when we act – and do so for a reason – but when the reason is not one we have contemplated in advance of acting. (Think here of suddenly squeezing the brakes on your bicycle when a pedestrian carelessly strays in your path.) It makes perfect sense to say that you were minded to make lunch, though it is doubtful that you were minded to bring your bicycle to a sudden stop. Yet both are clearly cases in which you acted intentionally, and both involve your having reasons. It is just that in the bicycle case, the reason you had to squeeze the brake was not itself the subject of your deliberative awareness. Rather, it was something plausibly attributable to you on the basis of attitudes and propensities to act which were (one might say) silently at work as you were bicycling along. So, when thesis (IV) speaks of the actions as intentional and when we connect 'intentional' with the having of reasons, we are not thereby committing ourselves to any very fancy story about the explicitness or deliberative awareness of reasons.

Identity and Individuation

As preparation for taking our next step, here are a few words – and a picture – of where we have got to. Figure 2.1 is intended as a representation of the cumulative wisdom of the four theses about action.

As the concentric circles in Figure 2.1 show, the successive restrictions we put on happenings have allowed us to narrow our focus until we can be fairly sure that the innermost circle contains actions. And being sure in this way that we have captured actions, we can now get to work on saying more precisely what they are. Since this last thought may come as something of a surprise to those who think we have been doing just that, let me amplify it a bit.

The contribution of theses (I)–(IV) was in helping us to locate actions by saying where to find them in our larger conception of the world. What we have said in thesis (I) is that the place to look is a certain range of happenings, namely those involving the mind in roughly the ways outlined by theses (II)–(IV). For example, we are now sure that Harry's reaching was an action because it was a happening suitably involving something we called a reason. However, though this helps us to recognize the reaching as an action, it doesn't tell us what a specific reaching is, and how it differs from, say, a grasping or

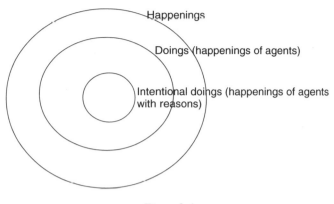

Figure 2.1

pointing. One way to put this would be to say that the story so far helps us to *identify* actions, but not to *individuate* them.

Here an analogy might help: you can identify something as a Beethoven symphony by saying who composed it, but this does not tell you what kind of thing a Beethoven symphony is — what individuates it. It does not settle disputes about whether it is a pattern of printed notes in a score authorized by Beethoven, or a performance according to that score, or a pattern of imagined sound in Beethoven's mind, or . . . Similarly, in saying that actions are happenings located by means of agents' reasons, we have gone quite far in identifying those happenings that are actions without yet saying what the individual nature of an action is.

Of course, in saying what you need to be able to identify something as an action (or as a Beethoven symphony) you have to assume that your audience has some inkling of what specific thing you're talking about. How else could anyone understand the story about identification? So, perfectly reasonably, discussion of the identification of actions (or symphonies) has proceeded on the assumption that you have some grasp of the individual nature of an action (or symphony). The trouble is that in the case of actions (and I think also in the case of symphonies) the inklings many people have are not sufficient to settle questions about individuation. For, as has been remarked, one gets nothing but dispute when trying to decide, for example, whether a specific act of reaching is a mental item, or is merely the physical result of something mental. And yet this dispute can take place against the background of complete agreement in respect of theses (I)–(IV).

Once Upon a Time

Where does this leave us? Well, the obvious thing to do is to set to work uncovering theses which bear directly on the issue of individuation of action. In this way, we might end up seeing what the real ground of disagreement is, and whether it can be resolved. Of course, this route has risks, for my main goal is to show that there are problems arising from uncontroversial thoughts that people have about action. If I were to begin now suggesting theses likely to be either technical or disputable (or both), this would ruin any chance of reaching that goal. Fortunately, we are not going to have to run that risk. As thesis (I) has it, actions are happenings. Though this perfectly ordinary thought is hardly rich enough to take us all the way to an individuating conception of an action, it will serve my nefarious purpose suprisingly well. For what I suggest is that a little further reflection on thesis (I) will show just what a mess we get into when we think about actions.

Bypassing all the complicated things we could say about happenings and actions, the following certainly seems beyond dispute:

Thesis (V)   When something happens, there is a time at which it happens.

This thesis is not meant to be particularly demanding. Certainly, it isn't meant to suggest that we can always be very precise in saying when something happens. If you ask someone when was the Battle of Hastings, you are most likely to be told '1066'. Though historians can no doubt do better than this, even they would be hard pressed to say exactly on which days and at what hours it began and ended. All that is fine as far as thesis (V) is concerned: battles are just too complicated to allow timing by stopwatches. Moreover, the thesis does not even demand that we should always be able to *say* even approximately when a happening takes place. There are things that go on in the world when we are simply not around.

None the less, even bearing in mind these qualifications, thesis (V) does assert something substantial. It reveals our commitment to the idea that happenings have locations in the temporal order – that it just wouldn't make sense to think that there could be a happening that didn't take place during some more or less determinate stretch of time. Moreover, if the happening is one we actually witness, then, within relevant limits of precision, we ought to be able to say when it began and when it ended. Finally, since actions fall into the class of happenings, it should always make sense to ask the question: 'when did someone intentionally do such-and-such?' Moreover, since actions, unlike 'mere' happenings, always involve an agent, this question should always be answerable. It just doesn't make sense to think that someone could do something intentionally, but that there would be no one around to count as a witness. Agents are witnesses.

Given all of this, what I propose is to consider some examples just to see how we fare in placing human actions in the temporal order. Somewhat surprisingly, it turns out that we do not fare very well. Moreover, the problem is deeper than it might at first seem – or so I shall argue.

Some Examples

(a)   Moving

Just to get us off on the right track, I shall begin with an example that doesn't seem problematic. On the table in front of me is a bowl. By bringing my hand into contact with it, and exerting some small, even pressure, I have managed to displace it several inches to the left. What have I done? I have moved the bowl to the left. When did I begin to do this? At that very time when the bowl, in contact with my hand, first began to move. And when did I finish this act? When the bowl came to rest. Nothing seems difficult here: the happening that is my action can be located (within reasonable limits of precision) in the temporal order. My intentionally displacing the bowl would seem to coincide in time with the observable displacement of the bowl.

(b)   Breaking

The second case raises more questions. Arm outstretched, I hold up a piece of chalk and then relax the grip of my fingers. The chalk falls to the floor and breaks. What I did – quite intentionally – was to break the chalk. When did this begin? Well, it is certainly tempting to think that I began the episode of breaking when I released my hold on the chalk. But when did I finish breaking it? At the moment when it began to slip through my fingers? This doesn't seem right, since the chalk is at that stage unbroken. At the moment when it hit the floor? This seems more like it, but there is a problem. For, having released my grip, there is a sense in which I didn't do anything at all during the time it took to reach the floor; it is only a short time, but it is not unreasonable to think that I was *inactive* during it. So it may seem odd to count that time as included in my action. Unlike the case in which I moved the bowl, the intended effect of my action seems not to coincide temporally with my being active. Still, since the time between my releasing my grip and the chalk's breaking is very small, we might get away with saying that I broke the chalk at ten minutes past the hour, and leave it at that. After all, I did say earlier that a high order of precision in our timing of actions is not required by thesis (V).

Or we could take another less evasive tack. We could say that, strictly speaking, the action was nothing more nor less than the releasing of my grip. This happened at a particular moment in time yet, as with many things we do, it had further consequences, among which was the breaking of the chalk. Knowing of this consequence, anyone who was a witness could *redescribe* the action – the releasing – as a breaking, even though the action itself ended before the breaking began. We go in for this kind of redescription all the time with particular concrete objects. Thus, we can describe one and the same object as 'the blue car in the drive' or as 'the car that stranded me on the motorway'. The same object but with two different descriptions, though the second of these is only apt if certain facts about the car are known. (Before I set out for the motorway, it would not have been possible for me to describe it in terms of the stranding.) Similarly, the releasing of my grip – that very particular happening – can be described in many different ways, one of which becomes available only after the chalk reaches the floor and breaks. That particular releasing *was* a breaking. This is something we come to know after it happens, and all will be well so long as we don't allow ourselves to think about other releasings which could have (but didn't) take place. These other releasings might have misfired; one of them might have involved a carpet that cushioned the impact, and the chalk might not have broken. But these other non-destructive releasings are not what took place.

Note that this way of dealing with the breaking was not apparently called for in the bowl-moving episode because the movement of the bowl and the action of moving the bowl were simultaneous. Of course, once we look at the bowl-moving case in this new way, we are committing ourselves to a distinction between some effect (the bowl's moving) and some action (moving the bowl), even though the effect and the action are simultaneous. Keep this in mind as it will be important later on.

(c)   Claudius

The following imagined case is meant to test the various suggestions made in respect of the chalk-breaking. Changing the well-known (though already fictional) story in *Hamlet*, consider the case of Claudius and the King. Claudius wants the King out of the way, but he wants to avoid any chance of being caught. So he acquires a very slow-acting poison which he administers by pouring it into the ear of the sleeping King. Having administered the poison, he retires to his own castle and awaits the outcome. Sure enough, after a period of some six months, the King succumbs to the effects of the poison and dies. As he expected, Claudius appears to members of the court to be in the clear: he has been miles away from the King for most of the six months. Yet we who are in the know have no doubt in saying Claudius killed the King. Yes, but when? Well, Claudius moved his fingers and hand in such a way as to empty the vial into the King's ear. Suppose this happened at 3 p.m. on the 5th of May 1360. It then seems perfectly plausible to regard this as what we might call the 'start time' of the deed. But a start time is not quite enough to get the happening properly settled into the temporal order. For we need to know when the killing ended, and many would be reluctant to say that Claudius killed the King on the 5th of May. After all, the King didn't die until the following November.

Someone might be tempted to say that the murder was a rather longish happening which began on the 5th of May and ended in November. The idea here would be that happenings can have parts, and that the pouring was the first part and the dying the second. This would be like the move made earlier which treated the chalk-breaking as beginning with the releasing and ending with the breaking. However, though it just about sounded all right in that case, the length of time involved in the murder makes this suggestion much less appealing. What seemed odd before was that someone should describe me as engaged in breaking the chalk – being active in this way – when I was standing there inactive, having already made my contribution to the activity by releasing my grip. Whilst it is easy to think this was just picky in respect of the breaking, it is a serious difficulty in the case of the murder. Do we really want to say that what Claudius did happened from May to November? Suppose you see him sitting peacefully in his castle in September reading a book: do you want to be committed to saying that he is then both reading a book and murdering the King? And what if, as is possible, he had died before the King? Posthumous publication is one thing, but would we really countenance posthumous murdering (other than supernaturally)?[4]

What about the second suggestion? Why not treat Claudius' activity as beginning and ending on the 5th of May when he poured the poison? The death was, of course, a consequence of this pouring, but is not itself *part* of the act. It is just that in November, when the King dies, we then have available a new way of describing the original pouring: we can now say it was a killing, indeed a murder. As before, this way of treating the matter makes more sense in connection with the chalk-breaking than it does in respect of the murder. For, whereas it may be just about acceptable to say that I broke the chalk when I released it, it seems odd to say that Claudius murdered the King on the 5th of May. This is because there seem to be so many things that must happen before the death occurs, and so many ways it could go other than as Claudius had hoped. Of course, we can stick to our guns here and say: 'Look, that very action – the pouring – had the death as a consequence. If the death had not occurred, then it would have been a different pouring of poison from the one that actually took place.' As long as you keep thinking of what Claudius did as a wholly specific thing which had the consequences it did have, then there is no harm in saying that he murdered the King on the 5th of May. It is just that this description of Claudius' act only becomes available in November.

It should be obvious that this kind of 'sticking to one's guns' brings with it a conception of action that goes beyond what is contained in theses (I)–(IV). We have now to think of each action as some kind of wholly particular thing which has its causes and consequences tied to it in some unbreakable way. If, even in thought, you change something about the consequences of an act, you are then barred from speaking about the very same action. For example, in connection with the present discussion, one might be tempted to appeal to a case of 'Claudius Interruptus': Claudius pours the poison in just the way that he did, but the King rolls over, or he later takes some substance which has the effect of an antidote, or his doctor figures out how to cure him. However, on the view we are considering, the very fact that the King does not die means that Claudius' act on 5th May is not the same act as the one which began our considerations – for that act resulted in the King's death.

Whether this conception of action is ultimately convincing enough to justify the claim that Claudius murdered the King on the 5th of May is, I would suggest, unclear. But remember that it or some other view is necessary to help us answer the question: when did Claudius murder the King? For no matter what deeper view we take of action, we are committed to the idea that actions have temporal locations, and we are certainly having trouble locating this dastardly deed. So, given that the view under consideration has less troublesome consequences than any other – for surely we do not want to say that the act took Claudius six months to complete – let us continue our discussion assuming that it is basically correct. It does commit us to saying some odd things, but maybe this is just the price to pay for having something to say about when the act took place.

(d)   Moving Reconsidered
We have settled for what can be called the 'act/effect' view. This requires that we distinguish an agent's act from the effects which follow such acts, *even when these effects are responsible for the descriptions we give of the original actions.* Thus, 'breaking the chalk' describes something that I did, but this is only appropriate because of the destructive effect of my loosening my grip. Indeed, according to the act/effect view, one should expect there to be lots of different descriptions of what will in fact be one and the same action: loosening my grip, releasing the chalk, breaking the chalk, making a mess on the floor,

making a point to a lecture audience, etc. And since all of these descriptions point to the same bit of my activity (my loosening of my fingers), we might as well distinguish this activity by calling it my *basic* action. In the light of the distinctions between basic acts and descriptions, it is worth reconsidering our first example, the case of moving the bowl.

When we discussed this example, it seemed to cause us no trouble at all. And now we ought to be able to see why. The timing of my action in that case coincided perfectly with the effect it brought about: my moving the bowl (my basic action) and the bowl's moving (the effect of my act) took place simultaneously, so, of course, we had no trouble in saying when I acted. Or so it can seem.

What we have to do now is to see how, if at all, the act/effect view applies to basic actions. Don't be surprised about this. We have been assuming that we know when these take place – that we know when I move my hand whilst it contacts the rim of the bowl, that we know when I release the grip of my fingers on the chalk, and finally that we know when Claudius does what is appropriate to inverting the vial over the King's ear. But it is now important to see what is going on 'inside' basic actions. And for this purpose, the bowl-moving episode will serve as the example.

The first thing to do is to forget the bowl and its movement. We have agreed that this is an *effect* of what I did, and our sole interest now is in what I did. Well, the obvious thing to say here is that I moved my hand – that was my basic action. However, let us look at this more closely. Focus on the the claim that I moved my hand. Can we see this – as per the act/effect view – as a complex consisting of some action and some effect? Admittedly it is a very small complex, but even so it does seem that there are two things discernible: one is that my hand moved and the other is that I moved it. And the first of these – the movement of my hand – could be seen as the effect of whatever it was that I did. On the act/effect view, it is perfectly reasonable to describe my action in terms of its effects, and in the present case we say 'I moved my hand' just because whatever it was that I did produced the hand movement as an effect. But what then did I do? And when? Neither of these questions is going to be easy to answer. In answering the first question, we need to find something that I did which can be described without mentioning its effect (the movement of my hand). But there doesn't seem to be any candidate description for this. Perhaps the best we can say is: I set myself to move my hand, and it was this which brought about the movement. And when did I do this? Well, precise temporal location isn't crucial, but, whenever it was, it certainly must have preceded the movement of my hand. Are these answers satisfactory?

Setting myself to move my hand at a time before it moves must be something that happens, as it were, 'inside' me; it would seem to be some kind of mental phenomenon. We could even imagine a case where this mental activity took place without its bodily effect. For example, suppose that some demon psychologist gave you a drug which paralysed your hand and arm, but did so in such a way as to leave you ignorant of this fact. She then blindfolds you and asks you to move your hand as if you were pushing a bowl across a table. What do you think you would do? Well, as far as anyone watching you was concerned, you would *do* nothing. But how would it appear to you? Well, you would certainly be able to set yourself to move your hand, and, if the drug really did leave you ignorant of your state, it would appear to you as if you were doing that very thing.

Taking apart basic actions in this way seems to have at least this advantage: it allows us to locate the onset of an action in the temporal order: setting yourself to move your hand – what has been called 'willing' your hand to move – begins in some small time interval before your hand actually moves. But when does it end? Does it continue even after the hand begins to move? Or are we to think of this act of will as somehow imparting its energy to the hand even though it ceases to work when the hand starts to move? It certainly doesn't feel the latter way in my own case: when I move my hand in the way required to move a bowl, it seems to me as if I am *guiding* my hand – as if my activity continues throughout. I can, of course, imagine what it would be like to have my hand move after just one initial mental exertion, but that is not how it seems in the normal case.

These questions are perhaps more difficult than the ones we asked of the chalk-breaking and of Claudius' felony. Moreover, even if we could answer them, we are still left with something very troubling. For, assuming that an action is something like setting oneself to bring about a movement – an exercise of will – this would seem to take place without anyone seeing it. In the normal case it will have effects on the body, and we will see these, but, on this assumption, the act itself will escape the scrutiny of everyone but the agent. And do we really want to treat an action as subject to all the problems of the inner/outer divide cited in relation to experience?

Of course the answer to this is certainly 'no', but in the end we might have no choice. Perhaps the best account we can give of acting will show it to have more of an inside – to be more like experience – than many imagine. If it turns out that the essential element in acting is setting oneself to move some part of one's body, then it is difficult to see how else to regard such an 'internal' exercise of will as other than something experienced. Moreover, this would accord well with that other category of action that we have not touched on in this chapter, namely those acts which are (apparently) purely mental. Adding up numbers in your head, deliberating about what to do next, as well as the activities of adopting attitudes and experiencing, are all things we do, though they are not things that require us to move our bodies or any other objects. If we come to think that the key element in all action is a felt sense of making ourselves active, then we will have found a way to unify these acts of mind with those whose effects are spread more directly onto the world.

Conclusion

We began with a few harmless theses about action and one thought about happenings in general. However, several straightforward examples later, we find ourselves in a bit of trouble. The theses told us that actions could be identified as happenings with the appropriate mental pedigrees, and further, that as happenings they ought to fit into the temporal order. But they don't fit – or at least not without great discomfort. And even stranger, we have found at least some reason to think that when we are genuinely active, the crucial ingredient in that activity is rather like an item of experience – something that raises the possibility that we will have some of the same problems with action as we did with pains.

This last result will no doubt appeal to those who insist that actions are mental phenomena. They might even take this as a victory over those who had maintained that actions were at most the visible signs of the mind. But things are not that simple. Recall that it was our need to assign a time to my breaking of the chalk that led to the doctrine of act/effect, and this doctrine seemed the only sensible thing to say about the case of Claudius and the King. For in that case the alternatives seemed to be: either say that the murder took six months or say that we cannot properly fit the murder into the temporal order. Admittedly, even the doctrine of act/effect has us saying that Claudius murdered the King six months before he died, but at least we saw the beginning of a more complex story about actions which might have made this palatable. Yet when we brought this apparently most plausible option to bear on the simplest of actions – the movements of our bodies which seem to be at the start of everything else we do – things seemed to dissolve in our hands. Instead of some well-behaved thing called a basic action, we ended up with an effect (a movement of the body) and a mental item (an exercise of will) neither of which meet all the criteria we expect in cases of action. The one is not really an action, just an effect, and the other is active, but it is not observable from an outsider's point of view except through its effects. In sum, it has turned out that when we try to say when actions happen, they tend to disappear from view. And even those who insist that actions are mental would not have been happy to think they were that elusive.

There are, of course, things we can do. But all of them involve a great deal more philosophy than one would have expected when we began. For example, we could just insist that an action is a *pair* consisting of an exercise of will and an effect on the body. Thus, we could simply refuse to count setting oneself to move a hand as an action unless it was successful – unless the hand moved. In this way, we could date the beginning of the action with the exercise of will and its end-point with the visible effect on the body. But we would then have to refuse to allow temporal assignment of this sort to any but basic actions, on pain of having to say that Claudius took six months over killing the King. Or we could bite the bullet and say that an action really doesn't belong in the physical realm, and that too much was being read into the idea that actions are happenings. Or, diametrically opposed to this, that much of the stuff about the mental pedigree of actions is misguided, and that actions are just bodily movements which are easily located in time.

These and many other options are all beyond my remit. For what they have in common is that they force us in one way or another to revise some of the things we ordinarily think true of actions, and my aim in part II is restricted to investigating the consequences of ordinary thought. But just as something must be done about the attitudes and experience, it should be no less clear that this most important feature of the mind – its acting in, and on, the world – is a suitable case for conceptual treatment.

Notes and References

1   This entity is sometimes called a 'proposition', but – confusingly – it is not the only sort of item that claims this title. Some think that we can get away with simply saying that a proposition is whatever it is that serves as the content of a proposi-tional attitude. The minimalism of this view has a lot to recommend it, but there are inevitably further questions about what kind of thing can serve that role. And the idea that a proposition is an abstract confection with real objects as it were baked into it is one way of providing this further specificity.

Another way in which to be less than minimalist about propositions is based on the idea of a *possible world*, and works as follows. Imagine all the ways in which our world could be different, whether greatly or only slightly. Then call each of these ways a 'possible world'. Finally, say that a proposition is the group or set of possible worlds in which the relevant content sentence is true. Thus, there are many possible worlds in which Anne has a coat and it is in the cupboard, and many in which either the coat doesn't exist or it is not in the cupboard. The sentence:

'Anne's coat is in the cupboard' is of course true only in the first set of possible worlds, and we can define the proposition that Anne's coat is in the cupboard as that set. Anne can then be said to be related to this set of possible worlds, and her belief will be true if our own actual world happens to be in that set.

The possible worlds treatments of propositions raises many questions which won't be discussed here. But then so does the abstract confection treatment. I use the latter in the text, but this should not be taken as a hint that there is something fatally wrong with the possible worlds conception. It is just that confectionary propositions – more often called 'structured propositions' – make it easier to pursue the discussion of attitude problems in the text. Possible worlds will return later in other contexts.

2   Philosophers who go in for the *de re/de dicto* distinction tend to try to convince us that there is an everyday linguistic device that does the work for us. Thus, the *de re* style is said to be captured by:

Monique believes *of* the British Museum that its entrance is guarded by lions.

and the *de dicto* by:

Monique believes *that* the British Museum entrance is guarded by lions.

However, most of those I have interrogated (before they were trained by philosophers) tend to use the 'believes of' and 'believes that' constructions interchangeably. Of course, the distinction made by philosophers is no less (or more) clear in virtue of the presence or absence of an ordinary language usage consistent with the distinction. It just would have been nice, for those who believe in it, if it were enshrined in ordinary language.

3   See 'The meaning of "meaning" in Putnam's *Mind Language and Reality* (Cambridge University Press, 1975), pp. 215–71.

4   Of course, Claudius might be *responsible* for the King's death, even after Claudius himself dies. The fact that our responsibilities extend beyond our lifetimes is intelligible on the assumption that an action undertaken during a lifetime can have consequences extending beyond it. But is it really intelligible that we can undertake actions after we have died?

3

Folk Psychology and Folk

3.1 Understanding the Folk

In chapter 1, we saw how folk psychological narrative wove together the items of the mental realm, thereby helping us in our efforts to make sense of human behaviour. The things we were told in *To the Lighthouse* about Lily Briscoe's state of mind, and the various conjectures about the unfortunately brief marriage, were examples of narratives that made sense of particular human actions – or tried to – by providing us with materials necessary to explain them. But how exactly does it work? What kinds of explanation does folk psychology provide?

Explanation

Starting at the beginning, let us think a bit about explanation in general. You have a very important meeting and you miss it. Asked afterwards why this happened, you say, 'The Underground train broke down between stations.' Does your claim provide an explanation for your not making the meeting? Probably, but there are some things that must be in place before we can be sure. First of all, your claim must be true. Your claiming to have been on a spaceship to Proxima Centauri would certainly have accounted for the missed meeting, but since you weren't, it doesn't.

Secondly, there must be a particular kind of connection between your claim about the Underground and the statement that you missed the meeting: the truth of the former must entail the truth of the latter. Some terminology will make it easier to describe this in a more general way. The claim or claims offered as an explanation are called the 'explanans' (Latin, suggesting 'thing doing the explain*ing*'); the statement describing the event needing explanation is called the 'explanandum' (Latin, suggesting 'thing explain*ed*'). The second requirement then is that the explanandum must be deducible from the explanans.

In the example, it is far from obvious that there is this deductive relationship. For example, you never did say that the underground broke down *today*, the day of the meeting. Nor did you actually say whether the breakdown lasted a short or a long time. Come to that, your explanans didn't actually say that you were on the train. Clearly, accepting what you say as an explanation will require these clarifications, and this is because the underlying relationship between explanans and explanandum is one of deducibility.

Deducibility is a strong requirement, but it would seem that nothing short of it will do. We would scarcely be satisfied with the following: 'my missing the meeting is explained by my going to bed late. How so? Because often when I go to bed late, I sleep through the alarm.' What we need to know is whether you actually slept in this morning, not simply that it often happens. (In the philosophy of science literature, the issue of probability and explanation is a complicated one. Here, and for current purposes, I am simplifying, though I do not think I am falsifying.)

Two things should be noted. First, we don't usually require informal explanations to display all the premises needed for a proper deduction. Even in the simple case above, a list of adequate premises would be enormously long. To satisfy a logician you would require, among many others, a premise claiming that a human being couldn't be in two places at the same time. But in accepting that the Underground breakdown explains the missed meeting, we are in effect accepting that these premises could in principle be provided. Secondly, there is another idiom of explanation in current use: sometimes we say that we have explained something's happening when we have cited its cause. Thus, you might say that the Underground breakdown caused you to miss the meeting, and you would rightly expect your audience to take this citing of a cause as your explanation. I shall not stop just yet to show how to relate the deductive and causal accounts of explanation, except to say that, as you might expect, they are not incompatible. For present expository purposes, we shall continue with the deductive notion of explanation, returning to the notion of causation as and when it is necessary.

The requirements of truth and deducibility are relatively obvious, seen at work as they are in even simple examples like that offered above. But there is a third requirement which is not easy to state, and can vary from one explanatory context to another. Suppose instead of the train-breakdown explanans, you offered this: 'I missed the meeting because I got to the office after it had finished.' Here what you say is perfectly true, and it undoubtedly has the right deducibility relation to the explanandum. But we would scarcely count it as a genuine explanation. At the minimum, we expect an explanans to have some independence from the explanandum. However, aside from the difficulty of spelling out what independence involves – remember that the deducibility requirement means that we had better not have too much independence – the explanans must be more than merely independent. A common thought, one that can be traced back at least to Aristotle, is that the explanans must somehow demystify the explanandum. But this is neither wholly right – explananda are not all puzzling in the first place – nor is it really much of an improvement on saying that the explanans must be genuinely explanatory.

Unable to provide any really general account of genuine explanatoriness, a perfectly reasonable way of proceeding is to consider specific examples that do in fact satisfy us. One such type of case, perhaps the most important, is characteristic of scientific explanation. Wondering, for example, why ice forms on the surface of a lake, we are told that ice is less dense than water, and that things that have this lower density float on the surface. Here the explanans tells us not merely something true, nor merely something that is independent of, and entails, the explanandum; it tells us that the world is governed by certain relevant regularities. The explanans includes these claims: *all* ice (water ice, of course) is less dense than water, and *all* things with a density less than that of water float.

Seeing the world as governed by the regularities alluded to in the explanans, and seeing the explanandum as following from them, confers on the explanans exactly what is needed for genuine explanatoriness. Our 'why-question' is resolved in a wholly satisfactory way when we come to see what happened – ice forming on the surface of the lake – as fitting into the dependably regular world described in the explanans. Moreover, this gives a pretty good interpretation of the Aristotelian idea that an explanation must demystify. After all, if the world is governed by regularities, then whether or not the explanandum is familiar (like ice forming on the surface of lakes) or deeply puzzling, it will count as all the more intelligible when we see it against the background of these regularities.

Looking back briefly at the example of the missed meeting – and allowing for the informality of that example – we can see it as in the same mould as the ice example. The world of times, places and transportation has a certain uniformity to it: one can only get from A to B by train in a certain time interval if the train doesn't break down. When it does, then we can't. In short, the explanans in the missed meeting case appeals to a certain pattern of regularity in the world in just the way that the ice example does. Also, using this example, we can see how one might connect the causal notion of explanation with the deductive-regularity one. It is more natural to say that you missed the meeting because the train broke down. But when you ask why citing a cause is a good way of explaining an event, you can easily see that this way of speaking is not necessarily in competition with the deductive-regularity conception. It seems perfectly reasonable to say that some event A causally explains another event B in virtue of the fact that the world works according to a certain pattern. Put in terms of our example: train-breakdown events cause lateness, which is, in part, to say that train breakdowns are regularly followed by lateness. This is, of course, a bit too simple, but it suffices to give the general idea. For if something like this weren't true – if there was no reason to expect breakdowns to go regularly with lateness – then it would be bizarre to count a mention of the breakdown as explaining the lateness.

Theories

As so far described, in a genuine explanation the explanans is a set of true statements, at least some of which establish that the world follows certain regular patterns, and these statements collectively entail the truth of a statement describing the explanandum. As far as it goes this is reasonable, but there is more. Consider again the explanation of ice forming on the surface of lakes. The explanation of this clearly conforms to the model just given, but many would regard this explanation, not as mistaken, but as somehow incomplete. A full or proper explanation would show us why ice – which is, after all, only frozen water – is in fact less dense than water in its liquid state, and it would also show us why density matters when it comes to floating. In short, the explanation so far offered assumes that the world is regular in certain ways, but it doesn't explain this regularity.

The demand that explanations must include regularities, whilst also explaining why they hold, must not be taken to extremes. If we are not careful, we will not count anything as explained unless we have explained everything. However, stopping well short of this, it would be reasonable to expect some greater depth to our explanations. And not only is it reasonable, it is typical: the history of our explanatory efforts is littered with such examples. Scientific cases are the first place to look, though very little scientific background is necessary to appreciate what you will see.

Think again about the explanation of ice forming on the surface of lakes. What explains this is the low density of ice, and what explains the low density of ice is, given the current theory, the peculiar way in which the molecules of water interact with one another. In essence, as the water approaches the freezing point, the H_2O molecules sort of spread out. The slight electric charge on each water molecule begins to have an effect when the lowering of temperature slows down the helter-skelter motion of the molecules constitutive of the liquid state. This charge, being repulsive, forces the molecules apart. This means that when the water actually freezes, the molecules are much less closely packed than they were in liquid water, and less close packing is a lower density.

The details aren't all that important (though without this unique property of water life probably wouldn't have evolved on earth). What is crucial is to appreciate the kind of thing typical of this further layer of explanation. And this is fairly straightforward, since, with one important addition, the deeper sort of explanation has pretty much the same general structure as its predecessor. In explaining the behaviour of ice, what we did was to tell a story about regularities in the world of water, a story from which we were then able to deduce the fact that water forms on the surface of a lake. (A story is after all just a set of related statements, and this is what we have in an explanans.) In what I have called the deeper explanation, we are also given a story about regularities, only this time the cast of characters has grown. Where before we had just ice and water, now we have *molecules* in motion and *electric charges*. We are able, using this further story, to deduce the regularities that counted for so much in our earlier explanation. The world of water is regular in ways crucial to the behaviour of ice, and the world of H_2O molecules and electric charge is regular in ways crucial to the regular behaviour of water.

Philosophers of science call the deeper explanation 'theoretical', much to the confusion of the ordinary public. For the story about molecules is not a theory in the common sense of being 'provisional', but in the uncommon sense of having characters that are the creatures of a theory rather than of observation. Molecules and electric charges are not things we can see or touch, at least not directly. Scientists began to talk about them because they were the main players in what are deeper explanatory accounts of the more superficial regularities observed in the world. As this talk developed, and seemed to explain more and more, the willingness to concede that there actually are such things has grown to a near certainty. And this conviction has not been shaken by the fact that the detail of the theoretical stories that introduced, e.g. molecules, has long since been altered in many ways.

Much more could be said about the issue of theoretical entities, and this discussion would take us deep into the history and philosophy of science. However, there is no need here for this undertaking. What was wanted was an outline of the main features of the notion of an explanation, and this we now have. The governing idea of explanation is that of seeing events as fitting into a world patterned and uniform in appropriate ways. This idea of fitting in can be expressed either in the idiom of regularity/deduction, or in the idiom of causal ancestry. Finally, as just described, the deepest level of our explanations of the physical world tend to show it to be uniform in ways we do not directly observe. Uniformity at this level makes an appeal to entities whose behaviour is only brought to our attention by theories, i.e. by stories that are often, but not necessarily, complex and mathematical, and that reveal the world to be regular in ways that couldn't have been anticipated by ordinary observation.

These features of explanation – here only sketched – are derived by careful thinking about what we count as explanations in everyday and scientific contexts, and thus it would appear that explanatoriness is itself a feature of the mind. Perhaps a better way to say this is: what counts as an explanation is something we find by examining human rationality – the human mind – at work. Of course, this is not to say that explanations themselves are discovered in this way. The uniformities which ground explanations are, as we might say, in the world; we discover them by means of our inquisitive and reasoning natures, but they are not simply the products of it.

Folk Psychological Explanation

As must be obvious, this model of explanation, and the suggestion about where it comes from, need more refinement and defence. But its wide acceptance in philosophy and science make it not unreasonable as a working model. So let us now consider how folk psychological narratives – stories which definitely have explanatory aims – might fit into this model.

Judging from the number of its advocates, it would not be unreasonable to think that folk psychology fits snugly into the model of explanation described above. Here is how the story goes. People are enormously complicated, and hence what they do is not likely to be easy to explain, much less predict. Yet in many cases we manage this quite well. Lily Briscoe winced at the approach of Mr Bankes, and yet she resisted keeping her painting hidden from his prying eyes. However, as soon as we were let in on the full picture of what she felt, believed and desired, we understood why she behaved in this way; her actions were thereby explained. Even more mundane cases of success make the same point: you can quite easily explain why a particular human being is sitting next to you at a restaurant when you take into account your having made the appointment with her by e-mail, your knowing her to care about keeping promises, your knowing that she is unlikely to forget this appointment because of how much she wants to eat at this restaurant . . . etc. Indeed, even before the event, you could have used this information to predict your friend's walking through the door, even though, like human beings generally, her states of mind are enormously complex.

We are sometimes less good at this. The one-day marriage is a case in which our explanatory abilities are stretched to the limit. Not only would no one have predicted it, we are still in the dark about why it happened. Still, in cases of both success and failure, what we *aim* to do in explaining human behaviour, according to the view under consideration, is to see it as a consequence of certain background uniformities, ones captured in the claims that together make up folk psychology. Moreover, this background does not merely consist of some, no doubt complicated, set of uniformities in human behaviour; explanation in folk psychological terms does not merely call on regularities as did our original explanation of ice's forming on the surface of the lake. Instead – and this is a particularly important feature of the view – folk psychological explanation is seen as theoretical; the uniformities described or presumed in our folk psychological narratives are more like the explanation of ice in terms of molecules and electric charges.

How is this possible? Think of the notions we use in building up these narratives. We begin by seeing certain movements, and even non-movements, as actions, and then we attribute experiences and attitudes to agents that are appropriate in the circumstances to explain these actions. Behind this notion of 'appropriateness' is a certain picture of how particular experiences and attitudes tend to go with certain kinds of action. To revert to an earlier simple example: we count someone's walking into a particular building as their meeting a friend for lunch, and we explain why this happened by attributing to the agent a whole set of beliefs, including one about the appointment, and a whole set of desires, including one about fulfilling the promise made by e-mail. What makes this an *explanation* is a sense that people with those beliefs and desires regularly do things like turning up; and what makes this a *theoretical* explanation is that we call on notions like belief and desire in framing these regularities. Beliefs and desires, and all the other items in the mental realm, count as theoretical entities like molecules and electric charges because, like the latter, they are not things we can directly observe, though they are things determining the background regularities that ground the explanation.

The Theory Theory and its Problems

This account of folk psychological narrative has come to be known as the 'Theory Theory' of folk psychology in virtue of its assimilating folk psychological explanation to theoretical explanation. (It might have been better to call it the 'Theory Account' of folk psychology, but many philosophers find the repetitious name appealing, and it has stuck.) Also, there is more to its appeal than the name since, as noted above, it has been accepted by a great many philosophers. Admittedly, much more needs to be said about the parallels (or lack of them) between scientifically sanctioned theoretical entities and those found in the mental realm; the status of consciousness is unsurprisingly contentious here. Also, there are important issues to be decided about whether agents and actions should themselves count as theoretical in the appropriate way. (This last issue is not often discussed, though it should be.) But in basic outline it seems to many to be just perfect: it suggests a model for thinking about items in the mental realm which allows for their observational elusiveness, and it allows us to remain faithful to our intuitions about explanatoriness in general.

However, aside from worries around the edges of the Theory Theory, there is a fly right in the middle of the ointment. So far only the minimum has been said about the regularities that underlie folk psychological narrative. But even that minimum might be too much if, as has been claimed, there simply are none, or at least none available to the folk who allegedly appeal to them in their explanatory practice.

In scientific explanations, explanatory uniformity comes from our access to universal generalizations true, either of the directly observed world, or of the world as described in theories. Our initial attempts to explain the behaviour of ice appealed to truths like this one:

(L)   All things less dense than water float.

Whilst our deeper explanation, finding the world to contain things like molecules and electric charges, requires the support of this:

(T)   All molecules of water have electric charges that lead them to repel one another.

In the philosophy of science literature, generalizations like (L) are usually called *laws*. The traditional view is that a law is an exceptionless universal generalization about the observable world, and though this view is not without its problems, nothing in our discussion will require abandoning that traditional conception.

(T) is also an exceptionless universal generalization but, given that its subject-matter is the only indirectly observable world of molecules, it is usually called a 'theoretical generalization' rather than a law. Still, whether they are called laws or not, what matters is the satisfying universality provided by these generalizations; combining them with premises describing certain initial conditions, we are able to deduce — and hence explain — why certain events took place. Against this background, the central problem for the Theory Theory is now easy to state: there are grounds for thinking that there are no such laws – no universal generalizations – about human behaviour. And, even if such laws exist, they are certainly not available to the folk who construct explanatory narratives.

Platitudes and Tacit Knowledge

The issue of whether there are in fact underlying generalizations about human behaviour, statable using the terms of folk psychology, is not one that can be settled easily. Human behaviour is bound to be complicated, and hence is bound to submit to generalization only when masses of qualifications are inserted. Some think this will succeed, some deny it. However, what does seem undeniable is that, even if these generalizations do exist, the propounders of folk explanations are not very good at stating them. The philosopher, David Lewis, in an early paper, claimed that one could display the relevant explanatory background by simply listing 'all the platitudes' of everyday human behaviour; claims about what people will tend to do given what they believe, want and experience. But it seems pretty impossible to list one, much less all of them, and thus the label 'platitude' can only have been a joke.

In recent papers, David Lewis, and a number of other writers, have abandoned the platitude suggestion, but they have done so without abandoning the regularities that they were supposed to embody. Here is a forthright statement of the new view:

> Think of it as a theory: folk psychology. It is common knowledge among us, but it is tacit, as our grammatical knowledge is. We can tell which particular predictions and explanations conform to its principles, but we cannot expound those principles systematically.[1]

The reference to grammatical knowledge – a reference everyone tends to make when they invoke the tacit knowledge defence – is to an idea mentioned briefly in chapter 1, an idea due to the linguist, Noam Chomsky. It goes as follows.

Think about the amazing fact that each of us knows how to speak a complicated language like English. How do we do it? Well one answer might be that it is just a kind of motor skill like riding a bicycle, and therefore calls for no more fancy explanation than one adverting to our general ability to acquire motor skills. But this seems unlikely. Though we do speak and understand English effortlessly, we are also pretty good at making judgements about whether certain sentences are acceptable as English, whether certain words fit into certain contexts, and a whole host of other things that have no analogue in the relatively brute world of motor skill.

What our ability with language suggests – at least to a good many in the linguistics community – is that we know a great deal about the rules and regularities that govern our native tongues. However, for all that we as ordinary speakers might be said to know the rules, we are hopeless at stating them. Linguistics journals are filled with suggestions, often wrong, about what these rules might be, and this is not what we would expect if the rules were articulable by just anyone. Faced with what looks like our ignorance of grammatical rules, but unwilling to admit that it is genuine ignorance, the now standard move is to insist that our knowledge of the rules of our native language is tacit. It is knowledge we *possess* in that it guides our speech, but it is not *available* to us in any conscious way. Hence, unsurprisingly, we cannot simply state the rules that in fact guide us.

Could the same thing be true of the regularities of folk psychology? Could they be known to us, but could their being known only tacitly account for our inability to state them? As noted, a number of philosophers think the Chomskyan model of tacit knowledge is a perfect way to reconcile the explanatoriness of folk psychology with the apparent absence of the regularities on which such explanation seems to be founded. Indeed, the appeal to tacit knowledge has become something of a mantra for those intent on saving the Theory Theory. But there are problems.

Considerable effort has been expended on issues raised by the notion of tacit knowledge. Some philosophers seem to feel that the very expression 'tacit knowledge' is an oxymoron – if it is knowledge it couldn't be tacit, and if it is tacit it couldn't be knowledge. Others, whilst admitting this is how it appears, investigate and refine both 'tacitness' and 'knowledge' so as to get around this almost too obvious obstacle to what is regarded as a seriously important notion. It has even been said that an appeal to tacit knowledge is 'one of the dominant paradigms in contemporary cognitive science'.[2] However, since our main interest is not in tacit knowledge generally, but in its relevance to folk psychological explanation, resolving this debate, while pertinent, wouldn't settle the issue now before us. Therefore let us, for the sake of the argument, agree that it makes sense to talk about tacit knowledge, and that, at least in connection with language, this notion is plausible and helpful. What we want to know is whether it is reasonable to use it to get the Theory Theory out of trouble.

An apparent lack of an analogy between the cases of language and folk psychology might give us pause here. It is not only possible, it is commonplace for there to be competent speakers of English who do not know any true generalizations about their language. And it is just as true that there are speakers – perhaps even the same ones – who haven't a clue about grammatical categories of even the simplest sort; speakers who don't know what a noun or verb is, and who therefore certainly don't know the difference between them. What this suggests is that, even aside from the generalizations themselves, competent speakers do not need to have explicit knowledge of any grammatical concepts.

Things seem quite different in respect of folk psychology. Here, though we are unable to state any of the background regularities, we do use the concepts of folk psychology all the time. Indeed, unless we could ascribe beliefs, desires, experiences and feelings to one another, and see our movements as certain sorts of action, we would simply not be competent users of folk psychology in the first place. So whereas in the language case, both the generalizations and the concepts with which they are formulated are only tacitly known to most language-using folk, we are asked to believe that we have mastered folk psychological concepts, and use them in our explanations, but are only tacitly aware of the generalizations which make these explanations explanatory.

This issue is very important, so it bears a closer look. Consider the following recent summary of the tacit knowledge defence:

> When I predict what someone will do, or explain why they have done something, I do so by deploying this theory [folk psychology]. Most of us are, of course, unaware that this is what we are doing; but as with grammatical theory, the fact is reckoned to be unimportant. Our relationship to the psychological theory is allowed to be 'tacit' or 'implicit' knowledge.[3]

Here the suggestion is that what is being compared are abilities that make up competence in speaking, and abilities like those of anticipating my friend's arrival in the restaurant, or of finding her arrival unsurprising. On this view, tacit knowledge of a grammar of English accounts for the first set of abilities, and tacit knowledge of folk psychology the second set. However, drawing the analogy in this way is awkward; it requires us to say that 'most of us are unaware of what we are doing' when we explain why people act as they do. Are we? Think of the perfectly ordinary explanatory activity that followed the one-day marriage. It seems not just implausible, but deeply mistaken, to say that when we formulate various stories about what went wrong we are unaware of what we were doing. It is, of course, true that we are unaware of the background regularities which supposedly provide the explanatory basis for our various stories, but the stories themselves make liberal use of the concepts of folk psychology. And we are surely aware of this.

Simulation

There are ways in which a defender of the Theory Theory can retrieve the situation. But before considering them in any detail, it will be useful to consider another, supposedly more radical, possibility. It has been suggested in the recent literature that if we begin by reconceiving the way folk psychology works, we can simply ignore the fact that we are unable to state folk psychological generalizations. Instead of viewing folk psychology as a theory of human beings, something resting on a mastery of the background generalizations, the suggestion is that we think of it as based on our ability to *simulate* other human beings. Since neither this description nor the label 'Simulation Theory' is likely to be that informative, it is helpful to begin with an example not involving folk.

Think of how someone might set about designing a hull for a competitive sailing boat. One way would be for the designer to set down all that is known about fluid dynamics and shape – all the general truths about these subjects – and then use them to work out a hull design optimal for speed. Having done this, not only would we end up with a particular shape for the hull, we would have a fully theoretical explanation for the shape's superiority. Another way – one perhaps easier, given the complexities of fluid dynamics – would be to build models of hulls and test them in a tank. What one does in this case is naturally described as simulating both the hull shape and the conditions under which it would normally operate in the sea. If all goes well, it should be possible, using this method, to come up with an optimum design, though at no stage would we be able, nor would we need, to state any of the generalizations about fluid dynamics which make the shape optimal for speed. Of course, it is likely that, during the tank trials, we would notice some truths about the behaviour of hulls, but these would themselves be products of the simulation, and not the exceptionless generalizations of fully theoretical fluid dynamics.

The idea that we might come to understand and explain a natural phenomenon by simulation rather than by deduction from laws or theory seems to have an application in the human sphere as well. No, we don't build model or replica human beings and put them in artificial surroundings. But, it is argued, we don't need to: for each of us is a human being, so we are all, in some sense, models of one another. Moreover, equipped as we are with imagination, we can conjure up circumstances in which to place ourselves, circumstances that then function something like the testing tank in hull design.

Think first about how I might use myself as a simulation model for understanding my own behaviour. Suppose that I am not well off, and basically just manage to meet each month's incoming bills (not a difficult supposition for most of us). However, I sometimes wonder what it would be like for this not to be so; in particular, I wonder about the ways in which my life might change if I were extremely well off. At least one part of this is no problem: I simply tell myself that I am rich, perhaps that I have just won 4 million pounds on the lottery. Against this background, I then imagine what I would do, where I would live, whether I would keep teaching or writing, which friends or charities I would support, etc.

This sort of activity – sometimes called 'daydreaming' – is perfectly familiar. My predictions of my own behaviour in quite specific, but not actual circumstances, flow from imagining that I am in those circumstances, and not from any general theory grounded on regularities in human behaviour. Here I am treating myself as the model in the simulation, and using the imagined circumstances as something like the test tank. But the same general procedure seems to be one that we can and do apply to others.

What would my closest friends do if they won the lottery? I go through my friends one by one and put myself in each of their places, when, as I imagine, the winning number comes up in the lottery draw. To take one example: one of my friends doesn't care for travel, or indeed for any kind of high life. He takes his editorial work extremely seriously and has all the financial security he needs to pursue this. So, in the unlikely event that he would even have bought a lottery ticket, it is pretty easy to imagine myself, *as him*, saying (at first): 'What do I need this for?' But then I allow the simulation to run a bit. Here I am not daydreaming, as it were, for myself but for him. 'Perhaps I shall set up a little independent publishing house where the books accepted, and their production, will be of the highest quality. Everyone says that such quality is a thing of the past because it just doesn't pay. But I can use this money to show they are wrong . . .'

This example is one in which the situation that figures is merely possible, but essentially the same procedure would work when it is actual. I have just heard that another friend has been made redundant. I pick up the telephone to ring her, and it comes as no surprise to hear her say, 'I hated working there, so they have done me a favour.' It came as no surprise because before I telephoned I spent a little time putting myself, as we say, in her shoes. This involved using myself as a model, having of course made allowances for the changes of character needed to fill those shoes, and then asking myself, 'What line would I take about this redundancy?' The result I came up with was completely consistent with what my friend said, but it was not what I would have said if I had myself been made redundant.

As noted, in using my own humanity as a basis for simulating what others do, I am able to predict their behaviour, or at least find it unsurprising. And

I am able to do this without apparently trying to embed their behaviour in a background of regularities furnished by some theory. In this respect, there really does seem to be a similarity to the hull design case: there too we are able to see how hull shapes would behave in various conditions, merely by using a model of each hull in a testing tank, and without at any stage appealing to the theoretical background given by fluid dynamics. But the similarities don't stop there.

Those practised at design using simulation in testing tanks come to recognize various truths about hull design; they can usually tell how a certain design is likely to behave even before it is put in a tank. These truths are perhaps best described as rules of thumb; they are certainly not a substitute for background explanatory regularities. This is important, for if one is not careful, one might take the presence of these rules of thumb for background generalities, and thus mistakenly conclude that simulation and theoretical explanation are not really that different. When a designer looks at yet another hull shape and says – before putting it in the tank – that the ratio of the beam to waterline length is all wrong, he is merely using his knowledge of previous simulations to anticipate what is likely to happen in the tank test. This can look like an appeal to the theoretical regularities of fluid dynamics. However, what the designer is in essence doing is running the simulation on the new hull design in his head; he is speculating about how the design would fare, and, if he is experienced, one would expect his speculations to be more right than wrong.

Such rule of thumb speculation shows itself in the folk psychological case in stories we often tell about people both before and after they act. These stories employ the language of belief, desire and other features of the mental, but they do so in the simulation mode, and not as part of a theory. For example, when I ask myself why I am not surprised to be sitting next to my friend in the restaurant, I might tell a story about her, involving the attribution of various beliefs and desires which, as I see it, resulted in her meeting me. Among the many things I would say is: 'She believed that the e-mail arranging the meeting was really from me.' On the simulation view, I could justify this by imagining my e-mail as it would look on my friend's screen, and also imagining myself to be her looking at it. Seeing the address and the content, I might say to myself, 'Here is a message from SG suggesting that we meet at the restaurant next Thursday.' I would in this way be putting myself in her shoes and speaking from her point of view. On the simulation view, I could, and often do, summarize this by saying, 'She believed the e-mail was from me.' In effect, my attribution of this belief is a summary of part of my simulation, the whole of which would involve my not merely speculating about this one belief, but about why she came to the restaurant.

Belief simulation is, of course, only a small part of the story, even in this simple case, and it is not really likely that I would bother to do this sort of simulation exercise for an event which was, after all, unsurprising. But it should give you the general idea of what we do in cases where we are genuinely surprised by some behaviour. Unable to find a satisfactory way to put ourselves in the shoes of either the bride or groom in the one-day marriage – unable to get the simulation right – we do our best by suggesting things that they may have believed or desired. As described above, this kind of talk is itself based on simulation: we imagine ourselves in their shoes and then say what we would think or want. In our attempt to understand this case, we then argue back and forth about the plausibility of these more limited simulations, with a view to seeing whether they are on the right track for simulating what happened on the day of the marriage.

In anticipating behaviour by simulation, or in reporting our simulations in the language of belief and desire, we are at no point appealing to law-like or theoretical regularities. My having anticipated my friend's meeting me in the restaurant is not grounded on my having, either explicitly or tacitly, embedded her behaviour in a matrix of regularities. And in the marriage case, our speculations about what the principals felt, believed and wanted are not speculations about which regularities we should call on. Instead, an appropriate kind of simulation lies at the bottom of both our unreflective predictions of behaviour and our highly reflective discussions. The rules of thumb that we have come to recognize through our wide experience suggest how we might speak if we were in the agent's shoes. And if we get these right, we can build on them until we come closer to a full-blooded story about what the agent did. But, to repeat, in none of this does the explanatory force come from proper theoretical generalizations. We count ourselves as having explained some act when we are satisfied that the simulations that re-create the agent's beliefs and desires – simulations using ourselves as models – are also simulations that recreate the agent's act.

Simulation and Theory: Compare and Contrast

There is much more to be said about the details of the Simulation Theory than I have room for here. However, even from the summary above, it does seem as if it is an alternative to the Theory Theory. In the latter, we explain by an embedding in a network of regularities; whereas in Simulation, we go in for no such thing.

That there is a difference between the theories at the level of practice is undeniable. But a difference at this level, however sharp, might not be all that radical. For it is commonly argued that, at some more fundamental level, the Simulation Theory is no less dependent on the regularity idea of explanation than the Theory Theory.

Think again about the hull design example which was used to introduce the Simulation Theory. A designer who used a tank to simulate the behaviour of hull shapes does not appeal to the theory of fluid dynamics, and might well not know the theory in any sense at all. Such a person would be carrying out the work in a completely different way from some more theoretical-minded designer who deduced the behaviour of hull shapes from fundamental theories. However, how would all this look from the point of view of someone who wanted a justification of each of these methods? The theoretical designer could say that he had explained the behaviour of this or that hull shape in the familiar deductive-regularity sense of explanation. Moreover, he could appeal to considerations that we offered earlier, and to the whole history of science, to argue that the deductive-regularity conception captures the very essence of our idea of explanation. What could the simulation designer say by way of justification?

If the simulation designer really knows nothing about fluid dynamics, or any other body of theoretical knowledge, there is little he could say. But in so far as we accept the efficacy of the tank-testing of hull design, it would seem that any justificatory story we would tell would at some stage have to appeal to this theoretical knowledge. After all, it is not magic that scale models and tanks give us a good idea of how real hull shapes will behave under various sea and wind conditions, nor is it magic that real hulls behave as they do. We count simulation as rational because we think that in principle a properly theoretical explanatory background could be provided.

Or so it would appear. The model and tank-testing example is typical of those chosen to illustrate the Simulation Theory, and in taking such examples seriously we end up finding that the differences between Theory and Simulation are real, but not particularly radical. Some conclude from this that the Simulation account ends up, at most, providing an alternative to the tacit knowledge defence of the Theory Theory. However, there is a way to understand the Simulation Theory which suggests that it is a more radical alternative.

Simulation and Explanation

We have seen that it is reasonable to think that the explanatoriness of an explanation requires the embedding of the explanandum in a network of regularities. The kernel of this idea reveals itself in our thinking about the most mundane examples, e.g. explanations of missed meetings, and it is present in its full glory in the more developed activities known collectively as science. Moreover, as just noted, even when we in fact do our explaining without explicit reference to the deductive-regularity conception, it seems to be there in the background. Whether the specific set of regularities are only tacitly known, or not known at all, it still seems true that our conception of explanation requires that there be a background of regularity.

Given all this, the Simulation Theory would only be a genuinely radical departure if it suggested, not merely a difference in explanatory practice, but instead a difference in the very nature of explanation. And, on one view of the Simulation Theory, that is precisely what we find. The suggestion is that if we look deeply enough into our intuitions about what counts as explanatoriness, we would find that there is after all an alternative to the regularity conception; one we can discern by thinking about the Simulation Theory in the right light. How might this intuition be brought out?

Think again about sailboat hulls. In our reckoning of that example, we decided that the behaviour of a real hull was genuinely explained by the model-in-the-tank simulation only if there was at least in principle a network of fluid-dynamic regularities in which we could appropriately situate the model, as well as the real hull. In essence, explaining here is a kind of fitting into a pattern of regularities. But a sailboat hull's behaviour differs in a fundamental way from human behaviour: the hull does not in any sense undertake or initiate its behaviour, whereas human beings do. Though we can and do try to explain human behaviour by fitting it into patterns – and though in this sense we do not distinguish it from the behaviour of anything else – the suggestion is that there is a second kind of explanatoriness that is reserved exclusively for human action. Explanatoriness in this alternative sense comes not from fitting into patterns, but from appreciating how an action appears to an agent. The connection between this and the Simulation Theory arises from the further claim that only creatures who are themselves agents can ever be in a position to have this sort of appreciation.

The idea of explanation as seeing actions from, as it were, the inside is not easy to appreciate without an example, so consider the following bit of A's autobiography:

Woke up this morning feeling tired and uneasy. For the past months I knew that there was something wrong with my relationship with Z, but I couldn't put my finger on it. When we were first going out we enjoyed each other's company, took pleasure in our joint activities, and began to imagine a life together. But, when we went to dinner at our friends' house last night, Z reacted strangely to their children. He seemed to resent the attention that the children demanded, and, when we were alone later, he was deeply critical of their behaviour. But, as far as I could see, the kids were, well, just kids. And rather sweet ones at that. I know that this was just one incident, but the more that I think about it, the more I now see Z as himself somehow childish and self-centred, and see too that I must have realized this for some time now. I know this seems crazy, but my feelings have now crystallized into a conviction that I just cannot continue seeing Z and planning a future. Much as it will hurt him, and difficult as it will be for me, I have now decided to break off our relationship.

No doubt this excerpt misses out lots of background detail, and not everyone will understand why A decided to call off her relationship to Z. But many will, and when they do, it will be by seeing how the relationship came to appear to A, and by putting themselves in A's shoes. For those who do see it, this bit of autobiography will suffice to explain A's action, and it will do so without a hint of any fitting into patterns of regularities. The lack of descriptive detail in the example of A–Z is itself quite important here. If explanation were always a matter of fitting into patterns, this lack of detail would be a serious fault. But because we are agents and therefore creatures who can imagine an action from an agent's perspective, we don't need much detail to get a grip on the explanation.

It might be thought that examples like that of A–Z point to there being merely a special route to explanation that is available to creatures who can get inside the reasons with which actions are done. And that this by itself is not yet strong enough to render some version of the Simulation Theory a rival to the regularity conception. However, this way of looking at the matter overlooks something important that is suggested by the A–Z example. It is not simply that seeing things from an agent's point of view offers us a way of understanding the agent's actions (and thoughts); on the view being canvassed, it is the *only* way. When this is taken on board, we really do seem to have an alternative to the Theory Theory. For, details aside, an appealing feature of the regularity conception is its suggestion that explanation is not parochial. The explanation of surface freezing of water holds good for anyone, whether human or Martian, given only an understanding of the generalizations on which the explanation is based. But the upshot of the A–Z example seems to be that there is a type of explanation only available to creatures who themselves are agents and act for reasons, since it is only as agents that we could hope to appreciate the force of reasons. Someone outside what is sometimes called the 'space of reasons' – perhaps the proverbial Martian – might, for example, understand every sentence in the narrative about A–Z, and yet have no clue why A acted as she did.

The conclusion of the last paragraph is by no means the end of the matter. For there is still more to be said on behalf of the regularity conception that underpins the Theory Theory. On the one hand, it might be argued that there is after all a kind of agent-relativity even in straightforward cases of scientific explanation. After all, explanations in science are constructed by us, and we are their beneficiaries, So, perhaps one should not be too ready to cast the regularity conception outside the space of reasons. And, on the other hand, it might be pointed out that the generalizations that figure in the Theory Theory, whether tacit or not, are framed in the vocabulary of the mental landscape; they cite beliefs, desires and experiences and the relationship of these to actions. Requiring as we do that an explanation can be explanatory only for a creature who understands the relevant generalizations, we would have reason to exclude the Martian, and not merely because he failed to be one of us. The idea would be that the Martian's inability to understand why A acted as she did is a sign, not of its failure to see the action in the light of A's reasons, but simply because of a failure to understand the generalizations connecting A's attitudes and feelings to her action.

Quite clearly we are not going to settle here the issue of whether the Theory Theory, and its notion of explanation, stand alone or whether the Simulation Theory is a genuine alternative. But, as with the topics of chapter 2, my aim is not so much solving as exhibiting puzzles. What we have seen is that we have a strong intuition about what makes an explanation explanatory: it must show how some event or action fits into (typically, is deducible from) a network of established and appropriate generalizations. Since it is in the nature of generalizations that they hold independently of any parochial point of view, this creates tension with a competing intuition that we also have, namely that only agents sharing our space of reasons could ever explain our actions. Even if we find some way to absorb the practice of folk psychology into a scientific framework, the tension between these intuitions will remain. However, instead of being between competing conceptions, it will be internal to our idea of what makes an explanation explanatory.

3.2 Persons

The notion of the self (or of a person) came on stage at the very end of chapter 1; it was a late appearance but, given what was said, it was a starring role. Linking together the items making up the mental realm, persons constitute the crux of any folk psychological narrative. It is persons that experience, attitudinize and act, and thus any kind of folk psychological explanation of an action makes sense only if the agent of the act is the same person as the experiencer and attitudinizer. Without this continuity the attribution of experiences and attitudes would simply not connect with the actions in question, and so any attempt to treat the one as explanatory of the other would be unintelligible. And this is true whether we think folk psychological explanation is theoretical – placing an action against a background of known or tacitly known regularities – or whether it is a very different projective or simulation-based kind of explanation.

Individuation and Identity

Being in this way pivotal to our explanatory practices suggests that we must have some idea both of the nature of persons and what counts towards the continuity of persons over time. These notions are related but not the same, so it is worth getting clear about them, and about how they figure in explanatory narratives. Imagine that every day you catch a train to work at precisely the same time. Whilst riding in one morning, you ask yourself: is this particular carriage the same one that I travelled on yesterday? Here I assume that you have no trouble at all in telling that you are inside a train carriage. As philosophers say, you have no trouble in *individuating* or identifying carriages, no trouble in telling them apart from buses and planes. But knowing how to individuate a carriage is not yet the same thing as knowing how to identify a carriage as one and the same over some time interval, as knowing how to *re-identify* it.

Individuation and re-identification are not necessarily as separate as the example suggests. If your individuative skills are such that you can tell one carriage apart from *any* other carriage, then you have what you would need to answer your original question; you should be able to put your knowledge to use in telling whether this particular carriage is the same as the one you took yesterday. Still, it is very far from obvious that anyone could have quite such an exhaustive individuative ability, and in any case, what matters here is simply the fact that individuation (or identification) and re-identification are distinguishable skills.

In the present context our interest is in persons, and the suggestion is that folk psychological narrative demands not only that we be able to individuate persons, but that we also be able to re-identify them. If you have any doubts about our needing both of these skills, think of the fact that any given explanatory narrative is almost certain to appeal to some set of experiences and attitudes entertained by a subject over some considerable time-scale. What you have believed since childhood, and desired for the past year, might well be crucial to explaining why you are now taking a particular book out of the library. Here we have not only to identify the person who has the beliefs, desires and acts, we have to do so in a way that presupposes a re-identification of a person over time.

(Note: I have spoken of individuation or identity, and contrasted these with re-identification. In the literature, and confusingly, the problem of the re-identification of persons is known simply as the problem of personal *identity*. This means that it is safer to think of the other problem as that of personal *individuation*.)

Personal Problems

Accepting then that folk psychological explanation requires both individuation and identification, the next natural thought would be that, since we are fairly good at giving explanations, we ought to be no less good at saying what counts as a person both at a time and over time. Unfortunately, as will be described below, there are problems with this thought. It is not that we cannot say anything about persons, that we just tacitly assume the needed continuity. Far from it. For a start, we are, if anything, 'too good' at it. When pressed we are likely to come up with very different ideas about personal individuation and identification, ideas which are simply incompatible. Nor is this the whole of the problem. What compounds the difficulty is that our incompatible thoughts about the individuation and identity of persons do not seem to allow retreat. Unlike the situation in respect of most subject-matters within which we hold conflicting views, when it comes to persons we do not find it easy even to think of dropping one of them, or suspending judgement on both, pending a final decision. Our two basic conceptions of persons have us in a kind of thrall, so that we somehow need both, yet know them to be incoherent when taken together.

You can understand how we end up in this parlous position only if you appreciate our opposing intuitions about persons, so that is certainly a place to start. But let me warn you before we begin that the literature on persons and personal identity is vast, and there is no way that my remarks here could survey it all. Instead, I shall adapt an example first given by Bernard Williams, as it promises the quickest route to the heart of our deeply puzzling conceptions of persons.[4]

Since the Williams example will almost certainly put a strain on your imagination – perhaps even on your credulity – it is important that we work up to it by beginning with some obvious home truths. In our day-to-day dealings with one another, the strategy we employ in our assessments of personhood is simple and straightforward. We think that our relatives, friends and neighbours, having as they do human bodies that function in complicated but expected ways, are each and every one a person. If through some mishap one of these happens to be fatally injured or dies of some disease, we think of this person on his death as still embodied, but ceasing to be a person in any real sense. Harry has died; he is no more. Why? Not because there is any deeply metaphysical trouble with Harry, but simply because, whilst Harry's body still exists, it no longer functions in the way we have come to expect of persons; nor, as things now stand, will it do so in future.

When we think about personal identity, the story gets a little more complicated, but only a little. Most persons we have known for some time (ourselves included) have bodies that have undergone considerable alteration. Some of this alteration might have been deliberate, but by and large the bodily transition from infancy to old age is well beyond our control. For this reason, our re-identification of persons does not depend merely on sameness of body shape from one time to another. Instead, it relies on our knowing or anticipating a certain pattern of change that is typical of the human species.

The fact that we have bodies, and that they function and change in predictable ways, is certainly the basis of most of our thinking about personal individuation and identity. But there is, of course, another sort of factor, namely our possession of minds. Persons are conscious of what happens to them, they initiate actions, and they have complex beliefs, desires, fears, hopes, regrets and memories. Indeed, as we have seen, it is constitutive of each of these items in the mental realm that they belong to a self or person. Moreover, each of us seems convinced of our own personhood without having to appeal (at least directly) to any sort of bodily continuity. We believe that we can just tell that we are persons, and that each of us continues as the same person, just by some presented or presumed unity in our experiences, thoughts and projects.

The fact that our judgements of personhood rely both on bodily continuity and on a sort of 'psychological' unity might make us wonder which of these is the more reliable, or which of them (if either) is in fact constitutive of personhood. But in the ordinary run of cases, the issue simply doesn't arise. Meeting a friend, we expect the fully functioning and recognized body to produce utterances and react in ways consistent with our conviction that we are in the presence of the very person we have known all these years. And when we wake up in the morning, even before we have had a chance to check, each of us rightly expects that a later glance in the mirror will hold no major surprises.

There are cases, not common but common enough to need comment, which seem to disturb the harmony between bodily and psychological criteria of personhood. Included here would be cases of so-called 'split personality', and also cases in which we are confronted with what seem to be persons in very non-standard bodies. What are we to make of a human being who claims to be different persons at different times, and whose experiences, attitudes and actions seem systematically different from one time to another? And what of the non-human creature (perhaps an animal or a computer or some extra-terrestrial) with whom we seem able to have a perfectly reasonable, even intelligent conversation? (Locke rather credulously passes on a story about a parrot whose conversation is just like that expected of a human being.)

Split personality disorder is not a possibility, but an actuality. However, as has been pointed out many times, there is nothing in the detailed descriptions of the those suffering from the disorder that forces us to count them as multiple *persons* in a single human body. In fact, the very idea of a cure (or remission) of this disorder suggests that this is precisely the wrong way to look at it. Split personality sufferers are single persons who are deeply disturbed; had they genuinely been many persons inside a single body, they would be more freakish than ill, and attempts to cure them by encouraging an integration of personality would be just bizarre.

A person without a human body is, in contrast, a possibility not an actuality, though the ubiquity of this in science-fiction books and films suggests that we view the possibility as unproblematically genuine. Still, whether it is a real possibility or not, the existence of such creatures would cause few problems for our usual assumptions about persons and personal identity. To be sure, if we really did come across a creature with which we could communicate, and which appeared to us to have experiences and attitudes typical of persons, but which was as unlike a human being in body as we could imagine, then we would certainly have to extend the boundaries of our provincial conception of persons. (Though in most science fiction, the extra-terrestrials end up physically more like us than one might have thought probable.) We would then simply have to revise our criteria of re-identification, allowing for a larger range of species and body types than we now do.

(Note: it could be argued that something like this has already happened – that it is less of a mere possibility than I have been supposing. For there is considerable evidence that Europeans, when first encountering the inhabitants of the Americas, did not think of them as human beings, though those who were enlightened did think they were persons. A similar response might be read into Europeans' first encounters with certain other primates, but it is less easy to draw consequences from this case because virtually everyone came to think – perhaps wrongly – that apes are not persons.)

The possibility of non-human persons is important to our discussion, not because it genuinely threatens the harmony in our everyday criteria of personhood, but more simply because it reminds us of the role of imagination in the story. One way to understand our own concepts is to see how we apply them to actual things. But since concepts are after all *our* concepts – we presumably have some idea of how to use them – it is no less valuable to see how we would apply them to things we only imagine to be possible. Admittedly, we have to remain alert to the issue of whether what we imagine possible is genuinely possible, but that is an occupational hazard of any sort of philosophical thinking.

(a)   Arnold and Benedict Contemplate their Futures

Imagining possible cases of non-human persons can lead us to see a certain provinciality, even if not incoherence, in our everyday decisions about personhood. But other cases might be more problematic. Here finally is the beginning of the example I have adapted from Williams:

> Arnold and Benedict are brothers who are not twins, but who physically resemble one another closely, and are only a year and a half apart in age. Having just had a spectacular failure in their joint business, they are in desperate need of money. At the same time – and it is a time some distance in the future – a large biotech company is in the process of developing what they call a Brain Recorder. When this device is attached to someone, it records every physical and functional detail, down to the least molecular interchange, of the subject's brain. As a research tool, the Brain Recorder has proved invaluable, but the company's scientists have recently gone one better. The human brain had so far been treated as a 'Read Only' device; the Brain Recorder read off, but was unable to alter, the complex functional patterns in the brain. However, the newly developed Brain Writer changed all this: this second device can take the enormous amount of information stored in a Brain Reader, and use it to change an otherwise normally functioning human brain. (The details are unimportant, but you can think of the Brain Writer as essentially erasing and then overwriting the functional patterns of a given brain.)
>
> Together the Brain Reader/Writer devices promise to be more than simply a research tool, and the company's scientists are anxious to test it. For this reason, and with complete openness of intent, they offer 10 million pounds to any pair of people willing to undergo the following experiment: Brain Readers will record the brains of each, brain 1 and 2, and then Brain Writers will impose the functionality of brain 1 onto that of brain 2 and vice versa. In order to give the experiment the best chance of success, the scientists require not only that the pair be healthy but that they be siblings of the same sex.

Arnold and Benedict talk it over and decide to volunteer themselves for this experiment. (They were contemplating the proverbial trip to the office roof when their business went bust, and the experiment seems a slightly better option.) On arrival at the biotech company's headquarters, they are ushered into a seminar room for a sort of pre-operative session, and what they hear takes them somewhat aback. You see, whilst the scientists are very excited about trying out their new gadget, they are very unsure what would constitute a completely successful outcome. Clearly, any successful outcome will presuppose the reading and writing devices actually work, but what is less clear is how to describe the result. One view is that they will have simply *changed* Arnold and Benedict dramatically. Nobody doubts that. But some of the team think the experiment would actually *switch* Arnold into Benedict's body and vice versa. There being no consensus on this, it is suggested that the experiment be preceded by in-depth interviews with the two subjects to see what they think.

As I said, Arnold and Benedict are taken aback to find that their opinions are being sought about the outcome. Surely, they think, if this is a scientific experiment, then the experimenters, and not lay persons like us, must know what they are aiming to achieve. Their disquiet is partially allayed, however, by the smooth-talking philosophical member of the team, the one who proposed the interview in the first place. She convinces the brothers that what is at issue is not merely a question of bodies and brains, but of persons. The experimenters are quite happy that the brothers' bodies and brains will remain perfectly healthy; what they are not sure of is the best description of the outcome so far as the persons Arnold and Benedict are concerned. Since our judgements of person-hood tend to revolve around both bodily and mental criteria, and since mental features are best appreciated from the person's own point of view, she thinks that a pre-experiment interview should form part of the experiment. She also assures them that there will be a post-experiment interview.

Told that no one has any doubt that their bodies and brains will survive, the brothers are less anxious. But the next thing they are told unsettles them again. After the Reading and Writing has taken place, one of two things might happen: either the Arnold-body person will be subjected to great pain and the Benedict-body person will be given an extra 10 million pounds, or the Benedict-body person will be subjected to pain and the Arnold-body person will be given the money. What the experimenters ask is which of these two possibilities would each of you – Arnold and Benedict – prefer?

Arnold thinks: if the device is successful, then all my character, memories, feelings and the like will be transferred to the brain of Benedict. Though it will feel funny – but not too funny, since we look a great deal alike – I shall be walking around in Benedict's body. Since this is so, the obvious thing for me is to ask that the Benedict-body person, that is me, be given the money and spared the pain.

Benedict is not so sure – he has a certain fondness for his body – but, as they are encouraged to talk it over with one another, he comes to think that Arnold's view is correct. Therefore he decides that he, Benedict, would like the Arnold-body person to be given the money, and the Benedict-body person to experience pain.

What made Benedict come down on this side was his imagining how it would be when the rewards and pain were handed out. If the machine worked, then the Arnold-body person would intimately remember everything in Benedict's life, and would express Benedict's hopes and fears. If this person were offered the extra money, it would be gratefully accepted, and put to use in fulfilling the plans that Benedict now had. On the other hand, were it to be the pain and not the money that was offered, then the suffering would be characteristic of Benedict's attitude towards pain. (It was common knowledge in the family that Arnold was more stoic when it came to physical pain.)

Benedict also tried to imagine what it would be like if he had not decided in this way, if he had asked that the Benedict-body person be rewarded and the Arnold-body person suffered the pain. Again, assuming that the machines worked properly, the Arnold body person would protest in Benedict's characteristic way about the pain being inflicted, and, though he would remember having chosen this, he would say that he now deeply regretted it.

These outcomes become more vivid as he thinks about them and his sentimental attachment to his own body less so. That is why he acquiesced when his brother summed up the view this way:

> If your experiment works, you will be switching our bodies. Since it is natural to want what is best for oneself, one will choose in favour of the destination body and not the present one.
> (He also added that, since the interviewer's question was purely hypothetical, they had discounted the fraternal feelings which would complicate their choices.)

Thus ends the first part of the example. In it, and against a science-fantasy background, we look on as two individuals ponder their fate. Or at least that is how it seems. There are two preliminary things we have to decide:

(a)   Are we right to view the story this way?
(b)   If we are, are the brothers right to decide as they have?

And if we do get satisfactory answers to these questions, the main issue will return in this form:

(c)   What does all this show about our everyday conception of a person?

A lot could be said about the science-fiction story that sets up the examples. For a start, the idea that individual mental lives go with the pattern of their brains' functioning (or even with their brains) is assumed without any discussion. This issue will come up with full force in part III, but even there it will be suggested that, in the form presented above, this assumption is pretty difficult to avoid. Note that the example does not try to identify personhood with any kind of brain activity, nor does it suggest that someone's mental life is somehow a mere add-on to brain activity. All it says is that, if the Read/Write machine works as it should, then the things the brothers will say about what they are thinking after the procedure will be as described. And, whilst the idea of the machine might strain our imagination, there is nothing particularly surprising about its assumption that in some way or other the brain is necessary to our mental life.

There is a second element to the story which is crucial to the brothers' decisions and to our thinking about the example, namely the idea that there are in fact two persons around after the machine procedure. Answers to question (b) presuppose this, but perhaps it is not justified by the facts. For example, couldn't it just be the case that the Read/Write machine essentially kills both brothers, and that the 'creatures' we find around afterwards are not persons, and therefore certainly not the brothers? It is very difficult to argue against this possibility, but it does seem counter-intuitive. Remember that after the procedure, there will be two healthy bodies with perfectly normal brains, and each such body will be indistinguishable in general behaviour from any one of us. If a stranger were to meet, say the Arnold-body person, a couple of days after the operation, he would be in no doubt at all that he was dealing with a person. Of course, this doesn't show that the Arnold-body person is in fact either Arnold or Benedict. Perhaps *they* did die and somehow new persons emerged. Still, Arnold's and Benedict's friends and relations wouldn't view it that way, nor of course do Arnold and Benedict.

Accepting that two persons emerge, it is difficult to argue against Arnold's and Benedict's view of the procedure as one of body-switching. When all the feelings, thoughts and memories, as well as an insistence that it is Arnold speaking, issue from the mouth of the Benedict-body, there is also little doubt that we ought to find this conclusion, if not obviously right, then at least more plausible than any other. If we do – and this is a reply to (c) above – this has an important further consequence for our everyday conception of persons. The possibility of non-human persons described earlier indicated the need for a liberalization in the range of body-types we would accept as persons. The story of Arnold and Benedict doesn't straightforwardly require us to change the basic elements of our everyday conception, but it does force a ranking on those elements that actual cases do not. Our reaction to the experiment shows that personhood shadows specific features of the mind more closely than it does bodily features.

The specificity of the mental features is important. It is only because there was a description of the route by which the feelings, thoughts and memories came to be expressed by the Benedict-body person that we could allow ourselves to think of this person as Arnold. Moreover, it is this same feature which impresses Arnold and Benedict. It is for this reason that the story of the experiment has two subtly different upshots. On the one hand, we come away thinking of it as a case of body-switching; on the other, we think that this is what any pair subjected to the experiment would themselves think. Not only does body-switching seem the right thing for us, it seems no less right from the perspective of the participants.

(h) This is your Life

Keeping in mind these conclusions − especially the last one − let us now consider a second possible case.

> Someone tells you that he is going to inflict great pain on you tomorrow. This terrifies you, as it would any of us. Seeing your apprehension, however, he sets about trying to mollify you. He says first: 'Don't worry, when the time for the pain comes, you won't remember this conversation.' But seeing that this does not have the desired effect on you, he goes on: 'Look, what you have to realize is that before the pain is inflicted, a very great deal will change. Not only will you not remember this conversation, you will have none of your present memories.' Again, he sees that you are no less anxious. (You are now terrified both about the pain and about the threat of your suffering total amnesia.) So, he says: 'I haven't made myself clear. It is not that your memories will be erased and you will have no past; tomorrow you will have a set of completely different memories. And not only memories: tomorrow you will have a completely different set of attitudes and feelings.' (You think that this would only help if amongst those attitudes was a very different one towards pain. But you know that this not going to happen, and what you now think is that you are to suffer both pain and madness tomorrow.) Finally, believing this to provide the ultimate comfort, he says: 'You see, the feelings, thoughts and memories that you will have are those of someone now living. This will come about through a process of brain content transfer.' (Not quite sure what you can do to get out of this terrible situation, you pretend to be mollified somewhat by this. But underneath, and quite reasonably, this does not comfort you at all. Madness takes many forms, and the fact that, as well as suffering pain, you will insist to anyone who will listen that you are some other person, seems a particularly cruel form of the disease.)

Somewhere near the end, this second story should have sounded familiar. It is simply one half of the previous story about Arnold and Benedict, albeit told in a slightly different way. The person telling you about the pain is the philosophical interviewer (a 'he' was used to disguise this fact), and we can assume that you are Arnold. But though the situation is the same, the reaction to it is not. You, Arnold, are now terrified by what is going to happen to you, and you would give anything to get out of it.

As in the first case, there is an enormous amount that we could quibble about, but also as in that case, I do not think that any of it would change the outcome.[5] But surprisingly, the outcome here runs completely counter to that of the first story: on this second presentation of the facts, you – Arnold – would not think that someone else was going to be subjected to pain. If you did, you would be more sanguine about it – subject of course to your sympathy for the other person – and you would certainly feel relief at some stage in the interview described above. However, unlike the first case, where we imagined that both Arnold and Benedict (and we) would see the situation of one of body-switching, here Arnold's continuing fear shows him to be committed to the idea that he and his body – Arnold's body – together constitute the locus of his personhood. (You might be tempted to think that this second story would be changed substantially if the interviewer had begun this way: 'pain will be inflicted on Arnold's body, but before this happens Arnold will not remember . . .' However, thinking of yourself as Arnold, you would simply find this a strangely impersonal way of speaking. You would take the interviewer as saying: 'pain will be inflicted on Arnold's body, i.e. *mine*, but before this happens *I* will not remember . . . and so on, as in the version above.)

Our capacity to take in both examples and come up with contrary views about persons is disturbing. Our everyday conception seemed to have two harmonious parts: persons are *both* human beings – creatures whose bodily forms and functions are determined by their membership in a particular biological species – *and* things whose mental landscapes have a special kind of coherence and unity. However, this harmony is threatened when we employ our dual conception of persons in deciding matters of personal identity. In actual cases of re-identifying persons from one time to another, the dual conception holds together, but cases like those above show how it falls apart. And of course it is not just that the two aspects separate; rather they turn out to be opposed to one another.[6]

Avoidance

What is to be done? It is of course entirely possible that the right answer to this is nothing. Our dual-aspect conception of persons serves us well enough in the actual cases we come across, and there might be reasons to demur from giving verdicts in the sorts of case thrown up by our imagination. Here the strategy is one of avoidance, and there are two ways in which this might be justified.

First of all, we might be able to show that the imagined cases are not in fact possible. Brain Reading and Writing machines, brain transplantation and cases of human fission fill the literature on personal identity, but they are certainly bizarre. If it turns out that they are in some deeper sense impossible, then this would certainly get us off the hook. However, for this way of avoiding the problem to carry any conviction, there ought to be some substantial grounds for thinking the problem cases are impossible. But what could they be? Most but not all of the cases rely on the background assumption that our mental lives depend upon a normally functioning brain. We will be discussing this further in part III, but, as already noted, this background assumption seems true, so an attack on it seems a poor strategy for showing that, for example, 'body-switching' is impossible. More subtle grounds might be imagined, but we have to be very careful, precisely because of the role of the imagination. The examples in the literature on personal identity seem coherent, and we do not want to declare them impossible simply because of the philosophical embarrassment they cause. Yet the danger of this is very real when the impossibilities are no less products of our imagination than the putative possibilities they are intended to rule out.

Without a demonstration that the troublesome cases are impossible, we might simply ignore them. This is not quite as intellectually disreputable as it might seem. Noting first that our concept of personhood has been developed in a world in which bodies and minds seem to march in step, it might be suggested that the best thing to do is simply to admit that our concept is not equipped to deal with cases in which these criteria come apart. What we should do now is agree to count these cases as undecided, perhaps waiting until they actually crop up before we would be prepared to issue any verdict.

Peter Strawson suggests that the concept of a person is primitive within the framework of concepts that make up what I have called 'folk psychology'. Roughly, to be primitive in this way is to be presupposed in, and not analysable by, both features of our mental life and features of our bodily existence. He sums up the view this way:

> The concept of a person is not to be analysed as that of an animated body or of an embodied anima.[7]

Of course, this primitiveness thesis tells us nothing about the identity of persons over time. It is in fact simply another way – perhaps a better one –

of expressing what I have described as the everyday idea that there is a kind of de facto harmony between mental and bodily features of those persons we are likely to meet. When Strawson does come to consider personal identity over time, he writes:

> . . . once that [primitiveness] thesis is understood and admitted, the residual problem of personal identity, though still debatable, appears as one of minor significance and relatively little difficulty.

And though he is reluctant to add much to this dismissal of the problem, he goes on to write:

> The criteria of personal identity are certainly multiple. In saying that a personal body gives us a necessary point of application for these criteria, I am not saying that the criteria for re-identifying persons are the same as the criteria for re-identifying material bodies. I am not denying that we might, in unusual circumstances, be prepared to speak of two persons alternatively sharing a body, or of persons changing bodies, &c.[8]

In effect, he is suggesting in these passages that we must simply be patient; that we must just wait to see what we would 'be prepared' to say when and if difficult cases crop up.

In general, a call for patience in deciding troublesome cases raised by the application of our concepts might be good advice, but the specific nature of each case is crucial. Unfortunately, I think that the concept of a person is one for which the advice in inappropriate. To see why, I would ask you to think about a different troublesome example – one often connected to the issue of personal identity – where the advice seems to me perfectly reasonable.

> Oxford tourist guides claim that Magdalen College Tower was built in 1492. Being the date that Columbus 'discovered' America gives this claim a certain resonance for Americans. But there is a little problem. Anyone visiting Oxford about fifteen years ago would have seen the major restoration job undertaken on the Tower. All the old and crumbling stones were removed and replaced, and this in effect meant all the stones. Moreover, this recent restoration was not the only one undertaken in the past 500 years.
>
> These restorations naturally raise the question of whether the Tower one sees today is in fact the same tower as the one built in 1492; whether it is reasonable to think of oneself as looking at the Magdalen Tower constructed when Columbus set sail.

There is, of course, a sense in which the replacement of any stone means that the tower of 1492 is no longer the same. But normally we do not let routine maintenance affect our judgement about the identity of things through time. More parts than I care to think about have been replaced in my old car, but it is still the car that I bought in 1985; it has simply been repaired. So it is not difficult to convince oneself that, in a perfectly respectable sense, the Tower now seen is the Tower built in 1492. Like my car, the restoration work – always carefully and accurately carried out – has served simply to guarantee the continuation of the Tower, and not its replacement.

However, let us let our imagination loose on this case. Suppose that, unbeknown to the College authorities, the foreman of the restoration team had carefully preserved each and every piece of old stone from Magdalen Tower, and stored them in a large warehouse on the outskirts of Oxford. He did this with no specific aim in mind, but, on retiring, a bold idea of what to do with the stones came to him. With some of his friends, he began the project of reconstructing Magdalen Tower, using the stones he had so carefully hoarded. After two years, the work is completed: there in a field just outside the Oxford city limits is a structure that anyone looking at a guidebook for, say 1950, would take to be Magdalen Tower.

But is it Magdalen Tower? Or is the Tower now restored and standing on the original site Magdalen Tower? These questions, themselves first asked of a ship that had received similar imaginative treatment, are actually quite difficult to answer.[9] Good arguments can be given for regarding both as Magdalen Tower, though we know that 'both' cannot be the correct answer, since the two Towers are certainly not identical to each other.

One perfectly sensible reaction to this sort of problem is to remain calm, and say:

> We are perfectly good at individuating towers. But if we come across some such case – remember that the 'second' Magdalen Tower is merely imagined – we will then have to look at what we are prepared to say. When we do, and given our clear grasp of the concept of a tower, the problem of the identity of Magdalen Tower will be one which 'though still debatable, appears as one of minor significance and relatively little difficulty'.

Of course, not everyone would (or does) have this reaction: many metaphysicians feel that honour will only be served by some definitive story about the *real* Magdalen Tower. However, for our purposes what matters is not whether patience is the best we can do, but whether it is reasonable. And when it comes to artefacts like Magdalen Tower – things which after all *we* make, use and sometimes discard – it does seem to be.

Unfortunately, in spite of Strawson's encouragement, the leave-it-undecided strategy doesn't really work when it is the identity of persons that is at issue. There are two ways to explain why this is so: the first is ultimately a bit unfair to the indecision suggestion, but it sets the stage for the second, more damning objection.

Imagine yet another interviewer discussing with Arnold and Benedict their reactions to the experiment. The interviewer says:

> When we sat you both down and told you what would happen in respect of pain and prize, you came to the conclusion that we were aiming to switch your bodies. But when the same story was separately aimed at *you* (here the interviewer points to Arnold and Benedict in turn) each of you expressed fears intelligible only on the assumption that no such switching was envisaged. Given these reactions, we cannot now decide what the outcome will be: maybe there will be a switch, maybe not. However, this shouldn't be cause for any alarm. Let us just do the experiment and see what happens. Perhaps, when we come to see what you and your friends are prepared to say, we will then be able to decide whether or not you have switched bodies. In any case, our metaphysicians think that this problem is no big deal. (This is then supported by the long story about the identity of Magdalen Tower.)

This bit of the interview is not likely to go over well with either of the subjects. Arnold puts it like this:

> I have been worried about this experiment from the beginning. Lots of things could go wrong, and either myself or Benedict (or both of us) might simply fail to survive. Now you tell me that, even if everything goes swimmingly, you don't know who I will be, and thus do not know whether I will suffer the pain or get the prize. This seems wrong – it seems now all too clear that it will be me suffering the pain. What your metaphysicians say therefore does not calm my nerves.

It is easy enough to sympathize with Arnold's sentiments here, but, from the philosophical point of view, this is not a wholly fair way to respond to Strawson's counsel of patience. Remember that the Arnold/Benedict example is a creature of our imagination. It has been used to prompt our intuitions about personal identity, and to show that there are two sorts of intuition, each pulling us in a different direction. Expressing sympathy with what Arnold is imagined as saying is essentially just reasserting one of the opposing intuitive verdicts. Arnold is imagined as treating the whole thing as about *him*, and this corresponds to the second interview, the one where the interviewer begins by addressing the subject as 'you'. But Strawson's advice is given from a standpoint that is meant to take account of the verdicts of both intuitions. Given that, from this standpoint, we are urged against trying to come down on one side or the other, it is wholly unsurprising to find that this advice is inconsistent with each side of the debate. (Strawson's position is no less in conflict with the view that the experiment is *definitely* one of switching bodies.)

Too direct an appeal to the verdict of an imagined participant is not that damaging to the wait-and-see strategy, but it does suggest a much more potent objection. Recall the conflicting intuitions about the identity of Magdalen Tower. One sort of intuition appeals to continuing location, ownership and function, the other to continuity of material constitution. For present purposes, the details of each position matter less than the fact that they both occupy a single perspective: they require us to look at the towers from what is recognizably the 'outside'. This can be put less metaphorically. The sets of features bearing on what we are prepared to say about the identity of Magdalen Tower are features assignable by observers of the towers; they are not assigned from the point of view of the tower. However, given that the towers are physical objects, this is scarcely surprising. There is no such thing as assigning features from such a point of view; it doesn't even make sense to ask about the tower's identity as seen from the inside. But with us it is different: there is such a thing as the 'inside' perspective.

In the first treatment of the Arnold/Benedict example, we – and the two participants – were invited to think about identity-relevant features *from the outside.* There was discussion of what would happen to one or other brain, what sorts of claims would issue from one or other body, and what would be judged about mental states as a result of interaction with one or other of the resulting persons. As Williams points out, in this first treatment we are encouraged to keep track of the experiences and attitudes of each participant, and the participants themselves are consulted. But, though some of these features are traditionally thought of as 'inner', the assessment of them in the first interview was firmly that of outside observers. We tried to imagine what Arnold and Benedict would say about the resulting persons, and we were guided in this by what we would say about them. But all of us, so to speak, were adopting the observer perspective.

In the second presentation, the perspective was firmly from the inside. Arnold was asked not what Arnold would judge, nor what we would judge, but what *you* – undergoing, as you will be, the relevant transformations – would experience and think. This is a perspective simply not available, to say the least, to physical objects like towers. From this perspective the outcome of the identity experiment looks quite different, but the details of this matter less than the mere fact that there is this perspective.

As noted above, the wait-and-see strategy tries to stay above the conflict of imagined intuitions in puzzle cases, and this puts it in some tension with both sides of the debate. But the crucial thing to notice here is that the strategy itself is not perspectivally neutral. In allowing that the puzzle cases are undecided, and could come out one way or the other, depending on what we will be prepared to say, it firmly adopts the stance of an observer. But this lack of neutrality has a devastating consequence for the inner perspective. The wait-and-see strategy is not merely in conflict with the verdict reached from the first-person perspective, it makes it impossible to understand how there could be such a perspective in the first place.

One way to see this is by working the other way around, by asking how the wait-and-see strategy might look from the inner perspective. Remember that the question here is not whether, starting from the inside, we would agree with that strategy; we have already seen that we would not. Instead, the question is whether one could so much as make sense of it. What you would have to do to get hold of the Strawsonian strategy is to think something like this:

> I have been told that I will suffer pain, and I am now fearful about this. But I am also told that I will have to wait until the experiment takes place for it to be decided whether it is me that suffers the pain.

But this is simply incoherent: you are told that you will in fact suffer pain but that it might not be you who suffers pain. (It would, of course, be coherent if you were told simply that it was undecided whether it is you who will suffer the pain. But, from the inside, being told just this would conjure up a completely different situation.) Nor is this an incoherence that could be patched up by reformulation. So long as you are looking at it from the first-person point of view, there is no way that you can at the same time make sense of the observer as speaking to someone who may turn out not to be you.

Returning to the original way around discussed above, this suggests that there is no way that one can make sense of the inside point of view from the perspective of an observer. To repeat, this is not because from outside one comes to a different verdict, 'it is undecided whether it is Arnold' instead of 'it is definitely Arnold'. Rather it is that, from the outside, there is no way to so much as understand an inner perspective that would be tempted by this definite verdict. Look at it this way: given that the observer adopts a wait-and-see attitude towards identity, what could he be thinking of when he tells Arnold, 'you will be subjected to pain'? The best he could do here might be,

'I hereby tell the person in front of me now [i.e. you] that if that person is still around, he will be subjected to pain,' but notice how the 'you' is forced to give way to 'that person' and 'he'.

What is so Special about Identity?

Our conception of persons as human beings – members of a certain biological species – endowed with certain experiences and thoughts serves us well enough for most of the identity issues we actually face. When our imagination throws up puzzling cases, there is a temptation to say that we just don't yet know what to say about identity. But we have seen that there is something deeply unsatisfactory about the idea that we can turn our puzzlement into policy; that we can simply let identity turn on what we would be prepared to say if we actually encountered one of these puzzling cases. This might tempt one to a more radical approach. Perhaps we can avoid the puzzle by revising our conception of persons so that it simply doesn't allow questions about identity to be raised, either in actual or imagined cases.

How might this work? First, think of the way rope is often made: many fibre strands, each one only inches long, are woven together to produce a length of rope many feet long. The strength (and unity) in the length of rope come not from there being single strands running its full length – for there are none – but from the fact that the frictional connection of the overlapping bundles of short strands prevents the rope from parting. Next, instead of strands of fibre, think of our conscious states and, in particular, memories. Each one extends only some way back, but because of the overlap of connected bundles, they appear to constitute a single personality starting at birth and ending with death.

More particularly, suppose that Arnold, the person, comes to be seen as wholly constituted by those memories that *at a given time* are in appropriate contact with one another, those that form, so to speak, a bundle. Since these memories will almost certainly not reach back all that many years, and since as time goes by new memories are added and old ones drop off, it will not make sense to speak of one and the same person, Arnold, underlying the whole of a biological history. This would be like imagining that the rope had at least a single strand running its whole length. But the succession of overlaps between the bundles of connected memories do generate the appearance of an identity, just as they suggest some single strand in the rope.

If we take the metaphor of the rope seriously, it will encourage a radically different way of thinking about persons and their continuity. Instead of seeing ourselves as single continuants of which it makes sense to demand criteria of re-identification, we will think of survival or continuity in terms of the degree of overlap between what are actually successive persons. Identity being an all-or-nothing notion is simply dropped in favour of this graded overlap.

The idea that each of us is really a nest of overlapping persons is likely to strike you as too radical, and as having too many counter-intuitive consequences. Think about something as straightforward as promising. Imagine that I borrowed some large sum of money from you, promising to pay it back in ten years. The ten years are up, and I insist that I no longer owe it you. What would be your reaction if, when you demanded an explanation, I said: 'It wasn't me who promised; it was a previous self'? Unless you have a very good sense of humour, it is not likely to be printable.

Perhaps this last paragraph is a bit unfair. In the actual world, there is sufficient connectedness in the memories of most human beings to prevent our taking seriously this kind of debt avoidance. And when there is real dislocation in the flow of mental life – as in Alzheimer's disease or in other clinical mental disorders – we might well consider some such defence. In any case, the plurality of persons view need not be aimed at reforming our present practices. We should see it as primarily designed to guide us in those cases that have so far proved intractable, cases like those of 'body-switching' and brain-content transfer. And its message here is clear enough: do not take seriously the idea of a single continuant which either is, or is not, re-identifiable. Think instead about a kind of fanning out of persons who are more or less similar, something we come across only in extreme cases in everyday life. If Arnold had adopted some such view then his question would not have been: will there be anyone identical to me around after the experiment, but will anyone similar enough to me survive? And if he had asked this second question, he would have found it easier to remain calm, since the answer, according to the plurality view, would almost certainly have been 'yes'.

Unfortunately, even if we let the view off the hook as far as practicalities are concerned, there is a problem, and it comes right at the beginning. Whilst it is easy to be swept along by metaphors, and by the promise of getting around the problems of personal identity, it is very difficult to make sense of the psychological 'strands' that are used to construct persons.

Think of any single psychological strand in the plurality conception; think of some memory. As a memory of, say some event, it will have a person as its subject. It is not that there is a memory of eating dinner yesterday, it is that *I* remember eating dinner yesterday. Now if the 'I' here is a person in the everyday sense we have considered, it will be useless to use this kind of memory as a basis for the nest-like conception of persons. For the everyday sense is precisely one for which all-or-nothing re-identification is presupposed. So, how does one coherently think of memory as the memory of a person, when that person might very well not be the one who had the original experience? What is needed is some notion of remembering an event which, like ordinary memory, has an intimate first-personal character, but which, unlike ordinary memory, does not explicitly represent the person who took part in the event. This latter requirement is necessary because only identity-neutral memories could serve as materials from which to construct persons. Anything short of this – any representation of the self in the memory – would disqualify the memory as a building block in the construction.

Though I won't pursue the point in all its detail here, there would seem to be good reason to think that the demand for this kind of memory is bound to go unfulfilled. This is because it is simply incoherent; there could not be a memory that was first-personal in the way necessary to make it a memory of some event, but which was identity-neutral in that it contained no representation of the subject of that event.

Conclusion

We have a notion of personhood which is central to our conception of the mind and to the explanation of action, but there is at least prima facie reason to wonder about the coherence of this notion. The few suggestions so far canvassed for dealing with the threat of incoherence seem to me inconclusive, but there does not seem any immediate reason to worry. It is certainly possible that I have been too quick to dismiss one or other option, and, in any case, the problems raised are more philosophical than practical, since we manage somehow to do the re-identification in daily life without much struggle. Many will find this simply a further reason to dismiss philosophical speculation as hopelessly out of touch. But this seems to me to be the wrong reaction. If there is genuinely some incoherence in our concepts, then in some way or other they are going to let us down in a quite practical way. So, whilst we can sleep peacefully, knowing for the time being that we will be correctly re-identified by our friends tomorrow, we had better take the threat seriously, either by considering changes to our concept of a person, or showing the incoherence to be somehow unreal.

Notes and References

1   Lewis, 'Reduction in Mind' in S. Guttenplan (ed.), *A Companion to the Philosophy of Mind* (Oxford: 1994), p. 416. The earlier view was prominent in essays in Lewis, *Philosophical Papers*, Blackwell, vol. 1 (Oxford University Press, 1983).

2   M. Davies and T. Stone (eds), *Mental Simulation* (Oxford: Blackwell, 1995), p. 1.

3   Ibid., p. 2.

4   The example occurs in 'The Self and the Future' in his collection *Problems of Self* (Cambridge University Press, 1973), pp. 46–63.

5   Many of the most obvious quibbles are raised and dealt with by Williams in *Problems of Self* on pp. 53f.

6   Williams makes an interesting point about the way the cases pit the two aspects of our conception of persons against one another. Looking at it from 'outside', the third-person perspective in the first story, we ended up thinking that the mental landscape takes precedence and that bodies are switched. But looking at it from 'inside', thinking of Arnold as me, suggests that the bodily aspect is not so easily dismissed. This surprising fact will be revisited in the next chapter.

7   P. F. Strawson, *Individuals: An Essay in Descriptive Metaphysics* (London: Methuen, 1959), p. 103.

8   Ibid., p. 133.

9   A more famous version of this sort of puzzle occurs in Thomas Hobbes' *De Corpore*. See vol. 1, p. 136 of *The English Works of Thomas Hobbes*, ed. W. Molesworth (London: Bohn, 1839–45).

4

The Marks of the Mental

The previous two chapters revealed something of what lies under the mental landscape, and in each case we found that matters were far from simple. The straightforward questions posed to each of experiencing, attitudinizing, acting, folk psychological explanation and personal identity did not return straightforward answers, and in each case the problems were different. But underlying these differences are certain commonalties and connections which it is the aim of this chapter to describe.

Up to now, what has linked the various features of the mind has been little more than the fact that each is true of persons. But this does not get to the heart of the matter; it does not give us any idea of *why* experiences, attitudes and actions are characteristic of persons. Nor does it even begin to explain why the identity of persons, and the explication of their actions, seem so different from questions about identity and explanation in other spheres. In the remarks which follow, some tentative steps will be taken to make up these deficiencies. What will emerge is some sense of a deeper unity in the mental landscape, and only with this as background will we be in a proper position to embark on part III.

To get the discussion started, I shall briefly survey each of the five problematic features, offering some hints as to what might underlie the problems in each case. After this survey, we will be in a better position both to appreciate the connections between the problems, and to begin in some small way to understand the thematic unity mentioned above.

(a) Attitudes

An attitude like belief or desire seems clearly enough a way of describing someone. As in our original example, to say that Anne believes that her coat is in the hallway cupboard is to say something true about her, and to do so by relating Anne to . . . well, that is the first problem we encountered. Exactly what kind of thing is it that is Anne believes? 'Believe' is a verb whose grammatical form is not unlike 'own' or 'touch', and as such it demands both a subject and an object. However, we don't get into any special trouble with the latter verbs: people own houses, cars, etc. and they can touch anything within reach. In these cases, the objects of the verbs are just objects, spatiotemporal items that we can keep track of straightforwardly.

In the case of belief and the other attitudes, however, the object is a more complicated grammatical structure: it is a sentence (which may or may not be preceded by 'that'). This makes the verbs of attitude more difficult to understand, and it pushes us to say, for example, that the objects of attitudes are states of affairs, ways the world is or might be, sentences themselves, or something called 'propositions'. None of these is without drawbacks, but deciding the nature of attitude objects was only the beginning of the real trouble. For whatever we come to say about attitude objects, we do want to see the attitudes themselves as describing stances towards the world adopted by a subject, as somehow relating a subject to the world. The precise nature of attitude objects might be left as a technical issue, but the underlying relationship between the subject and world described by attitude attributions is of crucial importance.

This feature of the attitudes – their directionality – was called into serious question by the examples of Monique in London and Richard in Paris. In each case, the circumstances described left us unsure how to ascribe beliefs correctly. Moreover, this was not merely because we lacked evidence; it was instead a matter of having, in a sense, too much evidence; of having good grounds for each of two incompatible attributions.

As described in chapter 2, these examples showed that the attitudes allow for a puzzling slack between a subject and the world towards which he or she has the relevant attitude. In some cases, two incompatible beliefs seem to hold of one and the same reality (Monique's predicament), whilst in other cases, a single belief seems not to distinguish between two different realities (Richard's predicament). It is as if our attitudes towards things answer only partly towards the things themselves, and partly to something else. And this contrasts sharply with more straightforward types of relationship such as ownership.

Let me spell this out in more concrete detail. On her first visit to London, and whilst sitting in the tourist bus, Monique was in direct causal contact with the British Museum. To be brutally specific about this, light reflected from the British Museum impinged on Monique's eyes, and, had the bus stopped, she could have touched the building. Having as she did, a perfectly determinate notion of the British Museum as a large public building in this part of London, everything points to our connecting Monique to the Museum by attributing to her a belief about it. Yet, the circumstances of her second encounter with the Museum called this connection into question. For when she walked by the Museum on the way to her meeting – and even though she was then in no less direct causal contact with it than on the first occasion – she formed the opinion that the building she was seeing was not in fact the British Museum.

To remind you, the problem here is not how such a thing could happen; the ease with which this case, and many like it, can be described suggests that confusions of this sort are common. Rather, what is problematic is that cases like Monique's make it difficult to think of belief relations – or any other attitudinal relation – as direct or immediate connections between a person and some feature of the world. Our attribution of attitude seems to depend on something other than the obvious connectedness of person and object that we find in Monique's encounters with the British Museum.

The first step in uncovering this further factor requires that we recognize that attitudinal relations in general are not attributed one by one. In deciding whether Monique is standing outside the British Museum, all we have to do is to identify both her and the Museum, and agree on what counts as 'standing outside'. This latter notion is of course vague, but that presents no insuperable obstacle. The main thing is that, in order to ascribe the 'standing outside' relation to Monique and the British Museum, we do not have to look beyond the situation itself. However, we have no hope at all of deciding what Monique believes about the British Museum merely by marshalling what might be called 'local' materials. And this is a general truth about the attitudes, and not simply a feature of the problem cases.

The most common way of learning what someone believes is by listening to what she says. But, of course, this works only if you have attributed – even if tacitly – a network of further beliefs and other attitudes to the speaker. If someone at Paddington station utters the words, 'the train for Oxford leaves from platform 2,' you can only attribute to him the belief that it does if you have already attributed many beliefs about English words, trains, stations, places and the like, as well, of course, as the desire to speak truthfully. Nor is this true only in cases where language plays a role in attribution. Seeing someone inserting a coin in a machine can only be taken as evidence of a desire to drink if you are also prepared to attribute a large number of beliefs (such as that it is a drinks machine, that it is working, that it accepts certain coins ...) and further attitudes (such as a willingness to give up the money in exchange for the drink). Moreover, it would require only a very little ingenuity to extend the range of these background attitudes, even in everyday cases, so as to include a great deal of what the protagonist believes about life, death and the fate of the universe, as well as his hopes, fears and other aspirations. The background network of attitudes that might be called on to support the attribution of even a single belief or desire seems to have no obvious limits.

Note that the point about attitudes coming in clusters does not by itself serve to distinguish attitude relations from many others. The fact that I am standing at the corner of Montague Place and Gower Street is a perfectly ordinary way to characterize a relation between me and a place. However, in order to make usable sense of this relation, I have to know where in a network of other locations this one figures. And this network – typically encoded on a map – is in effect a cluster of background facts implied by any single claim about my location.

The real importance of the point about attitude clusters does not lie in the mere fact of their clustering – something that is shared by many relational claims – so much as in what lies behind the clustering. To understand this, think again about the spatial case. When we use a map, we appeal to a background cluster of spatial facts in order to tell where we are, and this works because the relations among all the points shown on the map serve to fix each of them. But in the attitudinal case, what is at issue is not merely something like a point fixed by its relation to others so much as what it is natural to call a 'point of view'. And though we certainly characterize someone's point of view by attributing clusters of attitudes, there are constraints on these attributions arising from the notion of a point of view that have no analogue in the spatial case.

In the circumstances described in chapter 2, there was reason to attribute to Monique both the belief that a certain building was the British Museum and the belief that it wasn't. Yet we hesitated to include both of these in the cluster of attitudes that otherwise characterize Monique's point of view or perspective. The reason for this hesitation had nothing to do with our doubting the grounds for each attribution. Rather, it was because there is something about the very idea of a point of view that precludes the attribution of contradictory beliefs. Or, since that is a little too strong, there was nothing in Monique's circumstances – nothing in the background attitudes whose attribution we would have found plausible – to justify our seeing her as believing each of two contradictory things.

The kind of case in which we might be genuinely tempted to make a contradictory attribution usually, and unsurprisingly, requires us to see the subject as conflicted in some way. For example, M might seem both to believe that a lover is faithful and yet to give more than a little hint of believing the opposite. Imagine a case in which there is unmistakable evidence of infidelity, and it is clearly grasped by M. Those who know M have no doubt whatever about her belief in the unfaithfulness of her lover. However, it is also true that M cannot face the possibility of a break-up in the relationship, and hence has a strong motive for disregarding the palpable evidence of infidelity. The cluster of attitudes that go with a belief in infidelity are all present, but so is a strong desire to believe otherwise. And in some way or other, the latter produces behaviour suggesting that M does not believe the lover is unfaithful. Again, those who know M, convinced as they were that she more than suspects the unfaithfulness, find her behaviour puzzling, since it points clearly to M's not having any such suspicion.

In such cases – usually described as cases of self-deception – we might be willing to suspend the idea that points of view rule out the possession of contradictory beliefs. Perhaps when the general cluster of attitudes is as described for M – beliefs leaning one way, desires and fears leaning another – the best description will actually involve some kind of incoherence in belief. But this is certainly not the way it is with Monique and the British Museum. She is completely unconflicted in respect of the building, and thus has no motive for having these particular contradictory beliefs. Nor, as a fuller list of her background attitudes would show, is she intellectually challenged, illogical, or suffering any delusion.

Ruling out the too easy attribution of contradictory beliefs is only one of the ways in which the notion of a point of view constrains our attributions; other more subtle ways figure no less importantly. Though difficult, if not impossible, to spell out, they are familiar enough. A point of view requires paying attention to what is happening in the immediate vicinity, and forming beliefs about it, but not so much attention as to take up valuable, desire-satisfying time. It also requires bringing to these encounters a stock of organizing and categorizing attitudes. These attitudes – beliefs being the most salient – are then constitutive of the concepts displayed in a point of view. Finally, we associate with a point of view both ephemeral and settled aspirations and desires, the contents of which vary, but not without limit.

Having a point of view is not then just a matter of having clusters of beliefs, desires and other attitudes. Rather, it is having attitudes that fit with one another in certain unspecified but none the less intelligible ways. Belonging to the class of things which adopt points of view is like belonging to a club with certain rules; not just anyone or anything qualifies. For example, members must not believe contradictions without some good reason; they may not believe certain things without first having acquired the appropriate background of conceptual beliefs; they must desire only those things that are believed, from the relevant perspective, to be desirable; and, crucially, their attitudes must give expression to the possession of a coherent set of concepts.

The need to see attitudes as clustering around specific points of view, and conforming to the rules that go with them, is the key to understanding the slack we located in Monique's and Richard's beliefs. In the situations described, certain facts about Monique's (and Richard's) contact with the relevant building (and brasserie) encourage one kind of attribution. But the need to find in each of them a coherent point of view seems to undermine our first attempt at attribution. The very idea of a point of view imposes on us, not merely the need to attribute attitudes in clusters, but to attribute them according to certain rules or norms.

On first coming across them, many find it difficult to take the problem cases very seriously. Requiring special circumstances which are often improbable – even if possible – it is easy to miss their fundamental importance. For cases like those of Monique and Richard are symptomatic of a deep tension in our conception of the attitudes generally. On the one hand, attributing attitudes seems to be part of a descriptive practice; we use them to record often vital information about certain (admittedly special) objects in the world. On the other hand, as I have been suggesting, attitude attribution is also normative. Saying that Monique has this or that belief is not merely describing her, it is suggesting that something about what she does and says meets certain norms or standards. What we are doing is *crediting* her with a belief.

What the problem cases show is something that we might have realized even without them, that descriptive and normative practices that often function together can nevertheless be in tension. Here is a simple example – one not directly involving attitude attribution – which illustrates the contrast. Imagine someone describing a certain animal as both feline and dangerous. Both of these predicates might seem innocently descriptive, but there is a special problem about the second. It is obvious that judgements about what is dangerous vary from person to person, and probably would not extend to creatures without our particular set of frailties. Yet for all this, we do not think that a judgement about dangerousness is mere subjective whim, and this is because there are certain norms in place in the background conditions for the application of this predicate. The spot on the wall might be said to be dangerous by a frightened arachnophobe, but of course it isn't dangerous; it doesn't *merit* this predicate. To be sure, we can say that an object 'merits' the predicate 'feline', but this is merely a way of saying that the animal has the properties that make something feline. With 'dangerous' it is different: the application of the predicate depends on more than the properties of an object, it depends upon our judgement as to whether these properties rationally justify fear. And in speaking of rational justification, we are in effect speaking of norms guiding the attribution of the predicate.[1]

The notion of rationality figures as well in the attitude case, though it can lead to misunderstanding. In the literature you will comes across claims about the 'constraints of rationality' and, given that the most common example of these constraints is the one counselling against the attribution of contradictory beliefs, it is easy to think that 'rationality' here stands for some high standard of logical acumen. But this would be wrong. This talk of rationality is merely another way of making the point that a cluster of attitudes must have a certain shape in order to constitute a point of view. But this is in no way intended to rule out the possibility of irrational points of view; as used in the present context, 'rational' should be contrasted with 'non-rational' and not with 'irrational'. Holding what seem to be contradictory beliefs, the self-deceiver may well be irrational, but, as our interest in these cases shows, we do not think that the self-deceiver is simply disqualified from having any point of view at all.

(b) Experiencing

Attributing attitudes can seem simply a way of describing people by relating them to the world of objects and properties, and it takes some effort to see that this is far from the whole story. That is, it takes some effort to appreciate that attribution depends crucially on the notion of a point of view which normatively controls the practice. With experience or consciousness, the problem is quite the opposite. The identification of something that is recognizably 'inner' sits easily with our idea of experience. It takes little more than a couple of examples – cases like that of Simone and the colour blue, or Harry and his pain – to turn most of us into Cartesians. The really hard work comes in seeing that the 'innerness' of consciousness cannot be the whole story.

In chapter 2, the notion that was pivotal in getting us to recognize an outerness to experience was the notion of knowledge. Lots of things figure in our idea of knowledge, but one proved especially useful – the intuition that if we know something, then we ought to be able to communicate what we know. (When my nephew was four, and envious of the praise his older sister received for being able to read, he said that he knew what the printed words said, but that 'it just never shows.' Much to his dismay at the time, we just don't think that knowledge could be like that.)

As you might expect, it is easier to discuss consciousness by thinking about one's own case. So, leaving Simone and Harry behind, think of yourself and of your present conscious states. Sitting (as I will presume) and reading this book, you are aware of a certain pressure on your body, aware of the feeling of the book in your hand, aware of the print on the page, and also almost certainly aware of the ambient sounds in the room. These items of experience, among many others, figure in what is called your 'stream of consciousness'. Carrying this metaphor a little further, we might say that a stream of consciousness is like a real stream: we can imagine sitting by and noting the things that bob past, though, unlike a real stream, you are the only witness of what transpires. It is therefore not surprising that you will regard the contents of the stream of consciousness as private and inner.

That the contents of experience are inner and private is by itself unproblematic; the contents of your bedside table could well be described in the same terms. Of course, the parallel here would be regarded as hopelessly misguided. Nothing, except perhaps the possibility of embarrassment, stops us from displaying our most intimate possessions to the world at large; but with the contents of consciousness, such display would seem simply out of the question. Focusing on your own experience, it is easy to convince yourself that you are somehow witnessing something that no one else *could*.

It is here that the clash between Cartesian intuitions and the intuition about knowledge surfaces. Witnessing something generally results in knowing about it, and knowing suggests at least the possibility of communicating this knowledge to others. But if you witness something bobbing about in your stream of consciousness, knowledge seems a possibility, but communicating what you come to know does not. We seem here to have a straightforward conflict between the intuition that consciousness is inner and ineffably private, and the intuition that knowledge is communicable.

In chapter 2, we considered various ways of dealing with this conflict. One strategy was to challenge, in one way or other, the intuition about knowledge, or at least its relevance to the case at hand. Claims made in pursuit of this strategy included: knowledge of our conscious states is special and not subject to the communicability intuition; we can communicate our innermost experiences, but in some attenuated way, perhaps by using metaphors or some special, invented vocabulary; we don't really have knowledge of our conscious experiences, so there is no problem about communication; the kind of knowledge we have is of a completely different sort from that which figures in the communicability intuition.

This is not the place to repeat the objections raised against each of these moves, and it must be admitted that these objections only scratch the surface. Any more complete evaluation would have led us into some of the toughest terrain in philosophy, a journey inappropriate for this book. However, having admitted that this first strategy is not quite a dead-end, the case against it does at least justify a more careful look at the second. Here the idea is not to challenge the intuition about knowledge, but instead the intuition about conscious experience. In effect, this second strategy asks us to think again about the model of consciousness that comes to us so easily.

The negative part of this suggestion is that we must give up on the idea that consciousness – to shift to another prominent metaphor – is a stage on which the actors play out ineffably private roles before an audience of one. More positively, we must allow that even that most private of realms, our inner life, has an outer aspect. Taken in the right way, this outer aspect of experience is not merely some effect – some behavioural 'coming out' – of secret untransferable happenings in the theatre of experience. It is rather in some way constitutive of our conception of experience that it have this outer aspect. In what way? This is no easy question to answer.

Philosophers have for a long time said things which bear on it, for example, that the language we inevitably use to describe many so-called private experiences – especially perceptual ones – is anything but 'inner'. (Simone's claim that she came to know what blue was like is, after all, a claim about a publicly observable colour; and how can you characterize your sense of what it is like to be reading this book, except in terms which mention the reading of the book?) Further, they have noted that our conception of experience is incoherent without some 'outer' aspect. It would be impossible for each of us to so much as refer to the inner realm with any hope of being understood by anyone else, unless there was some accessible commonalty to our conscious lives; and any such commonalty would inevitably call on some outer aspect of experience. The very fact that I can write so confidently not only about my experience, but about yours, suggests that the model of a private stage and audience is misguided.

Whilst I think that this second strategy is the better one, I do not want to give you the impression that it is all plain sailing. As noted above, the difficult thing to appreciate about experience is that it has some kind of constitutive outer aspect in the first place. But once you have managed this, it is no less difficult to keep both the outer and the inner aspects in focus at the same time. There is an inevitable tendency to move from recognizing the outer aspect to letting it completely dominate our understanding of experience. This is the mistake of the view known as behaviourism (which will be discussed in a little more detail in the next chapter). And it is a mistake not confined to behaviourism.

(c) Acting

In the ordinary case of a simple physical action – say, reaching for a cup – we seem to have something whose credentials as a happening or event are impeccable. The hand's movement towards the cup, the contact with the handle, these are no less features of the world than the river's scouring of the bank or the movement of a tree branch in the wind. Yet, as we saw, things are not that simple, even in the simplest of cases. For whilst the movement of the hand towards the cup is an event just like any other, this movement is not itself the action of reaching for the cup. The lightly sketched argument described in chapter 2 suggested that actions were somehow not completely visible from the purely *objective* spatiotemporal perspective we normally adopt in respect of events. *Movements* are of course available from this perspective, but *movings* – acts of moving – are not.

That acting is in part only visible from a certain perspective is even more obvious when we consider the huge class of cases pretty much ignored in chapter 2, namely those actions which have no obvious physical upshot. You cannot reach for a cup without some movement of the body, but you can certainly imagine, decide, deliberate, experience, adopt an attitude and do all manner of other 'mental' acts without these requiring any specific movement of your body. The very idea of activity that may or may not have characteristic expression in the physical or objective world is something that seems inexorably tied to the idea of a subject or person ('agent' being perhaps the better word here). Reaching for a cup or deliberating about this evening are not things which merely happen – things located in the objective spatiotemporal order. They are undertaken by subjects or agents, and it is therefore reasonable to count them as in this sense *subjective*.

The argument which led us to identify these two aspects of action – the subjective and the objective – turned on a number of apparently straightforward intuitions. First, we set out to locate the class of actions within the larger class of events; and second, we applied the lessons thereby learned to the task of locating actions in the temporal order. This second stage involved some detailed manoeuvres, but the general shape of the argument wasn't complicated. Noting that the temporal location of an action (e.g. a killing) need not depend on the temporal location of events which are mere consequences of it (e.g. a death), we applied this to 'simpler' actions such as moving a bowl or raising an arm. The rather startling conclusion that emerged was that there seems no way to locate these simpler or 'basic' actions in the temporal order.

Of course, we can say that they take place in some not wholly determinate stretch of time, and this might satisfy those who would regard any demand for precision here as misguided in the first place. But there is something peculiar about the way in which basic actions resist temporal assignment. It is not usually required, or desirable, to work out to the millisecond when some everyday event takes place. Yet, though there doesn't seem to be any single generalizable reason for lack of precision, the fact of indeterminacy is intelligible. Thus, we wouldn't expect to be able to time, to several decimal places, a cup's striking the floor, because different cup-related molecules will hit the ground at different times. And for different reasons in each case, we wouldn't expect the passage of a thunderstorm or someone's death to be events we could time with a stopwatch. However, our problem with the timing of an action shares nothing with these ordinary cases of everyday indeterminacy. With the latter, what we know about each specific event is enough to justify indeterminacy and to help us appreciate its limits. When it comes to basic actions, however, we don't know enough even to see why they are only indeterminately locatable in the temporal order.

When I aim to move the cup by pushing it across the table, I first set myself to be active, and then I find that I am − I find that the cup is moving in virtue of my activity. Yet, even though the outlines of this are clear enough, there seems to be no event whose features would explain any temporal indeterminacy. Given that the mere movement of the cup is not itself an action, my setting myself to act − what is sometimes called an exercise of my will − is the most likely candidate. But, unlike the cup-falling or the thunderstorm, an act of will is not something we can take apart; it doesn't involve molecules or part-events to which we can appeal in showing why precise time-keeping is inappropriate. It is as if the activeness of an action − the feature in virtue of which an event is an action − just drops out of the temporal order.

But even allowing that actions are in this way elusive, one must remember that this is only part of the story. There could be no cup-pushing if there was no cup-movement; saying that actions have a subjective aspect is not the same as saying that they have *only* a subjective aspect. At least for physical actions, a spatiotemporally ordered objective world, and its constituent events, form a necessary framework for our activity. And, though there is no space to argue this here, this same objective framework plays no less a role in respect even of 'inner' or 'mental' actions such as deciding and inferring.[2]

(d) Folk Psychological Explanation

We describe people using notions like experience, attitude and action, and such description lends itself to explanations of what people do and think. The framework of concepts that make up folk psychology is explanatory as well as descriptive. However, as was discussed at some length in chapter 3, it is far from clear how to understand the notion of explanation that figures in folk psychology. One deep-seated intuition we have about explanation is that it consists in our seeing events, processes or actions as embedded in appropriate networks of regularities. This regularity conception of explanation is the one that has served us well in scientific contexts, and many feel that it is applicable to the folk with only slight modifications.

However, there seems to be another form of explanatoriness – one grounded on the very nature of the folk – which seems to be in some competition with the regularity conception. Here the idea is that one explains some human action, not by fitting it into a network of regularities, but by somehow sharing the point of view from which the action seems reasonable. This second notion of explanation presupposes that there is something special about the way that reasons explain. In particular, unlike scientific explanation, reason-based explanation can only be deployed by someone who is herself a person with a mental life. For this reason, it seems appropriate to distinguish the regularity conception of explanation from the reason-based sort by calling the first 'impersonal' and second 'personal'.

One has to be careful about the idea that these two sorts of explanation are in competition. It is certainly true that there is currently an active debate about the relative merits of the Theory Theory and the Simulation Theory, an outline of which was given in chapter 3. What has been central to this debate is the question of whether folk psychology employs one or the other pattern of explanation, and whether in fact the two are more than stylistic variants of one another. Indeed, many are now tempted by the idea that personal-level explanation is after all merely a way in which some form of the Theory Theory happens, for various practical reasons, to be deployed by the folk. However, too often lost amidst the flurry of argument is the fact that impersonal explanation itself is dependent on the personal level; the regularity (or causal) conception of explanatoriness is, after all, a *conception*. So, whilst the debate is important, it could never end up showing that what I have called impersonal explanation is only impersonal; that it owed nothing to the level of persons and their mental landscapes. For, at bottom, explanation itself exhibits a duality: not exactly a duality of normative/descriptive, objective/subjective or inner/outer, but a duality none the less.

(e)   Personal Identity
Our discussion of this issue revealed a stark divide between what we might call a *first-person* conception of our own identity and a *third-person* one. In the special circumstances of the example described in chapter 3 – circumstances which certainly seem to be coherently imaginable – different verdicts are returned, depending upon which conception is adopted. Hearing of the circumstances, and relying on one conception to think about their own futures, Arnold and Benedict came to the conclusion that the experiment would result

in their changing bodies. This, of course, led each of them to think favourably about certain future eventualities – for instance, that the Arnold-person (i.e. the person in Benedict's body) would win the prize – and with dread about the possibility of pain inflicted on that same body. However, when the same experimental circumstances were conceived of differently, the result was very different. For example, we elicited from Arnold, not the relatively sanguine idea that he would soon inhabit Benedict's body, but merely fear for his future.

The puzzles about personal identity differ sharply from similar puzzles about the identity of physical objects; it does not seem appropriate to think of resolving personal identity puzzles by making some kind of *decision* about how to settle the issue, whereas this seems fine for the case of physical objects. We do not now face questions like those raised by the experiment, but it seems wrong somehow to say: 'if and when the circumstances arise, we will just have to decide whether the case involves body-swapping or not; we will just have to adapt our concepts to these future possibilities.' What seems initially wrong with this response is that, thinking about the matter in the first person, we do not think that the very possibility of our own survival could be a matter of decision or convention. But, on reflection, an even better way of putting it is this: thinking that our identities could be a matter for decision is tantamount to thinking of the whole problem in a third-person way. And this unreasonably just rules out any first-person conception.

An interesting further feature of the example of Arnold and Benedict – one emphasized by Williams – is that the body-swapping verdict is one reached by asking both participants about the future course of their memories and other psychological states. In a way, this is asking them about each of their inner perspectives, albeit from a perspective that asks them to consider the matter from the outside. In contrast, the other verdict – the one disinclined to see the result as survival in a different body – is taken from a first-personal perspective, but it seems to deny the importance of continuity of memory and other psychological states. No amount of assurance about what the Benedict body will claim to remember, feel or say is enough to remove the dread with which Arnold anticipates the experiment.

What this suggests is that the ideas we have about the role of our mental states in our continuing identity – states which are paradigmatically 'inner' – does not really keep step with the perspective from which we view these states. Asked about the inner from the outside, Arnold and Benedict were quite happy to rely on it in their assessment of the situation, but asked about the inner from the inside, they seemed unwilling to rely on what looks like a continuity in mental life.

The fact that the inner/outer dichotomy characteristic of experience does not capture what is at issue in the re-identification of persons lies behind my preference for speaking of 'first'- and 'third-person' conceptions. But this is not to say that two dichotomies are completely different. Not unreasonably, philosophers tend to speak of experiences like suffering pain as 'first-personal', and our assessments of injuries that cause pain as 'third-personal'. There is also a tendency to connect the first person with the subjective and the third person with the objective. (That is why it struck Williams as odd that a first-personal approach should lend support to a criterion of person re-identification centred around the body. Bodies are typically supposed to be outer, objective and third-personal.)

Connections amongst the various dichotomies will figure prominently in the later sections of this chapter, but the slippage between the inner and the first-personal should serve as a warning. We should not think that these connections can be made by simply assuming that each pair of labels is appropriate to all the cases.

Duality and Unity

The above review leaves us with some intriguing dichotomies:

> The attitudes answer to *normative* considerations in so far as they express points of view, but attitude attributions are also *descriptive*.

> Our conscious experiences are undeniably *inner*, though a reference to something *outer* seems required in any coherent conception of experience.

> Actions seem to be events in the *objective* order, but, in distinguishing them from other events, we end up recognizing an aspect that is *subjective*.

> A kind of explanation that seems intuitively satisfying to the folk calls on *impersonal* regularities and causes. Yet, when it comes to explaining our own behaviour, only facts at a *personal* level seem adequate.

> Verdicts about the identity of persons which are based on *first-person* criteria do not always cohere with verdicts made from a *third-person* perspective.

What is particularly intriguing about them is that, despite their different origins, they seem to fit with one another. Normativity, innerness, subjectivity, the first-person and explanation at the personal level, and the contrast of these with the descriptive, outer, objective, the third-person and impersonal explanation, suggest some more basic duality which distinguishes and unifies the mental realm. But here one must proceed with caution.

As I have noted, the dichotomies are not the same, so any kind of unification will need further argument. Whilst it is true that experiences are not only inner but also first-personal and subjective, these three notions are different. Though experiences strike us as inner, we can talk about them in a third- as well as a first-person way, and it is not the mere fact of their innerness that makes them subjective. With normativity and explanation at the personal level, the connections to the other dichotomies are even less clear. Why should it be true that the innerness of experience goes with the normative demands of attitude attribution? Couldn't one imagine attributing attitudes to a creature – and doing so in a way that respected normative constraints – even though that creature had no inner life? And what is the argument that could connect consciousness with the personal, as opposed to impersonal, style of explanation?

Though offered in a merely tentative way, it seems to me that the key to answering some of these questions, and to appreciating the unity of the mental landscape, lies in the notion of a point of view (or perspective). This notion was used to give some intuitive justification to the idea that the attitudes are normative, but it is more fundamental than even this suggests.

Points of View (Again)

Attitude attributions are not distinguished from other relational claims merely in virtue of their forming some kind of network. Knowing our location depends on our knowing, or at least there being, some network of spatial relations determining a place. Yet the place itself, as it were, makes no contribution: it is merely a node in the overall network. In contrast, perspectives are not passive with respect to the networks or clusters of attitudes which help to define them. Instead, the very idea of a perspective imposes constraints on what counts as allowable in the network. And this is why relational judgements about what someone believes, desires, hopes, fears, regrets, etc. are normative as well as descriptive.

The notion of a perspective thus plays an important role in our understanding of the attitudes in general, and specific networks of attitudes help us to define perspectives in particular. Yet this is only part of the story. To be the sort of thing that could impose specific constraints on attitude attribution, a perspective must be more complicated than has so far been suggested. For all that has been said, anything that bears certain rationally describable attitude-like relations to its environment would count as having a perspective, and this seems wrong. Though some philosophers have felt themselves forced to countenance the idea that 'mere' things, e.g. thermostats, might have beliefs and desires in virtue of their responding causally to an environment, this seems, if not absurd, then at least a good reason to look elsewhere for an account of attitudes. And what grounds this reaction surely has something to do with its being unacceptable to speak of a thermostat's 'point of view' or 'perspective' in anything other than a metaphorical sense. Yet if perspectives were just nodes in a network of attitudes, there would be nothing to prevent someone's regarding thermostats or computers, as well as the less complicated products of evolution, as having them.[3]

My suggestion is this: in order for an organism to have a perspective that is more than a mere node there must be something it is like to be that creature. The expression 'what it is like', as we noted in chapter 2, is highly idiomatic, even colloquial. But it is also one we seem to understand immediately, and it is often difficult, if not impossible, to think of another way of putting it. So perhaps the best thing to do, rather than complain about this rather 1960s idiom, is to do what we can to understand it better, and see whether it helps to flesh out the idea of a perspective.

What is it Like?

The expression 'what it is like' is of course tied to the interrogative: 'what is it like?' Indeed, one supposes that talk of 'what it is like' in the philosophy of mind comes from particular ways of asking and answering questions of this form. Bearing this in mind, the first thing to notice is that, as used in connection with the consciousness or experience, the question 'what is it like?' needs to be completed with some verb in the infinitive. Thus we do not ask: What is it like dream? What is it like pain? Instead, we ask: What it is like *to* dream? What is it like *to* suffer pain?

This might seem an obvious and pedantic point, but it will be important. The second thing to notice is that, whilst 'what is it like?' questions seem to require adjectival answers, the range of such answers is highly restricted. Thus, think of the kinds of thing that might be replied to each of the following:

What is it like to eat an unripe tomato?

What is it like to see an unripe tomato?

We might answer the first by saying 'it is unpleasant,' but not by saying that it is bitter or astringent; this is, of course, because the unripe tomato is bitter or astringent, and not the experience of tasting it. Similar remarks apply to the second question: saying what it is like to see an unripe tomato is likely to require an appeal to other experiences ('it is like seeing newly formed leaves in spring'), but it is just odd to answer the above question by saying 'green'.

These remarks echo the discussion of the Simone case in chapter 2, and the difficulties that we had in finding words and concepts adequate to deal with knowledge of our own experience. However, it is not my intention to re-open a discussion of the properties of experience, and the role of the concept of 'qualia' in that discussion. Rather, I should like to focus on the relationship between the 'what is it like?' questions described above – the ones that apply to this or that experience – and the slightly different one which opened our discussion, namely:

What is it like to be X (where X is some kind or individual creature)?

It might come as a surprise that I distinguish the two questions; they seem after all to be of the same form (and they are not usually distinguished in the literature). But appearances here can be deceptive. When I ask myself:

What is it like to be me?

my question involves a verb in the infinitive ('to be'), but this verb does not lend itself to the treatment we gave to the earlier form of question. Being me is not something that I *do*, and it is thus in contrast to dreaming, remembering, seeing, suffering, etc. which are certainly things that I do from time to time.

There is a further difference between the two sorts of question. As noted above, asking about seeing an unripe tomato invites adjectival answers of a restricted sort, namely those suitable to an activity. That is why it is so odd to think that an answer to such a question could be, for example, 'green'; tomatoes can be green, not the seeing of them. But asking, 'what is it like to be me?' is different. It invites answers such as:

(Think of prefacing each of the following with 'It is'.)

Getting depressed too easily,
Believing that right will eventually triumph,
Struggling against the desire to smoke,
Being too worried about the car breaking down,
Being convinced that something will turn up.

These are adjectival phrases, but they are more appropriate to a thing (in the grammatical, not the physical sense) than an action. Indeed, my suggestion is that they would fit points of view or perspectives better than anything else.

Recognizing that the two kind of question are different is important because we can then properly appreciate how they are related. In particular, answers to questions of the first sort can be seen as forming part of the overall answer we might give to the second. Thus, fully understanding what it is like to be me would require some idea of what it is like for me to dream, to see unripe tomatoes, to suffer pains, etc. Notice, however, these latter answers to the mental activity form of the question do not exhaust the answer to the first. There is more to knowing what it is like to be me than knowing what it is like for me to dream, see, suffer, etc. Amongst other things, knowing what it is like to be me would involve knowing what sorts of thing I believe and desire, and these do not lend themselves so easily to the activity form of the question. There may be something it is like to have an obsessive or enormously powerful desire, but, in comparison with seeing objects and suffering pain, there is nothing characteristic of what it is like (for me or anyone, I suspect) to believe that right will eventually triumph, or to desire a new car.

Answers to the activity form of the question are *part* of the overall answer to what I shall now call the 'perspectival' form, but they are not merely optional. Any organism of which it makes sense to ask what is it like to be that organism must have conscious experiences, experiences to which the activity question is appropriate. This might appear to be a strong claim needing lots of support, but since I think it follows from our understanding of the notion of a perspective, I do not regard it as risky (and it is important). Desktop computers and thermostats might be credited with attitudes in an attenuated sense, but scarcely with experiences. It therefore makes no sense to ask what is it like, for example, for a thermostat to detect 70°F. And in the absence of these sorts of question (and possible answers) there is nothing to anchor the beliefs and desires of the thermostat in anything deserving to be called a point of view. This is so even if some desperate manoeuvre succeeds in showing the 'beliefs' of physical devices or simple organisms as liable to error, and not simply breakdown, and thus to that extent normative.

Making Connections

(a)   Normativity and the Inner

Recognizing that the perspectival question requires – but is not exhausted by – answers to the activity question, clarifies the connection between the normativity of the attitudes and the innerness of experience. More generally, it helps us to link attitudes and experience. The reasoning here is not complicated. Normativity is demanded by the idea of a perspective. But experience

– the possibility of there being something it is like to engage with the world in various ways – is necessary for filling out and anchoring a given perspective. Without something it is like to engage with the world, perspectives would be hollow and therefore unrecognizable. In short, there would be nothing to think of as a perspective. It is this dependence of perspectives on experience that shows why we can attribute beliefs, desires and the other attitudes only to organisms with conscious states. But, since networks of attitudes are themselves necessary to shape perspectives, it is also reasonable to think we can locate conscious states only in organisms to whom we can attribute attitudes.

This two-way relationship makes unnecessary some of the more desperate attempts to link consciousness and attitude.[4] In particular, it removes any need to insist – implausibly – that attitudes figure in streams of consciousness. (It would also shed some light on the temptation to see consciousness as something like a place   a Cartesian stream or stage – which is different from any other, and accessible only to the organism whose consciousness it is. A properly convincing explanation of this would be lengthy, but perhaps a brief comment will show the way. If it is required that there be a range of things it is like to engage with the world in order for an organism to have a point of view, one might be tempted to think of these qualitative features as features of the place at which the organism is, so to speak, located. This would be taking the metaphor inherent in 'point of view' too seriously, but this is easy enough to do.)

(b)   Subjective and Objective
The link between the normativity of the attitudes and the innerness of experience makes it possible to see how links to the other dichotomies might go. I shall begin with action and the subjective/objective distinction. Think about some simple case, e.g. raising your arm. As has been suggested, your arm's going up is certainly going to figure in this action, but does not constitute it, for your arm's moving is not the same thing as your moving it. What is needed in addition? (This is a natural way of asking the question, but we shouldn't take the arithmetical idea too seriously.) One thing seems a natural candidate: there is something it is like for your arm to go up; not just any old thing, but some specific quality to its going up in a case where you are raising it which differs from the case in which, say, it goes up because someone else brings this about.

That there is something it is like to raise your arm is no more surprising than that there is something it is like to see an unripe tomato, and this suggests that what you feel when you are active – cases when you move your body – shares features with other conscious states. In particular, it suggests that what it is like in a case of arm-raising (as opposed to arm-rising) is something inner. Further, since it is inner, it is likely to be subjective in some sense; it is likely to contrast with the objectivity or outerness of the arm's going up. However, the way in which this contrast is made, and the subjective/objective distinction that goes with it, differ from cases like the suffering of pain and the perception of colours.

There seems to be no problem in discovering *when* you see an unripe tomato, though it is far from clear *where* the experience occurs. With action, it is not exactly that things are reversed, but there is a difference. Considered as an inner experience, the sense of what it is like to raise your arm is like seeing the unripe tomato: it is locatable in time but not so easily in space. But the inner experience of activity does not by itself fix the initiation of the act in the temporal order; it merely constitutes our being active at the time. And it is the problematic placement of acts in the temporal order which led us to wonder about their objectivity.

These remarks about the temporal ordering of actions are, as you probably realize, no more than speculative. However, this doesn't matter for the point under discussion. For if we broaden 'objective' in a natural way to mean 'placeable in the spatial as well as temporal order', then it is plausible that each of what it is like to see blue, what it is like to suffer pain and what it is like to raise your arm all have this subjective aspect.

(c)   The First Person

The notion of the first person goes naturally with the inner and the subjective, whilst the third person seems more at home with the outer and objective. This suggests that the route from the first person to the perspectival is the same as the one from the innerness of experience to the perspectival. However, we must be careful here not to let this naturalness lead us astray. In particular, it would be wrong to conclude that the distinction between the first and third person is itself the same as the perspectival/non-perspectival one.

In the initial version of the experiment described in chapter 3, Arnold and Benedict came to the conclusion that they were about to change bodies. This was because they each had some conception about how to answer the question 'what is it like to be me?', and these conceptions gave a central place to experience. For instance, Arnold reasoned that, after the experiment, when he judged what it was like to see or feel, these judgements would issue from Benedict's body. So he concluded that he would be in Benedict's body. Note, however, that Arnold's judgements here, though they concern experiences, are made in the third person. Arnold is judging what *Arnold* would experience, and thereby what *Arnold* might do and say. These verdicts were reversed when Arnold was invited to consider these same experiences from the first-person perspective. When he thought of these experiences, not as Arnold's, but as *mine*, he seemed less eager to conclude that he would be selling up and transferring to Benedict's body.

In the experiment, we began by assuming that both Arnold and Benedict were able to shift between the first and third person. However, though it is difficult, imagine conducting the experiment with beings who were unable to do this. On the one hand, we would have an Arnold who spoke of himself (and others) only in the third person; not only was he convinced that he would end up in Benedict's body, the whole of any autobiography that he might write would be indistinguishable to the reader from a biography. On the other hand, imagine that Benedict is resolutely first personal. He never thinks of himself as Benedict, nor of anyone as 'he'; 'I' (and only this) accompanies all experiences, thoughts and actions. If Benedict wrote about himself, the result would be pretty much essence of autobiography, since there would be no place in it for other characters.

If they had been like this, I suspect that we would never have thought of either of them as persons. Arnold would come across rather as if he was animated by a computer program; aiming – but failing – to trick us into thinking of him as a person. The program sees to it that third-person pronouns occur in a certain range of descriptions issuing from Arnold, but, after a while, we would no longer take Arnold's uses of 'he' seriously, since it would no longer seem to us that the device 'Arnold' understood these pronouns. Similarly, Benedict's 'I' would come to seem only grammatically like our own; the panic about the experiment that issues from Benedict's mouth might fool us for a while, but Benedict's failure ever to use the third (or even the second) person would give the game away.

What this suggests then is what counts for our notion of a perspective is not so much the first person as the possibility of correctly employing both the first and third persons. When it is thought that the third person is the natural choice for the outer and objective, this is not strictly correct; the third person is no less important for our idea of the inner and the subjective, as witness our reluctance to count the avowals of the obsessively first-personal Benedict as the expressions of anything genuinely inner.

(d) Explanation

A great deal could be said about the connection between perspectives and personal-level explanations. But the shortest version will serve here. The point to keep hold of is that the explananda of folk psychology are attitudes and actions. Roughly, what we seek in our folk psychological narratives is to explain why people believe (and desire) certain things, and why they act as they do. First think about the attitudes. Given their normativity, it should be unsurprising that any attempt to explain them will make reference to the perspectives which they help to define. And since perspectives have an inner, subjective and first-personal aspect, it is equally unsurprising that the regularity conception of explanation – in so far as it is impersonal – is going to have difficulty in accommodating them. An example will make this clearer.

Suppose that I have a colleague who believes his philosophical work to be unappreciated, and is cast down by this. Suspecting that he is mistaken about this (or at least, wrong to believe it so strongly as to cause despondency), I search about for some explanation. The first place to look is for the evidence on which the belief is based, but in doing so I cannot simply treat what I find as I would evidence for some empirical claim. Since my aim is to understand why my friend holds a certain belief, I inevitably have to see the evidence from his perspective; it is no good treating it as evidence from just any perspective (or no perspective), because if I do so, the very thing that I am trying to explain will disappear. Of course, I might come to think that the evidence cited does not in fact support the content of my friend's belief. However, this conclusion is certainly not perspective-less: it is rather dependent on either my own perspective, or, more helpfully, on what seems a more rational or impartial perspective. But in either case, the constraints of normativity apply. If I come to be satisfied that the explanation of my friend's belief is his particular, and skewed, perspective on the evidence, then I might use the result of the more impartial perspective to try to readjust his attitudes. But of course that project too requires me to take seriously the personal or perspectival. In whatever way the details pan out, my understanding of this case – and the basis of any attempt at intervention – would not demand my knowing any of the regularities that figure in impersonal explanations.

The suggestion that personal-level explanation is unavoidable when dealing with people's attitudes carries over to action almost immediately. Explaining what someone does requires me to work out that individual's reason for the action. And it is no good thinking that I can isolate this particular reason by consulting generalizations that purportedly connect reasons with actions. That is just not how it works. A reason will be some mix of foreground beliefs, desires, experiences and feelings – all against the background of standing attitudes and experience. Since all of this is intelligible only when seen as the expression of a particular point of view or perspective, there would seem to be little hope of explaining the connection between reason and action in the absence of some appreciation of this perspective. Indeed, when it is remembered that, independently of reasons, actions themselves have an essentially perspectival aspect, it seems even less likely that their explanation could be a matter of embedding in a network of regularities.

These remarks should not, however, be taken as a conclusive argument against the Theory Theory and its pretension to explain human action. What has been suggested is that we can appreciate reasons only when they are seen as the product of some point of view, and we can only engage with these reasons by comparing one point of view with another. But it is still open to the Theory Theorist to seek for regularities that would make sense of points of view themselves. After all, the explanatoriness of impersonal explanation is one of the best ideas that human beings have come up with; being responsible for virtually all our successful dealings with the natural world, you would scarcely expect it to be left outside when we come home to discuss our own activities. To be sure, the task will not be an easy one: the notion of a perspective brings with it normativity, innerness, subjectivity and the rest, and these are each formidable obstacles for an impersonal framework. And as you might expect, the tussle between the personal and the impersonal has long since spread to the social sciences of psychology, sociology and anthropology (amongst others). Here my point has been simply that there is ample reason to think the personal-level notion of explanation is tied into the other dichotomies.

Unity and Duality

I did say a few pages ago that my remarks about the thematic unity of the mental landscape would be tentative. And now is perhaps the time to admit that the picture I have painted of how the various dichotomies fit together, and how they might support one another, is only one amongst various ways this might be accomplished. However, whether you agree with the details or not is less important than the aim of the exercise. For what I have been suggesting is that normativity, innerness, subjectivity, the first-person and personal-level explanation are each reflections of an underlying and unifying theme. Moreover, it is a theme which only makes sense against a background that also joins up the opposing partners in each dichotomy – descriptivity, outerness, objectivity, the third-person and impersonal explanation. For just as each separate feature of the mental landscape is characterized by a dichotomy, so it is with the whole. For instance, just as our concept of experience requires us to recognize both an inner and outer aspect, so it is that the mental landscape as a whole exhibits an underlying duality, though it is one for which we have yet to have a suitable label.

In previous chapters, it was suggested that what makes minds so different is that they are the one kind of thing in nature that has both an 'inside' and 'outside'. Or, as it was sometimes put, mental items are uniquely features of the world for which it makes sense to ask: what is it like to have that feature?

For obvious enough reasons, these ways of putting it are not all that helpful, repeating as they do terms used to characterize only a specific feature of the mental landscape, that is, experience. But perhaps we are now in a better position to suggest an alternative. Given the prominent role the notion of a perspective has played, it seems reasonable to say that what is essential to the mental is that it is perspectival. Understood against the background of the earlier discussion, this claim brings together normativity, innerness, subjectivity, the first-person and personal-level explanation. Moreover, it carries with it the wholly welcome suggestion that the mental is not *merely* perspectival, and therefore that, irrespective of this or that feature, the mental itself is characterized by a fundamental duality. For it only makes sense to speak of perspectives when there is something non-perspectival in the offing. The landscape metaphor that I find so congenial might help to clarify this.

On the one hand, a landscape is a terrain of some particular kind; it is, for example, some stretch of hills, valleys, trees, rivers, houses and roads. On the other hand, the idea of a landscape suggests a stretch of terrain that is not merely there, but is seen, or at least capable of being seen. The notion of a landscape thus has a kind of duality; it is both something depicted and a depiction. And it is a similar kind of duality that carries over to the mental landscape. On the one hand, we have seen that attitudes, actions, experiences, and everything else that constitutes the mental landscape, are themselves features of an objective world – a world that is in no sense tied to this or that point of view. But, on the other hand, it is no less true that these features can only be appreciated from the more restricted perspectives that they themselves define.

It is this duality, and not merely the notion of a perspective, that gives the mental landscape its special character. Trees and tables, for example, figure in the world – they causally interact with things in it – but they adopt no perspective on the world, nor on their interactions with it. Organisms with mental landscapes, that is, persons, figure no less in the world – they too causally interact with the things in it – but, unlike trees and tables, they have perspectival relations to the world. This is what was gestured at by saying that persons have an inside and an outside, or by saying that there is something it is like to be a person. It seems also to be something that the nineteenth-century philosopher Franz Brentano had in mind when he spoke of the 'intentionality' of the mental.

Many contemporary philosophers use 'intentionality' for what, since chapter 2, I have been calling the 'directionality' of the attitudes – the fact that the attribution of beliefs and desires in some way or another reflects relations between persons and the world. Without wanting to legislate against contemporary usage, I have resisted speaking about the intentionality of the attitudes simply because I suspect that Brentano intended this notion in a more general way. His thesis was that intentionality is the mark of the mental – not merely of the attitudes – and, though Brentano's work is not easy to follow, one way to understand his point fits in rather well with our present discussion. In particular, it doesn't seem unreasonable to understand him as searching for some one characteristic that applies uniquely to the mental, and finding it in a duality that seems true of the mental and of nothing else. Without detailed historical investigation, it would be presumptuous to claim that Brentano's duality was exactly the one described above. But there they are clearly very close. For if I am right, a crucial characteristic of any mental feature – one which is genuinely a mark of the mental – is that it exhibits *both* a perspectival and a non-perspectival aspect.

Unity (Again)

We seem to have ended up with the idea that the characteristic mark of the mental is a special kind of duality. But it is very important that we do not lose sight of the unity that lies behind this. Each feature of the mental landscape seems to be marked by its own duality – e.g. inner/outer, subjective/objective, first/third person, etc. – and the affinities between these separate dualities point to a single line separating the mental from everything else. But we can only properly draw this line when we have seen how the bits of the mental realm fit together. Without the fundamental duality of the perspectival/non-perspectival, there is no mental as we know it, and without a unity underlying the different features of the mental landscape, there is no such duality.

The division of the mental realm in chapters 2 and 3 was intended merely to make our task manageable. The fact that the landscape contains experience, attitude and action should not be taken to mean that these features are wholly independent, or can be studied in isolation from one another. This should have been obvious in our discussion of persons and explanation, but, as we are just about to embark on the final stage of our investigation, it needs to be emphasized. For there is a real danger that in trying to get to the bedrock supporting one feature, and doing so without reference to other features, we will end up losing sight of the mental landscape itself. In advance of the actual work of part III, it is not really possible to illustrate in detail how this might happen, but, in outline, the problem should be clear enough.

Suppose, for example, that someone offers us an account of the attitudes implying that they could be found in creatures (or computers) that didn't otherwise have a mental life. If you have accepted the idea that the features of our mental lives are integrated – for example, that there are essential connections between the normativity of the attitudes and the possession of conscious experiences – then you should be suspicious of any such account. Of course, being suspicious of an account is not itself reason to reject it. It may be that the attraction of some piecemeal account of the attitudes proves to be stronger than the interconnections of the mental landscape. Perhaps the unity of the mental lives of persons will turn out to be more apparent than real. (Indeed, many think that the progressive disintegration associated with, for example, the onset of Alzheimer's disease, suggests just this.) None the less, whilst it falls short of providing a firm argument, it should serve at least as a warning: accept only with great care a piecemeal account of this or that feature of the mental life of persons.

Notes and References

1   I think that normativity lies behind all uses of language and employment of concepts, but it is an intricate matter to spell this out accurately. The contrast between 'feline' and 'dangerous' brings normativity into focus without the need for any such intricacy.
2   It is somewhat disingenuous to suggest that there is merely no space for this argument, suggesting thereby that I could provide it if I so chose. However, whilst acknowledging that the argument is not one that I could provide in detail, the last two sections of this chapter suggest at least in outline how it might go.
3   Some might argue that the 'attitudes' of thermostats would not exhibit normativity, and that this would rule them out. But there are those who insist that there is nothing to stop our seeing normativity even here, though in some more primitive form. (Debates about the appropriateness of attitude attribution are made to turn on such issues as whether thermostats or bacteria can be 'credited' with the capacity to make errors. This, in effect, is asking whether their states of mind exhibit even minimal normativity.) Without going deeply into it, this seems the wrong field on which to do battle. The reason thermostats do not have beliefs is not that they are immune from error; it is because they do not have anything that deserves to be called a perspective, a notion that I have insisted brings normativity in train, but is not wholly defined by it.
4   I suspect that many will concede the dependence of attitude on experience, though resisting the converse. Surely, it will be said, there could be organisms for whom it is like something to see, or suffer pain, but to whom we feel no temptation to attribute attitudes. I strongly disagree with this, but I do concede that this direction of dependence needs more argument.

Part III

Bedrock

5

Science and the Mind

The present scientific story about changes and happenings is very impressive, and it tempts many to think that there is something especially fundamental about the scientific picture of the world. Physical, chemical and biological phenomena which were once deeply mysterious are now routinely discussed and explained in an array of specialist journals and books. Indeed, the scientific enterprise has been so successful that it is now a commonplace to say that no one person can fully grasp the details of all its sub-disciplines. But in outline the picture is clear enough: the world seems to consist of such things as particles, atoms and molecules governed by laws, and it this orderly and increasingly complex arrangement of energetic matter which gives shape to the world we experience. One science – physics – studies the configurations of energetic matter at the most basic level, and for this reason the scientific world-view is often called 'physicalism'. Other natural sciences – from chemistry to biology – attempt to unravel the laws which govern more complex configurations up to, and including, the organisms which have populated this planet. (I leave the psychological and social sciences on one side for now.)

Of course, many mysteries remain – there are many phenomena which are not explicable by the current physicalist picture of the world. And it this large reservoir of ignorance which might well encourage someone to reject the claim of this picture to any sort of comprehensiveness. This rejectionist line can seem particularly attractive, accustomed as we are now to suspicion of scientific experts. Yet, in spite of its appeal, I would urge that taking the rejectionist line simply because of what we cannot now scientifically explain is less rational than persevering with the scientific world-view. To understand why, some distinctions must be made between what actually comes with scientific perseverance and what is inessential to it.

First of all, one should distinguish between the physicalist view of the world that goes with science and the much more specific – and doubtful –

view that all of science itself is essentially reducible to that part of itself known as physics. It is unfortunate that the commonly used word 'physicalism' hints at the latter idea – the idea that everything is explicable by physics – but it isn't difficult to keep these things separate. Physics is the study of the laws governing such things as elementary particles and atoms, forces and fields. There may be every reason to think that the world is constructed out of such things, but one can think this without also thinking that such sciences as biology, zoology, chemistry, meteorology are themselves merely branches of physics – that there will be laws of *physics* which tell us about, for example, *biological* phenomena. All that the physicalist perspective requires is that whatever happens will be explicable by some science or other. How we should deal with the 'branches' of science will then be a further question, and not one on which we have to take any stand now. (Some prefer to speak of 'naturalism' or 'materialism' in place of physicalism here, but these labels can also be misleading, so I shall take the risk of continuing to speak of 'physicalism'.)

Talking in this general way about what science may in the future explain introduces a second distinction: that between the sciences we now have and the idea of science itself. At present we have a general idea of what physics, biology, chemistry and the other sciences say the world is like. But, in adopting the physicalist or scientific perspective, we do not necessarily commit ourselves to the correctness of the present picture. All that is claimed is that any phenomenon which is a genuine happening in this world is in principle able to be studied by a science, albeit by a science which might be quite different from any we now have at our disposal. Though it may be difficult to imagine, our present scientific perspective may be deeply misconceived. But all that the scientific or physicalist perspective requires is that the *methods* of science – not the laws or theories we now have – can in principle provide an explanation for whatever happens.

Finally, one must be careful not to misunderstand what it means to say that any happening must be explicable by science. It should *not* be taken – as it so often is – to mean that what science has to say about a certain kind of happening is all that there is to say about it. The colours, shapes and images of a painting can be the subject of our aesthetic judgement without this challenging, or being challenged by, the fact that science can explain everything about how the surface molecules and incident light produce (in us) the painting's appearance. Indeed, one may even believe that there is a scientific story to be told about aesthetic judgements themselves, without this undermining their truth (or otherwise). In short, the universality of science should not be mistaken for a kind of tyranny.

Keeping in mind these three points, the thought that all phenomena (including the mental) must be in principle explicable by some science or other is less controversial than it first appears. Whilst nothing I could say would constitute an air-tight argument in favour of it, I hope I have said enough to justify at least proceeding as if the scientific perspective were true. To do the opposite would certainly be rash, as we would have to believe *now* that some phenomena – say those of the mind – were not explicable by any present or future science. This last is certainly a possibility – one to which we may want to return when the going gets tough. But it is not sensible to start with it.

Why should the going get tough in respect of the scientific understanding of the mind? Answering this question will take a little time, but let us begin with the brighter side of the picture. The mental realm consists of a quite heterogeneous collection of things which share at least this feature: they are, in the broadest sense, things which happen. As you read this, as the light waves from the page strike your eye, you undergo various conscious experiences and, equally likely, you come to form beliefs and other attitudes as well as going in for actions such as turning pages. The question of how to understand all this scientifically is thus no less pertinent here than it would be in respect of purely chemical, atomic or biological changes.

Put in this way, there seems to be no especially pressing reason for investigating the scientific basis of the mental. There are these phenomena – the mental – and we have just as much reason to expect them to fit into a future scientific story as we now have in respect of the weather or the behaviour of proteins. Of course, if some special need arises – as when a major mind-affecting drug is tested then there is bound to be some more urgent interest in the various mental 'side-effects' that follow administration of the drug. But this kind of interest is much like the interest we all take in, say, seismology, when earthquakes threaten large population centres. Where human concerns figure prominently, the need to understand precisely why things happen – the need for scientific understanding – moves up the list of priorities.

The idea that the mental landscape rests on the bedrock of the physical world as described by science, and that we shall gradually, and in our own good time, come to understand more about the contours of this fit, is by and large the common view in the scientific community. However, this relatively sanguine attitude about the relationship between the mental and physical is not typical of those in the philosophical community. Whereas the representative textbooks on neurophysiology tend to suggest that we will one day come to know more and more about the mind's relation to what goes on in the brain, philosophical discussion of this issue shows no such calmness. Indeed, it is only a mild exaggeration to say that what one finds instead is an urgent, even frenetic, search for some way to reconcile the mental and the physical; there is even a hint in some quarters of despair that the project will never get anywhere. Of course, even though I use terms such as 'frenetic' and 'despairing', I do not for a moment mean to suggest that the philosophical attitude is merely pathological; that, having opted for the idea that the physical is the bedrock reality of things which happen, philosophers have given in to a collective neurotic anxiety about the present impoverished state of our knowledge in that regard. On the contrary, it seems to me that the philosophical attitude is, if anything, more justified than that of the neurophysiologists, and thus the most immediate task is to show why.

Just before we begin the substantive work, let me insert a comment here about the parlous state in which we left matters in the mental realm, for it might be thought that the philosophical worries about the mental and the physical arise from this lack of order. The everyday notions of the mental are shot through with problems. The simplest of questions and assumptions leads to difficulties which can make us wonder whether we so much as have a coherent conception of the mental realm. The loose behaviour of the attitudes, the elusiveness of actions, the apparent incompatibilities of the first- and third-person perspectives that show themselves in folk psychology and personal identity, these problems are only samples, and yet they might easily provoke someone to worry about the possibility of ever having a proper science of the mental. After all, if we do not have a firm grasp of the mental happenings themselves, how can we ever hope to understand their physical basis?

This last question seems calculated to invite the answer, 'we can't,' but honesty requires me to admit that this would be too hasty. Granted that success in scientific understanding is made easier by our having a coherent grasp of the relevant phenomena, it does not follow that the lack of such a grasp renders the search for a physical basis impossible. For example, though the eighteenth-century account of what happened when things were heated was largely incoherent, this did not prevent progress in the next century, and the eventual development of our now accepted ideas about heat and temperature. So, whilst it would be nice if our conception of the mental was less problematic, this would not be a good enough reason for the widespread malaise in the philosophical community.

Reasons and Causes

The real reason for philosophical anxieties about the relations between the mental and the physical can be best brought out by backtracking a bit, that is, by considering an issue which figured inconclusively at various points in part

II. I have in mind here the question of how acting is related to experiencing and attitudinizing. Consider the following mundane example.

> You are sitting on the sofa engrossed in reading. Whilst so doing you begin to be aware of rumblings in your stomach – they are almost audible – and a general feeling of emptiness. Could you be suffering from some sort of indigestion? You look at your watch and realize that you have lost track of time: it is now nearly 3 o'clock and you haven't had lunch. You decide that you are more likely to be suffering from *lack* of something to digest. Having been shopping the night before you know what is available, and you mentally run through the items. Believing that a sandwich would be the quickest thing to fix (though not necessarily the most tasty), you recognize that your desire for food *soon* is much stronger than for food *quality*. So, intent upon the idea of making a sandwich, you head to the kitchen and open the door of the refrigerator . . .

Clearly, as the dots show, the mental episodes reported in the example are followed by lots of activity. But, for specificity, let us focus on the action of reaching out and grasping the refrigerator door. This simple action is brought about in some way or other by the bodily feelings, beliefs, desires and intentions which you had in the minutes leading up to the action. It is clear enough that items of our first two categories – experiencing and attitudinizing – are in some way responsible for the eventual door-grasping behaviour. But in what way? That is, in what way is that amalgam of attitudes and experiences which could be called your 'mental condition' responsible for your subsequent action?

Two somewhat different-sounding answers have been proposed. On the one hand, it would generally be held that your mental condition – or at least some element of it – was the *reason* for your opening the door. That is, if asked why you opened the door, you would make some more or less complicated reference to your beliefs, desires and feelings, saying that they provided your reason for so acting. On the other hand, it might be said (perhaps more naturally by an observer than by you) that your mental condition was the *cause* of your acting. Here the idea is that, just as we explain an earthquake by an appeal to factors that cause it, so can we explain your fridge-directed behaviour by saying that your mental condition caused it. And it is fair to say that these alternatives exhaust the field: the philosophical community seems agreed that minds rationalize – contain reasons for – actions, or they cause them.

(Note: in chapter 3, we considered what appear to be two very different kinds of explanation, and you may feel that there are connections between these and the above answers. The idea of an action's having a cause might seem to go with the deductive regularity conception of explanation, and it invites thoughts of the Theory Theory; whereas talk of a reason for an action might well put us in mind of the Simulation Theory, at least on one reading of that account. Unfortunately, things are not this neat; both reasons and causes could play roles in either account of explanation. So, for the present, I shall continue the discussion without trying to integrate the notion either of a reason or a cause with our earlier discussion of explanation. But not to worry: these issues will come up again.)

Attempts to understand what constitutes a reason for action began at least with Aristotle, and discussions of causation figure prominently on any list of philosophers' perennial favourites. However, we do not need to spend a lot of time considering masses of background material. To set out the core problem of the mental and physical, all we need to recognize is that the answers given above are not necessarily incompatible: someone could hold (and many do) that a reason for an action can also be a cause of it.

The story goes like this. A reason for an action is some set of attitudes and feelings which together show the action in a favourable light to the agent. Your mental condition in the above example made opening the refrigerator door an intelligible first step in the sequence of actions which followed. However, reasons tend to be a bit unspecific. Your reason for opening the door by grasping the handle would have equally made intelligible a whole host of slightly different movements. A reason doesn't usually tell us precisely how we are to move our bodies in acting on it. And this is where the idea of a cause comes in, for our original question was: what was the relationship between your mental condition and the *specific* action of opening the door that took place? A not implausible first reply is that your mental condition makes it *reasonable or rational* (from your point of view) for you to go in for some sort of refrigerator-door-opening behaviour. But the full *explanation* of why you opened the door when, and in the way, you did must make reference to the cause of that very specific event.

Bringing in causes helps, as they are the kinds of thing we appeal to when we want to explain why some specific thing happened. For example, suppose we are investigating the burning down of the house on 23 Elm Street. We know that faulty wiring can result in houses burning down. This is a general kind of truth which might well be in the background along with lots of other general truths (such as that petrol and matches, when mixed with insurance policies, also bring about house-burning). Knowing these sorts of thing helps, but in order to explain this particular burning down we must locate that actual state or event which preceded it and was, as one sometimes says, 'the' cause. Supposing it was in fact a loose wire in the kitchen wall which short-circuited the electrical supply, then the explanatory job is finished if we can find evidence of this loose wire. If we can, we will have established a link one can almost visualize: the loose wire in the wall touches another, there is no fuse to break the circuit, gradually heat builds up in the inner wall, combustion point is reached, the fire spreads in the wall, no one is home to notice the charring, the timber frames ignite . . . the house on Elm Street burns down.

Applying this to the refrigerator example, what we need is to find the cause for the quite specific door-reaching/grasping behaviour that took place. Your mental condition functions to explain rationally why you went in for *the sort of behaviour* you did – it is (or contains) your reason for having acted. But it doesn't by itself explain the particular door-grasping that occurred. So why not, as it were, kill two birds with one stone and recognize that the reason could itself also be the cause of the action?

Philosophers have spent a lot of time considering what is involved in one thing's being the cause of something else, and at least the following three are generally thought to be necessary:

(1) A cause is some state, event or datable/placeable happening.
(2) It precedes its effect.
(3) It is such that if it hadn't happened then neither would the effect. (Since, in the typical case, both the cause and effect have already happened, this last condition is 'counterfactual' – it says what would happen if things had been different. It thus creates a very strong bond between cause and effect.)[1]

Unsurprisingly, these three conditions seem to be met by the very thing which is your reason for opening the refrigerator door. You reason is part of your mental condition – it is arguably a series of states and events which take place in you just before you open the door. This shows that conditions (1) and (2) apply. Moreover, it doesn't seem implausible to say that if you hadn't been in that condition you wouldn't have opened the refrigerator door. And this means that condition (3) applies as well. So, the very thing which is a reason for an action also seems to have the characteristics necessary to make it a cause of an action. At least that will be the hypothesis which we shall adopt for our present expository purpose, and which we can represent by figure 5.1 below.

Brains

Focus next on the point in our example where your arm is by your side and you are just about to reach for the handle on the fridge door. No one now knows everything about how our nervous systems work, but we do have some reasonable idea. Lots of electrochemical activity in the brain, channelled down appropriate neural pathways, causes the very complicated, and yet delicately

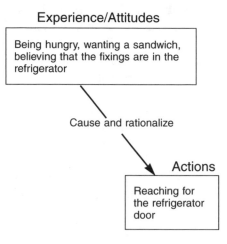

Figure 5.1

co-ordinated, contracting and expanding of muscles in your arm. The precise nature of this contraction and expansion is continuously controlled by the brain's electrochemical activity, and this, in turn, is partly dependent on the neural activity in the optical system. To cut a long story short: your muscles – acting on the brain's electrochemical commands – get your fingers to the fridge door-handle, and all of this is achieved with the help of your eyes and other systems which monitor the position of your body and arm.

What is important is that what has just been imagined is a causal story, indeed it is what we might call a 'purely physical' causal story. Tracing backwards from contraction of your muscles which force your fingers around the handle to the neural excitation in your arm, and brain, and optic nerve and so on, there is nothing here that anyone would regard as an activity of the mind. A textbook on the nervous system has no place in it for what would be a miraculous intervention of the mind in the causal chain just described. The physiologist doesn't even try to understand neural excitation and muscle contraction in any but chemical and physical terms. One would be stunned to read a paper in a journal of brain sciences which said: 'and just after this particular nerve sends its spiking pulse, the agent's belief about the location of the refrigerator handle sends a message to the muscles in the arm.'

Have we any reason to think that the neurophysiological story about your arm movements can be satisfactorily completed? After all, at present we know only a lot of general things about what goes on. I pointed out earlier that it may be an article of faith – a non-religious dogma – that all the happenings in this world are at bottom explicable in scientific terms. But I think that when it comes to that part of the world which is the human body, such faith couldn't be better grounded. For, unlike our picture of the sub-atomic basis of matter and energy, our *general* understanding of the biochemical basis of human biology is virtually complete. There are many details missing from the picture – and the details are crucial for such things as medical intervention – but there really do not seem to be the large-scale mysteries in biology that there are in physics.

In respect of the hand poised for opening the fridge door, the picture shown in figure 5.2 seems to just about sum up the way things are expected to be, scientifically speaking.

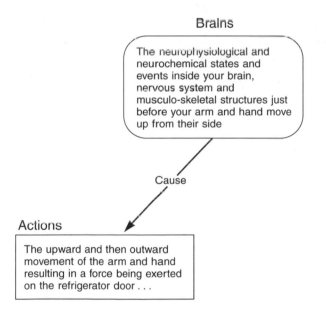

Figure 5.2

There are two things about the way the boxes are labelled in figure 5.2 which should be mentioned.

First, I use the label 'Brains' merely as a shorthand for the whole – and as yet unknown – physical story of what goes on. Clearly, where the mind is concerned, brains are going to have a large say, but I don't want you to think that I have forgotten about the rest of the nervous system, the muscles or the hormones. And there may well other important elements to the story about the causation of action.

Secondly, anyone who followed my detailed story about actions in part II will be somewhat surprised to see that the physical movement of the hand and arm gets the label 'action'. Given that discussion, it is far from obvious that the movement is itself an action; indeed, it may well be wrong to think this. None the less, there is reason to think that an action such as reaching for the fridge handle does include (or, less assertively, 'involves') such a movement, and that is the only thing intended by the label.

The Eternal Triangle

In matters of the heart, triangular relationships are celebrated for their difficulties. Two persons competing for the love of a third give the writers of soap operas all they need to get going; only the details need to be filled in to generate endless different plots. What needs to be appreciated now is that putting figures 5.1 and 5.2 together (see figure 5.3) we get a triangular relationship which, though hardly the matter of a soap opera, has at least at first glance something of the same tensions − and leads to no fewer variations of plot.

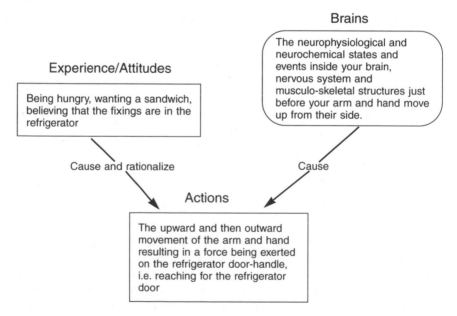

Figure 5.3

In figure 5.3, the left-hand arrow represents the claims of the mind to be the cause of what we do, whilst the right-hand arrow represents the claims of our neurophysiological make-up. Now human relationships can be surprisingly accommodating, but causal ones are not. It may really be possible for there to be something like harmony in a love-triangle, but no such possibility exists in respect of the causal claims shown in figure 5.3. Here is why.

Recall that among the very few things said about causality was this: some event or state − call it A − is the cause of another (call it B) when it is true that *were A not to have happened then B wouldn't have happened*. This requirement can be true even though both A and B have in fact happened − remember that it is 'counterfactual'. The trouble is that the situation in figure 5.3 makes it impossible for this feature of causality to apply to either the left- or right-hand side of the diagram. For example, suppose that it is really true that you have some reason for an action and that the reason causes it. Is it true that had you not had this reason, this action would not have taken place? No, because so long as your neurophysiological state were disposed in the appropriate way, then you would have acted, whether or not you had the supposed reason. Equally, it cannot be said of a case in which your neurophysiological state causes you to move your hand that if you had not been in that state, you wouldn't have so acted. This is because figure 5.3 allows it to be *possible* for a reason to have brought about some action, even in the absence of the neurophysiological state which in fact did cause it.

The problem here is known as that of *overdetermination*. It comes to this: effects cannot have two completely different causes competing for their attention. The counter-factual intimacy described above means that if there seem to be two completely independent causes, then one of them must give up its claim on the effect or, contrary to the original supposition, the causes are not fully independent. Here is a stark example to illustrate what I mean.

A house burns down, and the investigation unit of the Fire Department (FD) comes up with the view that it was caused by a short circuit in the kitchen wall. However, a neighbour has another idea. He believes that it was caused by a 'person or persons unknown' with a grudge to settle. Now, there seem to be three possibilities here: (i) the FD is right about the short circuit; (ii) the neighbour is right about the grudge; or (iii) they are both right, in that the grudge was settled by rigging the wiring so as to produce a short circuit. (They could of course all be wrong, but that is not worth considering here.) In possibility (iii), the causes are not independent − they are part of the same story − so this is not a relevant case of overdetermination. This is sometimes described by saying the causes are *overlapping*, which leaves the other two. Is it reasonable to think that both (i) and (ii) could obtain even when the causes do not overlap? That is, could the FD and the neighbour both be right about the cause, even though the grudge and the short circuit are both separate and independent causes of the fire?

An affirmative answer here would suggest a genuine case of overdetermination, but can you really conceive of this whilst keeping your grip on the idea of a cause? I suspect not. How can the short circuit have been the cause if some second, and wholly independent, chain of events also brought about the fire? And how could the cause be the grudge if there was also a short circuit, which had nothing to do with the grudge, and which would have burned down the house anyway? Clearly, if we are careful to insist on the non-overlapping condition, then overdetermination messes up the claims of both sides to be the rightful cause.

To be sure, there are cases where we might be tempted to think that we could rationally speak of overdetermination – cases where independent causes seem separately responsible for a single effect. For example, suppose that someone is very ill and suffers both a massive heart attack and respiratory failure – events which are followed by death. We may want to say that had the heart attack not killed the patient, then the respiratory failure would have – and vice versa – even though we would also insist that these do not overlap in the way the short circuit and grudge did in (iii) above. Is this a counter-example to the earlier claim about the incoherence of overdetermination? Not really. For even though the two conditions are different, there is nothing to prevent us seeing them as part of a larger condition which is itself the cause of death. Indeed, this is just how such cases are described when they occur: a doctor in such circumstances would cite the cause of death as 'a massive heart attack and respiratory failure'. Moreover, any attempt to press this verdict by asking which was really the cause of death would not unreasonably be resisted. For it would be downright misleading to single out one or other part of the larger circumstance as the real cause.

What this shows is that, faced with a putative case of overdetermination, our intuitive understanding of causality forces us to see the competing events as parts of a single complex cause. In effect, the very idea we have of certain events as parts of larger ones is one we appeal to naturally when overdetermination threatens. And this reaction shows just how deeply entrenched in our idea of causality is the rejection of genuine overdetermination.

On the face of it, the situation in figure 5.3 is one where non-overlapping causes compete to bring about an effect. Since overdetermination is simply not reasonable, this is not stable – it is not a picture we can live with. But notice that this unstable situation arose from what seemed perfectly reasonable opinions about the causal powers of both minds and brains. And it is this situation, arising as it does from these considerations, that grounds philosophical anxiety about the mental realm and its relationship to the bedrock of scientific description. When a philosopher thinks about how reasons cause actions, and about how our muscles are caused to move in response to brain events, these seem to lead inexorably to the precipice of overdetermination. It will not help here to maintain the 'laid-back' attitude that as we learn more about the brain, we will come to understand how the mind is related to it. For unless something is said *right now* about how to remove – at least in principle – the instability of figure 5.3, we aren't going to come to understand anything.

The triangle suggests that we cannot keep our conceptual grip on a world governed by a mindlessly described causal order that is none the less a world in which minds function more or less independently of the causal order. Something has to give. We have somehow to reconceive one or more of the features that lead to the incoherent triangular relationship between minds, brains and actions.

As you will soon appreciate, there is no shortage of proposals for how we should go about doing this. However, precisely because there are so many proposals, and because chasing each of them down will typically lead us into a maze of argument and counter-argument, it is important to keep some larger picture in view. This is where the starkness of the eternal triangle will prove especially valuable, even making up somewhat for the conceptual embarrassment it has brought us. For whilst specific proposals are many and various, the triangle itself hints at certain simple ways of organizing them. (There will be more on the details of this shortly.) My suggestion is that you keep a firm grip on the shape of each particular strategy, even if you initially find some of the details obscure. To be sure, talk of such a thing as the shape of strategy is metaphorical, but I think you will come to see that it is none the worse for that. Having a general idea where you are is no less important in following a philosophical argument than when walking around a strange city. Perhaps it is even more important. So, help from any quarter is welcome, and if it takes metaphor to keep us from getting lost, then so be it.

The Options

There are essentially three kinds of thing we can do to get ourselves out of the conceptual mess evident in the triangle. First of all, like the person who has two lovers making demands it is impossible to meet, we can simply remove one of them from the scene. In particular, we could find reasons to banish either the Mind or Brain, thus leaving the causal path to Action clear for the other. This strategy is generally known as *Elimination*. Contemporary philosophers who are attracted to it are often devotees of science, so they tend to look for ways of eliminating the Mind. (I do not expect that this strikes you as an appealing idea, but, for reasons which we will discuss later, some philosophers feel that their hand is forced here.) Of course, it is also possible to implement the elimination strategy by dropping the Brain, though this move doesn't sit easily with our present attitude towards science. There are doubtless many who do not regard the scientific story about our bodies and brains as the last word, but I don't think even the most spiritualist among them is likely to insist that the brain, and its related equipment, have *nothing* to do with how we move our bodies in action.

Elimination is a drastic strategy; no one in a triangular relationship, simultaneously and deeply attracted to two others, would embark on it without first considering less drastic alternatives. So a second kind of thing to do might be to keep both Mind and Brain on the scene, but to reassess the roles they have in relation to action. Perhaps when we look more closely at the notions of cause and reason, we will find a way to keep the work of Brain and Mind separate. For obvious enough reasons we can think of this general move as one of *Division of Labour*.

The third strategy – one might be tempted to say 'the third way' – is the most fashionable. Instead of eliminating one side of the triangle, or dividing labour, the idea here is to squeeze together two of vertices of the triangle. As you will see, there are various ways to do this, but the end result is the same: a *Coalescence* of two out of the three vertices. Described in this very general way, it would be easy to confuse coalescence with elimination, since both aim to rid us of the triangle. However, soon enough it will be apparent that coalescence, unlike elimination, aims to accommodate all three of the original elements rather than simply dropping one. And there is no doubt that the strategy is fashionable precisely because of this. (If only one could do the same in the triangular relationships of the heart.)

The next chapters will consider specific instances of the three strategies, including, as you would expect, those most likely to succeed. However, before we move on to them, it will be helpful to consider briefly two ways of dealing with the triangle which tend to be regarded as mistaken, but which have played important parts in the history of the philosophy of mind. I think it important to consider these attempts – failures though many think they are – not just for historical reasons, but because they will make the work of the next chapters easier to grasp. It will also give our classification of strategies a work-out.

Dualism

Descartes held that the mental and the physical were distinct substances, and it would be reasonable to wonder whether, by defending this sort of dualism, one could solve the problem posed by the triangle. Unfortunately, the answer here must be 'no'. For, even if you share Descartes' view, the triangle problem arises, not merely from the alleged independent existence of Mind and Brain, but from the fact that they both seem to have a causal interest in Actions. If you are inclined to be a dualist, then you will be happy to drop the 'allegedly' in my last sentence; Mind and Brain will be taken to be *in fact* independent existences. But this still leaves us in the dark about the rest of the picture. Indeed, in so far as we really do have distinct mental and material substances, overdetermination is, if anything, even more of a threat.

Descartes would never have thought that dualism alone would be of much use with our problem. Indeed, since he thought that the mind brought about effects in the physical world – it acted on, and reacted to, things which were undeniably material – one could say that he was amongst the first to recognise the difficulties (and importance) of the triangular relationship. He wondered how the mind could bring about effects in the physical world, given that it was itself a substance not belonging to that world. His worries began with his dualism, whereas the issue now is whether dualism can show us how to deal with the triangle. Still both ways of approaching the matter lead to similar questions:

Are there mental causes of actions as well as material?
If so, how does one deal with the threat of overdetermination?
And, in any case, how can something mental cause something physical?

Descartes' answer to the third of these questions implied his answer to the others. What he claimed was that there is a little, very 'subtle' organ in the brain – the pineal gland – which is where mental states acquire the causal power to affect the physical world. This interactive view of the mental and the physical, if successful, would avoid the problem of overdetermination, since the mental would, in actual cases, provide links in a *single* causal chain leading to action. In effect, the mental and the physical would be overlapping causes, rather like the unproblematic case in which the person with the grudge rigged the wiring in the house, so that it would short and bring about the necessary heat in the wall to set off the fire.

Of course, as one is trained in philosophy to point out, in the case of Mind and Brain, Descartes' suggestion just doesn't work, for the pineal gland is either a mental or a material substance. If the former, than the problem of how the mental has physical effects is simply pushed that bit further back – to the relation between the pineal gland and whatever is the first physical way station on the route to action. And if the pineal gland is material, as Descartes certainly thought it was, then the problem of causal interaction between the mental and physical doesn't go away – it simply takes place on the narrow stage of the pineal gland.

Mere dualism of the mental and the physical will not make the problems go away, and Descartes' attempt to add a kind of interactionism to his dualism is usually counted a failure. Of course, this doesn't mean that dualism itself must be rejected. For all I have said, dualism might be true. But if it is, then the resolution of the triangle is going to be that much more difficult, and many are convinced that some better way can be found.

It should be noted here, if only for completeness, that an even more thoroughgoing dualism than Descartes' own could provide a way to resolve the triangle. If one drops the idea that the mental and the physical interact, then one could convert the triangle into two stable pairwise relations in which the mental is partitioned from the material, rather as in figure 5.4.

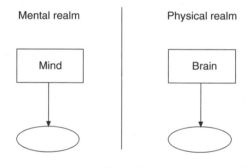

Figure 5.4

Following our earlier discussion of the options, this would count as employing a Division of Labour strategy of an extreme kind, perhaps too extreme to count as plausible. For example, suppose you were hungry and, having thought about it, reached for the refrigerator handle. It would seem to you as if your thought processes eventuated in a movement of your arm, but, on the view being considered, this would be denied. Instead, it would be maintained that your thought processes eventuated in a mental action of some sort (note that I have carefully *not* labelled the arrows and bottom boxes in figure 5.4, since it is unclear what to call them), and that this action just happened to be accompanied by perceptions as of your arm moving. The whole of this train would be purely mental, and it would be shadowed by, though would not causally interact with, a chain of purely physical events involving your brain, arm and the refrigerator.

Such a *parallelism* would certainly avoid the problem of overdetermination, but almost no one finds the idea acceptable. Aside from anything else, it would require us to believe there to be a fortuitous synchronization of mental and physical chains of events. Every time you reached for something, your action would be wholly mental, and would be followed by a lots of other mental states like perceptual experiences of the movement of your body and various external objects. But these movements of physical objects would have nothing to do with what went on in your mind before, during and after you 'initiated' some action.

The example of psychophysical parallelism should not prejudice you against the Division of Labour strategy. As you will come to see, there are more subtle and less objectionable ways of implementing this strategy. And to some extent it becomes more, not less, attractive when the alternative strategies are laid out. (You will, however, have to wait until chapter 9 for this further discussion.)

(Note that in spite of the implausibility of parallelism, it does seem that at least one person, the German philosopher, G. W. Leibniz (1646–1716), did hold some such view. Also, whilst on the subject of the history of philosophy of mind, it is worth pointing out that, in contemporary philosophy, the more prominent 'Cartesian' thesis is not dualism as such, but the insistence on the ineffable privacy and incorrigibility of our mental lives. This was discussed in chapter 2.)

An Attempt at Coalescence

As has been noted, our problem would disappear at a stroke if some rationale could be found for seeing the mental and the physical as somehow combined or co-operating, instead of competing. That is, if we could coalesce two of the vertices of the triangle, then all would be well, since of course we would no longer have a triangle on our hands. Of course, though it is easy enough to suggest such a rearrangement, the real work lies in making any kind of coalescing plausible. And, as one might expect, there are a bewildering number of ways in which this has been attempted. However, within this mass of detail, one can discern two main approaches. One is to see Mind and Brain as coalescing, as combining in some way to form part of a single causal antecedent of Action; the other is to attempt a coalescence between Mind and Action. The next two chapters will consider the first strategy in detail since, as has been suggested, this is by far the most popular, and offers what many regard as the best hope for a resolution of the problem. However, as you will see, there are good reasons for devoting a little space here to 'Mind into Action' coalescence.

Mind into Action

The label 'behaviourism' must be handled with care: there are views labelled as such that would have to be counted as instances of an Elimination strategy, and other behaviourist views that have little to do with the philosophical problem we are discussing at present (these latter being more advice to psychologists as to how best to do experimental work on our mental capacities). But on at least one understanding of the label, behaviourism can be seen as an attempt to resolve our problem by coalescing Mind and Action. This view is sketched in figure 5.5.

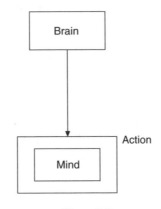

Figure 5.5

As a simple illustration, let's begin by imagining how a behaviourist would treat some attitudinal feature of the mental landscape, some specific belief. Suppose it is true that I believe my lawn needs watering, that I could be correctly described as being in that mental state. Being in that state it is pretty likely that I would indulge in grass-watering activity, at least in the right, non-rainy, not too busy circumstances. Or, perhaps being too lazy for that, I might simply do such things as complain about the dry weather, read the weather forecasts particularly carefully, try to get someone else to water the lawn, etc. Now it is these facts about what I am likely to do, given my belief, that the relevant sort of behaviourism exploits. For the coalescing behaviourist aims to *define* my mental states – e.g. my belief that the lawn needs watering – as a tendency to behave in certain grass-wateringly related ways.

This point about definition is the crucial one. It is not that I happen to have a belief   whatever kind of thing that is − and that my belief leads me to act in various ways. Rather, it is that a belief is nothing more nor less than a tendency to behave in certain ways. Talk of beliefs, attitudes generally, and all other features of the mental landscape is in this way really just a shorthand way of describing a whole range of complex and interrelated pieces of behaviour, as well as dispositions to behave.

Note that the notion of a 'disposition to behave' is no mere extra. For behaviourism to have any plausibility at all, we must allow that mental items are definable not merely in terms of what people actually do, but in terms of what they are disposed to do. And, of course, a disposition might never be actualized. For example, I might right now, on Wednesday morning, believe that the grass needs watering today, but never indulge in any grass-watering behaviour because, before I have a chance to do so, it rains. None the less, on that particular Wednesday, I did believe that the grass needed watering, and the behaviourist needs to say something about what defines this belief. Since there are no actions   nothing that I actually do − which could serve, the behaviourist must include in his definition my dispositions, 'things I would do if . . .', where the blank is filled in by appropriate possible circumstances.

Behaviourism which discerns the mind in action is at least concessive to the idea of the mental, since the mental is treated as genuinely present in patterns of action. But, as noted in passing earlier, there is a more ruthless kind of behaviourism which makes no such concession. Its adherents insist that there are brains and there is behaviour, but that mental states of any stripe are just surplus to requirements.

For obvious enough reasons, the concessive kind of behaviourism is sometimes called *definitional* behaviourism, but versions are also, and less obviously, known either as *logical* or *philosophical* behaviourism. There are slight differences in these views, but that won't matter much, since the real question is whether behaviourism is plausible enough to demand much further investigation. And nowadays the answer to this tends to be 'no'. There are three reasons for this.

First, it has been commonly accepted that the interconnections between items in the mental realm make it impossible to see how definitional behaviourism could succeed, even in principle. The problem here is that there does not seem to be any hope of allotting an inventory of action and disposition to each mental item, since things like feelings and attitudes often express themselves in terms of further feelings and attitudes, and not merely action.

Secondly, and less technically, there is the widespread incredulity that one could define experiences like pain in terms of action and disposition. No doubt after a particularly nasty encounter with the dentist, my pain leads me to take analgesics, to wince, to touch the sore area with my tongue and, of course, to complain at great length. But the idea that all this behaviour is by definition what it is to be in pain seems just too implausible. (The old joke about behaviourists greeting each other with, 'Hi, you're feeling fine, how am I?' is an expression of this implausibility.)

The third and final reason for behaviourism's losing its allure is a little more subtle. As has been suggested in many different ways, mind's landscape is populated with features that have what is best described as an inside and an outside. Conscious experiences seem most firmly to be inner, but further examination seems to demand that this cannot be wholly right, given that we apply shared concepts to what passes in our streams of consciousness. And, with fewer obvious complications, it is clear that attitudes and actions have public, or outer, manifestations. Behaviourism is rather good on these outer aspects of our mental life, but given the objections above, it could be said to concentrate too obsessively on them. Still, it long served the purpose of at least reminding those who were excessively committed to the Cartesian picture of our inner life that the outer is no less important to understanding the mind. In recent literature, however, this purpose has now been taken over by an account which is generally regarded as a front runner in the attempt to coalesce Mind and Brain. (We shall consider this account, known as *functionalism*, at some length in chapter 7.) What has in effect happened is that the felt need to recognize the outer side of our inner natures has been more than satisfied by the thesis of functionalism. So, no longer having a need to satisfy, and subject to many pretty damning objections, behaviourism has fallen on hard times.

Note

1   You would be right if you saw that there is a possible connection between this account of causality and the deductive-regularity conception of explanation discussed in chapter 3. However, as noted a few paragraphs back, we are leaving any deeper investigation of the connection of causation and explanation until later.

6

Identity

Aristotle seems to have thought the brain was a sort of radiator whose only function was cooling the blood, but now we know that some normal level of brain function is crucial for our so much as having mental lives. Moreover, the last fifty years or so have seen the idea of the mind's global dependence on the brain undergoing considerable refinement. The now charted effects of various drugs – legal and proscribed – suggest that certain states of mind depend on the presence of specific chemicals in the brain. And our growing awareness that localized brain damage, or direct stimulation during surgery, dramatically alters various specific features of mental life suggest that, not just the whole of mental functioning, but each state of mind depends on something quite specific going on in the brain.

Recognizing these palpable dependencies of the mind on the brain, there is a clear temptation to think that the resolution of our triangular problem lies in some kind of coalescence of Mind and Brain. (See figure 6.1.)

Indeed, reading articles that appear even in daily newspapers, you could be forgiven for thinking that, to all intents and purposes, such a resolution has already taken place. Each new development in techniques for monitoring brain function can be guaranteed to spark off journalistic claims about how brain scientists can now see into our very thoughts. PET scan images of brain activity are headlined as pictures of what someone is seeing or thinking at the time the images are taken. There would thus seem to be no doubt in the minds of the headline writers – nor presumably in the minds of a vast majority of their readers – that studying the brain just is studying the mind.

However, though there is I think a consensus in favour of some such view – amongst many neuroscientists as well as journalists – this consensus does not extend to philosophers. Far from thinking that recent developments in neurophysiology have put the problems to rest, philosophers continue, with increasing ingenuity and precision, to worry at the issue raised by the trian-

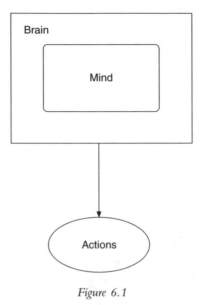

Figure 6.1

gle. Not all of them – one never gets unanimity in philosophy – but even those who do ultimately think that the secret of the mind lies in natural science do so only after engaging in quite complex philosophical discourse with their colleagues.

Is this apparent refusal to take the obviously true as simply true perverse? Philosophers certainly have a bad reputation in this regard. Long after most ordinary people are satisfied that there is a table in front of them, philosophers will go to great lengths considering ways of guaranteeing this to be so (often, in the eyes of other philosophers, failing in this task)! Still, when it comes to the issues of bedrock – of the placement of the mind in the natural world – I think this parody of philosophical thought is inappropriate. Whilst I can see the funny side of philosophical efforts to shore up the obvious – even whilst also noting a certain intellectual bravura in these efforts – the philosophical literature on the placement problem is neither merely virtuoso performance, nor does its value lie elsewhere.

Getting right an account of the mind which gives it an intelligible place in the physical world is a serious business. If we are precipitate in our treatment of the relationship between mind and brain – if we accept some view without really understanding it – then we might end up with a thoroughly shallow view of what it is to be a person. And this in turn could have dire consequences for how we think of, and treat, individual human beings. Perhaps in the end, there might be reason to think the mental landscape is less rich than it seems; that when we do come to see how it fits on the bedrock of our material nature, we will have to cut it down to size in some way. But it would be a terrible mistake to think any such thing is required before we have strained to get the fit right.

For this reason, the discussions in this chapter and those which follow will be detailed, even intricate. Whereas in other contexts, one might be willing to overlook certain twists and turns in an argument, here we will be fairly dogged in our pursuit of objections and counter-objections (subject, of course, to the fact that this book is intended as a first, and not the last, word on the philosophy of mind). And because of the intricacies of the subject-matter, it will sometimes happen that there will be several argumentative balls in the air at the same time, a situation we will handle by pausing at places in one argument whilst we pursue another. (I do promise that when this sort of thing happens, it will be well signposted.)

Identity

As always in philosophy, the first thing one must do is to find out exactly what is being said – in this case by those who think, for example, that PET scans show people's thoughts, that there are chemicals which alter our psychological states, and that, as summarized above, understanding the brain is understanding the mind. In short, we need a clear statement of how to conceive the coalescence of Mind and Brain which is, after all, only schematically represented in figure 6.1.

Amongst the list of candidates, the one generally considered first is this: the Mind just is the Brain. Or to put it in a less provocative and perhaps more intelligible way: mental states like your feeling pain, seeing sunsets, believing that you will finally clean out the attic tomorrow and desiring to get to the end of the month without having spent more than you earned, are each states of a normally functioning brain and central nervous system.

The key word in these formulations is 'is' (or 'are' when the need for a plural arises). But be careful here. In this context, 'is' does not count as marking predication; as when, for example, we say that Jones is hungry. This latter claim tells us something about Jones, that the notion of *hunger* applies to him. However, unlike this case, the 'is' relevant to present discussion marks a special relationship known as *identity*, a typical example of which might be: Uncle Fred *is* the person mugged yesterday on Main Street. One does not understand this as saying that Uncle Fred instantiates a certain property, one that might apply, as hunger could, to lots of different people. Instead, what is asserted is that Uncle Fred and the unfortunate victim of yesterday's mugging are one and the same person.

The basic idea, in respect of Mind and Brain, is that there is an *identity* between what are generally called 'states of mind' and specific neurophysiological states. Your pain, for example, is a firing of certain neurons in your central nervous system; your belief that the sun made an appearance last Wednesday is a certain overall state of some part of that same nervous system. Of course, we do not yet know exactly what these neural states are, but that doesn't matter for the present discussion. The thought is that if we can accept in principle that these identities are true, we will have a way to conceive the coalescence of Mind and Brain, a way that would thereby get us out of the difficulties posed by the triangle. For clearly, if these identities are plausible, then we do not have *two* things competing to bring about actions. Just as Uncle Fred and the man who was mugged yesterday on Main Street are not two persons, each leading separate lives, so mental states, being brain states, cannot compete with them. And on this view − known generally as the *identity theory* − it is obvious why, for example, a PET scan of someone's brain activity shows something about that person's mental functioning. Given that the mind just is the brain, monitoring the one is monitoring the other.

Initial Problems

Of course, as you might expect, there are problems. First of all, we have to be more cautious about the example used to motivate the identity theory. Uncle Fred is a specific individual, as is the unfortunate victim of the mugging. Finding out in this case that the identity claim is true is tantamount to finding out that there are not two individuals but only one (though there seem to be two different ways of referring to that individual). But it is far from clear that the identity of mental states and brain states suggested above is one that relates different individual or particular things. As you will appreciate later, there are lots of reasons to be concerned about this, but here is one obvious consideration: pains are most naturally thought of as a *kind* of mental state. When you play too much tennis, you get the pain generally called 'tennis elbow'. If you are incautious, this can happen to you each summer. So, if there is an identity in the offing between your tennis–elbow pain and some firing of neurons in your central nervous system, it will be an identity between kinds, and not simply between particulars. The relevant identity will be between the tennis-elbow kind of pain and a kind of activity (say, C–fibre firing) in your central nervous system. Hence, one might reasonably worry whether identity of the Uncle Fred sort is an appropriate model for what is going on in the Mind/Brain case.

(A brief note about C-fibres: some time ago, work in neurophysiology suggested a special role, in respect of pain, for a certain tract of neurons in the cerebral cortex. These were called C-fibres. More recently, neurophysiologists have abandoned this initial suggestion. But, for illustrative purposes – and that is all that matters to the thesis of identity – philosophers still tend to talk of pain and C-fibre stimulation. But, ironically, it is now assumed by many philosophical writers that 'C-fibres' were always merely an invented neural correlate of pain whose *only* purpose is illustrative. But this is no less mistaken than the original neurophysiology on which talk of C-fibre stimulation was originally based.)

Second, many people, on first or even second hearing, find the identity theory problematic. It is not that they think it wrong, it is just that they find it difficult to comprehend. Apparent as it is that our brains must be functioning more or less normally for us to be alive and to have mental states, it is not easy to understand the further claim that these mental items are one and the same as something neurophysiological. To put it simply: neurophysiology is about electrochemistry and biology; it is about the flow of organic molecules and electrical impulses rather than about anything mental. In the Uncle Fred example of identity, there was no such difficulty. Uncle Fred and the victim of the mugging are both individual human beings, so it takes no great imagination to understand how it could happen that they turned out to be one and the same human being. But our hopes and fears, not to mention pains and thoughts of the weather, seem so different from rhythmic movements of electrical charges along neural pathways, so it is just not easy to imagine how the one could be identical to the other.

These initial worries need to be refined, discussed and ultimately addressed before we can take some kind of identity theory seriously. And, as you will soon see, this is not something we can do in a few paragraphs. Moreover, our detailed examination will take us down various paths that will at times seem detours from the philosophy of mind. Of course, this is not how I see it, and I hope you will come to agree that the route chosen is ultimately the most rewarding, even if not the shortest. Most tours of the philosophy of mind tend to speed by the identity theory on their way to what are regarded as more interesting and rewarding destinations. But I think this is a mistake. Lingering over versions of the identity theory – appreciating the arguments against them and coming none the less to see their appeal – will deepen our understanding, not only of this particular coalescing strategy, but of all such strategies. It will also give us a slightly different perspective on the mental realm itself.

Opting for Identity

It was suggested above that the Uncle Fred case might not be suitable to illustrate the identity of, say, pains and brain states. Partly, this is because the latter is most plausibly seen as a case of identity between kinds or types, and there are important differences between type identities and Uncle Fred cases. But also, even aside from this issue, there is this further difference. It is possible to imagine assigning detectives, one to stake out Main Street and one to trail Uncle Fred, so that the identity would be discovered when notes are compared at the end of the day. But even if one thought of the identity of the mental and physical as an identity of particular items, it is simply not plausible to imagine this being established by such detective work.

These difficulties are at least implicitly acknowledged by advocates of the identity route to coalescence. Instead of the kind of direct, observational evidence that might be deployed in Uncle Fred cases, one finds a much less direct kind of argumentation. A certain softening-up strategy is employed: one is invited to consider various cases – mostly drawn from the history of science – in which identity claims have provided a kind of intellectual relief. In these cases, certain identities integrated domains that we were struggling to understand with those we had already understood, thus simplifying the intellectual scene. We are then encouraged to think that this same sort of relief could carry over to the troublesome relationship between mind and brain. Thus, it is not that we *discover* mind–brain identity to hold by staking out each of the relevant phenomena. Rather, we are encouraged to *opt* for the identity because of the kind of benefit it has been shown to provide in other disciplines.

Work on objections to identity will come in due course; the vague sense that there is something strange and incomprehensible about identifying features of the mental landscape with brain processes must be sharpened into something resembling an argumentative objection. But I should like first to look in some detail at a case commonly cited by identity theorists (and their opponents) as suitable for softening us up in the way described above. Whilst there are a number of cases cited in the literature on identity, I have chosen the story of heat as the most representative.

Heat and Identity

Even before the rise of science, we knew quite a bit about heat. Aside from common knowledge about the causes and effects of heat, quite considerable specialist knowledge had been amassed by blacksmiths, metalworkers and other artisans. More or less everyone knew that heat melts things, that metal objects left in the sun get too hot to touch and that fire can cause things to twist and distort. But blacksmiths and metalworkers understood how to use heat to transform the properties of substances in systematic ways. Taking common and specialist knowledge together, it seems reasonable enough to describe what was known as a folk theory of heat. Whilst even the most knowledgeable remained ignorant of the underlying nature of heat, the mass of accumulated generalizations about its behaviour would have compared favourably with those in other areas of folk endeavour. What was known of heat would have far outstripped in detail and accuracy the morass of claims which we now describe as folk medicine.

With the rise of science in the seventeenth century came the hope that we could gain a deeper insight into the folk theory of heat; as more and more came to be known about the underlying nature of physical change, there was the prospect that we could come to understand *why* the folk theory of heat was true. The foundation for this was, of course, the success of the Newtonian picture of the physical world. Treating matter in motion as fundamental, and accounting for it with mathematical precision using Newtonian mechanics, it had become possible to explain and predict phenomena that had up to then been only dimly understood. It was with some optimism then that early theorists set about looking for direct connections between the theory of heat and the motion of matter. But, unfortunately, these first efforts led nowhere. Heat from friction seemed to have something to do with motion, but there were many other heat sources, like fire and the Sun, and no one had a clue about how to connect these with the Newtonian world of matter in motion. Moreover, many of the changes brought about by heat – for example, changes to the hardness of metals – seemed completely unrelated to motion.

In the eighteenth century, progress at last seemed on the cards. Heat, which had by then come to be known as one of the 'imponderables', was being pondered using ideas that were recognizably Newtonian, even if they were off to the side of Newton's own work. The key here was the claim that heat was a substance made up of invisible small particles, albeit particles of a different sort from those that made up ponderable matter. The basic idea was that these heat particles exist in all substances, that they repel one another, and that there might be different kinds of heat particle, some more energetic in repulsion than others. Thinking of this substance as essentially a ubiquitous fluid, it came to be called 'caloric fluid'.

The caloric theory had some success. It could explain why heat flowed from hotter to colder bodies, and why an equilibrium was reached when the bodies were at the same temperature. After all, this is just what you would expect of a ubiquitous fluid whose constituent particles repelled one another.

It could also explain the difference between heat and temperature which had by then become well-known. Heat was a measure of the quantity of caloric, whereas temperature was a measure of the intensity of repulsion within it. But there were also a number of problems, heat generated by friction being chief among them. It was all very well treating friction as a way of 'squeezing' a certain amount of caloric out of an object, but there seemed no limit to the amount of heat that you could get by friction, and no one wanted to accept that we could produce an indefinite amount of a fluid in this way.

In the middle of the nineteenth century, various developments in physics and chemistry, as well as accumulated problems, led to a complete rejection of the caloric account, and also to a radical change in our conception of heat. Temperature came to be understood as a measure of the motion of the ponderable particles – the molecules – of which everything is made. And heat, now no longer a substance nor even a specific motion, came to be thought of as a transfer of motive energy. These features of what is now called the 'dynamical theory' of heat were at first greeted with scepticism. Though enthusiasm for the caloric theory was at a low ebb, it seemed to some just bizarre that temperature was merely a motion of molecules. Indeed, when an early theorist suggested the dynamical view to a colleague, he was told: but that would lead to the absurd consequence that you could raise the temperature of a liquid just by stirring it. (The German theorist to whom this was addressed treated it as a serious objection, but he set about seeing what would happen. And he returned the following week saying, with evident surprise, that one could indeed raise temperature this way.)

The idea that heat is itself nothing more than a transfer of motive energy is even more counter-intuitive. In effect, what the dynamical theory says is that there is no underlying difference between what happens when you are pushed, and what happens when you touch something hot. In the first case, the transfer of energy results in a co-ordinated displacement of all of your molecules from one place to another, whereas in the other a displacement takes place only within the molecules of which you are made. At bottom then, heat is neither a fluid-like substance nor even a force; it is simply a transfer of energy that sometimes, but not always, shows up as temperature change when molecules are displaced. (This is sufficiently counter-intuitive for many philosophical summaries to get it slightly wrong; there is a tendency to confuse the motion of molecules, which is temperature, with heat.)

The above story has three important stages, and identity plays a crucial role in two of them. In the first, we have a folk theory of heat – a theory that consists of all the true generalizations that were known about heat phenomena. (As the search for a deeper understanding of heat gathered pace, this folk theory gave way to a more sophisticated set of generalizations that came to be called 'thermodynamics', but this will not affect the basic point.)

In the second stage, and under the influence of Newton, scientists came to believe in the existence of an invisible caloric fluid; by connecting features of this fluid with features that figure in the folk theory of heat, they hoped to give us a deeper understanding of that theory. And this connection is made in terms of identity: the idea is that heat *is one and the same* as caloric fluid, and the properties of the latter are one and the same as properties (like temperature) that figure in the folk theory. The third stage differs substantially from the second as far as scientific content is concerned, but the role of identity is pretty much the same. Gone, and not missed, is caloric, but the connection between the folk theory of heat (by then transformed into thermodynamics) and the underlying physical reality is still framed in terms of the identity relation. 'Heat is a transfer of motive energy' and 'temperature is a measure of molecular motion' are both identity statements; they are used to tie the properties of a true, but not fully understood, account to properties of another account which is both true and more fundamental.

In thinking of this example, it is important to keep hold of the following:

(a)   The identities that figure are identities between properties or kinds, and thus stand in contrast to the Uncle Fred case.

(b)   In connecting properties by the relation of identity, one domain of knowledge is integrated into a second, and better understood, domain. Moreover, this integration allows us to understand the first domain in terms of the second.

(c)   The identities that we now accept took a long time to establish. Depending on when you begin counting, it took several hundred years for us to identify heat and energy transfer, temperature and motion.

(d)   At the outset, the integrating identities of the dynamical account seemed far from obvious. It is not uncommon for historians of science to bemoan the fact that elements of the dynamical theory were entertained in the seventeenth century, only to be lost for a century or so whilst the incorrect caloric theory held sway. But, aside from the obvious fact that the caloric theory was recognizably inspired by the Newtonian picture, this should not be surprising. It is understandable why one might find it counter-intuitive to think of heat and temperature in the way that we do.[1]

Heat and Mind

The lessons learned from the long, though here very much abbreviated, story of heat can now be carried over to the study of mind. In chapter 3, it was suggested that our talk of the mental can be viewed as part of an explanatory scheme we employ for understanding each other (and ourselves). Knowing what someone knows, believes, wants, fears, hopes, regrets and intends, as well as what she is feeling (or suffering) and what kind of mood she is in, gives us a pretty good idea of what further attitudes she is likely to adopt and what kinds of action she will engage in. As was noted, the application of the concepts of the mental realm to a particular individual might not always appear to be like the application of a genuinely scientific theory; the idea that folk psychology is in this sense a theoretical enterprise is itself controversial. None the less, there is a lot to be said for regarding the narratives we employ in making sense of what people do and suffer as owing something to the ways in which we explain the world generally.

The folk theory of heat existed, partly as common knowledge, and partly as the possession of experts, for thousands of years before any true and genuinely fundamental explanation became available. Similarly, it is claimed, the underlying truths about people contained in folk psychology now exist as a body of knowledge in need of some fundamental support. And armed with our current and exponentially increasing knowledge of biology, physiology and neural mechanisms, we are now in a position to give folk psychology that support by identifying thoughts and experiences with events in, or states of, the brain.

Like the identification of temperature and molecular motion, mind–brain identification often takes the form of property identity. For example, I happen to believe that the rain is easing off, and that the sun will come out shortly. Since there is some shopping that I want to do, it is therefore better to wait a while. These beliefs and desires are no doubt shared by other people in my street who, like me, are glancing out of the window from time to time. They are properties we have in common – properties which make it intelligible why those of us who share them will emerge from our flats – in the sunshine – in the next hour or so. What the identity theorist tells us is that these are in fact properties of our brains. They are enormously complicated properties, to be sure, but suited to play the role they do in producing the bodily movements typical of someone setting out to the shops.

The story is similar in respect of experience. When I play too much tennis, I get a dull ache in my forearm, just below or around my elbow. Its presence will lead me to put on the special bandage I once bought, and, if it gets bad enough, to desist from any kind of activity with that arm. Many others have the same kind of experience and react in the same ways. Even though the offending activity may vary from case to case, we all suffer from what is called 'tennis elbow', and, knowing this, an observer would find it fairly easy to make predictions about our behaviour. What the identity theory says is that it will be possible to discover something quite specific going on in our brains when such pain is experienced, something brought on by a certain kind of exertion and leading to a certain kind of avoidance behaviour. The claim then is that experienced tennis-elbow pain *is* that kind of event in the brain.

The analogy with the folk theory of heat encourages the idea that such identities need by no means be obvious, Just as it took a long time for us to get to the point of identifying heat and transfer of energy, so it has taken us even longer to reach our present state of neurophysiological knowledge, and to be encouraged by that knowledge to think that we can identify our mental lives with specific properties of a functioning brain.

The sceptical among you might think: how can an experience be something physical, something like a pattern of neural fibres firing in a region of the brain? Isn't pain just too different from any kind of electrically induced movement of chemicals? Here again the story of heat suggests something apt. It has turned out, contrary to the folks' initial intuitions, that heat is neither something substantial – e.g. a fluid – that moves from one place to another, nor a special kind of force. Yet, even if it there was some initial resistance, that has been no bar to the acceptance of the relevant identities. Just now, it might seem difficult to understand (and accept) that what I experience when my elbow hurts is in fact a pattern of chemical transfer and neural firing in my nervous system. But like the dynamical story of heat, this is something that will seem less strange with time. The imponderable phenomenon of pain (and, with some qualifications, other mental phenomena) will come to be thought of as properties of the very ponderable matter that we are made of.

Admittedly, the story of heat by itself is not an argument for the identity theory. Indeed, as one author has put it: 'The mind–brain identity theory is notoriously short of arguments, and some people embrace the doctrine out of little more than a pious regard or even reverence for the physical sciences.'[2] Nor is the fact that, if true, the identity theory would solve the triangular problem at one fell swoop any more of an argument for it; the utility of some thesis is scarcely evidence for its truth. Yet the lack of an overwhelming argument in favour is certainly not a reason to reject a view. So our final judgement about the identity theory will just have to wait until we know more; perhaps, like the dynamical story about heat, acceptance must be preceded by an intellectual revolution in our ideas about the mind.

Leibniz's Law and Identity

Whilst this might seem reasonable advice, patience of this sort is not a philosophical trait. Besides, the identity theory, containing at its centre the logical notion of identity, offers an inviting target. Think back to the case of Uncle Fred, and the claim that he is the very person who was mugged on Main Street. What kind of consideration might be used to show this claim as *false*? Well, if you could establish that Uncle Fred had been nowhere near Main Street on the day in question, or that the mugger's victim had dark hair and Uncle Fred is bald, the identity would crumble. Identity implies that any and every property of the one thing is shared by the 'other'. For if the identity is true, there is really only one thing in question.

Called 'Leibniz's Law' (after the seventeenth-century philosopher originally responsible for this way of thinking about identity), this highly intuitive idea can be expressed in a formal style this way:

$$\text{(LL)} \quad a = b \rightarrow (\emptyset a \leftrightarrow \emptyset b)$$

That is:

> If a is identical to b then: $\emptyset$ is true of a if and only if $\emptyset$ is true of b (where $\emptyset$ could be any property).

As a conditional, the antecedent of LL – the identity claim – is false whenever the consequent is false. And this makes it easy to see the general pattern of arguments that might be deployed against identity claims. In the case of Uncle Fred, this might work as follows. First, we assert LL for the case in question:

> If Uncle Fred is the person mugged on Main Street then: Uncle Fred is $\emptyset$ if and only if the mugger's victim is $\emptyset$.

If $\emptyset$ stands for the property of being dark-haired, then we have:

> If Uncle Fred is the person mugged on Main Street then: Uncle Fred is dark-haired if and only if the mugger's victim is dark-haired.

But finding out that Uncle Fred is completely bald and the mugger's victim is indeed dark-haired shows the 'then' part to be false. That is:

> It is false that Uncle Fred is dark-haired if and only if the mugger's victim is dark-haired.

So we conclude that:

> Uncle Fred is not the person mugged on Main Street.

I have taken some time to show how this works because the lessons learned will be important later on. But, as noted earlier, the Uncle Fred case is not quite the same as the heat/temperature or Mind/Brain identities, for the latter are most plausibly seen as identities of kinds or properties. So whilst the pattern of anti-identity arguments follows Leibniz's Law, strictly speaking we would need to write out a property version of that logical principle.

Though the logical formalism needed to write out LL for property identity is a bit more sophisticated, the general idea is going to be the same: if we can show that there is a property of temperature – a property of this property – which is not true of the kinetic (i.e. motion) energy of molecules, then temperature and kinetic energy cannot be one and the same. For example, if we could show that the temperature was rising, but the kinetic energy was not, then this would undermine the identity, and, with it, the whole of the dynamical story of heat. But, as you would expect, this is a purely imagined case; in the world as we know it, any rise in temperature is a rise in kinetic energy, and similarly for any of the *physical* properties of temperature that figure in natural science. (Note, however, that the idea of imagined cases – cases which we know to be false, but which *could have been true* – is going to be important later on in our discussion.)

Note also though that the application of LL is not always straightforward. Remember the adherent of the old, caloric theory who thought absurd the idea of raising the temperature of a liquid by stirring it? Let us call him 'Otto' (since the reported incident took place in Germany). Suppose we then argue as follows:

> If the 60°C temperature of a liquid *is* the kinetic energy of its molecules then: any property of the temperature holds if and only if it holds of the kinetic energy.

> Here is one property of the temperature: Otto thinks it is a measure of intensity of repulsion in caloric fluid. But this is *not* a property of the kinetic energy, since Otto does not think that such energy has anything to do with caloric.

Therefore,

> The 60°C temperature of the liquid is *not* the kinetic energy of its molecules.

Clearly, we cannot allow this argument to go through; we can scarcely reject profoundly important theoretical identities in physics on the basis of someone's mistaken beliefs about the relevant properties.

We could, of course, consider the above argument as a counter-example to LL: rather than rejecting the identity of temperature and mean kinetic energy, we could reject that logical principle used in the first premiss of the argument. But this is overkill. Leibniz's Law, as I have suggested, is pretty fundamental to our conception of identity, and it seems pretty obviously true. A less drastic move is to question the second premiss in the above argument. As the example was set up, someone named 'Otto' really did have these beliefs. But that is not the issue here. What the premiss claims is that in believing something about, e.g. temperature, Otto's beliefs should be counted as genuine properties of temperature. It is this feature that makes it inappropriate for use in the argument, and hence allows us to reject the above argument without threatening LL. What Otto, or anyone else, believes about something is not a property of the thing itself, and thus should not be allowed as a genuine substitution in LL. Moreover, this should come as no surprise, since we saw very early on that the mental 'relations' (desires, hopes, fears, intendings, as well as beliefs) in which we commonly stand to objects are distinctly slippery.

Refining the Objections

(a)   Dull Pains

Deploying LL – though taking care not to be fooled by only apparent properties – philosophers have used it as the central device for probing Mind/Brain identity theories. Historically, the first arguments tended to focus on what were regarded as certain obvious differences between the mental and physical. In effect, they took as their starting-point intuitions about the apparently unbridgeable gap between the mental and the physical, and LL served as the framework in transforming these intuitions into arguments.

The first kind of case involves certain commonly ascribed properties of experiences. Consider, for example, tennis-elbow pain. Unlike some kinds of pain, tennis-elbow pain is mostly dull, with only occasional twinges when the elbow is twisted suddenly in a particular way. On the identity theory, this pain is one and the same as a kind of brain state, a state whose precise nature we have yet to discover, but which, for the purposes of argument, we shall continue to describe as the firing of C-fibres. C-fibre firing, like any phenomenon in the brain, is bound to be a complex process involving the generation of electrical potentials by the movement of molecules across various axon/membrane boundaries and through inter-neuron gaps. Whatever the full and correct story, it seems perfectly true to say that these electrical phenomena will *not* be dull with occasional twinges. So doesn't this count as an LL case showing that my pain is not identical to any kind of event or process in the brain? The pain, but not the C-fibre firing, is dull. Moreover, arguing from the other direction, isn't it also unacceptable to describe a pain as having chemico-electrical properties?

Tempting though it is, this argument doesn't really work; it trades on a rather too hasty formulation of the identity theory. Strictly, we should not say that *pain* is identical to C-fibre firing, but rather that it is *the experiencing or having of the pain* which is identical to C-fibre firing. Put this way, the objection lapses: it is not my having or experiencing pain that is dull with occasional twinges, so the worry about whether dullness could be a property of C-fibre firing is not relevant. For the same reason, it is not relevant to worry whether my pain is said to have chemico-electrical properties, since it is the having of pain, and not merely pain, that is relevant to identity.

A couple of comments about this way of skirting the objection are in order, and they will lead us into the next objection. First, though I haven't mentioned it, the astute reader might have noticed an asymmetry in the treatment of the various properties. If you are inclined to accept identity theory, then you will be genuinely puzzled by the thought that dullness comes out as a property of C-fibre firing. Indeed, you are most likely to think that dullness simply couldn't be a property of C-fibre firing, and therefore that identity is in real trouble. For a devotee of identity, then, the more careful rewording will come as a real relief. But – and this is where the asymmetry comes in – you might not feel that we had ever needed to worry that pain might turn out to have chemico-electrical properties. After all, if the identity theory is true, then, as in the case of the discovery of other scientific identities, you would expect there to be some surprises. Who, before 1850 or so, would have thought that temperature is a property of molecular motion, or that heat is no different from the transfer of motive energy? If we can accept these, then why can't we also accept that pain, being C-fibre firing, has chemico-electrical properties?

This asymmetry suggests that we wouldn't have had to rework the identity claim to deal with initially odd-sounding attributions of physical properties to pain, but that we do have to take evasive action to get around attributing dullness to brain phenomena. But – and this is the subject of my second comment – what is the explanation of this difference?

'Pains', 'twinges', 'itches', 'tingles' are count nouns – nouns whose plurals suggest that we are dealing with a multitude of individual things or kinds of thing. Just as a the plural noun 'chairs' suggests there can be many different objects each of which is a chair, so the noun 'pains' suggests different items each of which is a pain. Moreover, it is a grammatical feature of nouns in general, and these in particular, that adjectives apply to them. Thus we speak of green chairs and dull pains, as well as icy tingles and sharp twinges. All of this is undeniable, and suggests that pains are a class of things which can be distinguished from one another by their specific properties – properties picked out by appropriate adjectives. And that, of course, is what creates trouble for the identity theory: for if a dull pain is a pain with the property of dullness, then we would have to swallow awfully hard to accept that a C–fibre firing was dull.

But grammar can be misleading. Our talk of pains seems less committed to the multitude model than our talk of chairs. Thus, whilst we do say, 'There was a pain in my elbow', rather on the model of, 'There was a chair in the sitting-room,' we also – and extensively – talk of pain *adjectivally*, and this way of talking does not carry over to most other count nouns. Thus we say that an experience is painful, but we do not tend to say such things as: 'The sitting-room is chairful.' This, in turn, suggests that when we use predicates such as 'dull' to convey information about pains, these predicates are not best treated on the model of object and property. Being made of wood, for example, is a perfectly genuine property of some chairs, but being dull might be not so much a property of some object called a pain as more a way of pointing to a kind of painfulness.

By itself, this grammatical point might not be quite enough to persuade, though when it is combined with another observation, the necessary conclusion is hard to resist. The second observation is this: talk of pains suggests that they are things or items that we can count, but it also suggests that they are at least as independent of us as chairs and tables. But, of course, this is non-sense. Pains, itches and the like are always tied to persons; pains are always someone's pains. Thus, though we naturally say, for example, that Smith has a pain in his elbow, we are not – or shouldn't be – fooled into thinking of this as on the model of 'Smith has a coin in his pocket.' For Smith can take the coin out of his pocket and give it to someone else. But (sadly for Smith) he cannot do this kind of thing with his pain. For this reason, a less misleading formulation of Smith's predicament is 'Smith's experience is painful.' This ascription not only avoids the temptation to treat pains as objects with properties, it highlights the role of a subject in such an ascription.

The upshot is this: when we reformulate identity claims as holding between someone's having a painful experience and someone's C–fibres firing, we are no longer treating predicates like 'dull' as properties suitable for substitution in LL. The linguistic point, and the fact that pains are essentially connected with persons, suggest that this reformulation is wholly appropriate. Moreover, though we could try the same manoeuvre with respect to the chemico-electric properties of C-fibre firing, it seems less pressing. Thus we might say that it is the *undergoing* of C-fibre firing that is at issue, and an undergoing does not have chemico-electric properties, even though the firing itself does. But this move is neither required nor particularly inviting. As the case of heat suggests, we ought simply to allow that someone's experiencing pain might well turn out to have chemico-electric properties.

(b)   Locating Pains
The reply to the first objection has taken us some time, but you will find that it is not time wasted. Though the objection does not stand, some of the issues uncovered in discussing it will come in handy later on. Also, one of the points raised will make the reply to the second LL objection easier.

This second objection, like the first, was made almost as soon as the identity theory was propounded in the late 1950s.[3] Following the structure of the previous LL objection, it appeals to the property of spatiotemporal location, rather than properties like dullness. On the one hand, it is claimed that we have no trouble in assigning a spatiotemporal location to such things as C-fibre firing. But, on the other hand, we have a great deal of trouble assigning spatial – though not temporal – locations to pains. And in so far as we do think we can assign them a location, we either do so in a misleading way or in a way completely at variance with the location of C-fibre firing. We do say, for example, that we have a pain in the elbow, but it is misleading to think of this as an attempt at locating our experience of pain. Instead, it is a location of the apparent and/or real site of the pain-causing damage. (We are all familiar with referred pain – pain which appears to result from damage to a place where there is none. Perhaps the most extreme such case, sadly familiar given the number of war victims in the twentieth century, is the pain 'located' in a limb which has been amputated.)

In any case, even if someone was convinced that his pain was itself actually in his elbow, this would scarcely let the identity theory off the hook. For on that theory the experience of pain is C-fibre firing, something going on in the cerebral cortex, not the elbow. But, of course, if the pain were really in the elbow, then since C-fibre firing is not, LL would show the identity to be false. Moreover, as seems more in keeping with how we do think of the matter, if we cheerfully admit that we find it merely difficult to locate the pain experience, this is equally damaging for the theory, since we do not find it difficult to locate C-fibre firing. Nor, finally, would the identity theory be saved by reference to a more realistic description of the physiology of damage. If we insist on locating the pain so as to include both the C-fibre firing in the cortex and the stimulation from the so-called 'nociceptors' in the real or referred area of damage, this spread-out location of pain is still unacceptable. For it still requires us to assign a pretty precise spatial location to something that we do not easily think of as in this or that place.

The key to answering this objection is contained in its very formulation. Note the phrases: 'we do not find it easy to assign location . . .' and 'we do not tend to think of [pain experiences] as in this or that place.' Both of these phrases suggest that the objection relies heavily on a certain epistemic inadequacy, and, if the lessons of the heat case have taught us anything, it is that we must not be misled by our own failures of understanding. As I have several times noted, the identity account of temperature and heat is very far from intuitive; knowing the story even in outline, it takes only a little effort to think of characters like the imagined Otto who would have found our contemporary view of heat incredible. But immediate credibility is not a good test in that case, and it is not a good test in the present one. If experiencing pain is in fact C-fibre firing, then, taking the best scientific advice about the location of the latter, we have thereby found a way to locate pain experience. And this surely must override any original disinclination we had to give our painful experiences spatial locations.

It would have been a different matter if it were simply *impossible* for pains to be located spatially. For example, if someone suggested that, in spite of our inability to find it up to now, the number two could be found on the surface of Jupiter, we would at best humour him in this madness. Numbers are not things we can imagine as located in space; nor is this merely an epistemic limitation on our part. It is true that we are unable to imagine the number two being somewhere, but this limitation is itself the result of a real impossibility: that of numbers in general having spatial location. Some evidence of this real impossibility, if it is needed, comes from the fact that numbers are no more easily located in time than in space. The very fact that we are unable to think of them in time as well as space – that they are simply not spatiotemporal items – is connected to their abstractness. But this kind of consideration does not carry over items in the mental realm. For a start, pains are all too obviously located in time and this immediately makes them quite different from abstract objects like numbers. But also the temptation we all have to think of our pains as located, as it were, where it hurts – at the site of damage – suggests that we find intelligible the idea of pains as being somewhere. To be sure, there are good reasons for being suspicious about such apparent location, so it might seem somewhat hypocritical of me to now use this as part of an argument in defence of the identity theory. But, in the present context, the point is not that we truly locate them in this way so much as that we can conceive of the possibility of location. Combined with the lesson of heat, namely that an identity theory can actually give us insight into some phenomenon, this should lessen resistance to the idea of a pain as at the place where C-fibres fire.

Experience isn't Everything

It seems then that, for slightly different reasons in each case, neither dullness nor spatial location present insuperable obstacles to accepting the identity of Mind and Brain. Yet I would expect that you have some residual dissatisfaction with the identity theory, and think that these two kinds of case only just scratch the surface. You might think that in the end we might well have to admit that the Mind is the Brain, but there still seems to be some obstacle to this thought that has yet to be canvassed. If this is how you feel, hang on, for I believe that the LL objection about to be considered will finally get to the nub of the issue. (Though, as you will see, we have not been wasting our time, since points raised above will figure in what follows.)

However, before we move on to the most current – and difficult – objection to identity theories, let me make explicit something that may already have been bothering you. Any identity theory is intended to show that the mental realm is not in causal/explanatory competition with a physiological story. As has been noted, identity provides the most straightforward way to implement the Coalescence strategy, and coalescence of some sort is the most natural way to deal with the problems raised by the triangle. But the whole of our detailed discussion so far has been about only one of the major categories of mind – namely experience   and even then it has focused almost obsessively on one kind of experience – pain. What has happened to the other features of mind's landscape? Are we to understand the attitudes as properties of our nervous system? And where do actions fit in the identity project? The identity account was offered without any disclaimer about attitudes and actions, so it ought to have something to say here. Yet for the most part, discussions of identity – and not merely the one offered here – tend to concentrate on experience. Speculating a bit, I think there are two interconnected reasons for this.

First, the papers that put the identity theory on the map in the first place tended exclusively to target experiences. There is reason to think that this focus on experience is evidence of a certain prejudice about the mind that we have noted more than once. It is the prejudice that the mental landscape is best represented by phenomena immediately available to consciousness. But – and this is a second reason – aside from this background prejudice it was, and to some extent it still is, supposed that experiences are the most difficult phenomena of mind for any coalescence account. The manifest nature of pains, and the introspective qualities of our perceptions of the external world, seem just so different from patterns of chemico-electrical activity that take place in our brains. And this difference can make it seem as if experience is the real, and perhaps the only, challenge for an identity account.

Of course, neither of these is a good justification for ignoring attitudes and actions. If an identity theory is to deliver the goods, it will have to say something about beliefs, desires, emotions and the like, and it will have to cope with the delicate problem of our active natures. (Remember that the triangle side-stepped the problem by simply noting that, whatever else was true, a typical non-mental action would include a movement of muscles, and ultimately of the body.) However, not being able to deal with everything at once, I suggest simply putting down a marker here: issues of attitude, action and the identity account will figure later, after we have taken the identity account of experience as far as we can in this chapter.

Essentialism

The message of LL is that identicals must share all their properties, and we have considered – and so far rejected – objections to the identity theory starting from this background assumption. But, in recent years, it has been recognized that LL provides an even stronger constraint on identity claims, and this constraint has been the centre of renewed attacks on mind–brain identity. Here is how Saul Kripke, one of the main contributors to this newer debate, sums up this stronger constraint:

> If $a = b$, then the identity of a with b is necessary, and any essential property of the one must be an essential property of the other.[4]

Since it will not be immediately obvious what an essential property is, and therefore what this claim comes to, let me spell this out with an example.

You are a wealthy collector of art – though one not known for being too fussy about the provenance of your acquisitions – and you are visited by a none too honest character who styles himself an 'art dealer'. Only half thinking that he might have something 'interesting', you are none the less startled to find yourself confronted with what looks like the *Mona Lisa*. Unsurprisingly, your first reaction is to think that the painting is a fake. Surely the painting in front of you cannot be the *Mona Lisa*, though the dealer insists that it is. So you set out to use (albeit informally) LL considerations to probe this possible identification.

The first and most obvious thing to wonder is about the location of the painting. As far as you know, the *Mona Lisa* hangs in the Louvre in

Paris. Doesn't this show that the painting in front of you simply cannot be the *Mona Lisa*? Here the dealer has a ready reply: where a painting hangs is a property of it that can vary over time. 'Sometimes it is in one place, sometimes in another,' he says, hinting broadly that his sources have been careful enough to conceal what would have been, if noticed, the art theft of the century. Being in your house is not a property you would have thought true of the *Mona Lisa*, but, given the dealer's claims, this property is not one you can rely on to challenge the identity. After all, he is right to insist that hanging in this or that place is an accidental, or non-essential, property; the *Mona Lisa* remains the *Mona Lisa* when it is moved from one place to another.

Unsatisfied that this answer settles it, though now even more fascinated, you ask the dealer who painted it. Not being particularly informed about art himself, he checks through some papers and announces that the papers prove that it was painted by Giuseppe Bloggs. Almost relieved, you say that you now know that the picture is a fake – that it is not identical to the *Mona Lisa* – because the latter was painted by Leonardo, and not Bloggs. The dealer is taken aback by this, but only briefly. 'I shall sort this out and be back tomorrow,' he says.

On his return, he tells you that he has some new papers that will prove the artist is now Leonardo. You point out that this is not possible, but he is unmoved. 'Yesterday,' he says, 'the painting was by Bloggs, today it is by Leonardo.' You laugh, but he goes on, 'Last week it hung in the Louvre, but today it is here. Properties change, and this painting is now by Leonardo, thus matching the property you claim to be true of the *Mona Lisa*. So what's the problem?'

The problem is, of course, that we regard the property of being painted by this or that person as an *essential* property of a painting. Given that the *Mona Lisa* was painted by Leonardo, it is simply not possible for this to change. It is, of course, possible that we are wrong about Leonardo; perhaps it will one day be proven that it was painted by Giuseppe Bloggs. But in this case, the fact that Bloggs painted it will be no less an essential property. If, as the 'dealer' claims, the painting in front of you can, as it were, change its artist, then it simply cannot be the *Mona Lisa*. One has identicals only if they share all of their properties, and also if they share the essentialness of any property that is essential.

It is often controversial whether some property is essential. I used the example of a painting, and its being executed by a particular artist, because I think this is one of the less controversial examples. But, in the context of identity claims, the point can be made without searching around too hard for any special kinds of essential property. If *a* is truly identical to *b,* then of course there is only one thing, so the claim that they are identical is itself a necessary truth. And there is a way to see this necessity as implying the existence of at least one essential property. The following paragraphs explain this, and also provide some background for the notion of necessity.

Necessity is often explained in terms of what are called 'possible worlds', a notion that we touched on in chapter 2. (In any case, philosophical depth aside, it is often simply more convenient to speak of necessity using this notion.) Counting our own world in all its circumstantial detail as one possible world, we can imagine endless other possible worlds. Our world and all its previous history up to and including my now sitting in my study constitute one possible world – the actual one – but think of everything being exactly the same except that I am now in another room. This is just one of the infinitely various possible worlds we can imagine. (Note: it is not that I have moved; in this second world I was never in my study at the relevant time.) Of course, there will also be possible worlds in which neither I nor my flat exists, so you should take this as merely an example.

Against the background of this talk of possible worlds, necessity is easily defined: a claim is necessarily true if it is true in every possible world. Foremost amongst such claims will be logical and mathematical truths. Thus, '2 + 2 = 4' and 'if P then P' are both true in our world and in every possible world; there is simply no world in which they are false. More to the present point, if an identity claim is true, then it too will be true in every possible world, and hence necessarily true. (That is to say, it will be true in every possible world where the object of the claim exists. I shall mostly assume this obvious proviso in what follows.) This should be unsurprising. Think of the identity claim:

(M)   The *Mona Lisa* is identical to *La Gioconda.*

Since this is true, there is only one object, one painting, which happens to be referred to in these two different ways. If you imagine this very object in any possible world, then, even if it happens not to be referred to by the denizens of that world (if any) by either or both of these names, (M) will still be true. How could it fail to be? We cannot imagine a single object in our world *which remains that object* whilst somehow being two non-identical things in some other world.

We can capture this by the following:

(N)   If *a* = *b* then it is necessarily true that *a* = *b*.

Using (N), we can concoct a couple of predicates that pick out certain essential properties. Here they are:

(i)   . . . is necessarily identical to a (. . . is Nec $= a$).
(ii)   . . . is necessarily identical to b (. . . is Nec $= b$).

The phrases that pick out these two properties are a little complicated, but the
idea is clear enough. Consider the object, whatever it is, that is named by a.
This object has the property of being necessarily identical to a, i.e. to itself.
And this is just what we would expect, since an object's being self-identical is
necessarily true if anything is. Using the fairly obvious notation given in (i)
and (ii), we can write it this way:

(iii) a is Nec $- a$ (i.e. a has the property of being necessarily identical to a.).

But by LL, and the accepted $a = b$, we know that b must have all the same
properties as a, so, we must also agree to:

(iv) b is Nec $= a$ (i.e. b has the property of being necessarily identical to
        a).

The properties that are ascribed in (iii) and (iv) are clearly not merely accidental properties of a and b. Given that b is necessarily identical to a, it is
obvious enough that an object in some possible world simply wouldn't be b
unless it were identical to a; being so identical is an essential property of b,
just as it is, of course, of a.

Notice that we are able to single out this essential property even though
we do not know what kind of thing a (i.e. b) is. The property picked out by
'is Nec $= a$', in being essential to a, is more like 'being painted by Leonardo'
(as said of the *Mona Lisa*) than it is like 'hangs in the Louvre'. But we did not
have to rely on any special intuition about essential properties of paintings to
get it. As noted, the idea that the creative origin of a painting is an essential
feature of it is not all that controversial, but controversy abounds in the broader
discussion of essentialism. Yet, once we recognize that any true identity is necessarily true, we have all we need to uncover at least a minimal essential property, that of being necessarily identical to the relevant object. And it is this sort
of essential property that can be used to make trouble for identity accounts of
mind and brain.

Generating the trouble unsurprisingly requires that we again appeal to LL,
only this time using an essential property. Thus, instead of worrying whether

pain and C-fibre firing can both be dull or spatially located, we must ask whether they both have: (i) the property of being necessarily identical to C-fibre firing; and (ii) the property of being necessarily identical to pain. Assuming it is true that pain is identical to C-fibre firing – assuming the antecedent of the relevant LL claim is true – these are the two candidate properties generated by the method described above. Clearly, if everything works the way as the identity theorist suggests, these two properties will come to the same thing, and will indeed apply both to pain and C-fibre firing. But we might as well explore our intuitions about whether this is in fact so using both of them.

Here are the pairs of claims that we must pass judgement on:

(1a)   Pain is necessarily identical to C-fibre firing,
(1b)   C-fibre firing is necessarily identical to C-fibre firing,

and,

(2a)   Pain is necessarily identical to pain,
(2b)   C-fibre firing is necessarily identical to pain.

Clearly, we can have no problem with (1b) and (2a), since each involves a logical truth, i.e. a claim which cannot fail to be true in every possible world. However, it is all too easy to have doubts about the others.

Other Creatures' Pains

Beginning with (1a), there is an obvious worry, one which should be apparent even without straining too hard to think about possible worlds. For right here in our world there are innumerable kinds of creature who certainly suffer pain, though they may not share our neural architecture. Primates certainly have nervous systems which have structures homologous to ours; and this is just what we would expect, given our common ancestry. So, stretching the point a bit, we might try to extend our notion of C-fibre firing to the firing of whatever fibres are homologous to them. But felines, canines and rodents, not to mention fish and fowl of various sorts, are surely capable of suffering pain, though they are unlikely to have nervous systems developed enough to have C-fibres or anything very close to them. Moreover, even if you were so committed to the identity theory as to question the presence of pain – or the absence of something close enough to C-fibres – in lower animals, there is always the Martian to contend with (or, perhaps, for followers of *Star Trek*, the

Klingon or Borg). What you have to do is to ask yourself whether it is simply incoherent to imagine that one of these alien creatures is in pain, even though you know for sure that it is made of materials, and structured in ways, that precludes having C-fibres or anything like them. If this thought is coherent – and most tend to agree that it is – then (1a) is simply false. And, though thinking about aliens requires more of a sense of what is possible than thinking about squirrels, the falsity of (1a) doesn't require our intellects to be stretched as far as possible worlds. Remember that a possible world other than the actual one is not a world we can reach by spaceship; by its very nature it is only reachable, if at all, mentally. In contrast, alien beings from other planets are, at least in principle, creatures we might someday come across. And the question here is whether we can imagine one of them suffering, as we do, with pain of some sort.

This worry about (1a) is usually called the 'multiple realizability' point, and it is usually considered a formidable threat to the identity theory.[5] Indeed, many authors think of it not merely as a threat, but as a definitive reason for rejection. Here, however, another point of view will be considered. (I didn't spend all this time setting up the discussion of essential properties just to drop a really powerful account of the mind at the first hurdle.)

Recall that the account we have been considering claims that various kinds of mental item – pain being so far our single representative – are one and the same as certain kinds of physical state. Pretending that C-fibre firing is the current favourite scientific candidate, the view is that pain is C-fibre firing in much the way that temperature is kinetic energy, or heat is a transference of motive energy. What we are faced with now is the claim that pain is not C-fibre firing because there are plenty of creatures (cats, dogs, squirrels, Martians – take your pick) who might well suffer pain though they do not even have C-fibres. The way this is often put is: pain is multiply realizable – realized this way in cats, that way in dogs, etc. – so the original identity just cannot stand.

In the literature, it is usually taken for granted that we know what it is for something like pain to be realized. But I don't think this is quite so obvious. Asked to give a specific example of what could be meant by 'realization' – outside the present context – I suspect we might think of the ways in which plans, dreams and fears are realized (or not). Seeing a piece of paper on my windscreen, I say that my fear of getting a parking ticket was realized, even though I was away for only five minutes. The use of this relation in the multiple realization point owes something to this common usage: my fear is realized by being made concrete in an appropriate way, and pain is said to be realized in being somehow made concrete by the firing of C-fibres. But not just anything can be made concrete in this sort of way; only something that is not concrete in an appropriate way in the first place will do the trick. This then raises the question of what it is that makes pain and other such mental states appropriate for being concretely realized. On the face of it, some work needs to be done to show why, for the purposes of realization, a pain is like a plan. This is because many would regard pain as quite concrete enough, or at least concrete in its own way, and therefore an inappropriate candidate for realization.

These observations are not intended to be more than suggestions. The whole thrust of our discussion up to this point has been about whether the relationship between the mental and the physical is one of identity. Talk of realization at this stage introduces many complications, not least that of getting clear what realization is, and what its relationship is to identity. However, since many of these issues will figure in the next chapter, I plan to leave further exploration of realization for now. This might seem a cheat, since multiple realization seems an obvious and devastating challenge to (1a) above, and hence to the identity theory. But it is not as bad as that. There is a perfectly reasonable evasive action that an identity theorist can take. As you will see, this move keeps the multiple realizability point at bay, though it by no means deals with all the issues raised by (1a) and (2b).

In fact, evasion is not at all difficult, since it was always optimistic to think that pain and other mental items are exactly the same kind of physical phenomena in every creature. Indeed, the very basis of the kind of identity theory under discussion suggests that this is unlikely. After all, what we first do is to think of how we might describe the psychology of various creatures, using the framework of folk psychology as our underlying theory, and then do some scientific investigative work to find out what kind of physical phenomena make that psychological description apt. Until considering (1a), we had spoken only about human pain and suffering, but this is only incidental to the general story. We can perfectly well allow that there are other sorts of pain and suffering, and that *extra* work must be done to find out what physical phenomena they are. But notice here that we are not forced to say that we are looking for those physical phenomena that 'realize pain' across the board, i.e. in a single population consisting of human beings, cats, Martians, etc. We could instead say we are searching for the physical phenomena which are pain in the population of human beings, and separately looking for pain in the population of cats, etc. In short, all we have to do to make our identity theory immune from the multiple realization point is to *relativize* pains and other mental items to particular populations of various creatures.

The details of such relativization can vary, but to keep it simple, just read the two problematic claims as:

(1a′)   Pain-in-human-beings is necessarily identical to C-fibre firing,
(2b′)   C-fibre firing is necessarily identical to pain-in-human-beings.

(Note: we do not have to relativize talk about C-fibres because these are already assumed to be quite specific to the human nervous system. Also, if the need arises, it is possible to think that relativization might have to be even more finely made. For example, suppose, as is perfectly possible, that research revealed there to be this basic difference within the human species: we each undergo one or the other of two distinctive sorts of neural activity when we are in pain. Based on such a finding, we could then think of humanity as divided into sub-populations for the purposes of the identity theory, and relativize our claims appropriately. The precise grounds for making such a distinction, and the fineness of it, generate questions about neurophysiological research and description – but we shall pass over them here.)

The new formulations (1a′) and (2b′) do raise questions. In particular, they seem to commit us to a way of looking at kinds of pain that is not anticipated in our ordinary folk psychological theory. In that theory, we quite happily differentiate between pains on the basis of their qualities – sharp, throbbing, dull pains – and on the basis of their apparent source – tennis elbow, sprained ankle, burn pains. But the relativization move demands that there are in addition cat pains, dog pains, squirrel pains and (possibly) Martian pains. And aside from being unanticipated by folk psychology, these new varieties would reasonably make anyone wonder what makes them all pain.

(Note: in spite of the claim just made, it might be argued that folk psychology does already make some room for relativization; we do tend to think of the suffering of other creatures as different from, though related to, our own. And similar remarks could be made about the attitudes (e.g. belief, desire, etc.) of non-human creatures on our planet, especially if they cannot speak. However, years of *Star Trek* and similar science-fiction programmes show that we are unlikely to make much sense of the idea that Martian belief is a different type of belief. By itself this point is not all that strong; there has always been something suspicious about the physical and intellectual nearness to us of science-fiction aliens. But it does hint that there is some difference between experience and attitude in respect of relativization – a difference not catered for by the relativizations the folk find natural.)

Other Worldly Pain

Further questions raised by relativization will figure in the next chapter, after the explicit introduction of a view known as *functionalism*. Anyway, there is still more to be said here about the identity account, and the idea of relativization will let us do this without the distraction of multiple realization. As before, though now with reference to (1a′) instead of (1a), the question we must ask is whether it is true. Is it the case that human pain has the property of being necessarily identical to C-fibre firing? Or, put in terms of the current philosophical idiom: is it the case that human pain is C-fibre firing in any possible world?

Some have the intuition that the answer to this is 'no', and this answer has nothing to do with dogs, cats or Martians. For can't we perfectly well imagine a world in which *human beings* suffer pain but that, because of certain neurophysiological differences from the actual world, C-fibres have nothing to do with it? And doesn't this show that this is a genuine possibility? Look at it this way: it is easy to imagine a possible world in which human beings have brains something like those we have in this world, but in which some of the wiring is switched around. In our world, it is C-fibres that figure in our suffering pain; in that other possible world, it is, say, the Z-fibres. But then in such a possible world, we have pain – human pain – but that pain is not C-fibre firing.

Notice that in suggesting this negative verdict for (1a′), I have treated imagination as a reliable guide to what is or is not possible. Some find this illegitimate: there may well be things we think we can imagine that are not in the end possible, and therefore not genuinely imaginable. Here is an example that happens, for good measure, to involve identity. Someone in your carriage on a long train journey tells you that he can perfectly well imagine being his cat, and he infers from this that it is possible for him to be that cat. Without going too deeply into this – something to be avoided on a long train journey – it should be easy enough to show him that this is nonsense. The cat, say Tibbles, is a kind of creature, and so are human beings. Moreover, it is essential to each that they be that kind of creature. (It wouldn't merely be difficult to imagine that Tibbles was really a wardrobe; it would just be impossibly silly.) So, whilst we can imagine a human being seeing the world from a cat's perspective, or even changing shape and size, and taking up an interest in chasing mice, neither of these is imagining a human being who was a cat. Since it is no more possible for a cat to be a wardrobe than for it to be human, such a feat of imagination is simply not genuine.

As a general point about the relationship between imagination and possibility, this vignette has an important moral: intuition and imagination are by no means sure guides to what is in fact possible (or impossible: think of those who hundreds of years ago couldn't imagine ____, and then fill in the blank with 'air travel' or your favourite example.) But though they are not 'sure' guides, they are the only guides we have. After all how, other than by thinking about it, could we ever come to a conclusion about what is or is not possible? And such 'thinking' or 'coming to a conclusion' are just other ways of speaking about the exercise of our imagination.

The correct moral to draw from the cat example is not that we shouldn't trust imagination and intuition in deciding what is possible, but that we must be careful when we do so. In some cases, it is probably not wise to rest everything on what we claim we can imagine. Descartes, for example, claimed that he could imagine himself to exist as a body-less thinking being. But many regard disembodied human existence as simply impossible, and would thus reject Descartes' claim. (I won't here go into their reasons, but it is not difficult to appreciate what they might be like. For instance, it seems sensible to regard action − making things happen in the world − as essential to the possession of a mind, so that, if someone were body-less, there would simply be no possibility of action and, hence, no mind in the first place.) Because strength of feeling on both sides runs high here, it is certainly not a good idea to rest our final decision about the possibility of disembodied human existence on what Descartes − or anyone else − claims to be able to imagine. But in other cases, the deliverances of our imagination seem on firmer ground. And the case of (1a′) seems to be one of those.

In contrast to the blanket claim that minds might exist without bodies, it puts no real strain on our credulity to think that a mind − allowing myself here Cartesian talk of the mind as an identifiable object − has to be embodied in some way, even though the precise embodiment of this or that mental phenomenon within such a mind can vary from one possible world to another. It thus seems we can imagine that human pain is C-fibre firing in the actual world, but that it is another neurophysiological process in some merely possible world. And this deliverance of our imagination does not seem to be opposed by any strong counter-intuition. After all, C-fibre firing is not that special; certainly it is not as crucial to a mind as having a body in the first place. Of course, if this is accepted then (1a′) seems to be just false. And, even without going on to consider (2b′), this would demolish the identity theory. Or so it seems.

(Note: Descartes' intuition is often reckoned to be the source of contemporary opposition to the identity theory. However, as we have seen, there is a world of difference between imagining that we do not have bodies, and imagining that our pains could be something other than the firing of C-fibres. So, whilst Descartes may have inspired anti-identity arguments, his claim is not a reasonable premiss from which to launch them.)

Essentialism and Identity

Fortunately – at least for a defender of the identity theory – this is not quite the end of the road it might seem. To see why, let us go back to the scientific models that have been used to encourage our acceptance of the identity theory in the first place. However, for the moment, instead of the heat example, let us consider another of these models – the chemical account of water (and other substances). Later on, I shall suggest that there are important differences between these examples – differences that are not generally noticed by those who lump them together – and that our understanding of mind is better served by the heat case. But you can, of course, appreciate this only if both accounts are in front of you.

   Just as the notion of heat figures in our folk physics, so the notion of water has a long history in what might be called 'folk ontology'. For what is probably the whole of human history, human beings have had the idea of water as a substance of some kind, one that fills rivers and lakes, dissolves other substances and, of course, is vital to human survival. However, it wasn't until the nineteenth century that chemical investigation had finally come to terms with this substance (amongst many others). The end result of this investigation is that we now know:

   (3)   Water = H_2O (that is, water is one and the same substance as hydrogen hydroxide).

Examining (3) to see if it passes the easier form of the LL test produces no special problems. Give or take some additives, the properties of the chemical compound H_2O share all and only the properties that human beings have always regarded as characterizing water. Both are liquid, solid and gaseous at appropriate temperatures, both are potable, both are solvents, etc. But what of essential properties? That is, does water share essential properties with H_2O? In particular, using the minimal kind of essential property that figured in the discussion above, is it the case that:

   (4)   Water has the property of being necessarily identical with H_2O?

A consequence of the truth of (3) is that it does, but intuition here seems to suggest otherwise. Many have little problem with:

(5)   Water might have turned out to be non-identical with H_2O (that is, it is possible that water is not identical with H_2O).

Yet, if (5) is allowed to stand without qualification, the identity in (3) cannot be true. This is a clear consequence of LL. So, saving the hard-won identity that resulted from chemistry – something we should certainly want to do – will require us to understand (5) and (4) in a way that explains why we are tempted think them both true, even though we know that this cannot be so. The hope is that once we find this way, we can deploy it in the mind–brain case to show that (1a′) might look false, even though it is really true. If this can be done, then not only will the water identity have encouraged our acceptance of mind–brain identity; it will in addition have provided us with an answer to an otherwise devastating objection.

There is a first move which can confuse the issue and which must be put to one side. It is important not to hear (5) as something like this:

(6)   Water might not be H_2O.

The possibility raised by (6) is one that we must always be prepared to admit, but it is not really relevant. What (6) suggests is that we might have got it wrong; that chemists, for all their certainty, might one day have to allow that their present account of the nature of water, and other substances, is just mistaken. Of course, it is not easy to see how this could be so, since so much of our success in dealing with the material world is based on our current chemistry. Still, there are deep puzzles remaining in physics, and, in ways we cannot now even imagine, we might have to revise our views. We might even come to think that the whole story of elements, compounds and chemical bonding is a plausible but flawed account of the material world.

If this did come to pass, then of course the identity expressed in (3) would of course *never* have been true. And this is why (6) is not the right way to understand (5). For the claim in (5) does not seek to challenge the present state of our knowledge. Indeed, it suggests that our chemical account is correct; that when you investigate the properties of water you correctly discover the central role of H_2O. The consequence of (5), if true, is not that we think current chemistry mistaken, but that we must give up on the idea that the right relation between water and H_2O is one of identity.

It could be said that (6) deploys a kind of epistemic possibility – a possibility related to our current claims to knowledge – and it raises the question of whether we are correct in taking ourselves to know that water is H_2O. In contrast, (5) is about possibilities related to the world itself – what is usually called metaphysical possibility. Thus, thinking of (5) this way:

(5′)   There is a possible world in which water is not H_2O,

there is no suggestion that in the actual world chemical theory might be wrong. (5′) is a claim about how things are in some possible world, not about what we know in the actual world. But of course if (5′) is true, then even in the actual world, we will have to give up expressing the chemical account by using the identity relation in (3). Since this seems to many writers to be unacceptable, the search is on for a way to understand (5) and (5′) that does not undermine (3). Moreover, as suggested earlier, even if we end up saying that (5′) is false, we must give some explanation of why it seems true.

Water Words and Worlds

The obvious place to begin any search for ways of understanding sentences is with an examination of the meanings of key words in those sentences. In the present circumstances, we would do well to look at the word 'water' and decide on its contribution to (3), (4) and (5). As I shall argue, what underlies the truth of the identity claim in (3) is not the precise way we take the meaning of 'water' (or any other word). But so much of the discussion of identity these days is bound up with words that we must begin there, even if it is not where we shall end up.

To start off, consider two ways in which 'water' might be understood. If, on the one hand, we think of 'water' as simply meaning *whatever* falls from skies during rain, fills lakes and rivers, is potable and acts as a solvent, then we can easily imagine a world in which the stuff that figures in these is not H_2O, but rather, say, XYZ. All you have to do is to imagine yourself in some alien world in which a more or less colourless liquid falls from the sky, fills lakes and rivers, is drunk in vast quantities by indigenous populations and which, on testing, turns out to be XYZ.

On the other hand, if we think of 'water' as meaning *the very substance* that falls from the sky in the actual world, that fills our rivers and lakes, and that we drink, then what we imagine in the previous case will be differently described. Instead of: water in the alien possible world is XYZ, it will be: there is a substance in the alien possible world that looks and feels enough like water to fool us into describing it as 'water'. In other words, there is in fact no water in the alien world, though there is a pretty good imitation of it.

Clearly, if 'water' is the name of *the very substance* that figures in our everyday and chemical encounters, then it is perfectly reasonable to regard (4) as true and (5) as false. But if it is the name merely of *whatever it is* that falls from the sky, etc. in any given possible world, then (5) is pretty likely to be true and (4) false.

Now, it can seem that in order to move forward we have to settle on a meaning for 'water'. But this is not quite right, and that is fortunate because this is not a good place to settle fundamental issues in the philosophy of language. What is crucial for us is not whether one or the other account of the meaning of 'water' is correct, but rather whether the facts of this case give *both* a certain plausibility. It will turn out that so long as the underlying facts of the water story allow both accounts of the meaning of 'water', we can rescue the identity of water and H_2O from the current objection, even if we might have to make a little modification in the way we report the claim. Having explained this, we will then have to see whether the same strategy works for mind–brain identity.

Think of how a chemist would go about checking whether the thought that underlies the identity in (3) is true. One would presume that she would first get hold of a sample of the relevant substance, and then do some chemical assays on it. In effect, she would be acting in roughly the way imagined earlier for the detective in the Uncle Fred case. What the detective did was to keep tabs on Uncle Fred with a view to determining whether or not he was the victim of the mugging. Similarly, the chemist keeps firm hold of a sample – keeps tabs on it – whilst determining whether it is H_2O. To appreciate how important this 'keeping tabs' is, suppose now that this same chemist is transported to an alien possible world, and given the job of determining whether the stuff that fell from the skies in that world was one and the same substance as the one she had tested in her lab in our world. What the chemist would have to do in this case is to make sure to bring her sample with her or, failing that, bring her vital laboratory notes. As you might expect in this case, after a quick assay of the alien 'rain', she would, of course, tell you that it was not the same substance, that it was in fact XYZ.

In cases like that of Uncle Fred, what matters for identity is that one be able to keep hold of the relevant item through different possibilities, track it in different possible worlds. Exactly how one names the item is therefore not all that important, though it is helpful to use a name which shadows the object closely enough to follow it through all possible worlds. (And it is more convenient than taking along Uncle Fred.) For then we can use that name to report our findings; we can say, e.g. 'Uncle Fred might not have been the person mugged' because, even though he was mugged in the actual world, it is easy to imagine tracking him to the more congenial possible world in which the mugging doesn't take place. The suggestion is that the identity in (3), and the essential properties it entails, requires in the first instance the same 'keeping tabs'. That is the reason why the chemist would do best if she could take along her sample, or at least the notes on the sample. However, if she can do neither, then there seems nothing to prevent her doing the next best thing, taking along a word that tracks the stuff in her sample through every possible world in which that stuff exists. Moreover, when it comes to reporting her findings about this stuff in the actual or any other possible world, such a word comes in very handy. Putting that word in the blank in:

(7)   _____ is identical to H_2O,

she can report the results of her chemical assay in the actual world, using the notion of identity. Further, and crucially, she can do so without fear of being found wrong, simply because of the behaviour of some substance in another world that is close enough in appearance to fool the average human visitor. In the judgement of the chemist, this other substance is not '____' because it does not have the chemical features of her sample.

This discussion leads to the inevitable question: is 'water' the right term to use in filling '____'? There are those who think it is – who say that 'water' designates typical samples of the stuff in this world and, therefore, in every possible world where there is something of the same kind as the sample. For this reason, they describe 'water' as a *rigid designator*. (Analogously to the idealization of a rigid body as one that keeps its shape when subjected to various changes in motion, a rigid designator is one that hangs on to its object, even as it moves through possible worlds.) But then again, there are others who think that 'water' is not a rigid designator, that it could very well designate different kinds of stuff in different possible worlds.

But this brings me to the vital next step: we simply do not have to settle this dispute in order to mount a defence of the identity account. For so long as the facts allow us to invent (if necessary) a term that – through different possible worlds – keep tabs on the stuff we gave to the chemist for testing, then we can mount a defence of the original identity claim. What matters is not whether the English word 'water' rigidly designates the stuff, but whether the stuff itself is something we can imagine tracking as we move from one possible world to another. And as an earlier scenario suggests, we can do this. Indeed, we can forget words, and just make sure that the chemist takes her sample with her; in effect, nothing stops us thinking of this as a case in which the stuff itself serves as a kind of rigid designator. (In one of the tales from

Gulliver's Travels, a group of academicians are so mistrustful of words that they carry around the objects themselves, rather than relying on words that purport to describe the objects. We could imagine the same thing done with the sample of stuff given to the chemist.)

Once this point about tracking is recognized, the defence of the identity claim is then simple. The stuff that the chemist (as it were, mentally) carries from one possible world to another is, and will everywhere be, H_2O. Thus, it will have the property of being necessarily identical to H_2O. This is enough to make the thoughts behind (3) and (4) true, even if we might have to be circumspect about using 'water' in formulating them.

What about (5), the claim that water might have turned out not to be H_2O? If we take it to be about the stuff that the chemist keeps tabs on, then of course (5) is simply false. But, given the still unsettled issue of how to understand 'water', it is not in the least surprising that many hear (5) as true. This is, of course, because it would be true if the word 'water' used in it were used as a name of whatever appeared to be water, whatever fell from the sky, sustained life in the indigenous population, etc. Of course, this is not to say that 'water' must be taken one way or the other. It is merely that the facts of the case allow us to have certain thoughts, and that these thoughts might be expressed.

(Note: the way that Kripke puts this point is slightly different, but the underlying result is the same. What he suggests is that there is a way of understanding (5) which makes it true, but no threat to the necessary identity of water and H_2O. The basis of this understanding is the imagined possibility of a substance which we would naturally mistake for water. Looking, tasting and feeling like water, any ordinary observer would have no hesitation in judging it to be such. Yet, like the famous example of fool's gold, this substance is really 'fool's water' and it wouldn't in fact be H_2O or water, so there is no threat here to (3) and (4). But the possibility of there being such a substance is enough to explain our readiness to judge (5) as true.)

Fool's Pain

Assuming, as we have been, that water is identical to H_2O, we have seen that the necessity of this identity can be defended by a plausible reinterpretation of any contrary intuitions. It seems that water might have turned out not to be H_2O, but this simply means that there could be a substance which was so like water as to fool us, but which was not in fact water. (This gives the word 'water' a more central place than it had in my treatment, but this is the quickest way to summarize that discussion.)

The question now is whether we can use this same strategy to defuse a similar contrary intuition in respect of mind–brain identity. That is, we begin with the identity theorist's claim that:

(7)   Pain-in-human-beings is C-fibre firing.

Then, just as we did in the water case, we make up a predicate – 'is necessarily identical to C-fibre firing' which we treat as applying to pain-in-human-beings, thereby getting:

(8)   Pain-in-human-beings has the property of being necessarily identical to C-fibre firing.

Finally, and parallel again to the water case, we are faced with this intuition:

(9)   Pain-in-human-beings might have turned out not to be C-fibre firing,

which seems to be directly at odds with the necessity expressed in (8). But then we set out to explain (9) away by treating it as:

(9')   There could be something that seemed to us to be pain but wasn't in fact pain. (That is, we experience something we think is pain, but discover it is not C-fibre firing, so we conclude that we were simply mistaken in thinking it was pain in the first place.)

In a more colloquial way of putting it, what (9) really asserts is that there could be such a thing as fool's pain, something which we would mistake for pain if we came across it.

Unfortunately, whilst all the moves made from (7) to (9') precisely follow those made in respect of the identity of water and H_2O, the final result seems deeply unsatisfying. We can certainly imagine coming across some stuff we took to be water, but which wasn't really water, but can we make sense of the idea that we can come across some pain – actually experience it – and then decide that it wasn't pain after all?

Kripke thinks not. He says:

To be in the epistemic situation that would obtain if one had a pain *is* to have a pain.[6]

And many are inclined to agree with him.

A few have challenged this conclusion by pointing out that there may well be cases in which we are mistaken about what we are currently experiencing; sometimes we are distracted and do not seem to notice that we are in pain, and sometimes, when shocked, we misdescribe what we are feeling as pain. But these observations about pain really seem to miss the fundamental point of the argument. Kripke uses the notion of pain – as do many philosophers – as a vivid example of a conscious experience. But the lack of a parallel with the water case is not dependent on the nature of any specific kind of experience. Let it be granted that, through lack of concentration or some such distraction, we can be mistaken about our pains, or any other experience. The point of an identity account seems to be that our conscious lives are in fact *and of necessity* events and states of our central nervous system; what we describe as our streams of consciousness are necessarily chemical and electrical patterns in our brains. Kripke's argument turns, not on the nature of this or that feature of the our conscious life, but on the sense we have that there could be no systematic distinction between what our conscious lives seem like to us and what they are really.

Our sense that there is this lack of an 'is/seems' distinction in the mental case is in sharp conflict with our ready acceptance of it for the water case. What could be more obvious than that, if we are not careful about keeping tabs on some substance, then we might find ourselves in a world where we judged some substance to be, say water, when it isn't. It is easy to imagine ourselves getting off a spaceship on some distant planet, and with nothing more to go on than looks, taste and feel, judging the stuff in the lakes and rivers on that planet to be water when it isn't. (The stuff isn't water because water is H_2O in *every* possible world where it exists, and this stuff just isn't H_2O.) But can we imagine a world in which we come to judge that what seem to be our streams of conscious experiences weren't really conscious experiences after all? Those who agree with Kripke – and with Descartes, who inspired, even if he didn't formulate, this argument – find this question merely rhetorical. How else could it be answered except negatively? Yet, according to the identity theorist, if we find, *for example*, that in some possible world our C-fibres are not firing, we will have to conclude that we are not after all undergoing the relevant conscious experience.

C-fibres and Essentialism

Just before we see whether there is any comeback to this argument, let me insert a few remarks about the other claim that we need to evaluate:

(2b)   C–fibre firing is necessarily identical to pain-in-human-beings.

Unlike (1a), this claim figures less prominently in the debate about the identity account, and the reason is obvious enough. Whilst we believe lots of things about the nature of our mental lives, most of us do not have strong intuitions about C-fibres, or about any structural or anatomical features of the central nervous system. So, when confronted with the question of whether you could imagine a world in which there were C-fibres firing, but no pain, we are unlikely to have any strong view. If C-fibres are anatomically distinct, we could I suppose imagine them dissected from the brain and kept alive in some nutrient, whilst being fired up from time to time by outside stimulation. And one presumes that in this case – with some isolated nerve cells in a vat of nutrient – we would have no expectation that pain would accompany the stimulation of these cells. Besides, if being a C-fibre is some anatomical feature of nerve cells generally, then it is easy to imagine a world in which some creatures have C-fibres that fire, but in which there are simply no human beings, and so no pain-in-human-beings.

Both of these intuitions would, of course, show (2b) to be false, but they don't carry much conviction. First of all, it is likely that C-fibres are more than merely an anatomical grouping. That is, isolated nerve cells simply wouldn't count as C-fibres unless they were incorporated into a functional system within a functioning brain. The second point – the one about a world without human beings – would require us to relativize C-fibres to human beings, just as we did with pain. Since such relativization works perfectly well with pain, there is no reason to resist it for C-fibres.

Imagine then a fully functioning human brain suitably equipped with C-fibres. What does our intuition tell us about the following claim?

(2b″)   C-fibre-firing-in-human-beings is necessarily pain-in-human-beings.

Not much, is the most reasonable answer, but when forced to go further, I might be able to come up with something. Concentrating as hard as I can on C-fibre firing in a human brain (which is not very hard, since I am not a brain scientist), the best I can do is to 'subtract' pain. That is, I picture the physical event taking place as described, but imagine that the person whose brain it is does not experience pain. Note, though, that, since we are presuming that the C-fibres are situated in the proper way in the brain, the connections to the muscles will guarantee that the firing of the C-fibres produces the movements that normally figure in painful experience. Thus, the subject will wince, writhe and even utter the sounds, 'It hurts.' So, when I subtract pain, I am at most subtracting the inner experience from all this neuromuscular activity.

Does this kind of subtraction really make sense? Can I imagine a human being whose neurophysiology and physiological reactions are just like mine, but from whom I have subtracted the experience of pain? Any answer here depends on a conception of experience, and not really on any particular conception of the structure and functioning of the brain. So, if we can find something to say about experience that allows us to block the essentialist argument in respect of (1a), it is likely that we can also apply these considerations to get around the weaker intuition that experience subtraction is possible. And if, in the end, the identity theory falls to Kripkean–Cartesian arguments, it will not be because of special features of (2b).

Not Quite so Fast

The Kripkean–Cartesian argument looks pretty devastating for the identity theory. In fact, I suspect that many philosophers, who had clung on to the identity theory in the face of the multiple realizability point, caved in when confronted with this essentialism argument. Still, there are things that can be said, and they are worth saying, whatever the eventual fate of the identity account. For the Kripke argument, complex though it can seem at first, moves rather too fast.

Clearly, any defence of the identity theory cannot simply brazen out the idea that there might be such a thing as 'fool's' experience, an experience that is judged to be an experience by some subject, but isn't really an experience at all because the neurophysiology isn't right. But it is worth recalling what got us into that particular trouble in the first place, since we may in this way get some idea of how to get out of the grip of the Kripkean argument.

The key step was the one which took us from the assertion that pain is C-fibre firing to the assertion that pain is *necessarily* C-fibre firing. We took that step because it exactly corresponded to the one we took in respect of water and H_2O. But maybe we were wrong to do so. Perhaps there is a real difference between the two cases – a difference that makes the step unreasonable in the pain case, even if it is reasonable in the water case.

To see how we could reasonably resist taking this step, think back to the Uncle Fred case. Suppose that someone claimed:

The victim of the mugging is Uncle Fred.

If we tried to run the essentialism argument here, we would have to agree to:

The victim of the mugging has the property of being necessarily identical to Uncle Fred.

But this is hard on Uncle Fred. Surely it is bad enough that he was in fact mugged in the actual world. But do we want to say that in any possible world in which there is a victim of a mugging (on Main Street, etc.) that victim is Uncle Fred? Wouldn't it be more reasonable – indeed, isn't it simply obvious – that in some worlds the victim is Uncle Fred, whilst in others it is someone else?

The explanation for this difference from the water–H_2O case is simple. In the latter case, the identity was asserted to hold between two rigid designators. That is, we imagined that we had some way of keeping tabs on the relevant substance as we moved from one possible world to another. Some think that the word 'water' does this; others disagree. But, as you recall, we do not need to settle this dispute about words. All we have to do is to imagine that we have some way of keeping track of the substance. Imagining that we keep track of the substance using the letter 'W', we find that the scientific expression 'H_2O' keeps track of the same substance in any possible world. So, the claim:

W is identical to H_2O in this world,

entails that:

W is identical to H_2O in any possible world.

In short, W has the property of being necessarily identical to H_2O.

However, in the Uncle Fred case, the expression 'the victim of the mugging' does not keep track of one and the same individual in every possible world. It is perfectly possible, indeed likely, that in different possible worlds, different individuals are referred to by this expression. This point is usually made by saying that the definite description, 'the victim of the mugging', is *non-rigid*. And this means that the identity:

The victim of the mugging is Uncle Fred,

does not entail that the victim of the mugging is Uncle Fred *in any possible world*, and thus that it is not the case that the victim of the mugging is necessarily identical to Uncle Fred. In short, in this case we have an identity claim that does not entail anything about essential properties.

If we were to think of applying this to the mind–brain case, we might be able to avoid the essentialism argument, but even to think about doing so requires that we answer an immediate and crucial question: is 'pain' a rigid designator of some quite specific experience in the way that 'W' is a rigid designator of a wholly specific substance? (Note that I am reverting to talk of pain. This is because it is easier to express my point in terms of a specific example rather than in terms of the whole of our stream of consciousness.) If it is, then of course 'pain' will keep track of the same experience in every possible world, and we will have no way to resist the essentialist consequence that pain is of necessity identical to C-fibre firing. (A conclusion which, as we have seen, would pretty well finish off the identity account.)

As the earlier discussion of the word 'water' showed, it is difficult to find some neutral argumentative basis for settling the issue of whether a word is a rigid designator; accounts of meaning are too contested for us to rely upon them. But, as we also saw with 'water', the issue can be framed in a less linguistic way. For our question should be whether we can keep tabs on pain (or any other experience) as we rummage through different possible worlds. It was fairly easy to do this with the substance that we call 'water'; either we imagine some sample of the substance accompanying us on our travels, or we just stipulate that 'W' designates that very substance in any possible world.[7] But it is less clear whether these moves could work for pain, since there are good reasons to think that our concept of pain (or of any other conscious experience) behaves very differently from our concept of substances like water.

Cartesianism Again

In chapter 2 we struggled with two deeply clashing intuitions. On the one hand, conscious experiences appear to take place in a private realm, surveyable only by the subject of those experiences. But, on the other hand, since the concepts of experience are public, there must be some sense in which experience itself figures in the objective world. Cleaving to the first intuition, whilst pretty much ignoring the second, is one way to distort the mental landscape, and this form of distortion is usually blamed on Descartes. (Though this supposedly Cartesian picture seems to crop up all too readily even amongst those who have never read a word of Descartes.) Thinking only about objective and external features of the mental, whilst leaving out the inner, is a second form of distortion, one that is usually laid at the doorstep of behaviourists.

In chapter 4, we came to the tentative conclusion that the best we can do is to maintain a delicate balance between these intuitions: we (i.e. persons) are special in having natures that make us part of an objective world, while yet having our own individual perspectives on that world. As was noted, saying this does not resolve our conflicting intuitions, since it is still mysterious how objective things one is able to study can have perspectives and inner lives. As one writer put it:

> An observer makes a detailed picture of the whole universe but when he has finished he realises that it still lacks something: his own self. So he puts himself in it too. But again a 'self' remains outside and so forth in an endless sequence of projections, like those advertisements that depict a girl holding a picture of herself holding a picture of herself holding a picture that only coarse printing prevents one's eye from making out.[8]

And tempting though it is, we should not allow ourselves to conclude that, like the picture of the girl, the puzzle just disappears when our thinking becomes too coarse to make it out after a large enough number of repetitions.

The message of the earlier chapters was that we must somehow keep both the inner and the outer in play, even if we have as yet no wholly satisfying way of integrating them. The relevance of this point in the context of Kripke's essentialist argument is this: the temptation to think that we can keep tabs on experiences like pain as we move through possible worlds is of a piece with the temptations of the Cartesian conception of the mind. I do not expect that this will be instantly obvious, but it is important to spell it out. For, in understanding it, we can see how a debate about identity – one whose details seem to turn on recondite logical doctrines – is in reality based on deep assumptions about the nature of mind.

Imagine that you experience a sharp pain in your thumb. As things stand in this world, this pain will be almost certainly be accompanied by other mental and physical states and events. You might curse the hammer that inflicted the injury, jump up and down whilst holding your thumb (and your breath), fervently desire the throbbing to ease off, worry whether the damaged thumb will allow you to finish putting up the shelf, believe you should never have started the project in the first place, etc. In addition, if the identity theorist is right, there will be something going on in you to which you do not have any direct access: your C-fibres will be firing madly, and indeed in his view this is what your pain is. Now imagine a possible world in which your shelf-constructing activity is no less clumsy, most of the rest of your environment is the same, but in which your brain is configured differently, and you have Z-fibres functioning in the place of C-fibres. When you hit your thumb, you feel-sharp pain that gives way to a throbbing, and we can assume that most of the accompanying thoughts and behaviour would be described as above.

Given these two worlds, is your pain the same in both? Could you tell? These questions should be treated with great caution, but they rarely are. The pain has the same kind of cause and effects in each world, but there are those who regard these as only peripheral to answering the questions correctly. A common enough view is that all we have to do to answer the questions is to introspect. As Kripke says: 'Pain . . . is picked out by its immediate phenomenological quality,' and it seems easy enough to think that we can focus on that felt quality, making sure that it is the same in both worlds.[9] It is this that leads us to think that we can indeed keep tabs on experiences like pain as we move from one world to another. However, what we are doing here is, I think, surreptitiously (and distortingly) relying solely on the Cartesian conception of our inner life. On this conception, it is as if we could take a snapshot of our pain (or other experience) which we could then consult (in our imagination) when we needed to compare pain in one world with that in another. Of course, the camera taking the snap, and the snap itself, could never be seen by anyone other than the person whose experiences were at issue. But it is all too easy to let this pass as mere detail.

With something like this story in the background, it is clear why the essentialist argument against identity is felt to be so strong. If by carrying around (so to speak) this snapshot we can just tell whether an experience is the same or different in this or that possible world, we have all we need to make out the analogy with the water case. Just as we can imagine keeping tabs on some substance – thereby guaranteeing that if the substance is H_2O in this world, it is H_2O in every possible world – so we can use the snapshot as a way of tracking our pain through possible worlds. And if we can do this, then if that very pain is C-fibre firing in this world, we will be committed to thinking that it is C-fibre firing in every world.

The snapshot conception makes the linguistic issue of whether 'pain' is a rigid designator a minor one. So long as we can imagine tracking a pain by keeping its introspective snapshot in our wallet, we can simply stipulate that some term or other rigidly designates that particular kind of experience. The parallel with water here is exact. Someone might successfully argue that 'water' was not rigid, but how could they argue against the possibility of our making up some other term which did rigidly refer to that substance? So long as we can track what we call 'water' in this world, through other possible worlds, we can make up a term which records this tracking. Similarly, our ability to track a painful experience seems to guarantee that there *could* be a rigid designator of this kind of experience.

Yet, however tempting it is to think of experience this way, there is good reason to believe that it is neither coherent nor all that plausible. If we focus too closely on the idea that pain experiences are inner objects accessible only to those who are suffering, we will end up without any account at all of the fact that the concept of pain – like our concept of experience generally – is shared and public. As in the example in chapter 2, how can one coherently come to the conclusion that Harry's pain – that very thing which we are thinking about – is something that only Harry can actually think about?

Moreover, if we manage to get past the initially tempting Cartesian intuition, and take a good look at the snapshot conception, it loses a lot of its appeal. The example above spoke of a possible world in which you hit your finger with a hammer and thereby came to feel pain and react in some of the ways described, even though it was your Z-fibres that were firing. But what of a world which was even more different from the actual, e.g. a world in which the feeling of pain just came whilst you were sitting and reading, and which raised a wry smile and a certain mild curiosity about its origin? It is easy enough to *say* that this could be how pain happens to be in that world. But how confident would we be that the 'sufferer' in this case experienced the very same feeling as our familiar, thumb-striking kind of pain? I suspect the answer is: not very.

Compare this with a case in which the substance that we call 'water', i.e. H_2O, is very rare in some possible world, and is in fact a deadly poison to the humanoid characters inhabiting that world. No matter how bizarre the story, it is pretty easy to keep our grip on the substance itself; the particular way that water happens to affect creatures, or its prevalence in certain environments, is no bar to our thinking we can track it through possible worlds. But as we have seen, the more bizarre the circumstances of a feeling of pain, the less confident we would be that it was one and the same feeling. Even if you find it impossible to let go entirely of the Cartesian conception, the difference between these cases should give you pause.

As has been noted many times, the issues surrounding the Cartesian conception are enormously complicated, and continue to be controversial. It would be foolish, therefore, to suggest that my remarks add up to a knockdown argument against it. But in the present context, the important point is not whether I have convinced you to reject the Cartesian conception, so much as getting you to see that the Kripkean essentialist argument depends on it for cogency. An identity theorist who is not willing to go along with this conception can therefore evade that argument. In particular, what such a theorist must do is to insist that neurophysiology, and the behaviours it causes, are no less important to the individuation of experience than feeling. This is not, of course, to say that there could be pain without feeling; just that we should be less confident of the idea that feeling alone can be used to individuate pains in different possible circumstances.

This last point is crucial to getting the issues between identity theorists and their opponents right. It might be thought that the identity theorists' evasive action commits them to the view that pain has no essential properties at all, not even that it is a feeling. But, as Kripke rightly says, 'this notion seems to me self-evidently absurd.'[10] Well, of course it is absurd to say that a feeling of pain might, in some possible world, not be a feeling. But the evasive action described above does not require this.

Think about the victim of the mugging. In this world, Uncle Fred is the victim, but in another possible world it is someone else. This would commit us to saying something like this:

> The victim of the mugging in the actual world (i.e. Uncle Fred) is not the victim of the mugging in some other possible world.

But this is certainly a far cry from what would be absurd, namely:

> There is a possible world in which the victim of the mugging is not the victim of the mugging.

Similarly, if we pick out experiences like pain by some non-rigid description, then we might end up having to say:

> Pain-in-human-beings in the actual world (i.e. C-fibre firing) is not pain-in-human-beings in some possible world.

But, of course, identity theorists would insist that pain is a feeling in any possible world – indeed, they would insist that being a feeling available from the inner perspective is essential to pain – so they have no problem in denying the absurd claim:

> There is a possible world in which pain-in-human-beings is not a feeling.

In effect, they are treating this as:

> There is a possible world in which whatever is pain-in-human-beings (i.e. whatever is a feeling that has an associated range of behaviour and a discoverable neurophysiology) is not a feeling.

And, whilst this is surely incoherent, there is no reason to think that an identity theorist is would have to think it true. In suggesting that the identity account is in fact committed to something like this absurdity, Kripke has surreptitiously, and unfairly, assumed all the stuff about our being able to track pain in the Cartesian way through different possible worlds. For he thinks it perfectly possible that there could be a world in which there is pain-in-human-beings – pain that we could recognize by a sort of trans-world introspection – which had no recognizable connection with the behaviours and neuro-physiology of pain as it is in the actual world.

Paying the Price

Evading the essentialist objection in the way described is not cost-free. On the one hand, it seems to require too definitive a rejection of the Cartesian conception of the experience. On the other hand, it has the unwelcome consequence of undercutting the argumentative ground used by many identity theorists to persuade us to accept their account. Both of these require further elucidation.

(a)　Feeling Our Way from the Outside

Calling the first of these points a 'cost' might well seem paradoxical. After all, I have spent some effort in this book suggesting that the Cartesian conception of consciousness is distorting. So, why I am now suddenly claiming that the rejection of that conception counts as some kind of cost for the identity account? More detail will follow in later chapters, but here is an outline answer to this question.

Whilst there are deep problems with the idea that our inner life consists of a moving show of object-like items to which we have exclusive introspective access, the Cartesian at least attempts to take seriously the inner perspective that forms an integral part of the mental landscape. However, the identity story, as so far formulated and defended, shows little sign of taking that perspective on board. You can appreciate why by, as so often, focusing on the experience of pain. The identity theorist treats pain as a phenomenon brought on in certain ways, and leading to certain further typical behaviours, attitudes and experiences. It is accorded a place in the larger scheme of folk psychology – and it is correctly said to be a feeling – but it is accorded its place from a third-personal or outside perspective.

As we have seen, a certain essentialist challenge to this account assumes that we can somehow recognize the nature of pain purely from the inside, and that we can do this with sufficient confidence to fix on any given kind of painful experience, even as we move through possible worlds in which the neuro-physiology of pain varies enormously. If this fixing were possible, it would of course rule out the identity account, so a proponent of that theory must disallow it. As just noted, an identity theorist like David Lewis will insist that we fix on something as pain by seeing it as a feeling with certain typical causes and effects, and this means that the neurophysiological changes imagined in different possible worlds are no threat to the identification *in this world* of pain-in-human-beings and C-fibre firing. But the worry is whether the identity theorist, in referring to pain as, among other things, a feeling, is paying no more than lip service to the idea that there is something it is like from the inside to suffer pain.

This worry is heightened by the crucial role played in the story by the supposedly typical causes and effects of painful experiences. It is one thing to insist that our inner lives come to be shared because they are expressed in publicly available ways; but it is quite another to think these outer expressions are in some way constitutive of the inner life. The price that the identity theory might have to pay for defending itself against Kripke's argument is that it becomes committed to the second of these thoughts. And if this is so, it will have no resources with which to account for the inner perspective on mind's landscape that is of such special importance to the phenomena of consciousness.

(In the next chapter I shall discuss various accounts of the coalescence of Mind and Brain generally grouped together under the heading 'functionalism'. Functionalism is often reckoned to be a better strategy than the identity account, but as you will see, there is a real sense in which the identity account discussed here is itself best counted as one version of functionalism. Moreover, as even the cursory remarks above suggest, it should come as no surprise that the greatest stumbling blocks to functionalism are the phenomena of consciousness.)

(b)   Heat Again
It took the human intellect a long time to figure out what heat is, and the result is certainly surprising. Heat is a transfer of energy. When a hot body comes into contact with a cooler one, what happens is not significantly different from one object colliding with another, though of course a collision produces a co-ordinated displacement of the whole object, and heat transfer doesn't. This is surprising because there seems a world of difference to us between, say, our colliding with one another, and our touching a hot object. None the less, accepting this somewhat counter-intuitive result, and identifying heat with energy transfer, we end up unifying important branches of science and making sense of a huge range of everyday phenomena.

Stories like that of heat, in all their historical and scientific detail, have been immensely important in making us receptive to the identification of Mind and Brain. If not precisely part of a straightforward logical argument, they certainly do the next best thing: they give us an analogical push towards accepting the identity account. However, as we have seen, faced with the essentialist argu-

ment, the only way out for the identity account seems to involve a repudia-
tion of the parallels with science, and this means that the defence comes at
the cost of having to give up one of the original motivations for the theory.

Recall the case of water. The scientific account has it that the substance we
call 'water' is identified with the chemical kind H_2O. And there is every reason
to suppose that this identification leads to necessities; in particular, to the claim
that the substance we call water is H_2O in any possible world, or, equivalently,
that if something weren't H_2O it wouldn't be water. If the identity of pain and
C–fibre firing followed this pattern – as it should if the analogy with scientific identities holds – then the identity is untenable. It is just wildly implausible to claim that not being C–fibre firing is enough to rule out a phenomenon
as pain. But, in resisting this argument by emphasizing the contingent nature
of the identification, the analogy with water goes out of the window, and with
it the support for the identity theory that comes from the history of science.

Or so it seems. One thing that identity theorists could say is that they are
not all that bothered by the loss of the analogy.[11] But I do not think this satisfactory, for it leaves the identity theory without the intellectual support that
it had originally, and which continues to encourage new adherents.

The other option is to go on the offensive; to find some grounds on which
to reclaim the analogy in spite of the essentialist argument. Fully canvassing
this option would take us deeply into issues only indirectly connected to the
philosophy of mind, so here I shall only suggest how the strategy might go.
But I do think it is the best course of action for any defender of the identity
theory, and the materials needed for it have all made an appearance in this
chapter.

Two kinds of scientific example have dominated discussions of the identity
account. One is the story of heat: the not quite straight path from the folk's
appreciation of everyday phenomena of heat to the explanation of these phenomena as fundamentally dynamical. The other arises from the recognition of
the chemical nature of various common substances like water. In both cases,
the suggestion is that our present state of knowledge is best understood as
based on appropriate theoretical identities, namely the identity of heat with
transfer of energy, and, as an example, the identification of water with H_2O.

In the arguments and counter-arguments about mind–brain identity considered in this chapter, both these examples have figured, but without discussion of any differences between them. Yet there are grounds for thinking, not
only that they are different, but that they might not serve equally well as models
for the mind–brain identity account.

The water example seems quite convincing in the context of the essentialist argument; it seems undeniable that, if we are willing to leave linguistic dis-

putes on one side, we can imagine tracking the substance water – a substance we have discovered to be H_2O – through every possible world, and therefore finding it to be essentially H_2O. But the heat case is less convincing in respect of essentialism, and that is perhaps the reason it is usually bolstered by an appeal to substance examples. To see why it is less convincing, think back to the beginning of the story of heat, and in particular, to the earlier attempts to understand it.

The story started with the folk thinking of heat as some kind of power or characteristic of things which gave rise to various real and specific kinds of changes in the world, as well as to changes in our sensations. If someone had then wondered how we could identify heat in various possible worlds, the answer would have been clear: if in some possible world things have a power to melt, vaporize or in similar ways affect other things, and if this power causes certain characteristic sensations in the inhabitants, then that power is heat. In the eighteenth century, this power came to be numbered among the 'imponderables', and it was thought of as itself some kind of substance (caloric fluid) inherent in, and transmissible among, more ordinary things. Yet even at this point, I think that most would have regarded heat as a phenomenon identified by its causes and effects.

What about our present situation? We know now that heat is not caloric fluid, and that temperature is not a degree of intensity of repulsion within such a fluid. Heat – as I want to say 'in our world' – is a transfer of energy. Suppose, however, that there is a possible world in which a very subtle fluid, much as the caloric account describes, has the capacity to transform materials, as does 'our' heat, and to cause sensations of heat in the denizens of that world. Since our conception of heat and temperature form such an integral part of physics, the laws of physics in that world would have to be very different from those in the actual world. Still, there does not seem to be anything incoherent about a world in which caloric exists, and in which everything is explained in terms of indivisible atoms of varying sizes and shapes. (In some ways, this world might seem even more coherent than ours, described as it is by quantum physics and general relativity.) Would the caloric fluid in this possible world be heat?

As noted above, this is a very controversial question, and I am not confident of my own intuitions here. But it doesn't seem bizarre to think that the answer might be 'yes'; that we might come to say that in that world heat is at bottom very different from heat in our world. But whatever you think about that case, it seems quite a different matter from our judgement about water. If in some world the laws of chemistry were wildly different from those in the actual world, and if there were none the less a watery kind of substance in that world, I find little temptation to say that 'water' in that world just happens to be something other than H_2O.

If I am right about the difference, at least in degree of controversy, what could explain it? Well, the obvious thought would be that we conceive of water as a substance *composed* in a certain way, whereas our conception of heat has no such compositional presupposition. In fact, though I have played along up to now in characterizing the claim:

(i)   Water is H_2O,

as an identity claim, this may not be quite right. Perhaps the best way to understand the claim is as:

(ii)   Water is composed of H_2O.

Interpreted in this way, the claim is no less a basis for a form of essentialism, for we can agree that the composition of a substance is an essential property of it. But, if (i) is best understood as (ii), then the parallel between the heat and water cases is less straightforward than many seem to assume. And the way is clear for someone to insist that the supposed identification of pain and C-fibre firing owes more to 'genuine' theoretical identifications, like those involving heat, than to compositional claims like those about water. If we do see matters this way, then the way is also open, even if it is not completely clear, for evading the essentialist argument, without giving up the analogical support that mind–brain identity theorists have claimed from the history of science. (Also, it should now be even more apparent why I thought it worth going into some detail in telling the story of heat.)[12]

Identity, Attitude and Action

As noted earlier, arguments concerning the identity theory tend to be conducted in terms of experience, and even more narrowly, in terms of experiences like pain. But even though I intend to break off consideration of these arguments until we have considered functionalist alternatives in the next chapter, it is important to have at least some idea of the special problems that attitudes and actions might present for the identity theory.

(a)   Attitudes
Going back to the original example in chapter 2, think about Anne and her belief that her coat is in the hallway cupboard. Anne's belief is a mental state

which we understand by locating it in the folk psychological story character-istic of Anne and other persons. It is a mental state brought on by various per-ceptions and memories – by certain inputs – and, in conjunction with certain other mental states, it will lead Anne to act in various ways that we could call 'outputs'. Thus, if she wants to go out, and believes it is cold enough for a coat, then her belief about the coat's location suggests that she will head down the hallway in the direction of the cupboard.

Following the lead given by the treatment of pain, the identity theorist seems committed to saying that Anne's belief is a state of her brain (or, more generally, of her central nervous system). That is to say, it is a quite specific state of her brain which is located by its position in a nexus of characteristic input and output. Thus, just as our researches might one day tell us what state resides at the brain-end of a hammer blow to the thumb, and an output of expostulation, anger and, commonly, hopping up and down, so these same researches should locate the brain state whose characteristic input and output match (at least approximately) Anne's belief in the location of her coat.

However, unlike an experience of pain, an attitude like belief has a content. In the language we used in chapter 2, it has a certain directionality, and this creates a prima facie worry for the identity account. To put the matter in terms of our example, if Anne's belief is a state of her brain, what happens to the coat and the cupboard? This question is both pressing and difficult. For definiteness, let us suppose that there is a state of Anne's neural system – call it N – which research shows is the candidate neural state for being Anne's belief that her coat is in the cupboard. Against this background, we need to know how we can get from N – an internal neural state – to the things in the world to which N would have to be directed in order to count as a belief.

One way in which an identity theory might try to cope is by denying the very thing we have been supposing; that is, by denying that the relevant physical state is in fact internal to the individual. In Anne's case, this would mean saying that her belief was one and the same with some physical state of the world which may well include N, but which also takes in the state of affairs involving the coat, cupboard, etc. Of course, in doing this, one would be saying that Anne's mental state is somehow spread out so as to include much more than is local to Anne, and this is not an easy consequence to accept.

The idea that Anne's belief somehow has objects and/or states of affairs built in is generally known as *externalism*, and it is important not to confuse exter-nalism with directionality. Directionality consists in the fact that attitude attri-butions are in form relational; it does not imply any particular story about what lies behind this relational form. As we saw in chapter 2, some of the ways of filling in the story take the relational form more seriously than others. That is, some stories treat the relation between a believer and a content as a genuine relation on a par with relations like ownership; whereas others treat it more like the relationship between a person and his weight in kilograms, that is, something which is only apparently relational. The notion of externalism is often entangled in this debate, but it should be kept separate. The externalist insists that the involvement of objects and/or states of affairs in the world is constitutive of attitudes *themselves*. And this is consistent with many different ways of accounting for the relational form of attitude *attributions*. One could even be an externalist, whilst at the same time insisting that the belief relation in attribution is merely apparent. The issue for the externalist is not the form of attributions, but the structure of the attitudes themselves; though, unsurprisingly, these two sometimes inform each other. If, as above, the identity account assumes that externalism is true, it will be forced to add objects and/or states of affairs to internal neurophysiological states like N, when working out which item is Anne's belief. And, as was also suggested above, this is implausible.

A second tack would be to insist that there is a wholly internal state corresponding to Anne's belief, and that the directionality of the belief is explicable by relations between this state, and a real-world state of affairs involving the coat. Thus, perhaps what makes some state of Anne's a belief about the whereabouts of her coat is that there is a *causal* relation between that state and the coat. One would here be trying to capture the directionality of the attitudes by citing causal relations between internal (presumably, brain) states and actual and possible states of the world. The project of explaining directionality in terms of causal relations between internal states and states of the world is enormously complicated. Here I will note simply that something like this 'naturalization' of directionality seems both more plausible than the previous option, and more in keeping with the overall thrust of a coalescing strategy.

However, naturalizing intentionality is no easy thing to bring off. No straightforward causal relationship between brain state and world seems adequate, since no such relationship will allow for the slack between attitudes and the world that was discussed in both chapters 2 and 4. More will be said about this issue in the chapters which follow.

I have saved for last the most radical option for the identity theorist. This consists in denying that attitudes and experiences should be accorded the same treatment. Experiences like pains and perceptions seem to be genuine events that occur at specific times – that can, as it were, be counted – and which are therefore perfectly reasonable candidates for the identity treatment. But it has been argued that, though we speak of beliefs and desires as if they were individual items that can be counted, this is misleading. The argument begins with a suggestion about the source of the attitudes. For example, suppose we say that Anne has some faculty – as an identity theorist, you would presume it was some subsystem in her brain – responsible for keeping track of the world and her place in it. But instead of supposing that this system works with discrete bits of information, suppose that it is more like a constantly updated map. This is crucial: a map contains lots of information, but the information is not organized into separable elements. In representing London as south of Edinburgh and north of Paris, a map also represents that Edinburgh is north of Paris; and it gives at the same time lots of information about the location of other cities. There is no way to cut up a map so that it represents just one piece of information at a time.

If Anne's beliefs are thought of as information read off by us from the tracking system that Anne possesses, and recorded in our attributions, then the idea that beliefs are discrete and countable looks distinctly lame. There will of course be some kind of relationship between Anne's tracking system and the world, but the pressure on the identity theorist to give an account of contents, belief by belief, will evaporate. And this makes it reasonable for the identity theorist to maintain that experiences are states of the brain, but that attitudes are more complicated. They are part-descriptions of a system in the brain. More must be said about this system, but, as far as attitude contents go, the identity theory is off the hook.

(b)   Actions

The problem that actions raise for the identity theory is more straightforward. Take the act of pushing the cup across the table. An identity theorist might say that this act consists of a brain state causing the muscles in the arm and hand to move in a way necessary to get the job done. Unfortunately, this would make it impossible for a dog to push the cup across the table; a dog would presumably do it with his nose. And it would certainly rule out some armless extra-terrestrial whose activities are served by a whirring of gears and wheels. We might well want to relativize experience to human beings, and perhaps even attitudes. But it would seem just absurd to say that actions should be relativized – i.e. that we should talk of 'pushing-the-cup-by-human-beings', instead of merely pushing the cup – as if this were an act that could not be accomplished by dogs and Martians. With apologies for the number of promissory notes that I have already given, I shall leave this problem to the chapters which follow. As you will see, whilst it is a problem for an identity account, it is an even more severe problem for some of the accounts offered in the next chapter.

Conclusion

After such a long chapter, one with so many twists and turns, a summary would be a good idea. The driving idea of this chapter is that of coalescing or integrating Mind and Brain by appealing to the relationship known as identity. This is not the particular identity of the Uncle Fred/mugger's victim kind, but the identity of kinds or properties that is typical in the history of science; the identity that obtains between heat and a transference of motive energy, temperature and molecular motion, water and H_2O. The fundamental claim discussed in this chapter is that, on the pattern of these theoretical identities, there is an identity between mental phenomena and states of the central nervous system. The example used was that pain is a firing of C-fibres in the cortex, but the account is intended to apply across the board to all features of the mental landscape.

As with any identity claim, the best way to probe it is via Leibniz's Law. When an identity is true, there is in reality only one thing in play, so features of one side of the identity should exactly match features of other side. Any failure here means that the original identity claim is simply false. In the early stages, we considered two ways which might induce such failure. What we were doing in these skirmishes was trying to sharpen the common intuition that there is something not quite right about the claim that an experience like pain could just be a process in the brain. Both of the early attempts to do this were themselves failures (or at least inconclusive), but we began to get to the nub of the issue when we came to consider essential properties. For Leibniz's Law is no less true of them than it is of 'ordinary' properties like dullness or spatial location.

Condensing what is a long and complex debate in the literature, I suggested that, in the end, the essentialist argument against identity was somewhat less conclusive than it is normally taken to be. What is at issue between identity theorists and their opponents is nothing short of the fundamental dichotomy that runs through the whole of our conception of the mind. On a certain conception of experience as inner, the essentialist argument wins hands down; but on a conception that allows a substantial role to the outer, the identity theorist is still in the game. Admittedly, the stakes at that point had been raised pretty high for the identity account; not only is it struggling to give the inner its due, it is in danger of losing contact with the scientific identities that set it going in the first place. (Only tentatively, I suggested that by noting the real difference between the heat and water cases, this last problem might be got round.) None the less, in spite of these and other problems, for example, problems with attitude and action, the identity account finished the chapter with a hand to play. And in the next chapter, though the centrepiece will be what many regard as the alternative to the identity account, you will see that the relationship of identity still has an important role.

Notes and References

1   This is especially obvious when you read about interstellar gases having enormous temperatures but very little heat. The temperatures are high because of the high velocities of interstellar gas molecules, but there are too few of them per unit volume to allow any significant transfer of motive energy.

2   B. O'Shaughnessy, 'The Mind–Body Problem' in R. Warner and T. Szubka (eds), *The Mind–Body Problem* (Oxford: Blackwell, 1994), p. 212.

3   The seventeenth-century philosopher Spinoza (in his *Ethics*) held a metaphysical position which can seem tantalizingly close to an identity account. However, since none of the scientific examples were available to Spinoza, it is difficult to judge how close his account really is to those of the 1950s. (I happen to think it is very close and, precisely because it is not based on modern scientific examples, it repays careful study.)

4   S. Kripke, *Naming and Necessity* (Oxford: Blackwell, 1980), p. 148.

5   Some use 'implementation' in place of 'realization', but for some reason it is the 'multiple realization' and not the 'multiple implementation' point. However, as far as I can tell the two words can be used interchangeably.

6   Kripke, *Naming and Necessity*, p. 152.

7   Of course, since we are not physically connected to different possible worlds, we cannot actually travel to them, and the sample cannot literally accompany us. But allowing some license, the idea is clear enough.

8   Vladimir Nabokov: *Speak Memory: An Autobiography Revisited* (London: Everyman, 1999), ch. 16.

9   Kripke, *Naming and Necessity*, p. 152.

10   Ibid., p. 147.

11   See D. Braddon-Mitchell and F. Jackson, *Philosophy of Mind and Cognition* (Oxford: Blackwell, 1996), p. 102.

12   On p. 133 of Kripke, *Naming and Necessity*, there is a tantalizing footnote which suggests that he at least recognized some such comeback to his argument. However, this footnote occurs before he embarks on his essentialist argument against mind–brain identity.

7

Functionalism

Identity theorists, in asking about the nature of experiences such as pain, or attitudes such as belief, expect (and defend) answers in reassuringly physical terms. Pain is a kind of activity in the central nervous system, belief and the other attitudes are perhaps a mixture of activity and disposition in that same nervous system. Somewhat counter to the current fashion, I have suggested that we must take these answers very seriously. The argument in the previous chapter was broken off without any final verdict, not because we had exhausted discussion, but because doing justice to the identity story requires a somewhat broader canvas. There are other ways of asking about experiences and attitudes, and only by understanding them can we hope to decide the fate of identity accounts.

What is . . .?

The following small advertisement once appeared in an Oxford newspaper:

> Wanted: bicycle or similar.

Why is this downright funny, or, if you do not quite share my sense of humour, at least peculiar? At the risk of ruining the joke, I suppose it is because we think of a bicycle as a physical object of a certain shape and size, made of certain materials, and it is therefore difficult to imagine something similar to a bicycle which isn't one.

In contrast, however, imagine that the newspaper had published this small ad:

> Wanted: word processor or similar.

Given that there exist (though they are less common now) dedicated word-processing machines, typewriters with small screens and memories, as well as computers with word-processing programs, there is nothing particularly remarkable about this request. What is wanted is something that can process words in some appropriately efficient way, and this request, unlike the bicycle advertisement, tells us what is wanted without suggesting any particular shape, size or physical makeup.

The simple idea that there can be this second way of approaching 'What is . . .?' questions lies behind much current philosophical (and psychological) work on the mind. It is the basis for a nest of views known as *functionalism*. Moreover, though there is fierce disagreement about details, there is a widespread feeling that functionalism is a better bet than identity for achieving coalescence between mind and brain. After exploring what I take to be the central insight of functionalism, I shall at least try to untangle the different strands of functionalism. And at some point in the discussion, we shall return to a consideration of identity.

Labour-Saving Devices

Functionalism is usually explained by reference to the widely used, even if not always understood, digital computer, and computers will certainly figure in later discussion. However, the basic idea can be illustrated more simply. Imagine yourself an inventor interested in the construction of what are often called 'labour-saving devices'. Clearly, part of being this kind of inventor consists in having ideas about which particular kinds of labour need to be saved. Running through the annoying little daily tasks that beset us all, you hit upon the following:

(O)   After a day of getting and spending, we often end up with lots of small change in our pockets. Wouldn't it be good if there was a little device into which we could dump this loose change, and which would automatically register its total value?

Perhaps this is not a brilliant labour-saving idea, but there are many less useful ones in the marketplace. Anyway, it will do for our purposes. Armed with this thought – let us call (O) your *objective* – you now set out to think of ways of fulfilling it. Put in somewhat fancy terms, what you have to do is to think of some way of harnessing the material world – some way of constructing a physical device – that regularly and accurately meets your objective. However, experienced as you are in inventing things, you realize that your goal would be more efficiently achieved by somewhat indirect means. Not setting off immediately to the workshop, you set out to analyse (O).

Analysis here means working out which features any device capable of doing (O) is likely to have. Typically these would be: sorting, counting and adding, and we can be a little more precise by noting that any device which achieves (O) is likely to contain:

(1)   A unit or module which sorts the coins;
(2)   A module which counts how many coins there are of each type;
(3)   A module which uses the counts in (2) to get a total value of the coins.

Also, it might be useful to see the task in (3) as demanding:

(3a)   A module which works out the total value of each type of coin;
(3b)   A module which keeps track of the results of (3a) so as to give the final total value of all the coins.

The precise details do not matter, but it should be clear enough how thinking in terms of some such analysis helps an inventor in the further task of actually constructing a device suitable for mass production. For example, we know that there are lots of coins in circulation, and they are distinguishable by one or all of size, shape, weight and material constitution. Since any number of any of these coins might be dropped in the finished device, the sorting module must use one or other of these distinguishing features in carrying out its task. One way might be a system of holes through which the coins drop; another way might be some optical device which can sense the difference in the material composition of each coin as it passes by. Similarly, after the sorting is completed, the counting module must somehow work out how many coins there are of each type. Thinking of the system of holes, it might be that all of the coins dropping through each hole are weighed; or perhaps the optical analyser has an attached counter. Finally, I leave it to your imagination to think of the many different ways in which the results of counting can be turned into a monetary total.

Ingenuity and cost are the typical factors determining how each module is turned into a physical device, but our interest here is more in the modular description itself. The description given in (1)–(3) can be thought of as functional characterization; it tells us about the 'parts' or modules of what you decide to call the 'Small Change Reckoner', but it does so in a way which falls short of any precise physical characterization. An inventor can design as many different actual Change Reckoners as imagination allows, but each of them will be Change Reckoners only in so far as they achieve (O), and they will only achieve (O) if they in some way perform the tasks described in (1)–(3).

Mental Reckoning

What does this have to do with the mental realm? The job done by the Change Reckoner is not particularly difficult, but none the less it involves mental tasks such as recognizing, distinguishing, counting, adding, etc. Given this – and setting our standards very low – imagine that there is a human being whose sole intellectual accomplishment is to act as a Change Reckoner. Of course, the most reasonable question to ask about such a person is how his mental life could be so impoverished. But playing along with the supposition, imagine instead that what we want to find out is how this person manages to be an accurate and tireless counter of loose change. Noting that he, like everyone else, is essentially a brain-controlled biological system, it is reasonable to suspect that in some way or other the reckoner's brain is responsible for this limited but real mental ability. Moreover, just as we imagined using a functional characterization in the *construction* of the mechanical Change Reckoner, we can appeal to this same characterization in our *deconstruction* of the human reckoner's brain.

Spelling this out, it seems reasonable to treat the functional characterization given by (1)–(3), not now as a constraint on constructing a Change Reckoner, but as a guide to research into the mental life of the human reckoner. Surely, the suggestion runs, there must be some subsystem in the human reckoner which distinguishes coins, and can therefore sort them; some subsystem which can count the total number of each type of coin; and finally some subsystem which works out the monetary grand total of any parcel of change. The aim of our research will be to find out which sensory and brain systems perform these tasks.

Not only does this kind of deconstruction serve as a practical guide to our continuing research, it suggests a way of thinking of the human reckoner's mental life that does not involve any immediate reference to the physical mechanisms in the reckoner's brain. The functional characterization does not itself mention the brain's chemico-electrical properties – properties that implement the counting skill – but it does give a perfectly good answer to the question: what is a mental ability to count loose change? And this suggests that this admittedly toy example might offer us a way to understand the relationship between mind and brain which differs in important respects from the identity story.

The coalescing strategy of the identity theory was represented by a figure in the previous chapter which is repeated as figure 7.1. However, the picture suggested by the story about functional characterization would look more like figure 7.2. In this configuration, a layer of functional characterization is interposed between the experiences and attitudes, here collectively called 'Mind', and the bedrock physicality of the human organism abbreviated as 'Brain'. It

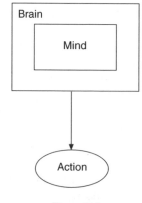

Figure 7.1

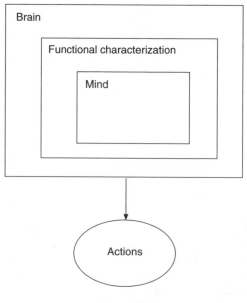

Figure 7.2

is the possibility of this interposition that lies at the heart of the view known as functionalism.

The central idea of functionalism, suggested by the Change Reckoner case, is that this layer affords us a better way of understanding the mental landscape, and thereby a new way of conceiving the relationship between Mind and Brain. Mind can be functionally characterized without commitment to this or that physical story; and Brain can be thought of as a kind of engineering implementation of the functional account. However, it is a long way from the toy example described earlier to a complete functionalist story about the relationship between Mind and Brain. So, before we can properly understand – and then evaluate – the functionalist idea, we need to be assured that we have a right to generalize from the toy example.

Leaving on one side for the moment any more philosophical discussion of functionalism itself, let us consider first the grounds for the widely shared view that functional characterization of something as complex as the human intellect is in principle imaginable. Without grounds for thinking that the whole of the mental landscape – experience, attitude and action – can be deconstructed in functional terms, there wouldn't be much point in taking our discussion of functionalism any further.

Turing Machines

Crucial to such a guarantee is a quite astounding story first told in a form relevant to our discussion by the logician and mathematician Alan Turing (1912–54). There are a number of reasons why Turing's contribution is so astounding. First of all, it is by and large quite simple; it takes little more effort to understand what he proposed than it does to understand the Change Reckoner case. Secondly, even though the story is simple, it allows one to see straightaway that there is virtually no limit to the scope of functional characterization. And it manages to create this conviction even though it does not actually set out to give detailed functional characterizations of the mental or any other realm. Finally, as my description of him suggests, Turing was not primarily a philosopher, and his work was not directed to the philosophy of mind. In fact, a significant consequence of his work was to show in a theoretical way the possibility of digital computers, an example of which he himself helped to construct. (Some time after he published his logical results, Turing did also publish a much-discussed paper relating the logical work to the philosophy of mind. There will be more on this later.)

At the heart of his work is what has come to be called a *Turing Machine*. In spite of the name, a Turing Machine is not a machine in any familiar sense; it would take up no space in an office. Instead, it is a detailed description of how various intellectual tasks can be performed; it is in effect a functional characterization – what I have called a 'deconstruction' – of these tasks. However, partly because of his fondness for gadgets and machinery, and partly because it was useful to his ultimate aim, Turing represented functional descriptions as if they were actually implemented in a simple gadget, one which seems constructible in reality, even if it isn't. Figure 7.3 is the starting-point or blueprint for the design of Turing Machines. The tape is divided into squares, though only a portion of it is shown, and one has to imagine it as indefinitely long in both directions. The printer moves across the tape in either direction, and it can detect, print or erase certain symbols on the squares of the tape.

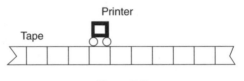

Figure 7.3

Figure 7.3 shows only the kind of thing that counts as a Turing Machine, though it does not represent any particular machine. To get a better understanding of Turing's idea, we have therefore to look at a determinate Turing Machine, one designed to carry out some given task. Only in this way can you appreciate the surprising resources of the two basic components – tape and printer – of the device.

As you will see, Turing Machines are in no sense limited to mathematical work, but it is perhaps easiest to begin with an example of a Turing Machine whose competence is confined to an elementary arithmetical task. Here is how to fill in the general description above in order to turn it into a dedicated 'machine' that is able to add '1' to any number. (This is a simple enough task, but useful for conveying Turing's idea in an uncluttered way.)

(1)   To begin with, we need some way to input a number to the machine: some way of representing a number to which, if all goes well, the machine will add '1'. One way would be to have an appropriate arabic numeral printed on the tape, but for reasons which will be clearer shortly this is too complicated, and would undermine the beautiful simplicity we are aiming for. Instead, let us use the fact that we have as much tape as we need, and we can therefore represent any number as a sequence of '*' symbols printed on the squares of the tape. We represent the input of '2' by figure 7.4 and '3' by figure 7.5. Notice that some section of the tape counts as an input if: (a) it contains

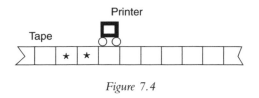

Figure 7.4

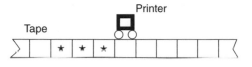

Figure 7.5

an appropriate number of squares on which '★' is printed; (b) the section is bounded on either side by at least one blank square; and (c) the printer is poised above the blank square immediately to the right of the last '★' in the sequence. (To keep matters simple, we shall assume that all the squares to the right and left of the input are blank.)

(2)   Next, we need some way to describe the operation of the printer, i.e. some account of what kinds of thing the printer does which enable it detect the input and add '1' to it. This will be described shortly.

(3)   Finally, we need some way of telling that a number produced by the device counts as the output. Here we simply use the same idea of numerical representation as that given in (1) above, but we count the representation as the output (or answer) when, after moving about, the printer comes to rest on the blank square immediately to the *left* of a sequence of '★' squares.

To illustrate how all this works, imagine that the input to the machine is '2' (as in figure 7.4) and the desired output is thus '3', as in figure 7.6. Clearly, we have to give the printer abilities to move, scan, print, and possibly erase, in such a way that, whenever it begins in the position shown in figure 7.4, it ends up in the position shown in figure 7.6. Moreover, our specification of these abilities must make it plausible that they could be deployed to get the correct answer for *any* input, since only then would we be able to see the machine as '1'-adder.

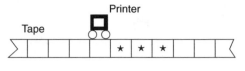

Figure 7.6

In order to finish our characterization of the Turing Machine, we need some way of specifying the operations of the printer. We shall say that the printer is able to follow certain *instructions*, each of which can be specified by a string of four items:

(i)   a name or label of the instruction,
(ii)   a state of the square of the tape immediately under the printer,
(iii) an action to be taken by the printer,
(iv)   a name of an instruction that is to be carried out next.

As an example, consider:

(a) $I_1/\star/R/I_2.$

This instruction is labelled 'I_1'. It requires the printer the detect what is on the square it currently rests over, and if it is '$\star$', it further requires the printer to move one square to the right. Finally, as indicated by the last symbol, it requires the printer to get to work on a new instruction, I_2. What if there is no '$\star$' written on the tape immediately under the printer? In this case, as you might expect, the instruction 'I_1' offers no guidance to the printer, and the latter moves nowhere and does nothing.

However, there is nothing to prevent us giving the printer this additional instruction:

(b) $I_1/-/L/I_2.$

This instruction has the same name as the previous one, but it tells the printer what to do in case the square immediately under it has no '$\star$'. When taken together, the above pair of instructions prepare the printer for every eventuality; they tell it what to do if '$\star$' is on the square, and what to do if there is no "$\star$" on the square.

What if, in addition to (a) and (b) we had this instruction:

(c) $I_1/\star/L/I_2$?

This would be bad news for the printer. Faced with this last instruction, and mindful of the instruction in (a) above, the printer would presumably try to move both left and right at the same time. Since, as you would expect, this would lead to a breakdown in any real machine constructed to carry out these instructions, we must avoid giving such an inconsistent set of instructions to the printer.

A set of instructions governing the operation of the printer can be thought of, using the familiar notion of a program. In the example under considera-tion we are looking for some program which will make the printer perform as an 'x + 1' (or 'Plus One') machine, i.e. a machine which will turn an input like that in figure 7.4 into the output in figure 7.6. Here is such a program for a 'Plus One' machine:

$I_1/-/\star/I_2$
$I_2/\star/L/I_2$
$I_2/-/-/I_2$

We can also represent this program in the following tabular form which makes it easier to keep track of the working of the program:

What's on the tape

		$-$	$\star$
Instruction	I_1	$\star/I_2$	
	I_2	$-/I_2$	L/I_2

The machine is started with an input as in figure 7.4, and the printer first follows instruction I_1. Given the way in which we defined 'input', we know that the printer must begin over a blank square, so I_1 is only defined for this case. And what this instruction tells the printer is to print '$\star$' in the blank square, and then to carry out a different instruction, namely I_2. The effect of I_2 depends on whether a '$\star$' is detected. If there is a sequence of '$\star$' squares, the printer will move left over all of them. But when this sequence comes to an end, and it detects a blank square, it will not move anywhere; it will halt.

But of course, halting in this way over a blank square with a sequence of '★' squares to the right is precisely what we count as the output in figure 7.6. And since the program increased the sequence of '★' squares by one, this output represents a number greater by one than the input.

The program, and above all the narrative description of how it works, is tedious. But that is the point. If I had said that all we had to do was to instruct the printer to move in such a way that it halted when it had calculated a number that was greater by one than the input, it would have been unclear how this was to be accomplished. The program and its description remove this lack of clarity, albeit at the cost of introducing a boringly repetitive sequence of instructions, the study of which would appeal only to someone who likes that sort of thing.

Any Task?

One can think of this – and any other program for a Turing Machine – as a very basic functional description of a task or ability. The abilities that we give the printer – moving left or right, checking for '★' and printing '★' – are not sophisticated, and it is no strain to imagine a physical device that could carry them out. Yet when we string together a program – a sequence of such instructions – we are able to describe how some imagined device can perform much more challenging tasks. What the above program does is to reduce the ability to add one to the simpler abilities of moving, printing etc.

Of course, it must be admitted that adding one to any number is not difficult. The description of the Turing Machine for accomplishing it is certainly much more complicated than the task itself. However, as noted earlier, the conclusions derivable from even such a simple example are astoundingly powerful. Using some ingenuity in specifying inputs and outputs, and allowing considerably longer lists of instructions, it is possible to imagine designing Turing Machines capable of performing a huge range of mathematical and linguistic tasks. (The inclusion of linguistic tasks shouldn't surprise you, since there is no limit to the sets of symbols that can be written on the tape.) But even this is only the beginning.

Turing's interest in his thought-device was that it allowed him to conceive of tasks as divided into those that could be performed by some Turing Machine and those that couldn't be. Though the latter were of most interest to him, setting as they did certain limits in formal logic, it is the class of tasks that *can be* carried out that is of interest here. What is suggested by Turing's discussion is that, so long as there is some appropriately systematic or intelligible relationship between some range of input and some range of output in any device, process or organism, it is possible to 'construct' a Turing Machine whose behaviour would match that of the original. Of course, as we have seen, a Turing Machine is not something one actually constructs; it is merely a useful way of displaying functional characterizations in tediously basic form. But it is precisely this that makes Turing's result so pertinent to our discussion.

Imagine that you came across some vast and hugely powerful computer with which you could interact in your own language and which was wonderfully patient in listening to you, answering your questions and, of course, correcting you when you were wrong. Think of it as something like HAL in the film *2001* (except suppose it to be without HAL's wicked secret). However ingenious such a machine is, however complicated its storage and retrieval mechanisms, it is none the less a machine. It is enmeshed in the causal world. When you ask it a question, you causally affect some part of it. When it answers or corrects you, it does so because in some mind-bogglingly complicated way, your questions cause a flow of electrons (or light) to course through its myriad circuits, eventuating in some output that you can hear or see, and which is appropriate to your question.

Could the behaviour of HAL be duplicated by a Turing Machine? Certainly. Any causally structured input–output network, no matter how complicated, could be mimicked by a Turing Machine of suitable complexity. Causal relations in a supercomputer will, of course, be much more difficult to mimic than simple ones like the 'Plus One' relationship between two numbers, but from the perspective of a Turing Machine, this difference is not important. I have described a Turing Machine that does the simple task, but, given this claim about causal networks, we can be sure that there could be a Turing-Machine description for HAL.

A detailed demonstration of this is beyond this book. But you can collect the flavour of an argument for it just by thinking about the relationship between the notions of explanation and regularity that were discussed in chapter 3. It was noted there that an appeal to regularities is what allows us to think that we have explained something, and it is also these regularities which make prediction possible. From Turing's point of view, it is precisely these regularities – wildly complex though they might be – which guarantee the availability of Turing-Machine characterization. One can sketch an argument for this as follows: (i) we certainly do think that anything that HAL does is explicable. However, (ii) in so far as we believe that some event is explicable, we think that it can be embedded in a background network of regularities. But, (iii) any network of regularities – any sequences in which there is a determined output given specific inputs – can be mimicked by a suitably complicated Turing-Machine program. So we can conclude that HAL itself, in all its amazing complexity, must be describable at some level as embodying a Turing-Machine program.

The idea that we can know that HAL is functionally characterizable, even before we have made any attempt to do it, might not seem so impressive. After all, HAL is a computer, and is therefore already animated by some sort of program. (More will be said about computer programs and software shortly.) However, the ideas behind Turing-Machine characterization in no way depend on such a restriction.

Forget HAL and think about human beings. Whatever else is true of us, we are certainly machines in the broadest sense of the word; we are biological machines. Moreover, we are not merely biological machines that live and reproduce by extracting energy from organic molecules, we are machines that believe, desire, experience, reason, deliberate and act. More precisely, we are machines whose actions are often explicable, and sometimes even predictable, when set in a folk psychological narrative. If we think of the hugely complex folk psychological story as basically a causal-explanatory account – something suggested by the Theory Theory of chapter 3 – then there is every reason to think that Turing's result will apply to us. Though no one seriously thinks that we will ever write out instructions for a Turing Machine that would accurately mimic some human being, the mere fact that human action is explicable suggests that some such description is in principle possible.

Viewing the huge range of things that we see, hear, touch, think and experience as input, and the things we do, as well as think and experience, as output, the functionalist suggestion is that there is some level of description of the relationship between input and output which could be described in Turing-Machine terms. That is, at bottom we could imagine a Turing-Machine description – a vast list of specific instructions – which captured precisely the mental features of a human being.

Turing Machines and the Mind

The earliest functionalists, among whom it is reasonable to include Turing, tended to think there was a very direct connection between our mental abilities and Turing Machines. To see what they had in mind, consider again the notion of an instruction as used in our 'Plus One' machine. We can think of an instruction given to the printer partly as a demand for practical action, and partly as a demand that the printer be receptive in a certain specific way. Thus, the instruction I_1 asked the printer to print '$\star$' on a square, and it also told it to prepare itself for following another instruction, namely I_2. One way to describe this would be to say that at the beginning the machine was in a certain state – namely a readiness to carry out I_1 – and that, having done so, it then moved into a different state – a readiness to carry out I_2. But these states of readiness bear more than a little resemblance to human mental states.

One way to think about belief, e.g. my belief that today is Sunday, is that it is a state which, given certain circumstances, will produce various actions or other mental states; it is, in short, a state of readiness. If I am asked about the day, the belief will lead me to say: 'Today is Sunday'; if I remember that I should book a restaurant table for next Saturday, the belief will lead me to make a note of this in my diary, given that I also believe that the restaurant is not open for bookings on Sunday; and, of course, the belief typically leads to other mental states, such as the mild depression that occurs when the pressures of the coming week seem all too close.

The original idea of some functionalists was that the analogy between Turing-Machine states of readiness and human mental states like belief was more than suggestive. They thought that any given human mental state could be understood as itself a state of some human embodiment of a Turing Machine. Of course, there was never the expectation that human beings had hidden printers and tapes, or even representations of printers or tapes, in them. The embodiment was not that immediate. Nor was it thought that some given mental state, such as the belief that today is Sunday, would be like a single instruction to a Turing Machine. Still, it was thought that any given belief might well turn out to be a complex of states – a sort of sub-routine of a program – running in the machine that constituted the human mind, and which was recognizably like some kind of Turing Machine.

The idea that mental states should be understood as Turing-Machine states is not the only way of putting Turing's work to use in the philosophy of mind, and there are reasons to think it a mistake. The more plausible view (touched on above) understands Turing-Machine description, not as a direct functional characterization of the mental landscape, but rather more as a kind of *guarantee* that there can be such a functional characterization. It is because we can be sure that at some level the kinds of thing we do, think and say could be characterizable by Turing's methods that we are free to take seriously the message of even simple examples like that of the Change Reckoner. And it is because of Turing's result that many find the analogy between computers and the mind irresistible and informative.

It is all too easy to misunderstand the way in which Turing's result has encouraged a computational conception of the mind. Some find the analogy between computers and the mind appealing because they think of modern computers as getting more sophisticated, and as therefore taking on an appearance of mentality to a greater extent than anyone would have thought possible a very few years ago. But whether or not this is true – whether or not actual computers impress you in this way – this is not the point at issue. Even if computers were still as they were in the 1940s – behemoths with fast-moving, one-track abilities – the Turing idea would have had the same consequence. In effect, what Turing did was to extend the notion of computation, so that it included anything that gave evidence of an intelligible regularity. From this point of view, not only do computers count as computational devices, but so does virtually anything that reacts in some systematic way to events around it.

To take an example which is as far as possible from computation in the everyday sense, think of the behaviour of earthworms. (My knowledge of earthworms is limited, but that doesn't matter for the example, and indeed that is part of the point.) Earthworm life is basic, but this does not prevent it being described in broadly functional terms. Moving through the soil, they absorb various nutrients, reject others, sometimes find mates, sometimes reproduce hermaphroditically, etc. If we think of the various things that affect earthworms as input, and the various ways they react as output, we are well on the way to characterizing them in terms amenable to Turing-Machine description. All we have to do to complete the task is to figure out how to encode the various inputs and outputs as sequences of symbols on a Turing-Machine tape, and then to draw up a list of instructions which create a Turing Machine that mimics earthworm reactions to these inputs.

No one would confuse a Turing Machine with an earthworm, not least because a Turing Machine is just an idea. But that doesn't matter, since the aim is not to make an earthworm by computational means. Instead, it is to mimic or simulate, and therefore come to understand, earthworm life by reducing it to a basic level of functional characterization – a level we could describe in Turing-Machine terms.

To make this idea more concrete, imagine the following scenario. In one room you place the world expert on earthworms – someone who knows everything about their structure and their behaviours. In a second room you have a tank with some earthworms in an environment you can control and monitor, but which is natural enough for them to be put through typical earthworm paces. Finally, in a third room you have a Turing Machine whose program is aimed at mimicking the typical input–output features of earthworm life. Suppose you then water the surface of the earthworm tank, whilst also telling the expert what you are doing, and whilst also running the Turing Program with an input suggesting that water is to be found in the upward direction. You then tell the expert what the earthworms actually do (move up towards the surface) and also what the Turing Machine would do (the same), though you do not tell him the respective sources of these pieces of information. If all goes as it should across a full range of inputs, it will be impossible for the expert to tell whether your information came from looking at the worms or reading off the output of the Turing device. The earthworm and the earthworm-mimicking Turing Machine are perfect functional duplicates.

This probably seems a fanciful example, and it is certainly not meant to show that earthworms have minds. However, it does bring out the point at issue, namely that the idea of Turing Machines enlarges our conception of computation. By means of it, we can see that not only do desktop computers count as computational devices, so do machines like the Change Reckoner, as well as any living organism. The relevance to mind of this notion of computation comes not from any special feature of present-day digital computers, but from the more general supposition that we too are computational devices. We are, of course, different in detail from earthworms and desktop computers, and of enormously greater complexity, but, if Turing is right, we should be able to be simulated (in principle) by some Turing Machine or other. Moreover, since what is characteristic of us is not our form of digestion or locomotion but our mental abilities, Turing believed that the construction of an actual machine which matched in an appropriate sense the input–output of a human mind would itself have mental abilities.

This last observation is fundamental. In his one venture directly into philosophy, Turing proposed a variant of the earthworm example as a test of this hypothesis. Called the 'Imitation game', it works roughly as follows. In one room there is a human being ready to answer questions about what he or she is thinking, thought, would say, knows, remembers, etc. In another is the implementation of a Turing Machine which the designer thinks is of sufficient complexity to mimic the mental abilities of a human being. You, the expert in this case, do not know which room contains the human being and which the machine, but you are able to put questions to both. The object of the game is to design questions that will allow you tell which set of answers come from the human being and which from the machine. (In Turing's original description of the case, these questions were put using a kind of teletype arrangement, so that the game wasn't given away.) If, no matter how cleverly you design your questions, you cannot tell the machine from the human being, then Turing suggested that the machine should count as having mental states.

Whilst superficially similar, the earthworm and human variants of the Imitation game are very different. The program of a Turing Machine that functionally duplicates an earthworm is certainly not an earthworm. But Turing believed that a machine which 'won' the Imitation game in the human case would not merely simulate the possession of a mind; it would in fact have one. This is a strong claim, and, whilst something related to it is central to the general functionalist line, the functionalist does not have to follow Turing here. And the most plausible versions of functionalism do not. This will be clearer after we deal with a few possible sources of misunderstanding.

(a) Mimicry or Mind

One such source has been touched on, but bears further comment. Turing himself was understandably keen on his Machines, and he probably did think that our mental lives are nothing more – nor less – than states of some Turing-Machine program. Certainly, his interpretation of the Imitation game suggests this. However, it is open to someone to think that features of the mental landscape are best understood functionally, yet to resist the identification of these features with machine states or programs. On this view, Turing-Machine programs at most produce something like mental features; they mimic them.

The fundamental claim of functionalism is that 'What is . . . ?' questions about the mind should be approached by something like functional deconstruction. And the ever-present possibility of Turing Machine simulation acts as a guarantee that this claim is not empty. But we do not have to draw from this the consequence that all there is to our mental life is to be found in a Turing Machine program. For a start, the specific way in which some functional story is implemented might be crucial to the full functionalist account of the mind. Whilst being grateful to the Turing idea for support, a functionalist might well insist that Turing-Machine functionalism – independent as it is from any particular implementation in the physical world – is at most suited to mimic the mental. Moreover, the most plausible form of functional deconstruction might well have sources other than those allowed for by Turing. What other sources? Here the picture gets more complicated.

One suggestion – perhaps the most common one – is that the correct functional account will emerge only as the result of empirical work on human subjects. The idea here is that by undertaking detailed psychological studies, we will come to recognize the functional units that combine to make up our mental lives. A second possibility is that all the materials needed for a functional account are already contained in the folk psychological story itself.

Both of these suggestions will be elaborated below, and as you will find in the literature, the details here occasion lively debate amongst functionalists. But here the important point is, to repeat, that there is room in the functionalist picture for regarding some functional stories as merely mimicking our mental life – rather as in the earthworm case – and others as themselves constituting it.

(b) Behaviourism Again

A second possible confusion concerns the relationship between functionalism and behaviourism. With talk of 'input/output' deconstructions of human mental abilities, it is natural to think that functionalism is little more than a new name for the old – and largely discredited – behaviourist view. But however natural it is to think this, it is mistaken.

Many functionalists, and the kind of behaviourist discussed in chapter 5, aim to solve the problem of the triangle by pursuing the Coalescing strategy. However, the behaviourist sets out to coalesce Mind into Action, whereas the functionalist is firmly in the Mind into Brain camp. One way to take in the difference at a glance is by putting the schematic representations of the two views side by side (see figure 7.7).

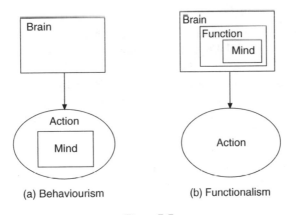

Figure 7.7

The behaviourist, whose view is captured in figure 7.7(a), does not doubt that, when we talk about our mental lives, we are making perfectly good sense, and are talking about genuine features of the world. But at the same time this behaviourist does not think that mental features compete with Brain for the causal generation of action. (Another sort of behaviourist sets out to solve the triangular problem by simply denying that there are, in any genuine sense, mental landscapes. I am leaving this aggressive behaviourist view for later consideration.) How could something real and mental exist and yet not be part of the causal story about action? The behaviourist of figure 7.7(a) thinks that each mental item is a kind of summing-up of some specific pattern of actions and dispositions to act. Thus, my belief that today is Sunday is nothing over and above certain characteristic behaviours and tendencies to behave.

In contrast, the functionalist (shown in figure 7.7(b)) aims to coalesce Mind into Brain, but to do so via a layer of functional description. That layer is most often described in an 'input–output' way where the outputs also include action, but crucially, the functionalist sees these inputs and outputs as including other mental states. Thus, my belief that today is Sunday is not only a state that leads to various forms of behaviour, it also arises from other beliefs and perceptions that I have, and it leads to other mental states. The functionalist, unlike the behaviourist, is not even trying to coalesce mental states simply into patterns of behaviour.

Deconstructing Harry

The discussion in the rest of this chapter will be clearer if we distinguish between two stages in the functionalist pursuit of coalescence. The first stage consists in providing a functional characterization of human mental features; and the second is an account of how the functional comes to be embodied in neurophysiological bedrock. These stages are equally important. Thinking, along with Turing, that purely functional characterization is all we need to know about Mind is, as we have seen, not necessary to functionalism generally. Moreover, even aside from this, it would not by itself help us to resolve the overdetermination problem. Mind causes Action and so does the Brain, so any plausible functionalism is committed to giving some story about how the functional rests on the physical.

Whilst keeping these two stages in mind, in this section we will consider ways of completing the first. That is, admitting for the present that functional characterization would illuminate the mental, we must see how we might arrive at such characterization.

To keep the discussion concrete, think again about Harry. If you recall, he was the somewhat clumsy character whose overexcitement led him to break the china figurine, and who suffered pain in the cause of our exposition. In the present context, you are to think of him as a typical adult human being. Thus:

> Though sometimes he is just not in control of his movements, at other times he initiates them through thought. That is, in thinking about what he is about to do, he comes up with plans and reasons, and these explain the movements he makes, and the actions he engages in;

He has a patchy memories of his late infancy and early youth, though he could produce a more coherent narrative extending from his late teens to the present;

He forms beliefs on the basis of his perceptions, as well as on the basis of the testimony of others, and these beliefs touch on the many subjects you might expect from an adult in our culture;

He has a whole range of wants, needs and desires, some of which are satisfied, and some of which he is working on;

He is a competent speaker of English, but can barely manage ordering a meal in any other language;

He is better than average at arithmetic, makes certain avoidable mistakes in his reasoning (and is no good at sports at all).

Ordinary as these accomplishments might seem, it is by no means clear how Harry — or any other human being — manages them. How is it that we perceive the things we do, that we keep track of events, persons and places in memory, that we can acquire a natural language when we are young, but have great difficulty with this same feat when we are older (and supposedly wiser), that we manage so often to make choices that bring together our beliefs and our needs, wants or interests, and yet that we sometimes fail so spectacularly in this same task?

These questions, and many others like them, set the agenda for much of contemporary cognitive psychology. The aim of this discipline is to provide an understanding of these adult cognitive capacities, and also to work out how they develop from infancy. Even the most superficial summary of this work would be a task well beyond the remit of this book, but what is relevant here is not detail so much as the characteristic shape of the work. For when cognitive psychologists search for answers to these questions, what they are looking for is precisely the kind of deconstruction required by the functionalist. Take, for example, vision. Among many other abilities, a normal adult like Harry is able to use sight to judge whether something in front of him is, say, a cat. This ability requires Harry to possess the concept of a cat, and to be able to recognize something in common in the different cat-like shapes that might occupy his visual field. As you will see by consulting any cognitive psychology text, even these most basic abilities concept possession and shape recognition — are the subject of enormously detailed research. That research aims to give more and more detailed accounts of functional units within the visual system subserving these abilities. And, of course, the aim is not merely to describe ways in which someone *might* come to decide visually that an object falls under a certain concept. Rather, it is to describe ways in which organisms like Harry *actually* manage the task.[1]

In resolving (or deconstructing) Harry's abilities by describing systems and subsystems that together accomplish the core tasks of cognition, what the psychologist is doing is something like what we did when we discussed the case of the human Change Reckoner. Starting with the Change Reckoner's ability to work out the monetary value of each arbitrary sample of loose change, we figured out that this abilitiy required the sub-abilities of being able to tell coins apart, to count them and to add up their values. How did we work this out? Partly by a kind of analysis of the task itself, and partly by our empirical guesses as to how such a task could be done. Of course, if we were serious about the *psychology* of this, we would have to find ways to test the Reckoner to see whether our guesses about these sub-abilities were correct. For all we know, the task might actually be accomplished in some completely different, and as yet unimagined, way.

With apologies to psychologists for using an example that does nothing to show off the intricate and demanding nature of their work, the Change Reckoner case displays the main outline of the kind of account they aim to provide. Starting with the range of mental abilities attributed to Harry, the aim of cognitive psychology is to come up with reasonable hypotheses, both about how these abilities work and about how they came to develop in the first place, and then to test these hypotheses by experimental work on normal, and not so normal, subjects. If all goes well, the result will be a complicated description of the functional layer that lies between the folk psychological characterization of organisms like Harry (a characterization of Mind) and the bedrock physical systems (abbreviated here as Brain) that in some way implement this functionality.

The description above is an outline, from a functionalist perspective, of the arena within which cognitive psychology operates. It shows cognitive psychology, and related disciplines, as sources of the functional characterization which sits between folk psychology and physical bedrock (see figure 7.7(b)). Accounts which look to the cognitive sciences for functional characterizations are usually grouped under the label *psychological functionalism* (*psychofunctionalism*, for short).

Though what we have is the merest sketch of psychofunctionalism, it highlights the advantages of the account, as well as its problems. Being able to call on the substantial body of work in cognitive psychology is clearly on the plus side, but this same feature leads to certain problems. However, before we get too deeply involved in any assessment, some refinements need to be made.

Hierarchies all the Way Down

So far we have spoken of functional organization as somehow a single level of description coming between the mind and the brain. But it is time that we noticed the more interesting possibility that there might be many layers of functional characterization occupying that space. Some functionalist writers encourage us to think of the mind as being like the software of a computer, and the brain as being like the hardware. This seems apt because software is functional rather than physical, and as a metaphor for the functional account it is arresting. But this metaphor also suggests that the detailed functional stories told by cognitive psychologists can be lumped together as somehow at one level – the software level – and that everything else is mere hardware implementation. This may be a convenient way to speak about desktop computers but, as applied to the psychofunctionalist account of the mind, it is a mistake, and it can lead to distracting and probably unfounded objections. If instead, as many functionalists now think, the right picture of the mind is one in which there are interwoven hierarchies of functional characterization, stretching from the folk psychological portrayal of the mental landscape to the neurophysiological bedrock, we get both a more realistic and a more defensible story. In terms of my schematic figures, one should think of a plausible functionalist account as in figure 7.8, rather than the simpler figures given earlier.

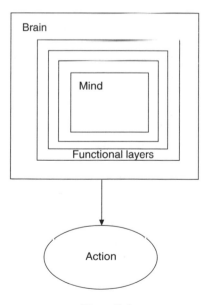

Figure 7.8

The functional layers shown in figure 7.8 are in fact different levels of description. The mental accomplishments of an organism at one cognitive level are broken down into component abilities which are themselves accomplished by various subsystems, which are then broken down into component abilities, which are then accomplished by various sub-subsystems, etc. For example, Harry's perceptual belief that there is a cat in front of him requiries that his visual system be able to pick out objects against a background, and this in turn requires some kind of depth perception, and this in turn requires some kind of shape perception, and this in turn requires some kind of line and edge perception, and so on. (And, of course, all of this is only one part of what is required to perceive a cat; there would have to be more said about concepts and perception.)

What governs the choice of components, and the postulation of the various subsystems, is the empirical methodology of cognitive science; and this methodology is in turn an application to the cognitive of scientific methodology itself. If all goes well, the systems described at various levels of description will reach right down to the brain level: we will uncover those functional neurophysiological units which make possible our higher-level cognitive functioning.

This is a more complicated (and realistic) picture of funtionalism and, in ways to be discussed, it allows the functionalist to evade various objections. But no amount of complication in the functional layers between Mind and Brain changes the basic shape of functionalism. The 'What is . . . ?' question is answered by the functionalist, not by any direct physical account of the mental, but by pointing to the levels of functional description. Harry's perceptual belief that there is a cat in front of him is not to be *understood* as a state of his brain. Rather, such understanding comes from seeing it as a state within Harry's functional organization that exists in virtue of the workings of various cognitive subsystems, and which is apt to produce certain other states and behaviour. On the more complicated picture, there will of course be no one level at which the input and output characterization of Harry's belief can be found. But that doesn't make much difference, since our understanding can be based on the hierarchy of levels working together to make Harry the kind of creature who can believe, by seeing, that there is a cat in front of him.

Of course, as we move down the hierarchy of Harry's functional organization, we come to a level describing what goes on in his brain. But this should not be seen as a retreat from the functionalist idea. For what counts from the functionalist perspective is not the physical nature of Harry's brain, so much as its functional organization. If Harry had non-standard brain chemistry, or if his brain was in some other structural way different from ours, then this would not prevent Harry from sharing our beliefs about cats. So long as we have in common a functional organization in which the lowest functional level supports those above, all the way up to the input/output structure of belief, then the specific chemical 'brainware' that Harry happens to have is not important. To be sure, it is important to his having a mental landscape that he has something physical supporting his functional organization. But, as has been said from the beginning, the functionalist looks to the organization, and not the stuff, for an understanding of the features of that landscape.

(This last point might remind you of an issue considered in chapter 6. One reason offered in favour of functionalism, and against the identity view, is functionalism's built-in recognition that there could be creatures with similar minds but very different physical natures. In the relevant lingo: mental features can be multiply realized. Following Lewis, I suggested that there is less to this point than meets the eye; the identity theorist need only relativize identifications to species or subspecies of creatures to get around it. And in any case it is not clear what the importance of multiple realization is until we know more about 'realization'. As you will soon see, we are gradually closing in on these issues.)

Including the Mind

Figure 7.8 shows Mind sitting comfortably on the top of the functional hierarchy, and this is, I suppose, just what you would expect. After all, functionalism ultimately aims to coalesce Mind and Brain, and you can scarcely count yourself as doing that unless Mind figures in the picture; we certainly do not want to get so carried away by our search for functional characterization that we lose sight of the very thing we set out to characterize. Yet there are tendencies in the philosophical literature suggesting that this is less easy than it seems and, even more surprisingly, might not in the end be necessary.

To understand how this could be, let's look more closely at what the hierarchical functionalist might say about Harry's cat belief. At the top level we have Harry and his perceptual belief that there is a cat in front of him. We have seen how the functionalist appeals to cognitive psychology to explain how it is possible for a creature like Harry to entertain such a belief, and we can summarize the explanation in the following picturesque way.

Harry is the agent of his belief: he is the organism who entertains it, and is in some sense 'in charge' of this folk psychological attitude. But inside Harry there are more specialized agents, each of which is in charge, not of the overall belief, but of some element which is necessary to Harry's belief-forming capacities. Thus, there is an agent whose task it is to detect objects, another which detects depth, another which detects shapes, another which detects edges and lines, and so on. Each of these agents can be thought of, for the purposes of this metaphorical description, as possessing some sort of mental ability; only as you move down the hierarchy, the level of sophistication diminishes. For example, the little agent or 'homunculus' which detects lines and edges does nothing else, and it reports upwards to the shape-detecting homunculus, who then reports up to the depth perceptor, etc.

The aim, in laying out this story, is to show how Harry's perceptual belief comes to exist in virtue of the behaviour of homunculi at various levels of functional description. Moreover, a vital further part of this story is the idea that homuncular 'intelligence' becomes less evident as we descend down the levels. If, at the lowest level, the homunculi require no real intelligence at all, then it would seem we have explained Harry's original capacity by gradual functional reduction. The stuff about the intelligence of homunculi at each level – about there being a little person who detects and reports on, e.g. shapes – turns out to be of only expository interest (which is of course all it was ever intended to be). Achieving the needed discrimination at the lowest level turns out to be purely mechanical, and, since each level supports the one above it, there seems no level at which a genuinely intelligent homunculus needs to re-enter the picture.

Unfortunately, it would appear that the same could be said of Harry. Looking at the work of the homunculi from the bottom up, we do not have to treat homunculi at each higher level other than metaphorically, and hence not as 'real' agents. But then how, when we get to the folk psychological level – the one where we find Harry – do we come suddenly to find a real, and not merely metaphorical, person who is the subject of thoughts and the agent of actions?

The problem arises because in appealing to the experimental work of cognitive psychologists, we make it possible for a gap to open up between their complex functional story and our folk psychological conception of belief. This gap was perhaps not envisaged by philosophers who thought of the functionalist story as offering us a way of reconciling Mind and Brain. But that goal looks distinctly odd if one of the parties to the reconciliation disappears.

Avoiding Gaps in the Story

There are ways of preventing the gap between the functional layers and our everyday conceptions from opening up in the first place. For example, it might be argued that as you move up the hierarchy of functional levels, something akin to belief enters the picture even before we get to Harry. Since one or other version of this strategy is common in the literature on functionalism, I should spell this out a bit.

It is an intrinsic feature of attitudes like belief that, as they are ordinarily understood, they are about a way the world is, or might be. Harry's belief is not simply a self-contained state of mind, it is directed towards a cat located somewhere in front of him. The gap in the functional hierarchy seems to open up if it is insisted that this belief can be successively reduced to descending levels in which this attitudinal feature simply disappears. After all, if the homunculi at the bottom level are mere shufflers of internal states, then where does world directedness re-enter the picture as we move up the hierarchy? However, there are other ways of looking at the hierarchy of functional levels.

One suggestion is that we were too hasty in assuming that world-directness dropped out of the hierarchy in the first place. Admittedly, the homunculi at some lower level are not apprised of cats or of spatial locations like 'in front of'. But, as described earlier, there is nothing to stop us thinking of them as directing their attentions to lines and edges. In being so directed, we can treat them as having attitudes in some minimalist sense. Taking these minimal attitudes to ground the shape-directed attitudes of the next level up, and taking the shape directed attitudes to ground attitudes towards the foregrounding of objects at a still higher level, we can continue up the hierarchy until we reach Harry. He has the attitude which we recognize, not from any cognitive psychological experimentation, but as ordinary human beings interacting with him. But if we get the details of the functionalist story right, the suggestion is that the directedness of Harry's perceptual belief is simply the same kind of directedness that exists lower down the hierarchy. The only difference between them is that Harry's belief is visible to anyone who knows some folk psychology, whereas the lower layers which support that belief are discernible only after some experimental research.

In outline, this strategy seems fine, but the devil is in the details. The rub comes when an advocate of this strategy tries to account for the directedness of the lower-level 'attitudes'. Most often called 'sub-personal' states (i.e. 'sub-Harry' states), they seem to gain their directedness from broadly causal relations to relevant items in the world. What makes it true, for example, that a type of sub-personal state is about edges is that the edges of objects cause that type of state. This is, of course, perfectly fine from the scientific point of view; one would expect causal relations – and the regularities which come with them – to figure in the subject-matter of an aspiring science like cognitive psychology. But, as we have seen, it is far from clear that the directedness of the attitudes that figure in folk psychology is itself a causal notion.

In chapter 2 I described two sorts of case suggesting that there can be a puzzling slack between beliefs and the world, and it is this slack which leads to trouble for the above programme. Recall the case of Monique and the British Museum. Monique's belief about the British Museum doesn't seem to be a merely causal relation between her and the British Museum, for causal relations do not seem to be sensitive to the way in which the cause is described, and thus do not allow the slack we found in the Monique case. If the British Museum causes something – say, Monique's belief – then it causes it no matter how the building itself is described. (If a brick breaks a window – causes it to break – then the fact that it breaks the window scarcely depends on whether the brick is described as 'a heavy object' or as 'a London stock'.) But the correctness of our attribution of beliefs to Monique's seemed to depend on whether we described the building as the British Museum or as a building with lions guarding the entrance. In this case, one and the same reality – one and the same building – figured in two different, indeed incompatible, beliefs. In the case of Richard and the Parisian brasserie, the slack was in a different place: two different realities – two brasseries – but apparently the same belief. Unless we can explain this slack in some way, consistently with a view of a believer as in effect a nest of sub-personal agents who are at most causally connected to different aspects of reality, the gap between the functionalist account and our everyday conception of the attitudes remains.

The above observation marks the beginning of a very long story, one with lots of twists in the plot and many suggested endings. Even the point about the mismatch between causality and belief is less clear than I may have made it seem. On the one hand, the literature contains ingenious attempts to conjure up, from merely causal ingredients in the functionalist hierarchy, a sufficiently complex relation to handle the directionality of belief. And, on the other hand, there are writers around who think that if the directionality of belief is not causal, then so much the worse for our ordinary notion of belief. (The 'so-much-the-worse-for' strategy can be difficult to assess, especially when the proponent at the same time suggests that the favoured, usually causal, notion of directionality is really all we need in the ordinary notion of belief. To learn more, you should follow up the works of Daniel Dennett which are cited in the reading list relevant to this chapter and to chapter 9. He is not the only philosopher who hints at the 'so-much-the-worse' strategy, but his writings are a good place to start.)

Alternatives to Psychofunctionalism

It would be disappointing if a functionalist had to admit that, after all the hard work of trying to coalesce Mind and Brain, a space opens up between Mind and the functional story whose job it was to bring about the coalescence. But this does seem to be a possible cost of taking the psychofunctionalist route. Spelling this out graphically, instead of the orderly situation shown in the earlier figure 7.8, we would have something like figure 7.9. And this offers us no immediate relief from the overdetermination problem.

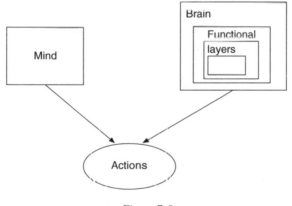

Figure 7.9

Of course, there are other ways of dealing with the triangle than coalescence, and nothing prevents the psychofunctionalist from pursuing them. Indeed, one such possibility has already been touched on. The 'so-much-the-worse' option in respect of belief might be extended to the whole of Mind. This would lead to a version of the radical strategy described earlier as Elimination; the problems of the triangle would be made to go away by dropping Mind from the picture. This is a radical move, but not quite as radical as my wording might suggest. For any sensible psychofunctionalist who adopts it will insist that the real nature of Mind is in fact revealed by psychological research, and that what is being dropped is merely a deeply problematic folk psychological account. (We can scarcely deny that this account is problematic, having spent some time in chapters 2 and 3 pointing out the trouble it causes.)

Another way to cope with the overdetermination represented in figure 7.9 involves our giving different jobs to the two arrows. Taking this route would make the psychofunctionalist a Division of Labour strategist. However, since the emphasis in this chapter, as in the last, is on the Coalesence strategy, I shall save both of these options for later. In any case, whilst recognizing that there may be ways of dealing with the tensions evident in figure 7.9, avoiding them might be an even better bet.

What landed us in trouble in the first place was looking to empirically based psychological research for the functional characterization of the mind. The core philosophical idea of functionalism is that the essence of the mental is functional; that 'What is . . . ?' questions about pains, beliefs and the rest are best answered by describing what these things do – what sorts of patterns of input and output they figure in – rather than by trying directly to say what they are made of. But the idea that the relevant patterns are those uncovered by cognitive psychology is additional to the philosophical core of functionalism and, as such, it is optional. Or, rather, it would be optional if we could think of some other source for the patterns we need to make a philosophical case for functionalism.

Unsurprisingly, there is indeed another such source, one that has been staring us in the face. The kind of identity account discussed in the previous chapter took as its starting-point the folk psychological description of the mental landscape. Just as the story of heat – a discussion of the phenomena of heat known for centuries – set the agenda for our eventual identification of heat and energy transfer, so the folk psychological account was seen as setting the agenda for the identification of, for example, pain and C-fibre firing. And it is this idea of 'setting the agenda' that can we can construe in a functionalist way. The story goes roughly as follows.

On one influential view of the notion of explanation, we explain some phenomena only when we have embedded them in a pattern of regularities. As you will recall from chapter 3, if this notion of explanation is taken as the appropriate one for folk psychology, we end up having to say that folk psychology consists of a vast network of true generalizations about what people will do, say, think and feel in appropriate circumstances. Seen in this way, folk psychology is a theory, and its generalizations are regularities into which we embed, and thereby explain, human action, thought and experience. Recall also that since our explanatory abilities do not seem to be accompanied by the ability to state these generalizations, this Theory Theory requires us to count the generalizations as known only tacitly by the folk.

Amongst the generalizations of folk psychology will be those telling us what sorts of things cause painful experiences, and what sorts of things painful experiences lead us to do and think. Of course, these generalizations will be enormously complicated and, as noted, there is no practical hope of our listing them all in advance. None the less, in so far as we find pain intelligible – as something which figures in our explanations of human behaviour – it seems reasonable to think that we have some kind of access to these generalizations. Moreover, unlike the results of empirical psychology, our access to these generalizations (when we do come upon them) is through reflection, rather than experiment. As a sufferer of pains, and as a witness to such suffering in others, I have in some way come to acquire the concept of pain. And, in reflecting on this concept, I can appreciate why certain sorts of pain have the causes and effects they do.

If you accept the above story, it is plausible to think of the network of folk psychological generalizations as itself a functional characterization of mind. Each of the phenomena of mind will take their place in the criss-crossed network made by these generalizations. For example, we can define types of pain, or the belief that today is Sunday, by seeing them as more or less stable features in a network of causes (inputs) and effects (outputs). To help in visualizing this, think of waves in the sea. The complex interrelations of parcels of water   a causal pattern of inputs and outputs – produces relatively stable features that we identify as waves. The suggestion is that our experiences and attitudes are like waves formed in the vastly more complicated flow of causes and effects that constitute the regularities of folk psychological generalizations. (A full and non-metaphorical consideration of this kind of definition raises interesting technical issues that are beyond the remit of this book; they can be pursued by using the reading list for this chapter. But suffice it to say that there do not seem to be any principled *technical* objections to the possibility of this kind of definition.)

In this way – and simply by analytical reflection on folk psychology – we will end up with functionalist answers to 'What is . . . ?' questions. Further, the very fact that we arrive at these answers by a priori analysis of our concepts rules out even the possibility of a gap between Mind and functional characterization. Whatever we come to say about the role of Brain in our final picture, we can be sure in advance that Mind and its functional description will always march in step. This feature of the view – a view called for obvious enough reasons *analytical functionalism* – is in contrast to the rival psychological functionalist account. For, as we have seen, the latter account leaves room for the possibility that Mind and functional description *might not* march in step.

Which sort of functionalism is the better bet? From what has been said so far, there are interesting pros and cons to both views. Psychological functionalism creates what looks like just the right space for the serious research now going on in cognitive psychology and related disciplines. To be sure, in creating this space it leaves open the possibility of a break in the link between Mind and functional description. But perhaps this is a possibility that we should at least take seriously. And, in any case, it is only a possibility; it may well turn out that the psychologists' results will vindicate, rather than replace, the folk psychological picture. (There are a number of philosophers of mind who are quite convinced now that this is the likely outcome.)

Analytical functionalism gives us the guarantee that Mind and functional description can never come apart. And this captures something that seems intuitively right. For it does seem odd to think that a psychologist's research on, say, pain could come to show that pains either do not exist or that they are not as we feel them to be. (This would be odd, but then again almost no position in this area is too odd to have adherents. Not only are there philosophers who think that empirical research could teach us that there no such things as the beliefs, desires, etc. of folk psychology; some of these same philosophers would also insist that pains and other experiences might not be anything like they seem.) On the minus side, however, the analytical functionalist's view comes with lots of costs, very few of which are hidden. The most expensive of these is its story about what the folk are up to in their explanatory practices: many find the picture of folk psychology as a tacitly known set of explanatory generalities just implausible.

Functionalism and Coalescence

You will not be surprised to hear that no decision will be made here about which functionalism is the better bet. (There will, however, be further discussion bearing on this issue in the next chapter.) In any case, any such decision made on the evidence before us would be rash. For our candidate functionalisms have so far been distinguished only as two different *sources* of functional description; nothing very specific has been said about how they relate functional description to the physical bedrock we have abbreviated as Brain.

This might not be obvious; it is easy to get lulled into thinking you have been told a story about functional description and Brain simply because of the kinds of examples that are used to introduce functionalism. Change Reckoners and other such devices motivate the idea that functional description is of the first importance in answering 'What is . . . ?' questions about the mental, and, in the course of developing these answers, the physical world does figure. After all, Change Reckoners and suchlike things are physical as well as functional devices, and the talk of 'implementation' or 'realization', can give one the sense that the physical world has been given due consideration.[2]

None the less, when we come to evaluate functionalism in general, and analytical versus psychological functionalism in particular, the notions of implementation and realization are perhaps not up to the task. Rooted as they are in folk psychological narrative – hopes and fears are realized, plans are implemented – they are not likely to inspire confidence in the larger project of reconciling such narrative to physicalism. What is needed is a clear and non-metaphorical characterization of the relationship between the functional and the physical, a characterization that takes us beyond the vague suggestion of the motivating examples. And, whilst we are at it, we also need to be more explicit than we have been about the *nature* – and not merely the *source* – of the relationship between the mind and the functional level.

Figure 7.10 represents the situation in a slightly different way from the schemata given previously, but it shows clearly what is required, and it will be crucial to the remainder of this chapter. The aim of the coalescence strategy is, of course, to pull the three sections of figure 7.10 together, and this requires defensible accounts of *both* the ?- and ??-relations.

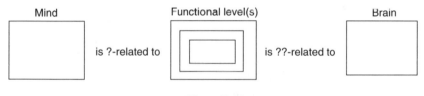

Figure 7.10

The ?-Relation

According to an analytical functionalist, functional-level description comes from an analysis of the concepts of Mind. This makes the ?-relation relatively straightforward: it is something like the relationship between the concept of *bachelor* and the concept *unmarried male human being*. That is, it is an a priori definitional-type link arrived at by reflection on the nature of Mind. (As suggested earlier, the technical details of this definition are complicated, and therefore are not just like the bachelor case. The items by Lewis on the reading list will help.) However, nothing we say about the specification of the ?-relation constrains us when it comes to specifying the ??-relation. It is open to an analytical functionalist to say that this second relation is one of *implementation by*, or being *realized in*, providing, of course, that we are told more about these notions. But, in fact, the most common analytical functionalist story about the

??-relation does not beat around the bush by beginning with these notions. Rather, it is said that the ??-relation is *identity*, the very relation that we spent so much time discussing in the previous chapter. And this has the effect of making the account into a version of the identity theory: concepts of Mind are definitionally tied to functional specifications, and these latter are simply identified with features of the Brain. Of course, unlike the ?-relation, the establishment of identities requires empirical, and not merely conceptual, investigation. As with heat and temperature, detailed and arduous scientific work is needed to find out which features of our neurophysiology should be counted as, for example, the functional state that constitutes pain. But as in the previous chapter, this is just what we should expect in an identity account of the mental and the physical.

The idea that, by pursuing functionalism, we could end up back again at the identity theory has caused enormous confusion in the literature. (It has led the archetypal identity theorist, David Lewis, whose view is also analytically functionalist in our terms, to wonder whether he is a functionalist.) This is because of the tendency to think of functionalism as somehow in competition with the identity theory. However, I would hope that our discussion (and figure 7.10) act to dissipate the confusion. If you think of functionalism as a view solely concerned with giving a non-physicalist account of Mind, then of course it is in some initial tension with the identity theory. But if you think of functionalism more broadly as an account aimed at reconciling Mind and Brain – an account which makes use of functional characterization along the way – then it is not surprising to find identity re-entering the picture. After all, the kind of identification found in the heat case – a theoretical identification developed in the course of scientific advancement – is a well-understood way to connect two otherwise disparate realms. Indeed, we could think of this kind of theoretical identity as providing a role model for any aspiring coalescence relation. One could say to any functionalist who resists identity: we understand what it is for Mind and Brain to be integrated using the relation of identity. But if you think this is wrong, then you must tell us what what you intend to put in its place, and your answer must be at least as clear.

I shall discuss ways of trying to meet this challenge shortly, but first let's see what the psychofunctionalist has to say about the ?-relation, the relationship between Mind and the functional level that does not by itself bring about the full integration of Mind and Brain. We have seen that the psychofunctionalist sees functional-level descriptions as resulting from hard graft on the part of psychologists and others. But, whilst acknowledging all the work required for filling in the functional story, we are still owed some account of how the psychofunctionalist would characterize the ?-relation. Gleaned from what is often implicit in the literature, here are some possibilities, arranged in order of increasing optimism and with some explanatory glosses:

(a)   There is no systematic relationship because the 'Mind' box just disappears.

The idea here – one that we have touched on before – is that the folk psychological concepts of mind set the ball rolling, but then scientific psychology and cognitive science take over. When the smoke clears, the presumption is that we will come to think of folk psychology as just a bad or confused, first attempt at understanding human beings.

(b)   The relationship is one of vindication, though this is not a precisely characterized notion.

Here the suggestion is that the functional level or levels will reflect enough of the folk psychological to justify the kind of explanation the folk employ. However, the fit between the two conceptual schemes will not guarantee that each phenomenon of interest to the folk will match precisely some particular functional deconstruction.

(c)   The relationship is in fact one of identity.

The hope here is that the concepts used in folk psychological explanation will turn out to *be* features of the underlying functional account. This will, of course, vindicate the folk psychological as in (b) above, but it will do so in a more robust way.

The first of these possibilities is eliminativist, a position that has so far figured on the margins of our discussion of both identity and functionalist accounts. However, its being marginal is an artefact of our focusing on the coalescence strategy, and I shall continue to reserve further discussion of it until later.

The vindication suggestion is really a family of positions, each defined by more specific proposals about the way in which folk psychological concepts are reflected in the functional characterizations of cognitive psychology. For example, suppose you think that belief and the other attitudes are not as such features at the functional level, but that something like the directedness of belief can be seen there. That is, you think that some functional states are (and must be) assigned contents, and that these contents work in something like the way the contents of the attitudes do. Then you will think that a crucial feature of the attitudes is visible in the scientifically demanding world of functional characterization. And this suggests something more hopeful than eliminativism: the folk are, after all, on to something when they talk about our beliefs and desires; it is just that this talk is only approximated at the more scientific level.

Elimination and vindication are possibilities we have come across before, and both are, among other things, ways of avoiding concrete specification of the ?-relation. But the third possibility is new; the identity relation is of course familiar, though in (c) it is employed in a different context. Unlike the identity account in the last chapter, or the analytical functional version of that account in this chapter, the identity in (c) connects the items of folk psychology with features described in functional rather than physical terms. Things like the belief that it is Sunday, or a pain in the elbow, are identified with states having specific roles in an overall story about functional organization. Whilst we have yet to be given such a story, when we are, it will be told in the language of cognitive psychology, and not using the narrative resources of folk psychology.

Interpreting the ?-relation as identity removes the vagueness that is typical in formulations of psychofunctionalism. Many accounts speak about the functional story as 'fixing the extension' of folk psychological notions, or of its telling us what the mental 'consists in'.[3] But it is difficult to see what these claims come to, unless they are merely variant ways of speaking in terms of an identity relation. Also, it is important to stress again that the identity relation used here connects the folk psychological to the functional; it is not a relation between either of these and the physical.

The ??-Relation

Whether we accept the psychofunctionalist identification of, e.g. beliefs and pains with functional roles, or insist instead on one of the other options, we now need to say something about the relation of functional role to the physical structure of Brain. As with the ?-relation, there is often a certain vagueness in formulation here: the physical is spoken about as 'implementing' the functional, but this is not good enough. We think we understand 'implementation' better than we do partly because it is a familiar folk term – we implement plans and designs all the time – and partly because we think we understand the Change Reckoner and desktop computer examples. But neither of these is an adequate basis for our confidence. Any transfer from talk about implementation of plans to implemenation of functional roles is quite simply metaphorical; and the relationship between Reckoner or computer 'software' and 'hardware' is at best evocative.

One move we might make at this point is simple and radical: count the ??-relation as identity. Doing this, whilst at the same time identifying Mind and functional role, would lead immediately to the coalescence of Mind and Brain. Treating the ?-relation as identity, the features of Mind are one and the same as functional roles, and these latter come out as one and the same as certain physical features of Brain. This proposal pulls the boxes of figure 7.10 together to give a unified picture of the Mind and Brain – a picture that fulfils an original functionalist ambition. (This proposal is subject to any counter-arguments both to identity accounts and to functionalism itself. But here the point is simply getting clear about the shape of the proposal, rather than viewing it as the last word about the mental landscape.)

In effect, this radical proposal would transform psychofunctionalism into a version of the identity account. So far as I am aware, no one has been tempted by it, but we can learn a lot by examining both the reasons it is unappealing to psychofunctionalists, and reasons why they should perhaps have taken it more seriously. I shall begin with the latter.

Change Reckoner-type examples get the functionalist idea rolling, but, as has been suggested, the model of the mind that is dear to many functionalists is that provided by the digital computer. The earliest functionalists often compared Mind to software and the Brain to hardware, and, though more sophisticated functionalists think this is oversimplified, the computational paradigm still persists. However, rather than taking us away from identity, there is reason to think that that computer analogy actually offers support for identity. Writing this text on a computer, my interactions with the machine are pretty 'high-level'; I ask it to do things to words, sentences and paragraphs, and it responds in kind. (It even corrects spelling and would, if I let it, correct grammatical 'mistakes'.) However, I know that underlying this level, there is a more complicated program written in a language (perhaps one called 'C +') which I have never mastered. And underlying this are still more basic 'user-*unfriendly*' functional characterizations, all the way down to some sort of 'machine language', that is, a set of procedures which are tailored to the central processing chip proprietary to my computer.

Given this hierarchy, it would be possible, though admittedly tedious, to trace each of my high-level interactions down to the behaviour of the electrons in the central processor. My asking for a word to be deleted is a sub-routine of the program written in C + which is a sub-routine of . . . which is a flow of electrons in particular places and directions. Notice that the links between the levels are each made by an 'is'; the story is essentially one in which identity figures all the way down. And it figures all the way up too, which is unsurprising, given that identity is the symmetrical relation *par excellence*. An engineer who knew about the flow of electrons at a given time in the central processor (and in 'peripheral' devices like screens and disk drives) would be able to say which procedures were being called upon in the machine-language program, which procedures were called upon in the C + program, and, ultimately, would know that a specific word was being deleted.

This linkage between between the physical and the functional in a computer is sometimes denied because some specific machine-language procedure might call on physically different parts of the central processor and memory. For example, noticing the typo, suppose I delete 'wrod' in this sentence, and then retype it in the same place, but again as 'wrod'. The first deletion might send a flow of electrons to one memory address, the second deletion might send a flow to a different memory address. And this can make it seem as if two different physical processes were united only at the functional level. This argument, however, assumes a too simplistic notion of the physical. The two electron flows are different at some very basic level – they each involve different electrons – but they can none the less be the same physical process. The details will, of course, vary from case to case, but here is an analogy which makes the point. The temperature of a gas is surely a physical feature of it. Yet the distribution of motions of the molecules of the gas might vary from case to case, even though the temperature doesn't. In one instance, a specific molecule might be moving slowly, whilst in another case that very same molecule might be moving quickly, even though the gas is at the same temperature in both instances. This is, of course, because temperature depends only on *mean* kinetic energy, and not on the movements of, as it were, named molecules. Temperature is a somewhat higher-order property than that describing the actual distribution of velocities, but temperature is none the less a physical, and not merely a functional, property.

Returning to the main theme: if a psychofunctionalist is impressed by the computational model, then this is one good reason to opt for identity all the way down. In addition, identity makes it easier to tell a causal story about Mind. Leaving eliminativism and mere vindication on one side, the first stage of the psychofunctionalist account identifies mental features with functional roles. Now it is not at all apparent how a mere functional role can cause things to happen. Using a simple illustration common in the literature, suppose that we have functionally defined a specific poison as a substance that destroys nervous tissue and brings about death. Now ask yourself what causes the death of a human being who ingests a quantity of this poison. It sounds absurd to say that the cause of death was the role of the poison as a lethal destroyer of tissue. Functional roles don't cause things to happen; they are compendious descriptions of causal/functional relations, and this makes them seem the wrong sort of thing to count as actual causes. A death certificate wouldn't cite the functional role as the cause of death, but rather the substance itself. This suggests that causal efficacy is to be found at the physical level – the level which is ??-related to functional role. And taking the ??-relation to be identity makes all of this fall nicely into place.

In spite of these reasons in favour of treating the ??-relation as identity, advocates of psychofunctionalism seem not to be impressed. Appreciating why they resist the temptations of identity will require us to think again about a notion only partly discussed in the previous chapter: multiple realizability. The psychofunctionalist takes very seriously the idea that mental landscapes can be attributed at least partially to various non-human species, and can in principle be attributed to the merely imagined creatures of science fiction. As one hears over and again, a supposed consequence of this is that features of the mental landscape cannot be identified just as physical features. If pain were nothing but C-fibre firing, then there could be no pain in creatures without C-fibres. But since it seems just obvious that non-human species and extraterrestrials might well lack C-fibres, and yet suffer pain, this seems a conclusive reason to abandon the identity account. And it is precisely at this point that the psychofunctionalist makes a pitch: what non-human species and extraterrestrials share is not a physical nature, but a functional one.

As we saw in chapter 6, this kind of argument is far from conclusive. The identity theorist need only relativize identification to particular species, or even to subgroups within the species. Thus, the claim is not that pain is C-fibre firing *tout court*, it is only pain-in-human beings. This leaves open the possibility that pain in other creatures is some other type of physical state. If this seems a cheat – if it seems to avoid the question: what do pains of all kinds have in common? – the identity theorist will simply point out that you have not been following the discussion closely enough. What pains have in common is that they are all pains. If you are an analytical functionalist, this commonality will show up in the functional analysis of folk psychological pain; and there is nothing to stop the psychofunctionalist from giving a similar answer, though the source of the functional account would be scientific investigation, not merely analysis.

The stalemate reached at this point indicates that something has gone wrong. Or at least that there are elements lurking in the debate that we have not yet considered, and to which we must now devote some space. Only after this can we return to the job of interpreting the ??-relation in ways that might be more congenial to psychofunctionalists.

Knowledge all the Way up?

In the debate, the psychofunctionalist was imagined as challenging the identity theorist to say what various different pains – human, feline, bovine and even Martian – have in common. And the reply was, predictably, that they were all pains, or that they all shared the same analysis-derived functional profile. But the commonality question is not really the important one. Instead, we should be asking: what do we learn about a mental feature when we come to see it as one and the same as something physical? If the identity theorist is serious about the scientific examples to which appeal is usually made, the answer should be: a great deal. But the suspicion of the psychofunctionalist is that this answer does not carry over to the Mind–Brain case. We learn very little about a mental feature by finding out which physical arrangement underlies it. So, for this reason, the psychofunctionalist resists interpreting talk of 'underlying' physical arrangements by employing the notion of scientific identity.

In the previous chapter, we pushed the identity theorist hard when it came to the use of scientific examples as support for the view. Many of these examples suggest that theoretical identification brings with it a key to the essence of a thing: knowing that water is H_2O suggests that any substance we could discover, or anything that could be discovered in another possible world, could be water only if it was H_2O. But if this were true of all scientific identifications, then there would be an important disanalogy between Mind–Brain identity and these cases. For, in order to preserve the identity theory in the face of countervailing intuitions, we forced the theorist to admit that knowing the physical nature of a mental feature did not constitute knowledge of its essence. Pain in us, in this world, might well be C-fibre firing, without this counting against its being something quite different in some other creature or world.

I bring all this up again because we need to disentangle it from the present issue. When it is claimed that knowledge of the underlying physical nature of something mental does not teach us much about it, and that this contrasts to real cases of scientific identity, this suggests that the issue is again that of essence. But it is not. Recall the discussion in the previous chapter where I (tentatively) urged that there might be a fundamental difference between the water–H_2O case and that of heat. The idea was that the water case, which does involve essence, might not really involve identity after all; and this left it open that the heat case could be one of identity, though not of essence. The aim was to show that, in certain scientific cases, identity and essence can come apart, and these cases could then give continued support to the identity theorist of Mind.

This view hasn't (as yet) got many adherents, but it merits further investigation. However, whether or not someone takes this speculation seriously, the issue of identity and essence is not the same as the one we are discussing at present. It is true that if identification gives us something's essence – its nature in any possible world – this would have to count as our learning a great deal about it. But even in cases where identity does not give us essence, we still expect to learn from the identification. Even if heat is transfer of energy only relative to our world, our finding out that heat-in-this-world is transfer of energy out has taught us a great deal about the phenomena of heat. Similarly, if pain-in-human-beings, or belief-in-human-beings, is identified with appropriate physical properties, then we should learn something about these mental features through this identification. What the dissenting psychofunctionalist claims, however, is that knowing about the physical item that accompanies a mental one leads to no real further knowledge of the mind. And this is why the psychofunctionalist refuses to go along with the identity theorist; why he dissents from a picture in which we have identity all the way down. (I am, of course, assuming here that the psychofunctionalist happens not to be himself an identity theorist. But, as pointed out earlier, this is not a big assumption, since all the psychofunctionalists I have come across – however they might disagree among themselves about functional characterization – resist the identity theory of mind described in the previous chapter.)

The discussion so far has been general, so here is an example to make the point more concretely. Suppose you believe that there is a cat on the mat, that the mouse in its hole believes it, and finally that the Martian who is monitoring your every move also believes it. If the identity theory is right, then there is no reason to think that you, the mouse and the Martian have any physical feature in common in virtue of sharing the belief. The only commonality is the belief that the cat is on the mat.

If we accept this, then we have to give up on the idea that the essence of the belief that the cat is on the mat is given by its physical manifestation, and this is a price my kind of identity theorist is willing to pay. But now ask what we learn about each of these creatures from our knowledge of the physical substrates of their beliefs? If you think that identity goes all the way down, then you would expect to to learn quite a bit. For example, having once identified the substrate of the human belief that the cat is on the mat, you would expect to be able to decide whether some other human being shared this belief; you merely consult their neurophysiology. If the identity account were correct, we could even take this to science-fiction extremes by imagining a 'cerebroscope': a device which scanned the nervous system of its subjects, thereby allowing us to read off their thoughts.

The psychofunctionalist (among others) will have none of this. Anyone's belief that the cat is on the mat leaves some kind of trace in the nervous system, but, it is argued, it is implausible to think that we can tell what someone is thinking, or whether the thought is shared by someone else, by examining physical traces. There are two related reasons for this. On the one hand, attitudes like belief have directionality, and this means that we need to take account of subjects' extra-neural contexts as part of ascribing attitudes to them.

And, on the other hand, each human being will have acquired and stored the concepts used in thinking in an indefinitely varied number of ways; our individual learning histories are just very different. Therefore, there is a vanishingly small chance that we could tell just by looking at physical traces what thought is currently running through someone's head.

A great deal more neeeds to be said about both of these considerations, and in doing so one inevitably has to put heavy weight on the imagination. One has to imagine a knowledge of neurophysiology that we simply do not have, and one also has to imagine a more detailed functional story than is currently available. This makes it very difficult to assess the issue between the psycho-functionalist and the identity theorist. (We do not want the whole thing to turn on the superficial plausibility of science fiction.) However, it is possible to get the flavour of the argument – and a deeper understanding of its conclusion – by appealing to a simpler kind of case.

In my hallway, there is a bowl of smooth stones which once contained a plant. I have done nothing about replacing the plant or disposing of the bowl because the stones on their own have come to serve a useful purpose. Often, just before falling asleep, I remember tasks that I absolutely must do the next day – things that I haven't noted in my diary. Rather than putting on the light and searching for pen and paper, I have found that if I remove one stone per task and put it on the floor where I am bound to see it the next morning, I can recall what it is that I have to do.

Imagine now that this 'system' comes to be studied by some curious investigator. Cutting through complications, this is the sort of thing that the study might reveal: one stone on Tuesday means don't forget to make the bank deposit; two stones on Wednesday means ring your sister for her birthday and bring copies of last week's handouts to the logic class; three stones on Friday means . . . etc. I said that the study *might* reveal this sort of thing, but to assess this we need to know more about the investigator's assumptions. If the investigator brought folk psychological knowledge to bear on the system of stones, then it is likely that the results would be roughly as indicated. But the picture would be entirely different if a geologist specializing in minerals was put on the job instead. Reports on the chemical composition and geology of the stones might be interesting, but they would certainly not tell us much about the mnemonic system. This is not because the physical properties of the stones are completely irrelevant: the stones being chemically stable – they don't breed or disappear overnight – and countable is necessary for the system to work. Rather, as the system was set up in the first place, the physical properties of the stones are at most necessary, but certainly not sufficient, for recovering the mnemonic properties of the system. That I have to remember to make a bank deposit on Wednesday requires that there be a stone on the floor, but no one would be tempted to think that studying the stone itself could reveal this.

The psychofunctionalist claims that the brain has the same role with respect to mental features as the stones do with respect to the tasks they mark. Of course, the roles are only roughly the same: there are an enormous number of physical properties of the brain that are necessary to the proper functioning of the mind, whereas only a couple of properties of the stones are needed to make the mnemonic system work. But so far as the transmission of information is concerned, the two are on a par: you cannot move from detailed physical knowledge of brain states to knowledge of the mind any more than you can move from knowledge of the physical properties of the stones to knowledge of the mnemonic system. Or so runs the argument.

Psychofunctionalists of the kind I have been describing are against seeing the ??-relation as identity because they want to resist *reduction* of Mind to Brain. That is, whilst they might well be prepared to see a reduction of Mind to the functional level, they do not want to see the latter reduced to the merely physical. Though the notion of reduction is not always as clear as it could be, in the present context there should be no problem about what is intended. You have reduction when you have an identification of the sort described in the previous chapter; heat was found to be nothing other than transfer of energy, and this has as a consequence that the study of the relevant kind of energy transfer is itself the study of heat.

If not Identity then what?

So far we have been told a lot about how the psychofunctionalist does *not* want to view the ??-relation. But this is far from meeting our original demand. We have seen that if the ??-relation is treated as identity, then the needs of coalescence are easily met. But it is a consequence of this coalescence that knowledge about the functional (and through it, about Mind) would flow directly from knowledge of the physical properties of Brain, and this is something the psychofunctionalist wants to rule out. So what then does the psychofunctionalist have to say positively about the ??-relation? There is no shortage of answers to this in the literature.

Whilst you will still find talk of 'implementation', the above discussion shows why this is at best loose talk. A builder implements an architect's plans, and electronic circuits carefully devised by computer engineers implement the functionality of some specific program, but in both of these cases there seems to be no epistemological barrier like that illustrated in the stones example.

Allowing for inevitable mistakes, the building is a source of information about the plans, and the movements of electrons in the computer's circuits can tell you what the program is doing. In its most common use, 'implementation' allows for two-way traffic between the functional and the physical, so we would do better to look around for some better way to describe the psycho-functionalist's idea.[4]

(a)   Types and Tokens

What we need is some relation which allows mental features to be physical (just as the reminder is a stone), but which none the less rules out the possibility that we can know about these features simply from a study of the physical (just as we cannot know about reminders by studying the stones). One common suggestion for meeting this demand for a non-reductive physicalism is confusingly stated in terms of identity. It is said that mental and/or functional features are token, and not type, identical to physical states. A standard way in which this would be explained is roughly as follows:

(1)   First, get clear about the type/token distinction. Examples are usually called upon here, so consider this sentence:

> The cat is on the mat,

and ask yourself how many words it contains. If you said 'six' then this is because you were counting word tokens; but if you said 'five' then you must have had word types in mind. (There are two tokens of 'the', but only one word of this type.) The type/token distinction is therefore something like that between universals and particulars, or properties and instances, but, even though it is not exactly like either of these, examples like the one above are generally thought sufficient for making it.

(2)   With this distinction in mind – and just for practice – focus on the identity between the temperature of a gas and the mean (something like 'average') kinetic energy of its molecules. This is said to be a type identity; nineteenth-century physics has shown us that the property of temperature and the property of mean kinetic energy of the relevant molecules are one and the same. However, imagine that you are less interested in this general fact than in the temperature at the present instant of a particular parcel of gas – the one actually confined in a small container on your desk. In the relevant lingo, this is said to be a token state. The gas in this container has millions of molecules in it, and they are flying about. But at the instant that you measured the temperature, each particular molecule had a kinetic energy all its own. The mean of these

kinetic energies at that instant is also a token state. Unsurprisingly, these two token states are one and the same. This is guaranteed by the well-established type identity. But it is still possible to distinguish between the ideas of type and token identity.

(3)   The truth of type identity in the temperature case gives us all the reason we need to accept the identification of:

>   token *a*: temperature of this gas at this instant,

with:

>   token *b*: mean kinetic energy of the molecules of the gas at the same instant.

And of course it works the other way around: if we could measure each and every token of mean kinetic energy for a parcel of gas, as well as tokens of its temperature, we would find they supported type identification. (This is of course a physical, not an intellectual, impossibility since we cannot keep track of all the individual gas molecules.) But we are then invited to think that there might be cases in which token identity held, but type identity failed. Here is one possible case:

>   token *a*: stone on floor on Wednesday morning

is:

>   token *b*: reminder to make bank deposit on that day.

Given the background facts, these two tokens happen to be one and the same, but of course there is no reason to conclude that there is anything like type identity operative here. It is certainly not true that all tokens of stones on the floor in the morning are reminders to make bank deposits.

This sort of story encourages many writers to think that, as far as the functional and the physical are concerned, token identity is just what we need. That is, they think it offers the most congenial intepretation of the ??-relation. On the one hand, the physicality of the functional is captured by the fact that token identity is after all identity; token states described at the functional level *are* token states of Brain. On the other hand, the failure of token identity to be type identity seems just what is required to put in place an epistemological barrier; knowledge of the physical properties of token Brain states cannot breach this barrier to produce knowledge of the functional account of Mind. In sum, we end up being able to talk of an identity theory of the Mind, and the only cost is that we have to distinguish between two kinds of identity theory: type and token.

In spite of its prominence in discussions of Mind and Brain, the whole idea of token identity seems to me to be shot through with confusion. (Its prominence in the philosophy of mind is such that many will be surprised that I did not introduce it in the previous chapter. And now the reason for this is revealed: I don't think that talk of token identity is helpful, nor even wholly coherent.) In the three-step introduction above, I glossed over some of this, but the problems stand out none the less. First of all, though the type/token distinction is perfectly in order – it works fine for words and other things – it is simply not the same distinction as that between, say, particular states of some gas and properties of the gas. The transition from (1) to (2) is therefore very problematic. Is the identity of Uncle Fred and the mugging victim a case of token identity because it is an identity between particulars? What then is type identity here? This question is relevant because there seems to be an assumption that if you have what is called a 'type identity' – as with temperature and kinetic energy – then it makes perfect sense to speak of token identities of temperature and pressure. It is as if both kinds of identity always make sense in any given circumstance. But there is real reason to doubt this, and to say instead that, in different contexts, identity is either a relation between properties or particulars.

Secondly, even if we think we can get to (2), the transition to (3) is shot through with difficulties. What, for example, is a token reminder? About the only sense that this expression could have is something like: it is a specific reminder, one applicable to a certain event on a certain day. But then what stands to this as a token of the word 'the' stands to its type? I cannot see how this question can be sensibly answered. This sort of problem is even more evident when the type/token distinction is used of mental and functional features. Writers commonly speak of 'token beliefs', meaning thereby (one supposes) beliefs held by particular subjects on particular occasions. This then implies that the type of a token belief is one not held by any particular subject at any particular time. However, such a thing not only fails to be a type of belief, it fails to be a belief at all.

Much more could be said here about the confusions, even mistakes, which spring from talk of types and token mental features. But the charitable thing to say about the token identity thesis is that whilst its aim is perfectly coherent, it is inadequate as a positive interpretation of the ??-relation. Understood as a place-holder for a relation that makes the mental ontologically, though not epistemologically, at one with the physical, it offers us no advance on the position of a few paragraphs back. For we still need to find some uncontroversially clear and positive way of specifying the ??-relation, and there is ample reason for thinking that the token identity relation is just not up to this task.

(b) Supervenience

Images on computer screens are created by patterns of activation in the tiny discrete elements of the screen known as pixels. This commonly known fact will provide the starting-point for the next (and final) candidate in our search for intepretations of the ??-relation.

To keep it simple, suppose that the computer screen displays a black triangle against a plain white background. This, of course, means that many thousands of pixels in the screen are 'on' and appear white, and certain of them are 'off' and appear black. It is tempting in this case to say that the arrangement of the pixels *is* the image, but we do not have to say this, and there is reason to think it might not be quite true. It would be better to say that the image supervenes on the pixels, where supervenience is defined in this way: there could be no change in the image unless there were some change in the activation arrangement of pixels.

Notice that, when we define it this way, the relation of supervenience is not symmetrical. The image supervenes on the pixel arrangement, but that arrangement does not supervene on the image. Moreover, this seems reasonable, since we know that a tiny change in the arrangement of pixels would not necessarily result in a change in the image.

The fact that supervenience is not symmetrical means, of course, that it cannot be identity. For whatever else is true, if A is identical to B then it follows that B is identical to A. And it is this feature of supervenience that recommends it as an interpretation of the ??-relation. Defined as it has been, we seem free to say that some mental or functional feature supervenes on a physical arrangment in the brain, thus capturing the dependence of Mind on Brain. (Supervenient dependence here means: no change in the mental without some change in the physical.) But we can do this whilst at the same time insisting that information about the physical arrangement of matter in the brain is not by itself information about the mental or functional.

This understanding of supervenience is congenial to the psychofunctionalist who doesn't share the reductive aspirations of an identity theorist. But, as you might expect, matters are not this simple. Some think that the pixel example, far from grounding a non-reductive interpretation of the ??-relation, is actually a good example of reduction at work. Lewis says of this example:

> The picture reduces to the pixels. And that is because the picture supervenes on the pixels.[5]

How can it happen that what looks like a simple enough idea could be interpreted in two such diametrically opposed ways? The obvious (and accurate) response is that supervenience is not as simple a notion as the image-pixel example makes it seem. Lewis and his opponents both accept that the image depends on the pixels, and that a change in the picture would require a change in the arrangement of pixels. This of course does not *entail* that you can predict changes in the image from knowledge of changes in the pixels, but it doesn't rule it out. And this is where the trouble starts. Some think that if you know enough about our perception of images – about how we work – then you would be able to predict changes in image from changes in pixel arrangement. Further, those who think this do so because they believe that the way we work is ultimately supervenient on the arrangements of matter, specifically matter in our brains. From their perspective, supervenience is merely a way-station on the way to full-scale, identity-based reduction.

Others think that we can resist this. Since supervenience per se does not take us all the way to reduction, they urge us to accept it as a perfectly adequate and complete account of the ??-relation. (They would view the pixel example as having this as its sole point.) That this requires us to see an epistemological barrier between the right-hand box of figure 7.10 (Brain) and the boxes on the left and in the centre (Mind and Function) seems to them perfectly reasonable. To be sure, this insistence seems to leave the supervenience relation in a sort of limbo: one asserts that the mental supervenes on the physical, and offers no deeper explanation of this fact. But supporters of this view are unmoved by this complaint. The only reason, they would insist, that we would look for an explanation here is if we had some independent reason to be reductionist about the mental in the first place.

Coalescence and Non-Reduction

The battle over the notion of supervenience is at least a battle worth fighting. This is in contrast to arguments about token identity, which I have suggested are likely to be too confused to yield much of a reward. But the literature on supervenience is vast, and there is thus little hope of our deciding here whether supervenience is an adequate way to understand the ??-relation. However, even without detailed study, you ought to be able to appreciate how a supervenience relation of the kind described above alters the functionalist strategy for reconciling Mind and Brain. Begin by supposing that supervenience does help us to understand the ??-relation non-reductively. It is a consequence of this that the coalescence we have aimed for is at best only partial. This might come as something of a surprise. The expository effort that we have expended on functionalism of one or another flavour has been driven by the need to solve the overdetermination problem. And it is the coalescing strategy for solving that problem that is most closely associated with functionalism; counting the Mind as in one way or another functionally characterizable, we had hoped to show Mind and Brain as working together rather than separately in the causation of action. But if a psychofunctionalist insists on treating the ??-relation as supervenience, and also inteprets supervenience in a non-reductive way, then the picture we end up with is something like that shown in figure 7.11.

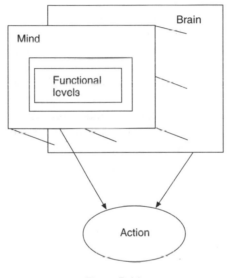

Figure 7.11

Coalescence is only partial here because, whilst it is true that Mind and the functional are counted as physical, they are also thought of as epistemologically cut off from the physical. (In figure 7.11, the lines showing the mental and functional levels as projecting from the physical should be thought of as supervenience lines.)

There is inevitably a certain awkwardness in trying to capture the non-reductive account schematically, but the important thing to focus on is the placement of the arrows. The essential point of the coalescence strategy is to get rid of one of these arrows, without sacrificing the claims on Action of either Mind or Brain. But it is not clear how to achieve this whilst respecting the proviso of non-reduction. We can scarcely erase the right-hand arrow, given that physicalism has been the driving force in our debate, and given the presumption that the world of causes is at bottom physical. But if instead we erase the left-hand arrow, then there is a danger that we are rendering the Mind and its functional deconstruction causally inert. Since this danger might not be immediately obvious, let me spell it out.

One way to explain why some event took place is to show how it is embedded in a network of regularities governing the occurrence of similar events; another way – compatible with the first – is to cite causes of the event. If we erase the left-hand arrow in figure 7.11, this is tantamount to saying that the causal explanation of some action lies wholly within the physical. By itself this wouldn't be a problem, but when it is combined with the epistemological isolation of the physical that is required by non-reductive supervenience, the result is unhappy. For, given this isolation, the explanatory significance of causal relations between Brain and Action is not transmitted upwards towards the functional and mental levels.

It is easiest to appreciate this in connection with a concrete example. Without the left-hand arrow of figure 7.11, my opening the refrigerator comes to be causally explained by some physical state of my brain, but not by the beliefs, desires and feelings that precede and are said to be my reason for this action. Admittedly, the mental states are physical but, without the left-hand arrow, the fact of their being mental states is given no explicit explanatory role. The causal explanatory account of how events in my brain come to produce my reaching for the refrigerator door-handle cannot break through the epistemological barrier separating the physical from the mental/functional.

If we keep both arrows, then the problem of inertness goes away, but then we are back where we started: overdetermination threatens to undermine all the hard work of superveniently balancing the mental landscape on physical bedrock.

There is a way out of this that has been widely discussed in the literature. Why not distinguish between the two arrows by seeing them as having separate jobs? For example, treat the arrow connecting Mind/Function and Action as explanatory in a different way from the more brute causal arrow between Brain and Action. However, whatever the merits of this proposal – and it can only be evaluated when some details are filled in – the important point for our purposes is that it does not fall under the coalescing strategy. Taking the arrows to represent fundamentally different relationships is a way of pursuing the Division of Labour strategy, and that is something we will discuss in the final chapter.

Conclusion

This chapter has no doubt left many loose ends, and, most evidently, it contains nothing much which is genuinely critical of functionalism. Objections to functionalism will be considered in the next chapter, where I shall also deal with some of these loose ends. However, as a way of helping you into that next chapter, I shall conclude this one with a brief summary.

The central idea of functionalism was introduced, as is usual, by its contrast with more directly physicalist accounts of the mental. The Change Reckoner example, simple though it is, sufficed to put the idea in play, and to suggest that functionalism does offer a radically different approach to questions about the nature of the mental. However, we followed this up with a consideration of Turing Machines, since we need to have some guarantee that the simple idea of functionalism, as illustrated in the Change Reckoner case, is adequate to the complexity of the mental. Turing's work suggests that any degree of complexity can be functionally characterized, so long as it is in some way governed by regularities, and this has proved enough of a guarantee for those committed to a functionalist account of the mind. (Turing thought that his work had an even stronger consequence, namely that the Turing-Machine functional is the mental.)

The functionalist approach to the 'What is . . . ? question differs significantly from the identity theory, but more than an approach to this sort of question is needed for situating the mental landscape on the bedrock of the physical. In this chapter, the working assumption has been that the functionalism operates within the Coalescence strategy. That is, functionalism is viewed as setting out to solve the overdetermination problem by integrating Mind and Brain. This assumption leads to several surprising consequences.

First, it turns out that that at least one version of the identity view must be counted as a kind of functionalism. Admittedly, this identity version of functionalism begins from an analytical account of the mental, and not one based on the results of research in cognitive psychology. Also, it continues to insist on the theoretical identification of mental features with physical features. But, since even the purest functionalism is going to have, at some point, to say how functional characterization is related to the physical, there is no reason to rule out the combination of analysis and identity as itself functionalist.

Second, the assumption that the functionalist aims to integrate Mind and Brain leads to two further kinds of difficulty. Opting for psychofunctionalism – the version more commonly associated with the functionalist perspective – threatens to open up a gap between the mental features described by folk psychology and the functional characterizations provided by research in the cognitive sciences. As we have come to expect of scientific research generally, there is no guarantee that cognitive science will 'vindicate' the folks' descriptions of themselves.

Third, the fact that functionalism gives us something interesting to say about the nature of the mental does not yet constitute an answer to the question: precisely what is the relationship between Mind and functional description? If you think there really is a gap between Mind and function, then this question is not pressing (though in that case, you will need to say what you intend to do with the folk psychological characterization of Mind. Elimination is always an option – about which there will be more in the final chapter – but then you will need a further story about what we thought we were studying when we began to be cognitive scientists.) However, if you believe that empirical investigation will match up with, and vindicate, folk psychology, then some specification of what I called the '?-relation' must be given. The most robust specification is a familiar one: the features of the mental landscape are one and the same as features described in psychofunctional terms. This is an identity account, but the identity relation comes in a different place from the account discussed in chapter 6. It is not, as in that account, a relationship between the mental and the physical, but is instead one between the mental and the functional. (Note though that, since it is an identity account, it is liable to face a version of the essentialist challenge. This will be discussed in the next chapter.)

The fourth and final point arising from our setting functionalism in the context of the Coalescence strategy concerns the relationship of functional characterization to the physical. Many discussions of functionalism rest content with noting the way in which mental features are reduced to functional characterization. Indeed, more than content, the functionalist seems almost to gloat over the fact that, in contrast to the identity theorist, he can tell us about mental features without having to descend to the physical level. In insisting that the functionalist give us a precise specification of the ??-relation, the final sections of this chapter suggested that adopting this superior attitude is unjustifiable. Any account which aims to reconcile Mind and Brain is going to have to say something about Brain. And it is not good enough just to say that the relation is one of implementation, token identity, or even supervenience, unless these are properly spelled out. However, it was argued that the computer examples used to clarify talk of implementation suggest an unwanted identity between the functional and the physical; and talk of token identity between the mental and the physical seems, for all its prominence in the literature, to be just confused, so that the only real contender for the ??-relation – one which is not simply reductive in the way identity would be – is supervenience.

However, non-reductive supervenience between the functional and the physical is not yet a solution to the overdetermination problem. Like the case of a recalcitrant bump under the carpet, appealing to supervenience simply moves the that problem to a different place. (Which is not to deny that there might be some version of the Division of Labour strategy that might finally iron out the bump; this is something we will look into in the final chapter.)

Notes and References

1   I have used the label 'cognitive psychology', but in fact the work of functional deconstruction often involves contributions from computer science, anthropology and even philosophy. Working together in this way, many speak here, not merely of cognitive psychology, but of cognitive science.

2   One often hears it said that functionalism about the mind is neutral in regard to the bedrock of the physical world, but this is misleading. In contrast to physicalism, functionalism approaches 'What is . . . ?' questions from a different angle, but the things it deals with − Change Reckoners and minds − are no less embedded in the physical world than bicycles. No one would take functionalism seriously if it insisted on this neutrality, and I have set the discussion of it in a context − the problematic triangle − which makes such neutrality untenable.

3   Here is a typical quote (from N. Block, 'Functionalism' in S. Guttenplan (ed.), *A Companion to the Philosophy of Mind* (1994), p. 325. 'The idea of psychofunctionalism is that the scientific nature of the mental consists not in anything biological, but in something "organisational."'

4   One must be careful here about the computer-program example. The claim is not that one can figure out the details of the program *ab initio* from a knowledge of the physical. Rather, it is that, if one knows that a certain type of physical configuration *is* a deletion of the word 'the' , then one can call on this relativized identity to recognize future calls on the deletion sub-routine. Contrast this with the stones example: knowing that a single stone is a reminder to make a bank deposit on Wednesday is in no way an indicator of what a single stone might indicate at some other time. It is, of course, unsurprising that computers work this way, since engineers have gone to a lot of trouble to get this kind of regularity built into them.

5   Lewis, 'Reduction in Mind' in S. Guttenplan (ed.), *A Companion to the Philosophy of Mind* (1994), p. 413.

8

Objections

In this chapter I shall review several objections to functionalism, and also deal with some unfinished business in connection with the identity theory. However, it must be admitted that locating this chapter has not been easy. On the one hand, it might be argued that we ought to have completed work on the identity account before the topic of functionalism was even broached. And, on the other hand, given that we have not yet finished with functionalism, discussion of objections might seem a bit premature. Both these considerations are reasonable, but they were outweighed by others. First of all, the fact is that the most plausible identity account is in effect a type of functionalism, so a just assessment of identity had to wait until we had at least an outline of functionalism in front of us. Second, the objections to functionalism to be presented are not particularly tied to this or that version of the account. We can therefore deepen our understanding of functionalism, in the way one does by confronting objections, without prejudice to the reappearance of non-reductive functionalism in the next chapter.

Functionalism and Understanding

For English-speakers, the mastery of the Chinese language has always seemed an exceedingly difficult task, and there are more people in China than in any other country. As you will see, these unconnected facts explain why the two most discussed objections to functionalism call on thought experiments known respectively as the Chinese Room and Chinese Nation. The first of these is the subject-matter of this section.

John Searle is responsible for the Chinese Room example, and it can be summarized as follows:

> A monolingual English speaker sits in a room, and slips of paper with Chinese symbols are passed in to him. He is intended to respond by returning the slips with something written in Chinese on the reverse side. Of course, he hasn't a

clue as to what these symbols mean, but the room contains a huge book of instructions (in English) telling him precisely what symbols he is to write. All he has to do is to look up in this book the symbols on each incoming slip, and write whatever it is that the instructions dictate on the reverse.

Though the English speaker is unaware of it, the Chinese symbols on the incoming slips are simple questions, and the symbols he copies onto the reverse of the slips are pretty sensible answers to them. Those Chinese speakers who write the original questions, and examine the answers, come to the conclusion that whoever is inside the room understands Chinese. But, as is obvious, this conclusion is simply false.[1]

You can probably recognize this example as a special case of the Turing's Imitation game. In that game, the idea is to see whether a computing device could be programmed so as to convince an outside observer that the answers it supplies are those of a human being. The book of instructions in Searle's example is in effect the program of a computing device, and Searle is in no doubt that the Chinese questioners will judge answers to have been written by a human being who is a Chinese-speaker. So, though the field of operation, namely language, is more restricted, Searle's case works very much like that of a successful run of the Imitation game. However, as the last line of the above description suggests, when it comes to interpreting this success, Searle and Turing part company.

Turing thought that any machine capable of 'winning' the Imitation game could be regarded as actually having thoughts; whereas Searle insists that computational manipulation of symbols is not at all the same thing as having thoughts. For Searle, those who judge that whoever or whatever is in the room understands Chinese are simply making a mistake. The person in the room does not understand Chinese, and the manipulation of symbols he carries out does no more than *fool* the Chinese-speakers who pose the questions. Moreover, though for dramatic purposes, there is a person in the Chinese room, this is inessential. Searle means us to see that if you replaced the person by a computational device – one that would do the very same looking up of symbols in a book of instructions – then it would no more understand Chinese than does the monolingual English-speaker.

In more recent writing, Searle has put the argument more directly, no longer relying on the Chinese connection:

Programs are entirely syntactical.
Minds have a semantics.
Syntax is not the same as, nor by itself sufficient for, semantics.

Therefore, programs are not minds.[2]

The first premise sums up Searle's attitude towards what in the original thought experiment was the consultation, whether by a human agent or a computational device, of a book of instructions. As was noted above, these instructions tell the person in the Chinese room neither what the incoming questions nor the outgoing answers mean. In fact, in a correctly austere version of the experiment, the inhabitant of the room does not even know that the incoming slips of paper contain questions to which the slips produced are answers. This is possible because the book of instructions requires only that the person or device match up symbols on the slips by comparing their shape or form with one another. Confinement in this way to the form of symbols is what is meant by saying that the book of instructions – the program – is purely syntactical.

The second premise will be discussed further below, but it is not difficult to see how it corresponds to a central consideration in the Chinese Room version. The human being in the room understands a language, albeit not Chinese. Understanding a language includes among other things the ability to field questions – to understand what they are about – and the ability to attempt answering them. Moreover, the possession of these abilities entails the presence of a mind. The person in the room, being in possession of a mind, does understand what sentences in English mean, and this is part of what Searle intends in saying that minds have semantics.

The third premiss in the above argument is in effect one of the preliminary conclusions you were intended to draw from the Chinese Room experiment – that merely consulting form-based, i.e. syntactical, instruction manuals is never going to be enough to yield genuine language use. Of course, the person in the room understands English, and he presumably leans on this understanding when given initial advice about how to employ the book of instructions. But this is inessential to the story. You can run the experiment using a mechanical device to look up Chinese symbols in the book of instructions, but then this device would neither be a Chinese-speaker, nor a speaker of any language. The semantics of questions and answers – what they mean – would play no role at all in its operation.

The conclusion of the argument is an explicit statement of what was merely the underlying moral of the Chinese Room case. In saying that programs are not minds, Searle is directly contradicting Turing's original conviction. Turing sought to reduce minds to some suitably programmed Turing Machine, a device which is a perfect analogue of the syntactical book of instructions in the Chinese Room. And it is just such a device that Searle insists can neither understand a language, nor for this reason possess a mind.

There are several things we have to be clearer about before we can connect this argument to functionalism. First, we must specify which feature or features of the mental landscape the argument addresses. Functionalism, as described in chapter 7, is certainly intended as an account of the whole range of mental phenomena; it is supposed to tell us about pain and conscious experience generally, as well as about the attitudes. But the Chinese Room example, and its less fanciful embodiment in Searle's three-premiss argument, give a central place to the idea of the mind as possessing 'semantical' properties, and this suggests that it takes aim at the attitudes, and not at experience. Second, as we also saw in chapter 7, there are functional characterizations which, unlike Turing's, are not merely syntactic. So, perhaps Searle's argument does not get much of a purchase on them. And, finally, we drew an important distinction between a level of functional characterization which was intended merely to simulate mental features, and a level which had the much more serious purpose of actually embodying some mental feature. Unless we can get clearer about this, someone might well dismiss Searle's argument as directed only at the more superficial kind of functional characterization. Since the evaluation of the Chinese Room example, and its consequences for functionalism, depend on these three points, it is worth pausing over them.

(i)   The Chinese Room and its accompanying argument gives a prominent place to language. Since we all know that words have semantical properties, meanings, it is all too easy to take the second premiss in the argument as essentially a claim about language. Thus, when Searle asserts that minds have semantics, one might hear this as: minds use language and language has semantics. However, this would be, whilst not completely wrong, not quite right either. The scope of the claim that minds have semantics extends beyond language to embrace the attitudes generally. In fact, the second premiss of the argument could have been: minds have directionality. Looked at in this way, the argument might be reformulated as:

> Programs are nothing but the formal or syntactical shuffling around of certain symbols (Think here of a Turing Machine and its printer and tape.)
>
> Minds have attitudes, and these latter are directed to objects and states of affairs in the world.
>
> No amount of syntactic shuffling will invest the symbols in a program with this kind of directional reference to things in the world. (No amount of printing and erasing of symbols makes it true that Turing Machine states refer to things.)

We are intended to view the person in the Chinese Room as like the printer in a Turing Machine animated by a list of instructions for carrying out some purely syntactic rearrangement of symbols. In saying that such a person will not thereby be able to understand Chinese, one is saying more than that there is a linguistic deficiency. When someone comes to understand a question (or answer), the network of beliefs of such a person will undergo some change. But, of course, the belief system of the person in the Chinese Room is unaffected (except incidentally) by the patient work of matching symbols on slips of paper. (And a Turing Machine doesn't even have a belief system in the first place.)

Notice that there is nothing in this way of spelling out the argument which implicates experience. Pains and other 'inner' sensations do not seem to have directionality, so, for all that the argument says, they are untouched by worries about programs and merely syntactic manipulation. Had the second premiss asserted that minds have experiences, and experiences are directional (or semantic), many would have regarded it as false. It is important to be clear about this, because it is not uncommonly assumed that the Chinese Room argument is as much about consciousness as it is about anything else. (Admittedly, someone might suggest – as I did in chapter 4 – that experience and attitudes are inseparable, and that showing the inadequacy of programs for the attitudes would be tantamount to showing them useless for consciousness. But, whilst this seems sensible enough, it requires that we embed the Chinese Room argument in a much deeper one about the nature of mind. There will be more about this issue later in the chapter.)

(ii)   The original target of Searle's Chinese Room argument was what he called the thesis of 'Strong Artificial Intelligence'. Almost certainly held by Turing, this thesis *identifies* our mental capacities with some suitably complex, though ultimately syntactical, computer program. However, as we saw in chapter 7, whilst there are functionalists who aim to reduce the mind in this way, it is not essential to functionalism that it take this reductive route. Many psychofunctionalists think that something like the directionality of the attitudes at the personal level can be found in the subsystems that subserve these personal-level mental features. For example, research in cognitive science might reveal that someone's perceptual belief, e.g. that there is a cat in front of him, consists in the operation of various sub-personal systems for detecting shapes and objects. Such functional characterization seems not to be merely syntactical; systems which detect shapes and objects are, after all, directed to features of the world.

(iii)   The imagined functional characterization of an earthworm in chapter 7 was certainly not an earthworm, and no one would have thought it was. The functional characterization modelled, or, as is commonly said, merely 'simulated' earthworm behaviour. However, faced with a functional characterization of some mental ability, the line between modelling (or mere simulation) and identification can become blurred. If a device responds to questions in a manner indistinguishable from human response, then many – not only Turing – would be tempted to attribute to it at least those attitudes that made the responses apposite. However, temptations are often best resisted, and it is possible to read the Chinese Room argument as little more than advice not to succumb in this case. Genuine belief, and the other attitudes that go with it, both lead to action and are often attributed on the basis of action. A device which responds like a human being – which declares itself to believe and desire various things – does in fact appear to engage in action, at least minimally; it acts linguistically. But this is surely not enough. For example, such a device might *declare* that it wanted an ice-cream, but, since the surest sign of wanting is trying to get, we are unlikely to attribute any such real desire to the device. How on earth could it want an ice-cream when it cannot actively engage with the world or consume the ice-cream if one were on offer?

Having made these qualifications to the Chinese Room argument, answering it would seem to be an easy task for a committed functionalist. (And many in the broad church of functionalism do regard it as answered.) One could insist that directionality figures, not only at the personal level, but at the level of functional characterization which Searle calls the program. This would make the first premiss of the argument is false. Or one could claim that a purely syntactic functional characterization can after all produce genuinely world-involving activity: just make sure to embody it in a device with sufficiently realistic input and output systems (perhaps some sort of robot with sensors and some means of locomotion). This would make the third premiss false. Yet somehow there is still a core to the argument which remains unanswered by these manoeuvres, and, even if we now leave the letter of Searle's argument, the remarks which follow are at least consistent with his spirited insistence that the Chinese Room argument is far from answered.

As has been remarked several times in previous chapters, the directionality of the attitudes is no straightforward matter. The folk insist on the one hand that attitudes are about, or directed to, objects and states of affairs in the world; hence the appositeness of the label 'directionality'. Yet they also put constraints on attitude attribution – constraints of rationality – which make it difficult to treat directionality in any simple relational way. Bearing this in mind, the really deep problem raised by the Chinese Room is not so much about the reduction of the attitudes to syntactically structured programs, but about their reduction to causal, i.e. relational, patterns of any kind. Laid out on the lines of previous versions, the argument can be generalized to become:

> Functionalist accounts are limited to describing the syntactical shuffling of symbols and/or the causal relations among these symbols, as well as the causal relations between the symbols and items in the world.
>
> Minds have attitudes that are genuinely semantic; they are directed towards the world, but they are not simply relations to items in it.
>
> Mere syntactic shuffling and appeal to causal relations do not suffice to capture the slack between subject and world that is a mark of genuine directionality.

These premises go well beyond anything that could be illustrated by a simple concrete example like that of the Chinese Room. But perhaps that is just as well, since focusing too narrowly on features of that example has engendered much of the confusion in the literature. In particular, the above form of argument suggests why Searle (and others) find certain responses to the Chinese Room example inadequate. The idea that directionality might exist at a sub-personal level in various functional characterizations would certainly undercut the original argument. If shape recognizers and edge-detecting systems are counted as having something like attitudes towards shapes and edges, then the obsession with mere syntax in the Chinese Room case looks misplaced. But a closer look at sub-personal attitudinizing shows it to be wholly unlike that envisaged by the folk. The causal/functional relations out of which sub-personal attitudes are constructed are just too straightforward to capture the more devious relations that believers bear to the world.

Similarly, we cannot evade the argument by, as it were, giving eyes and ears, arms and legs to a causal/functional program. At most this would causally embed such an input/output network in the real world; we would end up with a device whose sensors and motor equipment would allow it to occupy some environmental niche. But, if the above argument is right, the resulting behaviour of any such device would not add up to anything that we would recognize as attitudinal directedness. Not being subject to any of the constraints of rationality, its internal, dispositional states would be too predictably causal; there would be no sign of the slack that comes with genuine belief relations to the world.

You will find in the literature at least two lines of response to this generalized version of the Chinese Room argument. First, it might be argued that the argument is too cavalier in its treatment of causality. It might be true enough that simple causal relations between inner states and the outer world will not produce a genuine believer. But more sophisticated kinds of causal relation might yet do the trick. Second, it has been suggested that what is needed to bridge the gap between merely causal relations and attitudinal ones lies in the biological nature of true believers. A currently much-discussed view starts from the conviction that there is something special about the complex process of evolutionary change. In particular, the idea is that, in evolution, one sees a process which is not merely causal, and which in fact has something of the directionality of the attitudes. Thus, we might meet the challenge by arguing that the attitudes themselves, as features of the minds of evolved creatures, derive their directionality from this evolutionary history. (Exactly how far from a strictly causal path we are willing to allow evolution to stray is now a hotly debated issue. More will be said about the evolutionary account in the next section.)

Liberalism and Chauvinism

The second argument against functionalism requires us to make a fanciful supposition premissed on the fact that China is the most populous nation on earth. What we are to imagine first is that the complex functional characterization of some specific human mind has been worked out. That is to say, we have managed to write out a vast description of the input/output relations which are embodied in some typical human being. We are then asked to imagine that the whole of the Chinese population sets out to duplicate this same functional story. Each individual member of the population is assigned some small task or calculation, and the results of these are passed on to a next higher authority – probably a committee – which in turn carries out some further task and passes the result on, etc. In some versions of this story, the outputs of sufficiently high-level committees in the functional hierarchy are transmitted in real time to a sophisticated robotic device. Animated by this flow of instructions, the robot moves and speaks; and also because it is equipped with visual, tactile and other sensory devices, the robot takes in information which it passes on to relevant committees, who pass it on down the line for further processing.

Though the robot produces as life-like a performance as could be imagined, the objector none the less thinks that any question about the mind of the robot could only be rhetorical. After all, how could this robot have a mind, given that it is merely the product of distributed – and highly co-ordinated – piece-work in a vast army of dedicated workers?

In philosophy, however, there are no rhetorical questions. It may seem obvious that the China robot has no mind, but we must avoid being swept along by this appearance. For a start, we have to ask which features of the mental landscape most readily support it. That is, are we inclined to dismiss the idea that the China robot is minded because it couldn't possibly have attitudes, because it doesn't really do anything, or because it would make no sense to treat it as having an inner life of experience? Whilst there could be grounds for doubting the genuineness of all three of these features, experience must surely play the crucial role. By straining hard – and here it helps to think that Searle's Chinese Room objection has been overcome – one might be able to convince oneself that the robot does have beliefs and desires, and that it acts on the basis of these. But what makes this objection completely independent of the previous one is the intuition that no such robot could be in pain or have perceptual experience. Faced with a robot most fervently complaining about this or that injury, or writhing in some quite convincing way, we cannot strain hard enough to convince ourselves that the felt experience of pains lies behind these performances. Each time we try, the thought of the vast army of workers who are producing this behaviour returns. Each of *them* might suffer pain, but their co-ordinated efforts to produce the simulacrum of human behaviour in the robot distributes mental function too widely and too publicly for there to be a locus of pain in the robot.

The Chinese nation example suggests that functionalists are too liberal in what they would regard as implementations of genuine mentality. And if functionalism is *inherently* liberal in this way, then it is difficult to see what can be done to save it. Whilst it seems possible to convince yourself that the robot might actually have beliefs and desires, and – if you are not too careful about the nature of action – that it acts on them, the problem of consciousness is just too big an obstacle.[3] Because of this, the best, and perhaps only, functionalist defence requires some retreat from this liberalism. But such retreat is not without costs, as will be apparent from the following survey of two prominent options.

(a)   The Need for Brains
In chapter 7, I was careful to insist that the most plausible kind of functionalism distinguishes a hierarchy of functional levels. The highest level is closest to folk psychology, and the lowest, whilst not descending to talk of mere physical stuff, touches on the functional architecture of the brain. Right now we do not know enough about the details of this hierarchy, but when cognitive

scientists manage to fill in the picture, we will see precisely how certain lower-level functional units subserve the more complex functionality found at levels further up. Purely speculatively, let us imagine that object recognition is at least partly achieved by functional subsystems whose job it is to detect shape, and this in turn is achieved by some kind of edge-detecting system, and so on until we reach a level at which systems at the neuronal level play the role of supporting everything higher up. In the present context, the importance of this hierarchical conception lies in the lower levels. By insisting that functionalism include quite detailed specifications of neurophysiological function, the threat of the Chinese nation example simply lapses. At some level, one might be able to imagine functional relations being distributed in a large enough population of dedicated workers, and one can even imagine these input/output relations being implanted in a single robotic device. But the Chinese nation does not include anything like the brain; indeed, the vast army of workers is, if anything, a substitute for fine-grained neurophysiological function that is described at the lowest level of the hierarchy. No one would be fooled into thinking that an audience in a stadium is a single organism merely because it conveys messages in virtue of individual members holding placards aloft. And the Chinese nation, even with the robot attached, is no more a single organism than the audience in the stadium.

Whilst a hierarchical functionalism that gets down to the level of neurophysiology disposes of the charge of excessive liberalism, it has a tendency to lurch in an opposite — though no less problematic — direction. If the Chinese nation is ruled out because it fails to constitute a suitable organism with a brain, then so will be any genuine organism that happens not to have the functional neurophysiological architecture of a human being. Most likely the primate, perhaps the cat or dog, and certainly the Martian think, act and feel, though they probably do not do this with brains organized in the same way as human beings. A feature that many regard as functionalism's strongest suit, that is, an ability to discern mind in different physical systems, seems to be thrown away. Whereas before we had excessive liberalism, now we have just the sort of chauvinism about our own species that functionalists find unacceptable in identity theories.

Of course, when the final word is in on the functional hierarchy that actually describes human mentality, it might just be that we will have sailed between the Scylla of liberalism and the Charybdis of chauvinism. Primates, cats or dogs, and Martians will be seen to share enough of that functional organization to count as thinking, acting and feeling creatures; but the whole of the Chinese population working in concert simply falls outside the pale (as perhaps do certain kinds of computer program). Yet, whilst I do not think we can close out this option here, there is room for pessimism. Many function-alists make a point of avoiding mere physicality, or at least giving it the most menial of tasks, that of implementation. And it is difficult to see how, without some reference to the actual physical structures in human neurophysiology, one is going to rule out examples like that of the Chinese nation.

(b)   Function and Evolution

A second option – one based on an idea touched on in the previous section – accepts that mere input/output functionalisms are always going to fall short of what is required for dealing with the liberalism objection. However, pro-ponents of this option insist that what is missing in these sorts of functional-ism is a recognition of the fact that human beings (and any other minded creatures) have the functional organization that they do in virtue of their having evolved. Features of the mental landscape have the shape they do because they are the products of various evolutionary pressures. For example, the functionality of beliefs and desires comes not merely from a complex nexus of input and output, but from the fact that they have a biological purpose or, to use the usual Greek name for this feature, a 'telos'. One can therefore no more understand them in the input/output way than one can understand hearts and kidneys, or, taking a more realistically complicated example, the immune system. To be sure, hearts and immune systems can be understood to some extent merely in virtue of the work they actually do. But, unless one also includes some account of their evolved biological function (often called the 'proper function'), one's understanding is certain to be limited.

A more detailed account of this view, known generally as *teleofunctionalism*, is beyond our remit here. But it is easy enough to see why teleofunctionalists think they can successfully evade the charge of being too liberal. The Chinese nation might perfectly replicate the actual input/output network of some human being, and that functionality might then be embodied in a robot, but there is no sense in which either the system itself or the robot are evolution-ary products. They are at most an ingenious attempt to mimic or simulate real features of the mental landscape. Though vastly more complicated, they are like a toy that possesses the simulacrum of human language and movement in virtue of computer chips, levers and motors. But we, and all other creatures who have mental landscapes of one or another sort, have evolved; and, if the detail of the teleofunctionalist position is right, our mental states are no less products of that evolutionary process than our hearts and kidneys.

Given that evolutionary pedigree is required to distinguish real mental phe-nomena from mere imitation, the teleofunctionalist has no difficulty in avoid-ing liberalism. Unfortunately, many objectors to teleofunctionalism do not see why such a pedigree is required. It may be true enough that we did evolve, and also true enough that our minds evolved along with our bodies, but why does there *have to be* evolution for mentality? Why, for example, couldn't a humanoid creature – one like us in every respect except evolutionary history – just pop into existence? Bizarre though it might be, imagine that lightning strikes in a swamp, and a creature emerges – Swampman – who happens to be a molecule-by-molecule replica of some actually existing human being. Isn't the teleofunctionalist committed to denying that Swampman has any mental states at all? And isn't this absurd? (Imagine that Swampman is a molecule-by-molecule replica of a philosopher who holds a teleofunctionalist view, and who insists that he has no mental states at all.)

Moreover, the lurch to chauvinism seems just as much a danger for the teleofunctionalist as for the functionalist whose functional characterizations stray too close to the actual neurophysiology of the human organism. Though we have a long way to go before have anything more than the merest speculation about the evolutionary history of the mental landscape, it seems likely that the real story of that history will implicate human neurophysiology. Darwin's great insight, and most of the research that has transformed mere ideas of evolution into real scientific theories, all suggest that evolutionary pressures work at a fairly basic and certainly species-specific level. So the likelihood that the evolutionary story about my beliefs and desires, experiences and emotions will be the same as that told of members of other species (including of course Martians) seems to be heading towards zero. And the closer it gets to zero, the more the charge of chauvinism becomes apposite.

Neither hierarchical nor teleological functionalism are quite convincing in the face of the Chinese nation argument. But then again we cannot completely dismiss these options on the basis of the few paragraphs devoted to them. Moreover, since there are related, but still different, options that we haven't pursued, the best we can say at this stage is that functionalism is threatened by the charge of liberalism. Whether it is fatally damaged is still a subject of intense debate.

Zombies

A third objection to functionalism turns on the possibility of zombies, that is, creatures who are exactly like us functionally but who possess no inner life whatsoever. Added to robots controlled by the whole of the Chinese population and Swampmen, you would be forgiven for thinking that philosophers watch too many old grade-B movies. But, as you should by now anticipate, talk of zombies is merely a dramatic way of emphasizing what is a serious point. (Shortly, we will consider what may be a case of 'real' zombie-like human behaviour, so there are grounds for thinking that the example is less bizarre than it first appears.)

What you are to imagine is a population of creatures who resemble human beings physically, and who instantiate a complete and accurate functional characterization of human mental life. That is, they interact with the world and each other just as we do, and what they say about their experiences and attitudes suggests that they do not differ from us in any mental respect. But then you are to imagine that they have no conscious mental life at all. When they strike their thumbs, they cry out, hold the thumb, complain, and seek sympathy. Yet, for all this, there is nothing going on inside; they are in a perfectly good sense of the term 'zombies'. If it is really possible for there to be creatures who are our functional duplicates, but who have no conscious experiences, then functionalism can scarcely be the whole story about the mental landscape. Are zombies a real possibility? Before trying to sort this out, we have to sharpen the objection somewhat.

The problem raised for functionalism by the possibility of zombies is closely related to that of the liberalism objection, but they are not the same. The Chinese nation example turned on the apparent possibility of achieving functional duplication of human behaviour, even though it is absurd to regard the duplicating mechanism – the whole of the Chinese population – as itself conscious. The zombie problem too turns on the issue of consciousness; many find no problem at all in thinking of zombies as having beliefs and other attitudes. (One has to strain to think of the whole Chinese population, engaged in the functionalist project, as having attitudes. But there seems less absurdity in this than in trying to convince yourself that genuine pain is instantiated in that population.) However, in the Chinese nation case, the functionalist can cheerfully accept the possibility envisaged, and then appeal to further grounds for disqualifying the population from counting as a single, conscious creature. In contrast, in the zombie case, any functionalist counter-argument must come earlier: reasons must be found for denying that such a zombie is possible in the first place.

The zombie argument can be seen as an application of Leibniz's Law. Many functionalists implicitly or explicitly regard the relationship between Mind and functional characterization – the '?-relation' considered in the previous chapter – as an identity relation. Thus, beliefs about the weather, as well as perceptual experiences and pains, are said to be one and the same as various complex functional states. Using pain as our handy example, a functionalist might well claim:

Harry's pain in his elbow = the specific functional state defined by these inputs
. . . and these outputs . . .
(Where the blanks are to be filled in one day by research in cognitive science.)

And, by LL, this claim entails:

Any property of Harry's pain is a property of Harry's functional state, specified
by filling in the above blanks.

However, if zombies are a real possibility, then the above-mentioned functional
state exists in some zombie-like version of Harry, without being felt as pain;
that is, without having the introspectively available qualitative or phenomenal
characteristics of Harry's pain. In effect, then, it is possible that Harry's functional state could exist without being felt as pain, whereas, of course, Harry's
pain of necessity is felt as pain. So, since the functional state and Harry's pain
do not share all their properties, the identity above turns out to be false.[4]

There are two ways to get around this argument. One could deny that the
relationship between the mental and the functional is identity; or one could
argue that, despite an initial plausibility, there could be no zombie duplicate
of Harry. The first of these options is uninviting for anyone who wants to take
the folk psychological account of the mind seriously, whilst at the same time
being a functionalist. As we saw in the previous chapter, unless we treat the
?-relation as identity (or as in some way involving identity), there is a real risk
that our everyday conception of the mind will be simply left out. So, as suggested above, the battle tends to be joined over the second option. Many functionalists insist that if you get the functional characterization right, there simply
couldn't be creatures who were our functional duplicates but who lacked conscious experiences. And those on the other side insist that no amount of complication in the functional story could guarantee conscious experience in all
its inner and qualitative reality – in all its 'what-it-is-like-ness'.

Since no one has got much beyond the *idea* of a functional characterization, it is difficult to join this argument with any hope of resolution. One side
is attracted by various outline proposals for treating conscious experience as
nothing over and above the functionalist operation of various kinds of thought.
Since thoughts of the appropriate kind – attitude-like representations of how
things are – seem more amenable to functional characterization, these proposals hope to demystify the otherwise deeply puzzling nature of our inner
lives. On one view, you are conscious when you are entertaining immediate
and non-inferential thoughts about your present representational states. Given
that what you are doing here is entertaining thoughts about your thoughts,

the view is generally known as the 'higher-order thought' or 'HOT' account. A closely related but less demanding idea is that you are conscious when you have what is called inferential access to your present representational state, when, for example, a visual representation of how things are is one that is available to the central functional processes that produce choices and actions.

The other side – the defenders of the irreducibility of conscious experience – think these functionalist stories simply miss the point. No amount of higher-order thinking, nor moving around of information in a functionalist scheme, could ever add up to there being something it is like to feel pain or see colours. That is why they find the idea of functionally duplicate, but zombie-like, creatures perfectly intelligible. It is even suggested that the possibility of zombies receives some support from current research on a phenomenon known as 'blindsight'.

Briefly, a blindsight patient is one who, due to neurological damage, has no conscious experience of seeing, but who none the less performs better than chance when determining whether some object is present in his line of 'sight'. (Blindsight patients take themselves to be merely forced into *guessing* about the presence of objects by the questions of the experimenters; as far as they themselves are concerned, they are just blind.) The thought of some philosophers is that blindsight patients are in some small way like zombies: they detect objects, and so are functionally like the sighted, but they have no visual experience.

Unfortunately, both for the patients and for philosophers, only the most primitive kind of detection actually goes on in these experiments: a typical patient might 'guess' that there is something rather than nothing in the line of sight. There is certainly no example of a blindsight patient who can tell what kind of object is present, or whether it is moving. Undeterred, philosophers simply postulate the possibility of 'super' blindsight patients – patients whose functionality does in fact match that of a sighted person, and who can learn to rely on this functionality for getting around, but who none the less have no visual experience. However, such postulation goes so far beyond the actual as to be unhelpful. The functionalist who thinks of consciousness in one of the ways described above finds support for this thesis in the poverty of vision in actual patients. The thought is: what else would you expect, given that conscious visual experience is a key functional element in the story about how we come to navigate our environment? The opponent who finds the super-blindsight case perfectly intelligible has no better reply to this than to restate the conviction that zombie-like behaviour is a real possibility.

Whilst we cannot even begin to resolve this debate, some light can be shed by comparing it to the essentialist criticism of the identity account described in chapter 6. (And the illumination goes the other way too.) The essentialist argued that pain should not be identified with any brain process because pains are necessarily felt as pain, but any candidate brain process might not be felt as pain. Put the other way around, pains and brain processes have different essential properties, and so cannot be one and the same. Supporting this argument is the claim that we can imagine a possible world in which the relevant brain process takes place, but within which the subject feels no pain. In the present context, the issue is not that of brain processes, but of functional characterization. Still, the logic of the zombie objection is the same: it is supposed to be easy to imagine a possible world in which the functional works as it should, but in which there is no pain. If what we thereby imagine is genuinely possible, then the functional does not share all its properties with the phenomenon of pain. For, as before, pain is necessarily felt as pain, but the otherwise relevant functional arrangements are not necessarily painful.

In both arguments, most of the attention is given to the move from what is imagined to what is possible; objectors to identity accounts and functionalism find this move unproblematic, and supporters have doubts. But, in spite of the shared logic of the two arguments there is an obvious difference: the zombie argument exerts pressure on the identity between the mental and the functional, whereas the essentialist argument of chapter 6 takes aim at the identity between the mental and the physical. (As the picture was drawn in chapter 7, the zombie argument is about the ?-relation, and the other about the ??-relation.) Moreover, this difference could be crucial: it might well be easier to imagine a functional duplicate who didn't feel pain than a physical duplicate similarly deprived.

Just how crucial is this difference? The answer here depends on the kind of functionalism at issue, and on more general considerations about the nature of experience. The psychofunctionalist who aims to reduce conscious experience to thoughts, or thoughts about thoughts – that is, to something attitudinal – seems most at risk. For, as noted earlier, overturning this kind of reduction would only require imagining a creature with a full range of attitudes who was nevertheless a zombie. It would not require a zombie-like creature who was our neurophysiological duplicate. However, the analytical functionalist described in the previous chapter does not aim to reduce experience to attitude; she is perfectly happy to follow the lead of folk psychology in giving separate and independent existence to both experience and attitude. So the pressure of the zombie objection can be exerted only on the eventual identification of the functional and the physical. And this means that, for analytical functionalism, the intuitions that support the possibility of zombies and the intuition behind the essentialist objection come to pretty much the same.[5]

In particular, everything here turns on our willingness to accept the Cartesian–Kripke intuition discussed in chapter 6. That intuition suggests that we can imagine re-identifying any particular inner experience without reference to anything 'outer'. To take the familiar concrete example, the Cartesian insists we can imagine recognizing pain in some other possible world, even though it exists in that possible world without the usual behavioural, physical and, of course, functional features that pain happens to have in our actual world.

We will return to the debate about Cartesianism – thereby tying up the loose end we left in chapter 6 – after a brief discussion of functionalism and action. But, even before that, here is a summary of where we stand in respect of the three objections to functionalism so far given.

(i)   The Chinese Room argument – when certain superficialities are cleared away – suggests that functionalism does not in fact capture everything that the folk think is true of attitudes like belief and desire. The functionalist replies that, if there is something missing, it is probably no great loss. In the end, the debate here turns on the just how seriously we take the constraints that folk psychology appears to put on attitude attribution. As we saw in chapter 2, the slack that figures in our ordinary practice of attitude attribution can lead to difficulties, even to incoherence. This is why certain functionalists would be willing to trim the attitudes as necessary to fit in with some kind of causal or teleological account.

(ii)   The Chinese nation argument sets out to show that functionalism is too liberal; that the functionalist standard for membership in the society of minds would let in undesirables. The typical functionalist response is to find ways of raising the standard. But, as with most clubs, the danger is that the new standard will be too strict – the restricted membership will come to undermine the original rationale of the functionalist project. Whatever grounds are found for keeping out the Chinese nation, and other equally outlandish candidates for mindedness, had better not lead to a chauvinism that counts only human beings as having mental landscapes. (The issue of chauvinism will turn up again in the next section.)

(iii)   The zombie argument is perhaps the most difficult to assess, not least because its target is often unclear. Both previous objections could be understood as objections to functionalism in general. But the zombie argument can be interpreted as aiming either at a particular version of functionalism or at the account in general. Everything here depends on the materials thought appropriate to functionalism. On one view, it is of the essence of the functionalist story that its characterizations are restricted to representational phenomena – items which broadly share with the attitudes the feature of directionality. As noted earlier, this restriction seems to many to be natural, if only because attitude-like representational phenomena are seen as more amenable to functionalist treatment than the phenomena of experience. Given this, the problem for the functionalist is to tell a story about conscious experience using only phenomena that are representational; the aim is to reduce in some way the qualitative character of experience to attitudes we adopt either towards our own representations or, more generally, towards features of the world. (Consciousness consists then either in our being able to think about our thoughts about the world, or in our being able to call on our thoughts about the world in our plans and actions. From this perspective, the possibility of zombies then becomes the possibility of creatures with beliefs, including perceptual beliefs, as well as other representational states, and who act in ways indistinguishable from our own, but who have no inner conscious experience.)

On another view, however, the problem of zombies arises from the general, and not the specific, nature of functionalist materials. It is on this interpretation that the problem of zombies becomes indistinguishable from the essentialist objection to the identity account. For, whatever we might say about the content of this or that functionalist story, there can be no doubt that functionalists set out to describe the mental landscape from the outer or impersonal perspective. And it was this feature of neurophysiological description that put the identity account at risk from Cartesian intuitions about the essentially inner nature of experience. Whether one says that our consciousness of pain is a state of the brain, or an interanimation of inputs and outputs, or both, the Cartesian insists that something vital has been left out – the ineffable presence, the what-it-is-like-ness of the pain – that can only be appreciated by the sufferer. As we saw in chapter 6, and as reprised above, this intuition plays the crucial role in what is a Leibniz Law objection to the identification of pain with either the neurophysiological or the functional: pain is said to have the essential property of being felt as pain that is simply lacking in either the physical or the functional candidate for identity.

Because of the uncertainty of a target, the zombie objection is not easy to pin down. Many have the strong intuition that experience cannot be reduced to anything attitudinal, and so they are tempted into thinking that zombies are not only imaginable, but genuinely possible. But however strongly this intuition is held, and however much it partakes of the more general Cartesian intuition, it falls short of what is required to overturn functionalism itself, or the identity theory.

Legless Martians

Functionalist accounts have problems with action. Moreover, though these problems resemble those that beset the identity theory (see chapter 6), they are potentially worse. The first concerns the specificity of action. Any account which sets out to tell us about the underlying nature of experience and attitude also owes us some account of what it is to act on the basis of some individual creature's attitudes and experiences. But the physical actions that our beliefs, desires and feelings lead us to undertake include what looks like irreducible references to the means by which we achieve them, namely arms and legs. Needing to get to a post office in a strange town, and believing it to be just off the main square, you take a walk. That is, your belief and desire combine to get your legs moving so that they will carry you into the post office. However, whilst the functionalist suggests lots of things about inputs and outputs characteristic of believing and desiring, little if anything is generally said about the specific nature of the 'output'. Nor is this surprising, given that those of the functionalist persuasion count some degree of liberalism about the mental as one of its strongest suits. According to the functionalist, anything we say about our mental life should not rule out the possibility that it is shared by the proverbial Martian. But if reference to legs is counted intrinsic to the specification of output – i.e. to what constitutes specific acts of walking or kicking – then legless, though wheel-endowed, Martians simply cannot act as we do.

Psychofunctionalist accounts which specify output in terms of some highly general functional characterization will find actions very difficult. But a version of essentially the same problem besets analytic functionalism. Moreover, since the most plausible identity account involves analytic functionalism, the identity account itself has a case to answer here.

On the analytic functionalist view, one first analyses the folk psychological notions, thereby getting functional characterizations, and then one does some empirical research to find the physiological item with which the functional characterizations are identified. Given that the first step is analysis, there can be no concepts in the functional characterization not already known by the folk (at least tacitly). But the results of the empirical research will of course go beyond anything that the folk envisage. It is this empirical feature of analytical functionalism that requires us to relativize folk psychological notions to populations. As far as the folk are concerned, pain is an experience with certain characteristic causes and effects; nothing in the folk notion rules out the possibility of Martian pain. However, when we discover that pain in human beings is C-fibre firing, we can only accommodate this, and the possibility of Martian pain, by relativizing: human pain is one thing, Martian pain another, even though they share a functional characterization.

With action, though, matters are less simple: the folk notions of walking and kicking are not so easily transferable to legless Martians. And it would be going beyond the folk's usual characterization of actions to relativize the various populations. Unlike our discovery that pain is C-fibre firing, we do not discover by empirical research that walking involves the use of the legs.

There are different ways of dealing with this problem, though none of them is completely satisfying. One way would be to characterize the mental output of a functional story in terms of a hypothetical relation to the environment. Thus, in the example above, you could say that the belief and desire produced an output such that *if* you were near a post office, and *if* there the physical situation allowed, *then* you would move your body in such a way as to end up at the post office. There would of course be a problem here in distinguishing walking from running or crawling, but, with some ingenuity, this characterization might be patched up. (Though it is unclear to me how we are going to distinguish between walking and running for a wheel-endowed Martian who can none the less share our beliefs and desires about getting to the post office.) However, any functionalist story about action along these lines is going to have another problem with action, one that circles back to a more general difficulty.

The 'if . . . then' characterization suggests that actions can be defined as effects on (or in) an environment; effects which are brought about by functional states corresponding to mental items like belief and desire which go to make up what the folk think of as reasons. But our interrogation of the folk psychological story in chapter 2 led us to think of actions as having an irreducibly inner, experiential aspect. And we have seen that neither the identity theory, nor functionalism of any sort, is comfortable with the inner or private nature of experience. So both our brief discussion of action and our unfinished discussion of the essentialist objection to identity and functionalism demand that we return to the issue of experience.

The Inner and Outer (Again)

The ultimate defence of the identity theory in chapter 6 required us to go on the offensive against the Cartesian conception of experience. For it is impossible to sustain the identity account, once we allow that introspective grasp of conscious states is alone sufficient for recognizing those same states in different possible worlds. And functionalists must avail themselves of the same defence in their battle against zombies. If we convince ourselves that our grip on consciousness is strong enough to imagine it simply not present in creatures who otherwise move and speak just like us, then we will end up with functional duplicates who, unlike at least most of us, are zombies.

Moreover, there is ample reason to oppose Cartesianism independently of any need to defend either or both of functionalism and identity. As has been suggested several times, and argued for in outline, cleaving too closely to the Cartesian conception threatens the notion of experience with incoherence. The idea we have of our inner life as immediate, private and to some extent ineffable is after all *shared*; and this idea cannot be shared if of necessity it can only be grasped by each of us individually. The first-person perspective is not even intelligible as a perspective without there being something outer and third-personal to provide its objects, and to ground our notion of what is happening, as it were, inside.

Still, though there seem to be reasonable grounds for being suspicious of the Cartesian conception, we should not get carried away. Trying to understand the mind wholly from an illusory 'inside' is not sensible. But it is no more sensible to pass over everything inner in favour of the objective and third-personal. And this contrary mistake is one to which both functionalism and the identity account are perhaps irremediably prone. For, in identifying experience and other features of the mind with processes that are physical and/or functional, there seems simply no room for even a tamed first-personal perspective. Descriptions of our neurophysiology, or of the functional relations evident in it, are wholly 'outside' and objective. Nothing in an observer's account of the processes in our brains would prepare that observer for a fact that there is something it is like to undergo such processes. And the same applies to every kind of functionalist account. Moreover, it is the apparent absence of the first-person perspective, and not simply a Cartesian conception of it, that is the deepest source of our unease with identity and functionalist accounts. Our readiness to accept that one could genuinely recognize pains in the most changed of settings in some possible world, and the perennial appeal of zombies, owe as much to a failure to come to terms with the inner perspective as to an adherence to Cartesianism.

To appreciate just how difficult it is to account for the first person using impersonal resources, one need only look at a common suggestion in this regard. In the passage below, the aim is to offer a basis, from within an identity account, for the asymmetry of first- and third-person access to our mental lives. Admittedly, this asymmetry of access is only part of our conception of the first person, but it is clear that the authors, as well as many others, regard the proposal as a coherent and positive contribution to the larger issue.

Setting aside telepathy and invasive brain surgery, how else could I discover anything about the nature of your brain states other than by going by their 'surface'
manifestations . . . On the other hand, it makes good evolutionary sense that
subjects should have special access to the nature of their own internal states,
that they should have self-monitoring devices that generate beliefs about what
is going on in their own brains by a kind of internal scanning process. Of course,
this self-scanning process does not reveal them in their guise as states of the
brain.[6]

At first glance, this seems an appealing idea. The fact that my brain is hooked
up to me in a way your brain is not seems sensible as a way of accounting for
both the intimacy with which I am in contact with my mind and the lack of
such intimacy on the part of others. But a moment's thought shows this to be
hopelessly confused.

What is wanted in any serious attempt to come to terms with the first
person is an account of how it could happen that, unlike the case with tables
and towers, or Change Reckoners and computers, there is something it is like
to be me. We have never doubted for a moment that each of us is embodied,
and that the brains in our bodies are crucial for our having mental lives. When
a hammer strikes my thumb, C-fibres begin to fire rapidly. (I continue to
pretend that this specific physiological story is true.) This is something that
anyone equipped with a suitable device for studying the brain could detect.
What the identity theorist says is that this activity is my pain. Yet how could
the existence of this perfectly objective happening be something that is inner
and subjective? How could there be something that it is like to undergo C-
fibre firing? The answer suggested in the above citation is that this particular
C-fibre firing is one which is somehow scanned or monitored by certain other
of my brain processes. But then how does it come about that these have the
requisite inner and subjective nature? Come to that, what does it mean to
describe them as 'self-scanning'?

To see just how difficult it is to answer these questions satisfactorily,
one has only to think of other cases in which we have the same kind of
merely 'physical' privacy, and also have 'self-scanning', but which do nothing
to anchor the first-person perspective. For example, my temperature-
regulating mechanism is one that is exclusive to me, and this mechanism
requires that certain processes in my body monitor other processes. (This, of
course, makes good evolutionary sense.) But the fact that one process scans
another, and that this results in my heart-rate increasing, or in my sweating
profusely, has nothing to contribute to the understanding of the inner perspective.

Someone might protest that this example is not fair to the identity theorist. After all, the processes involved in temperature regulation in the body are scarcely cerebral, and the brain is where all the action is, as far as the mental is concerned. However, this is precisely to miss the point of the example. What is at issue is how any objectively described physical process can be at the same time something inner and subjective. If the 'scanning' story given above were right, this comes about in virtue of the fact that one physical process – a process which is as a matter of fact integral to a specific subject – is monitored by some other physical process. Yet in the temperature-regulation case, we have the monitoring, but not subjectivity. If it is protested that the monitoring in this case is not itself performed by a physical process that is itself identical to something inner and subjective, we will then want to be told why subjectivity figures as a feature in this particular process of scanning, and not in that of the temperature case. What is it about the cortex that makes its physical processes first-personal? The thought had been that it was their physical intimacy, and the fact that they were connected in the right way to certain processes of internal monitoring; rejecting the temperature case shows that this had been mistaken, but now we begin to suspect that the identity theorist had begged the question all along. It had been assumed that certain objective physical processes had a subjective side, when what was needed was some reason to believe this.

Functionalists probably fare no better here, though they perhaps have a little more room for manoeuvre. This is because some functionalists will insist that functional characterizations appeal to representational states – states which resemble attitudes – and there are various proposals around for reducing experience, in all its subjectivity, to these representations. However, these states are sub-personal and their representationality, or their directionality, is wholly causal. For this reason, as we have seen, they have difficulty in accommodating the slack typical of genuine, personal-level, attitudes. So there is no more reason to think that these states and their purely causal linkages can satisfactorily account for subjectivity than the physical states and processes implicated in the identity theory. (Indeed, the self-scanning proposal of the identity theorist bears a certain uncanny resemblance to the higher-order thought story about experience told by many functionalists).

The Unity of the Mental (Again)

The subjective and inner nature of experience is a headache for both identity and functionalist accounts, and this is reflected in the extensive literature devoted to the issue. But, though somewhat neglected, there is another related difficulty for these accounts which is no less problematic, and which, in the end, might well be more fundamental. I have in mind here the unity of the mental.

As noted towards the end of chapter 4, the mental landscape does not simply consist of different and separable features laid out for view, either from an outer or inner perspective. There are deep links between these features. Thus, there can be no attitudes without consciousness, even though this does not mean that attitudes are themselves features of experience; actions are intertwined with both attitude and experience, and only really count as actions when these linkages are taken seriously; and perhaps most important, something counts as a feature of the mental landscape only in virtue of its being possessed by a person.

This is only a sample of the linkages that exist, and even this sample is controversial. But what does seem true is that, correctly described, these linkages together constitute a real, even if elusive, unity. The trouble is that it is difficult to see how any such unity can be constructed using materials available to identity and functionalist accounts. Attempts to mirror the unity of the mental at the level of the functional or physical encounter the problem of mere contingency. Any functional or physical linkage which is intended to underpin this unity will be contingent, or matter of fact, whereas the unity of the mental is a conceptual matter. This difficulty was already visible in the identity theorist's attempt to capture first- and third-person asymmetry of access.

Suppose for the moment that pain is a C-fibre firing, and suppose also that there are other processes in the brain which monitor these C fibre firings. (Suppose, that is, that we think that the problem of subjectivity is soluble within the identity account.) Finally, suppose we accept that what makes for asymmetry of access to this pain is simply the fact that it occurs in a brain which happens also to have the relevant monitoring processes in place. (Others who are not so intimately connected to the C-fibre firing in this brain have to rely on word of mouth and behaviour for their access to it.) Now, against the background of these suppositions, what can be said about the connection between this pain and the person suffering it? Remembering that persons are in part loci of attitudes and initiators of actions, this question in effect asks for an account of how this experience of pain is conceptually integrated into the perspective constituting one individual rather than another. Yet the only kind of answer that the identity theorist is in a position to give is something like this: this particular C-fibre firing occurs in a brain, monitored by its own internal process, and which also contains identity correlates of various attitudes and reasons for action. Essentially, what is being said is that the pain belongs to one rather than another person because that person is hooked up to a brain containing that particular C-fibre firing, as well as containing various other states and processes.

Leaving aside the issue of whether it is coherent to speak of a person as 'hooked up' to a brain, this sort of answer is inadequate. It treats all actual and potential connections between mental features, and between persons and their mental lives, as merely contingent. It suggests that it could come as an empirical discovery that a pain belonged to someone, and this simply does not do justice to the folks' conception of their pains or themselves. Moreover, though I have illustrated the difficulty in the context of the identity account, it should be obvious that it applies, apart from some details, to functionalism. Any account of mind which is restricted to using the materials of the outer and impersonal will be forced to capture what is a conceptual matter in contingent terms. (Such accounts also encourage the idea that one can deal with features of the mental landscape in a piecemeal fashion; that the identity account, for example, might be best at handling pains and other experiences, whilst the functionalist account fares best with the attitudes.)

Conclusion

No one currently has any idea of how to accommodate the subjective and perspectival using resources composed solely of objective features of the world. So, whilst the previous two sections seem confidently to conclude that we cannot salvage identity accounts or functionalism, it is a little unfair to blame them for more general shortcomings inherent in our way of thinking about the mind. Still, we can scarcely come away from the above discussion convinced that we have genuinely integrated the mental and the physical through the intermediary of these accounts. It was recently claimed that:

> functionalism's besetting difficulties are significant but not daunting. Functionalism is not merely alive and well, but still and rightly the reigning paradigm in the philosophy of mind.[7]

Though I think that we should be less hasty in dismissing the identity account – which in its most defended version is also a type of functionalism – this does not seem an unreasonable stance. However, given the size of the problem of somehow getting from the objective to the subjective, there is less to being the reigning paradigm in the philosophy of mind than this expression suggests. Perhaps it would be better to have written: the problems facing functionalism are not only significant but daunting.

Notes and References

1 A source for the original presentation of the example is Searle, *Minds, Brains, and Science* (Cambridge, MA: Harvard University Press, 1984).

2 Searle, *The Mystery of Consciousness* (London: Granta, 1997), p. 11.

3 Attitudes are most at home in individual persons, but the possibility of their being somehow 'spread out' in a population is one we do allow. Remember the citation from Lewis Carroll in which he spoke of 'Anglo-Saxon attitudes'. These are presumably not attitudes held by each of the descendants of the Anglo-Saxons, but are attributed on the basis of bits of behaviour and attitude spread across the population. Admittedly, the Chinese nation example is not exactly like this, but one might use the one case to convince oneself of the possibility of the other.

   A brief comment here about action: virtually all of the discussions of functionalism tend to portray action in superficial terms as overt bodily movement whose cause is physiologically internal to an agent. The role of the will in action, and the connection between will and experience, are features of action which do not figure. This is a shame, but it is unsurprising. Action theory tends to form a separate preserve in philosophy of mind, and the arguments in that preserve are often highly detailed and controversial, so the larger philosophy of mind community tends to overlook them.

4 The text suggests that this argument is directed against versions of psychofunctionalism, accounts which treat the identity of experience and the functional as a discoverable empirical matter. However, it does have consequences for versions of analytical functionalism as well. Getting the precise target right is a surprisingly delicate matter, and will be discussed towards the end of the section.

5 There could also be psychofunctionalists who did not aim to reduce experience to states that are representational (i.e. have attitude-like directionality). However, I don't actually know anyone meeting this description. I suspect this is because the most plausible forms of psychofunctionalism are committed to using representational materials, and so there is an in-built pressure to reduce the whole of the mental landscape to the representational.

6 Braddon-Mitchell and Jackson, *Philosophy of Mind and Cognition* (Oxford: Blackwell, 1996), pp. 94–5.

7 Lycan, 'Functionalism' in S. Guttenplan (ed.), *A Companion to the Philosophy of Mind* (1994), p. 322.

9

Division and Elimination

The Coalesence strategy offers the most direct way to deal with the problem of overdetermination: if we could successfully integrate Mind and Brain, there would remain but one claimant to the titles both of reason and cause of Action, and the problematic triangle would disappear at a stroke. However, there are other strategies deserving of our attention. In this final chapter, and if for no other reason than completeness, we must consider both Division of Labour and Elimination. But completeness is only part of the story. Even aside from the general worry raised at the end of the previous chapter, the objections to identity and to some functionalisms make it reasonable to look elsewhere. Perhaps by some less direct means, we will end up with a more satisfactory resolution of the overdetermination problem, and thereby the smooth integration of mind into the natural world.

Anomalous Monism

In chapter 5, I described a radical proposal inspired by the philosopher Leibniz. As sketched, this suggestion involved splitting the Mind–Brain–Action triangle, so as to create two completely independent realms. In one realm, experiences and attitudes provide reasons for action; and in the other, the physical properties of our brains cause changes and movements in our bodies.

On this extreme view, something very strange happens when, say, you decide to open the refrigerator. As you might expect, your experiences and attitudes come together to give you a reason for opening it, but, less expectedly, this reason operates, not so as to produce a movement of the refrigerator door, but rather a flurry of further mental states that you take to be your opening the door. That is, having decided to open it, you have the perception as of your hand going out, and as of the handles being grasped, and as of the door's opening and so on, but none of this quite adds up to your actually making it open. To be sure, the door does open. However, this is in effect merely coincidental to your mental exertions. For what causes the door to move is your arm and the neurons firing in your brain that control it. Imagining a god's-eye view of this whole business, there is a kind of wonderful harmony – though no interaction – between your thoughts and the movements of things in the world.

This is generally regarded as too radical a way with the problem of overdetermination. The required 'pre-established harmony' between our thoughts and the physical workings of the world strikes many people as just crazy. However, it gives you the idea of what is demanded of a Division of Labour strategy – some way of splitting the Mind–Brain–Action triangle that preserves all the elements, whilst keeping them from getting in each other's way. Achieving this in some sane way is less easy than you might think, but, as noted, the problems with Coalescence make it worth a try.

At an apparently opposite extreme from Leibniz is the view known as *anomalous monism*, which can be found in the writings of Donald Davidson. As I shall explain the view here, it is in fact an ultra-minimalist way of implementing the Division of Labour strategy, though, for all its minimalism, we shall see that it hasn't completely shaken off some of the Leibnizian problems.

Anomalous monism is the result of trying to reconcile three claims:

(i)   There is causal interaction between the mental and the physical. For example, when I decide to open the refrigerator, and succeed, I do actually bring about a change in the physical world.

(ii)   Whenever one thing causes another, there is a law connecting the two. (Here by 'law' is meant the kind of universally general regularity described in chapter 3.)

(iii)   There are no laws – no exceptionless universal generalizations – connecting features of the mental landscape with either physical features, or with other features of the mental landscape. Thus, there will be no universal generalization, however narrowly set out, which will connect beliefs and desires with movements of arms and the opening of refrigerator doors; or connecting experiences with attitudes or attitudes with actions. (Mental/physical and mental/mental relations are thus said by (iii) to be 'anomalous', that is, not subject to laws.)

These three claims have been challenged, qualified, and challenged again. (Though, perhaps as a result of wanting to avoid the problems with Leibniz's view, philosophers have tended to let the first pass without much comment.) In particular, (iii) has been the one most worked over, not surprisingly, by those who for one reason or another have a commitment to the Theory

Theory. For accepting anomalousness is tantamount to denying the Theory Theory; if there are neither psychophysical laws nor purely psychological laws, then it would seem that folk psychological explanation couldn't work like theoretical explanation in science.

The claim about cause and law in (ii) makes explicit something that has been in the background at various points in this book, namely that there is a connection between explaining something by appealing to regularities and by appealing to causes. Indeed, (ii) takes the strongest possible line on this issue, declaring as it does that if you have the one you must have the other, and there are those who think that this is too strong.

In spite of the uneasiness generated by at least two of Davidson's claims, my interest here is not in the truth of each, so much as in seeing how Davidson tries to effect a reconciliation among them. For, at first glance, it is difficult to see how they could all be true. After all, the first says that there is causality, the second that there must therefore be laws, and the third that there can be no laws.[1]

As Davidson sees it, the key to the reconciliation is a version of the identity theory that he describes as 'token identity'. (Note that having already expressed strong reservations (in chapter 7) about this expression, it might be thought that I would be deeply unsympathetic to Davidson's project. But as I also indicated in chapter 7, it is usually possible to reconstruct so-called 'token identity' views using some notion of implementation or supervenience. So scruples about the expression 'token identity' will not get in the way here.)

In outline, the story goes as follows. Events, states and processes, whether mental or physical, are particulars. Moreover, though they can be grouped into kinds – we can speak of a kind of pain or a kind of brain process – it is as particulars that they are causally related to one another. Thus, when (i) claims that the mental causally interacts with the physical, the typical instance will be a case in which some particular mental item causes some specific change in the physical world. For example, it is Jones's coming to have the perceptual belief that there is a tennis ball approaching that causes him to move the arm holding the racket so as to contact the ball and send it back over the net.

However, the law-like universal generalizations mentioned in (ii) are sensitive to the ways in which we refer to, or classify, causes and effects. Some ways of grouping causes and effects result in a reasonable law; others do not. Here is a simple example. Begin first with this claim: the temperature's falling to 20° F last night caused the surface of the New River to freeze solid. This is a perfectly reasonable causal claim about two particular events. Next think about the low-level law that seems to be in the offing here, that whenever the temperature drops to 20° F, the surface of the New River freezes solid. Clearly, this is not the stuff of sophisticated science, but it seems to be true enough and law-like enough to offer at least the beginning of an explanation. But now think about the fact that the particular event which took place last night – the suddenly falling temperature – was the first event forecast by the new BBC weather man. This is a perfectly true, and in virtue of it we could recast the causal claim in terms of temperature so that it became: the first event forecast by the new BBC weather man caused the New River to freeze solid. But, finally think about the generalization: whenever an event is first forecast by a new BBC weather man, the New River freezes solid. This is just plain false; even though it might be used for ironical purposes, it is scarcely a law-like generalization.

Putting together these thoughts about (i) and (ii) provides Davidson with what he needs for a reconciliation with (iii). For he insists that, in asserting the anomalousness of the mental he is saying simply that there are no laws *whose terms make use of mental vocabulary*, and this is compatible with there being other ways of classifying mental particulars which do yield laws. Indeed, given the fact that mental items causally interact with physical particulars, Davidson takes (i)–(iii) to entail that there must be such laws, and hence that every mental item is classifiable in purely physical vocabulary. This is the consequence he calls the 'token identity' of the mental and the physical, and, somewhat differently described, we have come across it before.

The mnemonic system that employed stones to mark tasks had similar features. On the one hand, each stone stood for a task; when a stone was left on the floor on a certain night, it became the marker of the need to make a bank deposit the next day. On the other hand, the task-oriented vocabulary used in describing stones does not match up with, and certainly wouldn't illuminate, a classification based on physical predicates.

The stones example clearly illustrates the so-called token identity claim of anomalous monism, but it also sheds some light on wider issues. Though talk of regularities and laws is inappropriate to the mnemonic system, the epistemological barrier that exists between tasks and stones is something like the barrier that Davidson discerns between minds and the physical world (including, of course, brains). For him, specific mental features are physical features, but one should not expect to learn anything fundamental and systematic about the mind by studying either brains or the physical world in which they operate.[2]

For the moment, leaving aside the question of its plausibility, how does the anomalous monist picture help with the problematic triangle of Mind–Brain–Action? Answering this is not straightforward. On the one hand, the monist part of the view seems to rule out the possibility of our being anything except the physical stuff of which we are made. On the other hand, the mental landscape is counted no less real or important; it would make little sense to insist on the independence of our concepts of mind – and that is what the anomalousness thesis comes to – if there was no reality in whatever answered to those concepts. Perhaps the best we can do by way of representing the anomalous monist position is something like figure 9.1.

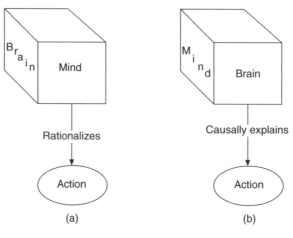

Figure 9.1

The two parts of figure 9.1 are intended as two different views of one and the same representation. In 9.1(a) what one sees, when looking at the cube face-on, is Mind, and, when you see this face, the connection to Action appears as reason–giving or rationalization. In 9.1(b), however, one sees another face of the cube, this time one labelled 'Brain', and from this angle the connection to Action appears as causal explanation. (That is, as the impersonal form of explanation described in chapter 3, placement in a network of law–like regularities.)

The solution to the problem of overdetermination suggested by figure 9.1 is not exactly a coalescence of Mind into Brain (or vice versa), so much as an attempt divide labour between these categories by assigning different roles to each. In fact, it is perhaps the most minimal such division that one could make. The idea is (roughly) that when you consider the world from a purely physicalist angle (figure 9.1(b)), you see only states, events and processes set in a network of law-governed regularities. From this angle, the mental landscape is not visible, but this does not mean that it, or anything else, is left out. Rather, engaged as you are in the business of physical science, your study of human beings is essentially neurophysiological, and, since the only kind of explanation relevant to this is of the regularity sort, you should not be expecting to encounter anything characteristically mental. However, when viewed from the angle shown in figure 9.1(a), what is set out before you is the whole of mind's landscape, and, from this angle, what matters is not the existence of general laws, but properties of persons and rational relations between persons and their actions. (The physical world is, of course, not wholly absent from this angle of view, but it figures only in so far as it is necessary for the folk's everyday dealings with the world.)

Anomalous monism is certainly an attractive view; as presented in figure 9.1, it seems to be a solution to the overdetermination problem that is as economical as it is effective. But one should not be carried away by what is no more than a sketch, and, in any case, this same sketch highlights, rather than hides, several difficult problems. First, though the faces of the cube are labelled as 'Mind' and 'Brain', such labelling is no more than metaphorical. What remains a substantial difficulty is spelling out in a transparent way what it means to say that the mental and the physical could be present to us as different faces or aspects. Second, and related, is the issue of whether it is ultimately reasonable to treat the connection between Mind Brain and Action in the ways suggested by figure 9.1. If causality needs to be backed by law-like regularities, and these are only visible from the physical angle, it is unclear what kind of explanatory role is being left for reasons. These two points merit further discussion.

Spinoza seems to have thought that the world, and everything in it, was a single self-subsisting substance which had the potential to be conceived of in an infinite number of ways. These ways were called 'modifications', and, limited as we are, only two are available to us – the mental and the physical. However, the Spinozistic thought that there is a substance independent of, yet supporting, what appears to us as either mental or physical is certainly not Davidson's. For him, as for many others, the world is at bottom physical; it does not consist of some 'neutral' (as between physical and mental) and only dimly knowable stuff. However, it is very difficult to understand how we can give the physical this fundamental status, whilst still insisting on the irreducible reality of the mental. A thought that many have come to have about anomalous monism is that it ultimately gives the mental landscape a second-class status; that we end up treating it as in some sense optional (perhaps not optional for us in our everyday dealings, but optional in some more fundamental ontological sense).

This first problem is echoed in the second. According to Davidson, if one event causes another then, though we might not be able to state it, there must be some exceptionless universal generalization – a law – connecting these events. However, he also insists that the concepts figuring in these laws, if and when we do manage to state them, will not be those of the mental realm. This asymmetry between mental and physical concepts is of a piece with the fundamental status accorded to the physical, and it leads pretty immediately to a problem known as the 'inertness', or lack of causal efficacy, of the mental. For, though Davidson insists that mental features are real enough to cause, as well as rationalize, actions, it is puzzling how this can be true. It is puzzling because mental concepts are ruled out of the laws that are needed to back up such causation.

Perhaps the best way to grasp these problems is to think about some specific case. Suppose, for example, that you have just reached for a glass of water, and that your reason for doing this was a combination of your thirst and the onset of the belief that the glass in front of you contained water. Did you reach for the glass because of this reason? Was the content of this reason – its water-directedness – efficacious in producing your movement towards the glass? Whilst the anomalous monist wants to answer these questions affirmatively, something inherent in the view seems to get in the way. To understand what, begin with a claim central to anomalous monism, namely the thesis that every specific mental event is also correctly describable in physical terms. (This captures what is intended by 'token identity', though without at the same time embroiling us in the problems that come with talk of 'token' states.) This describability thesis makes it possible to keep the mental independent enough of the physical to count as anomalous, yet close enough to benefit from the network of law-governed regularities that characterizes the physical. Figure 9.1 is again helpful here.

The fact that there is both a 'Mind' and a 'Brain' face to the cube displays the describability thesis. And the fact that the down-arrow can be seen as 'rationalizes' from the Mind angle, and 'causally explains' from the Brain angle, displays the minimal way in which labour is divided: your reaching for the glass is done for a reason when looked at one way, and is a causally explained feature of the physical when looked at in the other. However, the question that we asked above was about causation, not about causal explanation. Where in 9.1 does it figure?

At first the answer seems obvious: for Davidson, mental features are causes as well as reasons, and so we could add 'cause' to the label for the down-arrow in 9.1(a). Thus, the entertaining of your belief and desire in respect of the glass of water serve both as the reason for, and the cause of, your reaching. Of course, causality needs to be backed up by law-like regularities, and there are none discernible on the Mind-side shown in 9.1(a). But, as we saw above, the day is saved by the fact that explanatory regularities do exist when we shift our point of view to the Brain side shown in 9.1(b); the existence of physical laws, together with the describability thesis, ensure that we have the right to speak about mental causation.

All of this goes swimmingly until we ask about the possibility of adding 'cause' to the label for the down-arrow *in 9.1(b)*. Surely, if there are law-like regularities connecting features of the physical world with the physical movements that figure in actions, then the relation between Brain and Action will qualify as causal. But this spells trouble. If the regularities that underwrite the causal credentials of *reasons on their own* are the same as those that underwrite the causal credentials of these *reasons described physically*, there is a worry about whether reasons on their own are doing any work at all. In terms of the example: given the causal competence of your reason as physically conceived, the content of your reason – its water-directedness – is surplus to requirements. Your arm's moving is both caused and explained by what went on in your neural system and muscles. So, in making this causal claim, we need not advert to mental descriptions in general, nor contents of reasons in particular.

As you might expect, Davidsonians refuse to draw this conclusion, though they do not dispute the premises leading up to it. In their view, all that is required for the efficacy of the mental is that mental events can be causes and effects. The belief-desire event on a particular occasion causes (among other things) the glass to move towards you. And this suffices for our counting mental events as genuine functionaries on the world stage. To the objector who says: 'yes, but mental causes do not bring about physical effects in virtue of their mental properties – in virtue of their content,' the Davidsonian reply is:

> There is no room in my philosophy for talk of events causing other events 'in virtue of properties'. Causality is a nothing more nor less than a relation between events, however they are described and whatever properties they possess. It is a purely extensional relationship between particular events, and it bears none of the complications of, for example, belief relationships between persons and states of affairs. However, as insisted upon earlier, it is explanation not causation that is sensitive to properties, and to the predicates used to pick them out. Explanation requires law-like generalizations, and these depend for their truth on the right choice of properties. So, talk of 'causation in virtue of' is nothing more than an avoidable confusion between causation and explanation.

In reply, an objector might say:

> It is an essential part of the anomalous monist project that causality be backed by laws, by universal generalizations connecting the particular events. To be sure, there is no presumption that we must be able to state these generalizations; that

without such articulation we would have no right to make the causal claims in the first place. Rather, in asserting a causal relation we are committed only to there being some such generalization, even if it is not then known. Now accepting that we do need this backing, we still can reasonably ask why. And the answer seems obvious enough: there must be some connection between the causes that figure in our initial claim, and the predicates or properties figuring in the (perhaps not yet discovered) laws. One way to put this connection is to speak of a particular event as causing another in virtue of some property. However, since that seems unacceptable to the anomalous monist, we should be willing to accept alternatives. What does not seem acceptable is to say that causes must be backed by laws, yet there need never be any connection between the properties by which some cause is picked out, and the laws which back it up.

No verdict will be issued here in respect of this confrontation, though it does seem as if the anomalous monist is in some trouble. It is not the common philosophical trouble of employing a bad argument, but rather the unusual one of having too few argumentative resources to draw on. The distinction between causation and explanation is not one that everyone would accept, but the problem is that, even if we do, the case for the anomalous monist is far from assured. For it leaves unanswered questions about the connections between causation and explanation, and its only defence against certain ways of answering these questions seems to be to advise us against asking them.

As was obvious enough from the beginning, the root problem with anomalous monism is that it promises more than it seems to deliver. It promises us a way of being physicalist, though without reducing the mental to the physical, and it promises this, whilst insisting on the reality of the mental. The first of these promises is the joint result of so-called 'token identity' between mental and physical events, and the absence of laws, physical or otherwise, governing the mental. Token identity calms the physicalists, and lawlessness (anomalousness) keeps the mental out of reach of the reductionists. However, one might at this point ask: if the world is at bottom physical, and the mental is not reducible to the physical, then what is the point of the mental? This is where the anomalous monist's second promise – the one insisting that the mental be taken seriously – comes in. The mental, we are assured, is not only safe, it is substantial, because it has its own job of work to do – the work of providing reasons for, and causing, actions. The other task – that of providing the laws which ground causality – is turned over to the physical, which is competent here because of its potential for completeness and systematicity. Unfortunately, as we have seen, this second promise looks empty when it becomes apparent that the physical seems perfectly capable of doing both its own work and that originally assigned to the mental. Indeed, the worry is that having competence both with laws and causes, the physical is doing *all* the real work. The mental, like the four-year-old who insists on helping with the cooking, is at most allowed the appearance of a job of work.

Functionalism and Division of Labour

It would be unreasonable to count anomalous monism a complete failure on the basis of a brief discussion, but it is certainly no great success. In addition to the second-class status it seems to accord the mental, at least two of its central claims are far from obvious. None the less, even if it is a failure, anomalous monism and its difficulties can be extremely useful in helping us understand the kind of functionalism which cropped up at the end of chapter 7. (And it can guide us in some of the other directions we might want to take; more on this later in the chapter.)

As I chose to introduce it, functionalism counted as an attempt at coalescence, and as such it came to be entangled with the identity theory. For on one perfectly coherent interpretation, the identity theory is itself a kind of functionalism. Whilst this would no doubt please authors who never did see functionalism as superseding identity, we saw that there are versions of functionalism which do not aim at coalescence, and which do not therefore have any truck with mental-physical identity. As we left the matter in chapter 7, these views fall under either the Division of Labour or Elimination strategies, but we have now to be more specific.

The place to start is with, as they say, the big picture, and this is given as figure 9.2 (which incorporates elements of several of the figures in chapter 7). All options are left open here. At one extreme, if we specify both the ?-relation and the ??-relation as forms of identity, then we effectively collapse Mind–Function–Brain into a single category, and there is then only a single arrow aiming at action. Certain details aside, this is where we will find the analytical functionalist who is also an identity theorist. At the other extreme, if one insists that neither of the relations do any integrating, we end up with the complete independence of Mind, Function and Brain, and therefore with three claimants on Action. No one seems to have adopted this position – at least not intentionally – and this is not surprising. Whilst the analytical functionalist resolves the overdetermination problem, going to the opposite extreme intensifies it.

Of interest to us now are Division of Labour views which take up a position somewhere between these two extremes. In particular, we are concerned with those functionalisms which meet the following desiderata. First, they do not treat the ??-relation as identity, or as anything strong enough to weld the

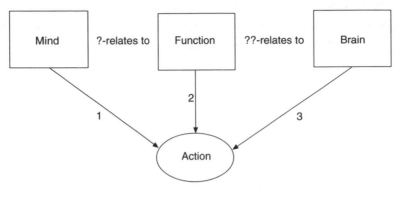

Figure 9.2

functional and the physical into a single unit. As suggested earlier, the most promising candidate for such a ??-relation is supervenience: the functional is said to supervene on, but not be reducible to, the physical. Second, these in-between functionalisms treat the ?-relationship as weak enough to prevent a complete collapse of Mind into Function, but strong enough to vindicate the folk characterization of the mental, and thereby prevent a slide towards elimination. Initially, we might as well just continue to say that mental is deconstructed into the functional, but we will consider other possibilities later.

One position which might seem to meet these desiderata counts the deconstructional relationship between Mind and Function as based on analysis – somewhat in the manner of the analytical functionalist – but resists the further step of identifying what results with physical features of Brain. However, this position does not seem to have any out-and-out support. Whatever we come to think of the identity theory of chapter 6, there can be little doubt that its main appeal lies in the fact that it offers us a way to solve the overdetermination problem. Were we to let this go, as we would if we insisted on non-reductive supervenience, the remaining analytic project looks distinctly frail. The idea that we can generate substantial functional characterizations merely by a priori analysis of the folk account of the mental is not an appealing one on its own; it was, and is, the weakest link in the analytical functionalist/identity account.

Without analysis as the way to get from the mental to the functional, we end up with some version of non-reductive psychofunctionalism, that is, a position which treats the ?-relation as an empirically discoverable relation of deconstruction, and which treats the ??-relation as neither identity nor anything else that promises reduction. This is the type of position that we touched on in chapter 7: the work of cognitive psychology shows how the mental landscape as described by the folk can be, unbeknown to the folk, deconstructed into a complex, probably multi-level, functional characterization. The functional, however, turns out not to be itself reducible to the physical; instead it merely supervenes on it. A schematic representation of this position (figure 9.3) shows both why it shares a difficulty with anomalous monism and how it comes to have a special one all its own.

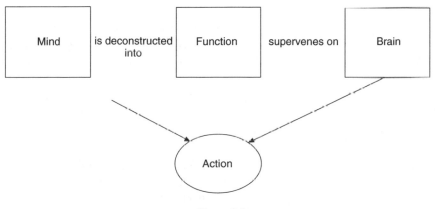

Figure 9.3

The difficulty it shares is that of having to deal with overdetermination. The vindicating link between Mind and Function suggests that we can drop one of the arrows in the big picture (figure 9.2), but the non-reductive supervenience relation on the right of figure 9.3 forces us to keep at least two in play. Remember that, as it was explained, non-reductive supervenience – or simply 'supervenience', since many count this relation as inherently non-reductive – puts up epistemic barriers. Knowing what goes on in the physical world does not provide us with knowledge of the functional nor, a fortiori, of the mental. Thus, any productive relation between the mental-functional and actions must in some way be separate from the productive relation between neurophysiological events and arm movements. (I have spoken here of 'productive' relations, rather than reasons, causes or anything else, so as not to prejudice the further discussion that will follow.)

The difficulty that non-reductive psychofunctionalism can call its own arises from the fact that it includes a category of the functional, as well as the mental, in the picture. This is in contrast to anomalous monism, which has no truck with anything resembling functional deconstruction. This difficulty is shown in figure 9.3 by the fact that the left-hand arrow has yet to be connected to either Mind or Function. On one view, the mental is a kind of gloss on an underlying functional story, and the almost certainly causal arrow linked to actions – the 'outputs' – takes off from Function. On another view, the mental is, as the folk imagine, rationally responsible for actions, and we are right to see the arrow as starting from Mind. In this case, we appeal separately to the functional story as a way of deconstructing both the reason relationship and the mental features that supply the content of reasons. Both of these options are problematic, but until we know more about the deconstruction relationship, we cannot even begin to deal with them.

If one ignores for the moment this second difficulty, there is a striking resemblance between anomalous monism and a certain version of non-reductive psychofunctionalism. Both insist that the mind is not reducible to the physical, though both insist that the mental must be taken seriously. Indeed, it would be open to the psychofunctionalist to adopt a partly Davidsonian line by attempting to divide labour between the mental-functional on the one hand and the physical on the other. Here is one way such a story might begin:

> A human being can be looked at in several different ways. Call these 'stances'. Adopting one stance, we are purely physical devices whose internal states and the movements they bring about are thoroughly explicable in terms of cause and effect. Adopting another stance, however, human beings can be seen as attitude-takers, as having beliefs and desires that lead them – give them reasons – to engage with the world in ways that are predictable from within this 'intentional' stance.

(There is also a third possibility, that of the design stance, where this is in effect what we see from the functional perspective. However, since nothing in anomalous monism corresponds to the functional level, I am temporarily ignoring this third stance.)

The division of labour implicit in this story allots causal tasks to the physical stance, and reason-based, predictive tasks to the intentional stance. And pretty much the same problem that besets anomalous monism shows up here. Pressing hard, though justifiably, on the notion of prediction, we want some reason to think that the predictions we make whilst adopting the intentional stance are well-grounded. Yet the way in which predictions are usually grounded is by their placement in a network of law-like regularities, and this is on offer only from the physical stance. So, as with anomalous monism, for all the talk of different stances, it seems as if we have failed to give real work to the mental.[3]

Keeping mental-functional features fully in play by insisting that they bear a non-reductive supervenience relation to the physical, whilst also dealing with the problem of overdetermination, might be thought problem enough for psychofunctionalism. Indeed, taking our lead from a discussion of anomalous monism, we saw that psychofunctionalism seems in no better shape here. A non-reductive psychofunctionalism threatens to demote the mental-functional to a second-class status in much the same way as anomalous monism threatens the mental on its own. Still, we cannot simply ignore the other problem that besets non-reductive psychofunctionalism, and, partly because it is specific to this range of views, it might even be thought more interesting.

This second problem concerns the deconstructive relationship between the mental and the functional. Though we have yet to be told about this relation in any detail, we do know that deconstruction is not an identity relation, whether established by a priori analysis or otherwise, and that it is unlikely to be some weaker analytic relation. Before getting down to the business of positive characterization, a few comments about these excluded possibilities are in order.

In earlier chapters, I suggested that identity might be one possible interpretation of the ?-relation. It then seemed reasonable that functionalists might be willing to identify mental features with functional ones, even though they are unwilling to identify them with physical features. Moreover, though no arguments were offered, it seemed that, if we countenanced mental-functional identity, the reality of the mental would have been vindicated. Yet, at the point when we are discussing these versions of functionalism in more detail, I have ruled out identity as one of the candidates for the ?-relation. Why?

The answer here is based on nothing deeper than a judgement of plausibility. When considering functionalism as a theory with the potential to vindicate folk psychological concepts, it was reasonable to imagine that there was an underlying identity relation between these concepts and the functional. If nothing else, the idea of a 'functional state identity theory', as it is often called, serves a useful expository purpose. Having simplicity and familiarity, identity shows what is required of any serious contender for the ?-relation. However, when contenders need to be plausible as well, identity seems just too strong. Having already put analytic functionalism on one side for reasons of plausibility, functional state identity would have to be established by the hard graft of empirical research. We would, for example, have to show by experimental and scientific means that what we think of as pains or beliefs are in fact enormously complex functional states, probably arranged in some hierarchy of levels. What are the chances that when all of the experiments are in, the functional hierarchy will match exactly the story the folk tell about their pains and beliefs? It would be foolish to think that they would be anything other than nil; to think otherwise would be like expecting the contemporary scientific notion of heat to have matched up precisely with the notion of heat entertained by blacksmiths in 1400.

This is not to say that psychofunctionalism leads directly to some kind of eliminativism, thereby completely by-passing the Division of Labour. Even though it is unlikely that cognitive science will establish functional identities, it is perfectly reasonable to think that they will find functional characterizations that in some way vindicate the folk psychological story. One might reasonably expect the kind of vindication we found in the case of heat: some central item in the folk story does in fact match up with something in the scientific one, and, even though the settings are completely different, we can see why folk thought as they did about heat.[4] Besides, though we won't pause over this here, many regard straightforward elimination of folk psychology as itself implausible, if not downright incoherent.

It is because any plausible candidate for the ?-relation must fall short of out-and-out identity that psychofunctionalism's special problem arises. If the Mind and Function boxes in figure 9.3 were coalesced, we would not have had any special worry about the starting-point of the arrow leading to action. However, as things stand, the most plausible versions of psychofunctionalism have two balls in the air – Mind and Function – where anomalous monism has only one, and this puts a lot of pressure on the deconstruction relation. Not only must it be strong enough to vindicate at least the core of the folk psychological story about experience and attitude, it must also vindicate the folk's ideas about the power of the mind to produce actions, and thereby to produce changes in the physical world generally.

Perhaps disappointingly, it will not be possible here to consider the particular ways one might spell out the deconstruction relation, and this is not simply due to the size of the task. It is because saying anything useful depends crucially on what turns up in cognitive scientific investigations, and it is still early days. In some areas, like those of perception, memory and language, there are already interesting and widely discussed experiments and hypotheses that bear on the relation of the mental and the functional. However, though there are extensive and lively philosophical discussions of these empirical studies, the overall picture is not clear enough for anything but speculation about the deconstructional relation.

(Note: even though we must be patient, there are a couple of caveats we can enter right now about the deconstruction relation. First, it will have to bear the weight of the general objections to functionalism raised in chapter 8. Any detailed functional account that includes some vindication of the folk psychological picture will have cope with worries about the directionality of the attitudes, the subjectivity of experience and the uniqueness of persons as objects in the world who none the less adopt perspectives on it.

Second, we should be chary of the suggestion that deconstruction is a form of non-reductive supervenience. If we did adopt this view, one would have the rather neat picture of the mental as supervenient on the functional and the functional as supervenient on the physical. But this neatness would come at a cost. For the whole point of *non-reductive* supervenience is that, whilst it is ontologically concessive, it creates epistemic barriers; it allows us to say that the mental is physical, even though we cannot learn about the mental by studying the physical. Linking the mental and the functional by a supervenience relation, we would make it difficult — perhaps impossible — to make any kind of case for vindication.)[5]

Experience and Attitude

Before considering other general strategies, it is worth pausing over a way of dividing labour that is commonly discussed in the literature and has the potential to cause a great deal of confusion. In this chapter, we have so far treated 'Mind' as a label for the whole of the mental as it would be characterized by the folk. This meant that when we considered the relationship of Mind to the other categories, we did not make finer discriminations; we made no separate provision for experiences or attitudes, or indeed for emotions and the myriad other items that populate the mental landscape. However, as was hinted earlier in the book, we might be able to avoid some of the problems that beset functionalism — and other views — if we accord special and different treatment to various items in the category of Mind. In doing this we would thereby be dividing labour, not *between* the categories shown in figure 9.2, but within each of them.

It will not be possible to survey here all of the ways in which fine-grained distinctions might be pressed into service, but one example will serve. The notable differences that obtain between experiences such as pain and attitudes like belief suggest that we might be better off if these phenomena were given different treatments. Pains and perceptual experiences have a immediacy and a presence which encourage the thought that, when they are undergone, there must be some process 'corresponding' to them going on at either the functional or the physical level. But attitudes like belief do not inspire quite this degree of confidence. It may certainly be true of Harry that he believes that right will prevail, but many do not think it sensible to set off looking for some one functional or physical state which appropriately corresponds to that belief. Instead, the thought is that we would be better off to think of this belief attribution, and a whole range of others, as part of a looser scheme for characterizing Harry. It is not that each attribution corresponds to some one, potentially isolable, state, within Harry's functional and/or physical architecture; rather the scheme as a whole is supported by that architecture.

The analogy that motivates this treatment of the attitudes made its appearance in chapter 6. Maps give us information by representing political, geographical and topological features; if you want to know where Toulouse is, you consult a map. But, though we talk of maps as giving us information in virtue of their representative capacities, we do not think of them as constructed out of discrete representations. Compare, for example, a map of France with a computer that has been programmed to answer questions about the country. When you interrogate the computer by typing in: 'Where is Toulouse?', the computer prints out: 'It is 675 kilometres south of Paris', or 'It is 1°30′ east longitude and 43°40′ north latitude.' Given what we know about how computers work, it is a reasonable assumption that internal states of the computer at some instant correspond to these answers, and we can think of these states as representing the relevant information. The computer has been designed so as to store bits of information in memory – perhaps in structures that are the electronic equivalent of sentences – and, when you ask your question, the central processor retrieves the relevant electronic bit of information. But with a map it is completely different. The information 'stored' in a map is not stored in anything like this way. If someone were to say: 'send me that portion of the map which shows where Toulouse is, and shows nothing else,' then however sharp our eye (and scissors) we could not do it. Cutting out a portion of the map which showed Toulouse in relation to Paris (or Toulouse and the grid co-ordinates) would be bound to go beyond what was required.

If we think of the part of Harry's internal functional or physical architecture that supports his attitudes as map-like, then we can explain why we are tempted to think of experiences and attitudes so differently. Harry's attitudes are at least partly representations of the world; he depends on them to guide him in acting, and he generally aims for some kind of accuracy or truth in his beliefs. But, though we talk of his attitudes or beliefs in the plural, thereby suggesting that we might find in him discrete, quantifiable representations, the map analogy suggests otherwise. When we attribute attitudes to Harry, we are in effect reading off information from the map-like structure which is, or realizes, Harry's representation of the world. Just as a map can give us lots of information without itself being made up of discrete representations, so the representational system within Harry is information-rich without containing anything that we should think of as pieces of information. In this, the attitudes do seem to contrast with experiences. When Harry reports that he is suffering a pain in his elbow this morning, we find it natural to think that there is some quite specific process in his functional or physical make-up which is that pain (or on which that pain supervenes). Though counting here is not a precise art, Harry's experiences of pain seem genuinely quantifiable in a way that, if we accept the map analogy, his attitudes are not.

But not everyone accepts the map analogy, and its main rival is in fact derived from the computer example used earlier. A geographically astute computer, unlike a map of France, contains information by containing bits of information; it stores what are either sentence-like representations, or materials out of which these representations can be constructed as interrogation demands. If we apply this analogy to Harry, then we will treat our attributions of attitude to him as descriptions of sentence-like bits of information 'stored' in the right place in Harry's physical or functional insides. For example, when we say that Harry believes that right will prevail, we are in effect saying that stored somewhere in Harry's belief system ('belief box' is the more usual expression) is a sentence-like entity which means that right will prevail. On this picture, the relation of experiences and attitudes is closer: though there is plenty of scope to distinguish them, they are alike in that each will be grounded in some identifiable feature of our physical or functional organization.

The computational account raises immediate questions: if Harry's beliefs are stored as sentences in his belief box, then what language are they stored in? It had probably better not be the English that Harry speaks, since we think that speakers of different languages can share his belief. Also, whatever is stored in Harry's belief box is bound to be sentence-like in a purely formal sense, so something additional must be said about where it gets its meaning.

Whilst these are daunting questions, and might be reason enough to accept the map-like nature of attitudinal representation, the matter is by no means clear cut. Talk of map-like representation is at best metaphorical; no one thinks that we actually have maps in our heads. But it is unclear how to fill out this proposal in clear physical or functional terms. The computer language proposal – the *language of thought* hypothesis, to give it its proper name – can at least call on the fact that computers are non-metaphorically functional and physical. And it can also call on the proposals that have been offered for assigning meaning (or semantics) to formal languages. After all, we do think that the internal states of computers are purely formal – *à la* Turing – but, when the computer program animating them has been appropriately designed, they are useful sources of information about various subjects.

There is no possibility of our deciding between these competing views here. This would take a book-length study, and even then one would not expect to do more than deepen the arguments on both sides. However, they nicely illustrate how a more piecemeal division of labour might figure in an overall strategy. If one accepts the map analogy, then we seem to have a way to take the attitudes seriously, without at the same time having to assign some causal or productive task to each attitude instance. Indeed, the map analogy suggests that it would be just a mistake to think of this or that belief as a physical or functional particular apt for causing anything, even though it is true that attributing beliefs is a perfectly reasonable way to characterize the information that someone possesses.

The consequence of this for the overdetermination problem depends, as you would expect, on the more general strategy that one adopts, but it is bound to be positive. If you lean towards the identity account, then it helps by relieving you of the obligation to find physical particulars with which each attitude must be identified. If you count yourself a non-reductive functionalist, then pursuing the map analogy will not help with the troublesome overdetermination that comes with the supervenience of the functional on the physical. But it will help with the deconstructional relation between the mental and the functional. For any real causal or productive work will be assigned to a functionally characterized map-like system, and attitudes attributed folk psychologically will owe their point to the workings of that system.

It was noted at the beginning of this section that this kind of piecemeal division of labour can cause confusion. Though I have discussed only a single example, the reason for it should be clear. Partisans of the map analogy seem to be in some way removing the attitudes from the causal storyline, whereas the language of thought theorists seem bent on giving each of them starring roles. This, in turn, might suggest that pursuit of the map analogy is eliminativist, and that folk psychology is only safe in the hands of the language of thought theorist. But this would be wrong.

It is true that the language of thought theorists considers that the folk psychological account employs the notion of causality. Adapting a common saying, they think that the folk are committed to the idea that not only sticks and stones break bones; beliefs and desires can do so as well. However, the evidence that the folk are committed in precisely this way to the causal powers of the attitudes is not conclusive. The folk refer to attitudes when they seek to understand one another, but, as has been seen, causality is not necessarily what they appeal to in pursuit of this understanding. However, if we are not forced to regard beliefs and desires as doing their job causally, the map-based picture can cope perfectly well with the explanatory role of the attitudes. So, whilst treatments of the attitudes along language of thought lines are definitely anti-eliminativist, we should not be confused into thinking that they are the only bulwark against elimination.

More Serious Divisions

Anomalous monism and non-reductive psychofunctionalism are pretty minimalist in their commitment to the Division of Labour strategy. For both, it is the physical world – the world described by science – which makes true the things we say about the mental landscape, and it is the physical world which carries the burden of causal/explanatory responsibility. Indeed, it is only by, as it were, standing in a certain place – by occupying the folk psychological perspective – that we can see the mental as having any kind of responsibility at all. However, given the problems with these views, shared and otherwise, it is certainly tempting to see if a less timid approach within the Division of Labour strategy might not fare better. It is tempting, but dangerous. For, as we know, if one divides labour too thoroughly, the result might well be some sort of Leibnizian parallelism in which Minds and Brains function like clocks wound up to keep the same time, though making no reference to one another.

Throwing caution to the winds, perhaps the most common way to make a more thorough job of the Division strategy is to challenge the claims of science to the comprehensiveness that identity theorists, functionalists, anomalous monists and non-reductive functionalists all seem to accept. Thus, instead of saying that the physical world makes true everything we say about the mental landscape, why not say instead that the physical world says true things about the physical world, and that there are also true things said by the folk about the world of experience, attitude and action? Paraphrasing Hamlet to Horatio, one says to the natural scientist that there are more things to be said about the world than are in your textbooks.

One might begin to implement this strategy by thinking again about the category of Action, a category that I have left pretty much untouched since the earlier chapters. Thus, one might insist, with considerable justification, that when you look at the world in purely scientific terms, there are simply no such things as actions. To be sure, there are movements of limbs – things are pushed and pulled about – but strictly there are no pushings and pullings. For the latter, we require the wilful activity of minds, or better, of persons, engaged in making things happen. Moreover, as we have also seen, whilst human bodies are unquestionably material, persons are no more material constituents of the physical world than their actions. Though nothing written so far adds up to a satisfying account of personhood, it does seem right to say at least this: persons are special in being both things in the world and things which adopt perspectives on that world. And whilst science is perfectly competent to study persons as things in the world, there are many truths about persons and their perspectives about which science has nothing to say.

Very roughly, these sorts of musing lead one to a position one might represent as in figure 9.4.

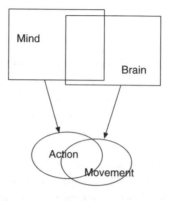

Figure 9.4

The overlaps are intended to suggest that holders of the view do not want to end up with a Leibnizian schism between Mind and Brain, Action and Movement. Also, I have left out any specification of the arrows, because this can vary without changing the overall effect. Thus, someone might insist that the right-hand arrow be labelled 'cause' and the left-hand one 'reason for'. Holders of this position would reject the idea that reasons for action are also causes of them. Or someone might insist that the right-hand arrow is one of explanation by law-like regularity, and the left is both reason and cause. This labelling resembles Davidson's, but only superficially. For holders of the view I have in mind here would reject the idea that causal claims must be backed by law-like regularities. Cause is for them a notion belonging to the folk, and, though it is used in science, it is always replaced in mature sciences by regularities which commonly take a mathematical form. (Scientists do talk about causes, though this should be unsurprising; they are after all folk, and the notion of cause has at least an expository role to play.)

The outline view shown in figure 9.4 is attractive, but it becomes elusive – perhaps unacceptably – when subjected to closer scrutiny. What one wants is a straightforward answer to this question: what do the overlaps signify? And answers tend either to make one think that the pass has been sold to the Leibnizians, or that we are being offered nothing more novel than the kind of non-reductive supervenience which has already been seen to be problematic. (One hears it said that the physical has an 'enabling but not constitutive' role with respect to the mental. However, it is difficult to hear this other than as a form of words that would happily fit non-reductive supervenience.) So, whilst I am sympathetic to this general strategy, more must be done before it can count as any kind of a solution to our problem.

Elimination

Quite often, when philosophers hold off discussing some view until the end of a chapter or book, this is because they think the view is closest to the truth. Arguing against other views along the way is often the best way of persuading readers of the attractiveness of the one left standing. However, I should not like you to draw any such conclusion from the fact that eliminativism is the last of the strategies to be considered. For it sometimes happens that the order of presentation of philosophical views is dictated, not by any increasing confidence, but out of a sort of desperation. Beginning with the most plausible – views that non philosophers might regard as already established – it can just happen that, as objections mount, one is inexorably pushed in a direction one never wanted to take. So, it is with the eliminativist strategy.

Beginning in chapter 6, we have tried to see how to fit the mental landscape into a scientifically characterized physical world. There were ample reasons to think that this could and should be done. Aside from the continuing explanatory success of science in general, it is perfectly obvious that without certain neurophysiological states, processes and events, there would be no mental life at all. Yet each time we have tried to show how neurophysiology (and the physical world generally) manages to support the mental landscape, we have encountered serious difficulties. The concepts we use to characterize ourselves seem not to fit in any acceptable way into the conceptual framework we use to describe the physical world. Yet simply leaving the folk psychological and the scientific side by side threatens us with the incoherence of overdetermination.

Early on, we canvassed a brutally simple way of dealing with this impasse: treat mental concepts as dispensable. This kind of elimination is not unprecedented. Under the pressure of science, we no longer regard the natural world as animate; no doubt thunderstorms continue to engender awe, but they are no longer thought of as an expression of someone's anger. Or, calling on our discussion of heat in chapter 6, having found that the theory of caloric fluid violates certain precepts of scientific methodology, we find it perfectly reasonable to say that there is no such fluid.

Such radical eliminativism is more than a hypothetical suggestion for dealing with overdetermination; it has genuine supporters. Why, they argue, do we treat the folk theoretical scheme which was put in place thousands of years ago, and left largely unchanged, as a genuine challenge to the constantly revised and obviously successful enterprise of science? One answer seems to play into their hands: saying that the folk scheme was designed for purposes other than that of description – that its concepts are not in any competition with the factual claims of science – seems really just a way of admitting defeat. For if our talk of the mental landscape is just a way of talking, then, however important it is to us in our daily lives, it need not be taken as fundamentally serious.

Critics of radical eliminativism have challenged these arguments in detail. Folk psychology is not stagnant: certain of its fundamental notions may not have changed – notions like experience, attitude and action – but the specific explanatory purposes to which they are put require the intelligence and imagination typical of scientific investigation. Here is an analogy: our contemporary theories of grammar say very different things from the grammars of the past, but both speak of words, sentences and other parts of speech. Opting for eliminativism would be like saying that because certain grammars have been shown to be inadequate, there simply aren't any words or sentences. Besides, even if folk psychology has changed very little, perhaps this is not so much 'stagnation ' as success.

Aside from detailed rebuttals of the eliminativist arguments, anti-eliminativists seem to have a trump card. If there is no such thing as belief, there is no such thing as having true belief. So eliminativism makes it impossible to believe truly that eliminativism is true. There are many variations of this argument, but all suggest that radical eliminativism is in some way 'self-defeating', and, if it could be made to stick, this would indeed put paid to the view. Unsurprisingly, though, this argument is not quite as powerful as it first appears; there are various replies available to the committed eliminativist, and so the debate goes on.

The intensity of these arguments tends to obscure another form of eliminativism, one which is more cautious than radical, and which, because of its cautiousness, is often not acknowledged as out-and-out eliminativist. Forms of this more insidious view have surfaced from time to time in previous chapters, and they tend to revolve around the deconstruction relation. Here is a rough outline of how it works.

First, you set out to deconstruct some feature of the mental landscape, e.g. beliefs, by telling a story about an underlying complex functional organization.

Any serious attempt at this will involve empirical research, but there is nothing to stop one making guesses about the outcome. Let's therefore suppose that you lean towards a language of thought view; you think it likely that beliefs will be functional states that include some syntactic, sentence-like elements. Of course, deconstruction of beliefs cannot stop short at this point. Functional states containing formal sentence-like elements are not about anything – they do not yet have semantic (directional) properties. Here you have yet another choice. On the one hand, you might argue that the interanimation of these formal elements, together with general input–output relations to the environment, is enough to turn the trick. The key notion here is *holism*: the meaning of each element comes from its relation to all the other elements. Or you might insist that the only way to get semantics into the functional picture is by some complex causal relation that each formal object bears to the environment.

Whatever your view – and the arguments here tend to be fierce – when looked at from a distance, the differences are less important than the similarities. For what has been effected is in essence a deconstruction of belief relations into broadly causal relations to an environment. However, since we have seen that belief relations, as understood by the folk, tend not to be as orderly as causal ones, the whole project looks to be in trouble. (We have also seen that this kind of functional deconstruction tends to just ignore many of the subtler connections that attitudes have to experience and action, but we will let these pass here.)

Faced with this, there are several reactions that one might have. You might insist that you are only dealing with some core notion of belief, a notion that is orderly enough for functional deconstruction, leaving the 'genuine' folk psychological notion for later treatment. Or you might go back to the examples that show belief relations to be disorderly – to have what I have called 'slack' in their relations to the environment – and find some reason to take the examples less than seriously. Both of these moves are fraught with difficulty, but they do show a certain non-eliminativist respect for the everyday concept of belief. However, in contrast to these, you might argue that the everyday notion is basically confused; that if it cannot be handled by some kind of causal or causal-teleological relation, we are better off without it. This is the 'so much the worse for belief' move that was described in chapter 7, and if this is your view, then there is every reason to think of your position as eliminativist.

Admittedly, this last position is at most cautiously eliminativist: belief does in fact count, only it is a notion cut down to what you regard as the right size to fit in the scientific framework. If this strategy is applied – as it often is – to the whole range of mental notions – then one ends up with a very different mental landscape from that with which we began.

Is this a bad thing? There are no simple answers to this question, and this is unfortunate. After having taken the story this far, I do not want to end by suggesting that the fundamental questions of the philosophy of mind turn on one's taste in landscapes. But that is often the way it can seem.

Notes and References

1   The main business of 'Mental Events' (in Davidson, *Essays on Mind and Action*, 1980, pp. 207–27) is just such a reconciliation, so I am pretty much following Davidson's advice. He admits right at the beginning that (i)–(iii) are bound to be controversial.

2   Davidson does allow that, by studying brains and the physical world generally, one might come by certain non-systematic and non-fundamental information about certain mental features. But this falls a long way short of what the identity theorist of chapter six thinks possible.

3   Dennett is a writer who has urged something like the position characterized here. (See especially Dennett, *The Intentional Stance*, 1987.) And it is interesting, not to say surprising, to see how, despite certain fundamental differences, as well as differences of emphasis, his views and Davidson's share a basic form. Moreover, the resemblance can be useful in understanding what looks like Dennett's vacillation, at least in respect of the attitudes. On the one hand, he wants us to take them seriously; they are a source of predictions about human beings that we depend on. But, on the other hand, he has sometimes spoken of them as mere glosses on the more basic physical and functional story. And this disparagement of folk psychological attitudes hints at an underlying allegiance to eliminativism. My suggestion is that by connecting Dennett's and Davidson's views, and taking on board the problem of causal inertness, we can understand why his views are difficult to pin down.

4   Strictly speaking, the identity of heat and transfer of energy is an identification of an already scientifically 'refined' notion – 'heat' as used in thermodynamics – with a mechanical one. The original folk notion seems vindicated by this, but was not itself coherent enough to figure in the scientific identity. This point was made but not emphasized in chapter 6, simply to avoid having to add a long story about thermodynamics to one about heat and mechanics.

5   The picture of a great supervenience chain leading from the physical up through a hierarchy of functional levels and right to the mental is not uncommon in the literature. But if the supervenience relations in this chain each set up epistemic barriers, the problem of transmitting intelligibility – an epistemic notion if every there was one – up through the hierarchy will be formidable. Yet, at least as between the functional and the mental, we do want something like intelligibility.

Further Reading

The following list of readings is arranged by chapter. Included are those works cited in the text of the chapter, as well as books and articles that will help you further your study. However, the philosophy of mind has in recent years seen an explosion of publication, and this reading list is not intended to be anything like a complete bibliography of the subject. (Some years ago an informal bibliography appeared and it had many thousands of citations, even though these were 'selected' for their importance.)

1   The Mental Landscape

There are a number of collections of articles, reference works and general introductions to the philosophy of mind, each of which could be helpful both for their contents and as sources of yet more detailed reading lists. Though they include much more material than is strictly relevant to this first chapter, this seemed the best place to include them. Also, given the fact that chapters 2 and 3 go more deeply into the topics of chapter 1, many of the following will also be useful for these later chapters. (Note: general collections and reference works are marked below with an asterisk★.)

Anscombe, G. E. M. 1963. *Intention*. 2nd edn. Ithaca, NY: Cornell Unversity Press.
★Block, N. (ed.) 1980–1. *Readings in the Philosophy of Psychology*. 2 vols. Cambridge, MA: Harvard University Press.
★Block, N., Flanagan, O. and Güzeldere, G. (eds). 1997. *The Nature of Consciousness*. Cambridge, MA: MIT Press.
Braddon-Mitchell, D. and Jackson, F. 1996. *Philosophy of Mind and Cognition*. Oxford: Blackwell.
Bratman, M. E. 1987. *Intention, Plans and Practical Reason*. Cambridge, MA: Harvard University Press.
Churchland, P. 1988. *Matter and Consciousness*. 2nd edn. Cambridge, MA: MIT Press.
de Sosa, R. 1987. *The Rationality of the Emotions*. Cambridge, MA: MIT Press.

Descartes, R. 1985. *Philosophical Writings*, trans. J. Cottingham, R. Stoothoff and D. Murdoch. 2 vols. Cambridge: Cambridge University Press. (See especially *Passions of the Soul* and *Meditations on First Philosophy*.)

Gardner, S. 1993. *Irrationality and the Philosophy of Psychoanalysis*. Cambridge: Cambridge University Press.

★Goldman, A. (ed.). 1993. *Readings in Philosophy and Cognitive Science*. Cambridge, MA: MIT Press.

Gordon, R. 1987. *The Structure of the Emotions*. Cambridge: Cambridge University Press.

★Guttenplan, S. (ed.). 1994. *A Companion to the Philosophy of Mind*. Oxford: Blackwell.

Heil, J. 1998. *Philosophy of Mind*. London: Routledge.

Hume, D. 1978. *A Treatise of Human Nature*, ed. P. H. Nidditch. Oxford: Oxford University Press. (See especially Book II.)

Kenny, A. 1963. *Action, Emotion and Will*. London: Routledge and Kegan Paul.

★Lycan, W. G. (ed.). 1999. *Mind and Cognition*. 2nd edn. Oxford: Blackwell.

McGinn, C. 1982. *The Character of Mind*. Oxford: Oxford University Press.

★Rosenthal, D. (ed.). 1991. *The Nature of Mind*. Oxford: Oxford University Press.

Searle, J. 1983. *Intentionality: An Essay in the Philosophy of Mind*. Cambridge: Cambridge University Press.

Spinoza, B. 1985. The *Collected Works of Spinoza*, ed. E. M. Curley. Princeton, NJ: Princeton University Press. (See especially *Ethics* I.)

2   Attitude, Experience and Act

Attitude

Brentano, F. 1995. *Psychology from an Empirical Standpoint*. London: Routledge. (First published in 1874.)

Burge, T. 1986. Individualism and the mental. In D. Rosenthal (ed.). 1991, *The Nature of Mind*, pp. 536–68.

Dretske, F. 1988. *Explaining Behavior*. Cambridge, MA: MIT Press.

Fodor, J. 1975. *The Language of Thought*. New York: Thomas Y. Crowell.

—— 1987. *Psychosemantics*. Cambridge, MA: MIT Press.

Frege, G. 1968. The thought: a logical inquiry. In E. D. Klemke (ed.), *Essays on Frege*. Urbana, IL: University of Illinois Press, pp. 507–35.

Kripke, S. 1979. A puzzle about belief. In A. Margalit (ed.), *Meaning and Use*. Boston: D. Reidel pp. 239–83.

Pessin, A. and Goldberg, S. (eds). 1995. *The Twin Earth Chronicles*. New York: Paragon House.

Pettit, P. and McDowell, J. (eds). 1986. *Subject, Thought, and Context*. Oxford: Oxford University Press.

Putnam, H. 1975. The meaning of 'meaning'. In *Mind, Language and Reality*. Cambridge: Cambridge University Press, pp. 215–71. (Also reprinted in Pessin and Goldberg, 1995, pp. 3–52.)

Quine, W. V. O. 1960. *Word and Object*. Cambridge, MA: MIT Press.

Salmon, N. 1986. *Frege's Puzzle*. Cambridge, MA: MIT Press.

Searle, J. 1994. Intentionality. In S. Guttenplan (ed.), *A Companion to the Philosophy of Mind*, 1994, pp. 379–86.

Stalnaker, R. 1984. *Inquiry*. Cambridge, MA: MIT Press.

Stich, S. 1983. *From Folk Psychology to Cognitive Science: The Case Against Belief*. Cambridge, MA: MIT Press.

Woodfield, A. (ed.). 1982. *Thought and Object*. Oxford University Press.

Experience

Budd, M. 1989. *Wittgenstein's Philosophy of Psychology*. London: Routledge and Kegan Paul. (See also: Ludwig Wittgenstein, in S. Guttenplan (ed.), *A Companion to the Philosophy of Mind*, 1994, pp. 617–22.)

Davidson, D. 1984. First person authority. *Dialectica*, 36, 317–27.

——1987. Knowing one's own mind. *Proceedings and Addresses of the American Philosophical Association*, 441–58.

Davies, M. and Humphreys, G. 1993. *Consciousness*. Oxford: Blackwell. (See especially the introduction.)

Flanagan, O. 1997. The robust phenomenology of the stream of consciousness. In N. Block et al. (eds), *The Nature of Consciousness*, pp. 89–93.

Heil, J. 1999. Privileged access. In W. G. Lycan (ed.), *Mind and Cognition*. 2nd edn, pp. 395–404.

Jackson, F. 1986. What Mary didn't know. *Journal of Philosophy*, 83, 291–5.

James, W. 1997. The stream of consciousness. In N. Block et al. (eds), *The Nature of Consciousness*, pp. 71–82.

Kirk, R. 1996. *Raw Feeling*. Oxford: Oxford University Press.

Lewis, D. 1999. What experiences teaches. In W. G. Lycan (ed.), *Mind and Cognition*. 2nd edn, pp. 447–61.

McGinn, C. 1990. *The Problem of Consciousness*. Oxford: Blackwell.

Nagel, T. 1974. What is it like to be a bat? *Philosophical Review*, 83, 435–50.

Shoemaker, S. 1988. On knowing one's own mind. *Philosophical Perspectives*, 2, 183–209.

Action

Anscombe, G. E. M. 1963. *Intention*. 2nd edn. Ithaca, NY: Cornell University Press.

Davidson, D. 1980. *Essays on Actions and Events*. Oxford: Oxford University Press.

Davis, L. 1979. *Theory of Action*. Englewood Cliffs, NJ: Prentice-Hall.

Goldman, A. 1970. *A Theory of Human Action*. Englewood Cliffs, NJ: Prentice-Hall.

Hornsby, J. 1980. *Action*. London: Routledge and Kegan Paul.

Mele, A. R. 1992. *Springs of Action*. Oxford: Oxford University Press.

O'Shaughnessy, B. 1980. *The Will*. 2 vols. Cambridge: Cambridge University Press. (See also: The Will, in S. Guttenplan (ed.), *A Companion to the Philosophy of Mind*, 1994, pp. 610–17.)

3 Folk Psychology and Folk

Explanation and Folk Psychology

Carruthers, P. and Smith, P. (eds). 1995. *Theories of Theories of Mind*. Cambridge: Cambridge University Press.

Chomsky, N. 1975. *Reflections on Language*. New York: Pantheon.

Davies, M. and Stone, M. (eds). 1995a: *Folk Psychology: The Theory of Mind Debate*. Oxford: Blackwell.

—— 1995b. *Mental Simulation: Evaluations and Applications*. Oxford: Blackwell.

Goldman, A. 1992. The psychology of folk psychology. *Behavioural and Brain Sciences*, 16, 15–28. (Also in Davies and Stone 1995a: see above.)

Gordon, R. 1986. Folk psychology as simulation. *Mind and Language*, 1, 158–71. (Also in Davies and Stone 1995a: see above.)

Greenwood, J. (ed.). 1991. *The Future of Folk Psychology*. Cambridge: Cambridge University Press.

Heal, J. 1986. Replication and functionalism. In Davies and Stone 1995a: see above, pp. 45–59.

Hempel, C. 1979. *Philosophy of Natural Science*. Englewood Cliffs, NJ: Prentice-Hall.

Lewis, D. 1983. *Philosophical Papers*, vol. 1. Oxford: Oxford University Press. (See especially: An argument for the identity theory, pp. 99–107.)

—— 1994. Reduction in mind. In S. Guttenplan (ed.), *A Companion to the Philosophy of Mind*, pp. 412–31.

Von Wright, G. 1971. *Explanation and Understanding*. Ithaca, NY: Cornell University Press.

Persons and Identity

Anscombe, G. E. M. 1975. The first person. In S. Guttenplan (ed.), *Mind and Language*. Oxford: Oxford University Press, pp. 45–65.

Parfit, D. 1971. Personal identity. *Philosophical Review*, 80, 3–27.

Rorty, A. (ed.). 1976. *The Identities of Persons*. Berkeley: University of California Press.

Strawson, P. F. 1959. *Individuals: An Essay in Descriptive Metaphysics*. London: Methuen.

Wiggins, D. 1980. *Sameness and Substance*. Oxford: Blackwell.

Williams, B. A. O. 1973. *Problems of Self*. Cambridge: Cambridge University Press. (See especially: The self and the future, pp. 46–63.)

4 The Marks of the Mental

Brandom, R. 1994. *Making it Explicit: Reasoning, Representing and Discursive Commitment*. Cambridge, MA: Harvard University Press.

Grandy, R. and Warner, R. (eds). 1986. *Philosophical Grounds of Rationality*. Oxford: Oxford University Press.

McDowell, J. H. 1994. *Mind and World*. Cambridge, MA: Harvard University Press.

Nagel, T. 1979. *Mortal Questions*. Cambridge University Press. (See especially: Subjective and objective.)

—— 1986. *The View from Nowhere*. Oxford: Oxford University Press.

Searle, J. 1992. *The Rediscovery of Mind*. Cambridge, MA: MIT Press.

Sellars, W. 1997. *Empiricism and the Philosophy of Mind*, ed. R. Brandom. Cambridge, MA: Harvard University Press.

Stich, S. 1990. The *Fragmentation of Reason*. Cambridge, MA: MIT Press.

Strawson, P. F. 1974. *Freedom and Resentment and Other Essays*. London, Methuen.

5   Science and the Mind

Block, N. (ed.). 1980. *Readings in the Philosophy of Psychology*, vol. 1. Cambridge, MA: Harvard University Press.

Byrne, A. 1994. Behaviourism. In S. Guttenplan (ed.), *A Companion to the Philosophy of Mind*, pp. 132–40.

Churchland, P. 1979. *Scientific Realism and the Plasticity of Mind*. Cambridge: Cambridge University Press.

Davidson, D. 1980. Actions, reasons and causes. In *Essays on Actions and Events*, pp. 3–19.

Dennett, D. 1978. *Brainstorms*. Montgomery, VT: Bradford.

Descartes, R. 1985. *Philosophical Writings*, trans. J. Cottingham et al. (see p. 348.)

Dretske, F. 1988. *Explaining Behaviour: Reasons in a World of Causes*. Cambridge, MA: MIT Press.

Hart, W. D. 1988. *The Engines of the Soul*. Cambridge: Cambridge University Press.

Heil, J. and Mele, A. (eds). 1993. *Mental Causation*. Oxford: Oxford University Press.

Leibniz, G. W. 1989. *Leibniz: Philosophical Essays*, trans. R. Ariew and D. Garber. Indianapolis, IN: Hackett.

Lennon, K. 1990. *Explaining Human Action*. London: Duckworth.

Nagel, E. 1961. *The Structure of Science*. New York: Harcourt, Brace and World.

Robinson, H. (ed.). 1993. *Objections to Physicalism*. Oxford: Oxford University Press.

Ryle, G. 1949. *The Concept of Mind*. London: Hutchinson.

Skinner, B. F. 1971. *Beyond Freedom and Dignity*. New York: Alfred A. Knopf.

6   Identity

Armstrong, D. M. 1968. *A Materialist Theory of Mind*. London: Routledge and Kegan Paul.

Borst, C. V. (ed.). 1970. *The Mind Brain Identity Theory*. London: Macmillan.

Braddon-Mitchell, D. and Jackson, F. 1996. *Philosophy of Mind and Cognition*. Oxford: Blackwell.

Campbell, K. 1970. *Body and Mind*. 2nd edn. London: Macmillan.

Kripke, S. 1980. *Naming and Necessity*. Oxford: Blackwell.

Lewis, D. 1983. *Collected Papers*, vol. 1. Oxford: Oxford University Press.
—— 1994. Reduction of Mind. In S. Guttenplan (ed.), *A Companion to the Philosophy of Mind*, pp. 412–31.
Singer, I. 1959. *A Short History of Scientific Ideas*. Oxford: Oxford University Press.
Smart, J. J. C. 1959. Sensations and Brain Processes. *Philosophical Review*, 68, 141–56.
Warner, R. and Szubka, T. 1994. *The Mind–Body Problem: A Guide to the Current Debate*. Oxford: Blackwell.

7   Functionalism

Block, N. 1994. Functionalism. In S. Guttenplan (ed.), *A Companion to the Philosophy of Mind*, pp. 323–32.
Block, N. (ed.). 1980. *Readings in the Philosophy of Psychology*, vol. 1. Cambridge, MA: Harvard University Press.
Cummins, R. 1983. *The Nature of Psychological Explanation*. Cambridge, MA: MIT Press.
Dennett, D. 1978. *Brainstorms*. Middlebury, VT: Bradford.
—— 1991. *Consciousness Explained*. Boston: Little, Brown.
Garnham, A. 1994. Cognitive Psychology. In S. Guttenplan (ed.), *A Companion to the Philosophy of Mind*, pp. 167–76.
Kim, J. 1993. *Supervenience and Mind*. Cambridge University Press.
—— 1996. *Philosophy of Mind*. Boulder. CO: Westview Press.
Lewis, D. 1994. Reduction of Mind. In S. Guttenplan (ed.), *A Companion to the Philosophy of Mind*, pp. 412–31.
Lycan, W. 1994. Functionalism. In S. Guttenplan (ed.), *A Companion to the Philosophy of Mind*, pp. 317–23.
Lycan, W. (ed.). 1999. *Mind and Cognition*. Oxford: Blackwell.
Osherson, D. N. et al. (eds). 1995. *An Invitation to Cognitive Science*. 2nd edn, 3 vols. Cambridge, MA: MIT Press.
Putnam, H. 1988. *Representation and Reality*. Cambridge, MA: MIT Press.
Rey, G. 1997. *Contemporary Philosophy of Mind*. Oxford: Blackwell.
Rosenthal, D. (ed.). 1991. *The Nature of Mind*. Oxford: Oxford University Press.
Shoemaker, S. 1981. Some varieties of functionalism. *Philosophical Topics*, 12, 93–120.
Turing, A. 1950. Computing machinery and intelligence. *Mind*, 59, 433–60.

8   Objections

Block, N. 1981. Troubles with functionalism. In *Readings in the Philosophy of Psychology*, vol. 1, pp. 268–305.
Braddon-Mitchell, D. and Jackson, F. 1996. *Philosophy of Mind and Cognition*. Oxford: Blackwell.

Chalmers, D. *The Conscious Mind: In Search of a Fundamental Theory.* Oxford: Oxford University Press.

Dennett, D. 1996. *Kinds of Minds: Towards an Understanding of Consciousness.* New York: Basic Books.

Hodges, A. 1985. *Alan Turing: The Enigma of Intelligence.* London: Unwin.

Lepore, E. and van Gulick, R. (eds). 1991. *John Searle and His Critics.* Oxford: Blackwell.

Levine, J. 1983. Materialism and qualia: the explanatory gap. *Pacific Philosophical Quarterly*, 64, 354–61.

Lycan, W. 1994. Functionalism. In S. Guttenplan (ed.), *A Companion to the Philosophy of Mind*, pp. 317–23.

Millikan, R. 1984. *Language, Thought and Other Biological Categories.* Cambridge, MA: MIT Press.

Papineau, D. 1993. *Philosophical Naturalism.* Oxford: Blackwell.

Searle, J. 1984. *Minds, Brains and Science.* Cambridge, MA: Harvard University Press.

——1997. *The Mystery of Consciousness.* London: Granta.

9 Division and Elimination

Antony, L. 1989. Anomalous monism and the problem of explanatory force. *Philosophical Review*, 98, 153–87.

Baker, L. R. 1995. *Explaining Attitudes.* Cambridge: Cambridge University Press.

Churchland, P. 1981. Eliminative materialism and the propositional attitudes. *Journal of Philosophy*, 78, 67–90. (Also in D. Rosenthal (ed.), *The Nature of Mind*, 1991.)

Davidson, D. 1980. *Essays on Actions and Events.* Oxford: Oxford University Press. (See especially 'Mental Events', pp. 207–27.)

——1993. Thinking Causes. In J. Heil and A. Mele (eds), *Mental Causation*, pp. 3–17.

Dennett, D. 1987. *The Intenational Stance.* Cambridge, MA: MIT Press.

Fodor, J. 1975. *The Language of Thought.* Cambridge, MA: MIT Press.

——1987. *Psychosemantics.* Cambridge, MA: MIT Press.

Fodor, J. and Lepore, E. 1992. *Meaning Holism.* Oxford: Blackwell.

Heil, J. and Mele, A. (eds). 1993. *Mental Causation.* Oxford: Oxford University Press.

Hornsby, J. 1997. *Simple Minds.* Cambridge, MA: Harvard University Press.

Lepore, E. and McLaughlin, B. (eds). 1985. *Actions and Events: Perspectives on the Philosophy of Donald Davidson.* Oxford: Blackwell.

McDowell, J. H. 1994. *Mind and World.* Cambridge, MA: Harvard University Press.

McLaughlin, B. 1994. Epiphenomenalism. In S. Guttenplan (ed.), *A Companion to the Philosophy of Mind*, pp. 277–88.

Stich, S. 1983. *From Folk Psychology to Cognitive Science: The Case Against Belief.* Cambridge, MA: MIT Press.

——1996. *Deconstructing the Mind.* Oxford: Oxford University Press.

Index